INDIAN SOLDIERS IN WORLD WAR I

Studies in War, Society, and the Military

GENERAL EDITORS

Kate Lemay
Smithsonian Institution

Richard S. Fogarty
University at Albany, State University of New York

EDITORIAL BOARD

Peter Maslowski
University of Nebraska-Lincoln

David Graff
Kansas State University

Reina Pennington
Norwich University

INDIAN SOLDIERS IN WORLD WAR I

Race *and* Representation *in an* Imperial War

ANDREW T. JARBOE

University of Nebraska Press
Lincoln

© 2021 by the Board of Regents of the University of Nebraska

All rights reserved

The University of Nebraska Press is part of a land-grant institution with campuses and programs on the past, present, and future homelands of the Pawnee, Ponca, Otoe-Missouria, Omaha, Dakota, Lakota, Kaw, Cheyenne, and Arapaho Peoples, as well as those of the relocated Ho-Chunk, Sac and Fox, and Iowa Peoples.

First Nebraska paperback printing: 2024

Library of Congress Cataloging-in-Publication Data
Names: Jarboe, Andrew Tait, author.
Title: Indian soldiers in World War I: race and representation in an imperial war / Andrew T. Jarboe.
Other titles: Race and representation in an imperial war
Description: Lincoln: University of Nebraska Press, [2021] | Series: Studies in war, society, and the military | Includes bibliographical references and index.
Identifiers: LCCN 2020040402
ISBN 9781496206787 (hardback)
ISBN 9781496241368 (paperback)
ISBN 9781496227171 (epub)
ISBN 9781496227188 (mobi)
ISBN 9781496227195 (pdf)
Subjects: LCSH: India. Army—History—20th century. | Great Britain. Army. British Indian Army—History—20th century. | World War, 1914-1918—India. | World War, 1914-1918—Campaigns—Western Front. | World War, 1914-1918—Participation, Indian. | India—History, Military—20th century. | Great Britain—Armed Forces—Minorities—History—20th century.
Classification: LCC D547.I5 J37 2021 | DDC 940.4/1254—dc23
LC record available at https://lccn.loc.gov/2020040402

Set in Lyon Text by Mikala R. Kolander.

CONTENTS

List of Tables	vi
Acknowledgments	vii
Introduction	1
1. Peasants into Sepoys	27
2. India's Splendid Rally	54
3. In Flanders Fields	83
4. Healing the Empire	117
5. In the Hands of the Enemy	153
6. The Empire's Fighters	184
7. The War's Most Critical Phase	216
8. Into the Face of Bayonets	243
Conclusion	267
Notes	281
Bibliography	305
Index	315

TABLES

1. Total mentions of "Indian troops" in UK and Irish newspapers   109
2. Deaths in the Indian camps   168
3. British prisoners of war in Turkey   170
4. Number of combatants sent for service overseas from India   187
5. Army enlistments and recruitments in the British Empire as a percentage of population   218
6. Enlistments in the Indian Army by province   220
7. Total enlistments for the British Army (and Territorial Force)   225
8. Total combatant enlistments for the Indian Army   225
9. Total recruits obtained throughout India   238
10. Total combatant Indians killed and wounded   275
11. Summary of all Indian casualties   275

ACKNOWLEDGMENTS

I would like to thank my editor Bridget Barry at the University of Nebraska Press for her initial enthusiasm and sustained belief in and support for this project. Thanks to the anonymous readers of UNP, all of whom helped make this a better book. I am especially grateful to the exemplary teachers and scholars who have mentored me since the topic of Indian soldiers in World War I caught my interest more than a decade ago, among them Timothy S. Brown, Richard Fogarty, Heather Streets-Salter, Laura Frader, Katherine Luongo, and Santanu Das. I am also grateful to the undergraduate students at Berklee College of Music, with whom I have enjoyed teaching a course on World War I since 2014, and my high school history students at Match High School in Boston, Massachusetts, for whom I endeavor to be the history teacher they might one day acknowledge in a book. I have been blessed with good friends and co-conspirators from graduate school at Northeastern University with whom I shared laughs, beers, and ideas (those followed usually by another beer or two, of course): James Bradford, Malcolm Purinton, Rachel Gillett, Samantha Christiansen, Burleigh Hendrickson, Zachary Scarlett, Satya Som, Stacey Farenthold, and Stephanie Boyle. And then, of course, I owe a special thanks to Mom and Dad, who have always been in my corner. Mom taught me gumption and nerve. Dad taught me how to tell a story. Dad also read drafts of this book as it made its way through one revision after another. Last but not least, I must thank my wife, Melanie, and my children, Maren and Phineas, for their own special brand of belief in and patience with me as I pursued this project. I am quite useless to everyone, I'm afraid, when I dive into research and writing. I am sure my children did not mind the evenings when I phoned-it-in or served up mac 'n' cheese for dinner. But I know

Acknowledgments

there were times when they wished I could have been more present than I was. That I was actually able to finish this book during a pandemic, when we were all at home together, all the time, is a credit to them, not to me. All my love to you three, forever and ever and ever. I dedicate this book to you.

INDIAN SOLDIERS IN WORLD WAR I

Introduction

> To-day it has been my great good fortune to assist at the making of history. I have seen the troops of one of the world's most ancient civilizations set foot for the first time on the shores of Europe. I have seen proud Princes of India ride at the head of thousands of soldiers, Princes and men alike fired with all the ardor of the East, determined to help win their Emperor's battles or die.
>
> —From a special correspondent to the *Times* (London), October 2, 1914

More than one million Indian soldiers deployed overseas to fight on behalf of the British Empire in the Indian Army during World War I. They fought in France and Belgium, Egypt and East Africa, Gallipoli, Palestine, and Mesopotamia. This book is about their contributions to the imperial war effort on the battlefield, the contested meanings contemporaries drew from the soldiers' wartime experiences, and the impacts these had on the British Empire's racial politics and on British colonial rule.

Britain's Indian Army fulfilled three vital functions as part of the imperial war effort. In 1914 and 1915 Indian infantry and cavalry fighting on the Western Front in France and Belgium provided vital manpower at a time when the British Army was desperate for able bodies in the trenches. Indian soldiers also secured important imperial holdings along the periphery of the Indian Ocean, without which the British Empire would have been unable to make war, among those the Suez Canal and Persian oil fields. Indian Army operations then fueled British imperial expansion. Even though the Indian Army was unprepared for extensive and protracted operations overseas at the war's outset, British policymakers and battlefield commanders spurred its soldiers into a hastily conceived and incompetently led war of imperial expansion in the Middle East.

Introduction

In 1915 and 1916 British imperial ambition produced one disaster after another on the battlefield. When the British press at long last (too late, some might say) shifted its focus to Indian Army operations there, policymakers finally prioritized supplying Indian soldiers with the resources they required to win important victories. By 1918 the Indian Army had transformed into an effective spearhead of British imperial expansion. Its Indian soldiers contributed decisively to Britain's final victory over Ottoman Turkey.

In some ways, war proved a great leveler. Soldiers deployed to France, East Africa, and the Middle East struggled in their letters home to narrate "sufferings beyond the power of words to describe." While the encounter between human tissue and high explosive shell was always a one-sided affair, the Indian soldiers who deployed overseas encountered dangers beyond those hurled at them by their German and Ottoman opponents. Between 1914 and 1918 thousands of Indian soldiers lost their lives to the racism of British civil and military commanders. Indian soldiers in France had little hope for relief from the trenches, for example. The racist assumptions of army recruiters in India made it impossible to secure their replacements. In the Middle East the racial prejudice of one battlefield commander contributed to the destruction of an entire division of the Indian Army—a loss of some thirteen thousand troops. All the while the colonial medical establishment denied Indian soldiers the kind of life-saving health care white soldiers enjoyed. For all this, many Indian soldiers fought bravely. But just as many resented the racism they encountered in the king's service, especially if it impeded their chances of returning home safely. To that most basic end—staying alive—Indian soldiers resisted racist army policy and the dictates of their military commanders when they thought it was safe to do so. Some soldiers malingered in hospital. Some deserted to the German or Turkish lines, lured by the promise of a decent shot at making it home again by way of Berlin and Constantinople. Some wrote home, begging friends and family to hide from army recruiters. Strategies like these, what we might call everyday forms of resistance and self-help (as opposed to outright collective defiance), rarely made headlines.¹ But otherwise loyal soldiers did engage in these sorts of behaviors when it was clear that no one else was looking out for their best interests. Sometimes something as simple as foot-dragging saved lives. Sometimes soldier resistance forced the British to change army policy. In any event, Indian soldiers were adept and savvy far beyond what newspapers like the *Times* reported.

The British press and Indian press were likewise interested in the fates of Indian soldiers. Applauded by British newspapers and statesmen alike, the deployment of Indian soldiers to battlefields in Europe, Africa, and Asia provided rich fodder for the colonial imagination. In England the wartime press boasted that India's participation in the war permanently linked India to "that singular and wonderful chain" known as the British Empire. A wartime rhetoric that routinely peddled in racial stereotypes about Indian soldiers obscured longer patterns of racial hierarchy and the Indian Army's prejudicial recruiting practices. Indian families prayed for the good fortune of their soldiers overseas, of course, and Indian newspaper reporters and publishers tried earnestly to satisfy the demand for war news. But where newspaper reporting in England tended to reinforce prewar racial stereotypes, the deployment of Indian soldiers overseas—most notably to the Western Front in France and Belgium—galvanized Indian demands for a realignment of the British Empire's racial hierarchies and the repeal of some of the racist immigration policies Indians encountered as they sought opportunities abroad.

Indian Army operations also fueled Indian national aspirations. At the start of the war, the Indian National Congress (INC) pledged its unconditional support and unwavering commitment to the British Empire. As late as 1918 Gandhi toured India on a pro-war propaganda campaign, encouraging young men to join the Indian Army. Indian nationalists wanted "self-government" within the empire, along the lines enjoyed by Britain's so-called White Dominions—Canada, Australia, New Zealand, and South Africa. In the Indian soldier Gandhi believed he had found a vehicle to advance this nationalist cause. But the war did not weaken British commitments to white supremacy. Instead the British Empire's dogged adherence to racial inequality, the sidelining of Indian nationalists at the postwar peace conference in Paris, and the brutal suppression of antigovernment demonstrations in India by the Indian Army in 1919 led Gandhi and the INC to conclude that cooperation with the empire was no longer possible. In 1921 Gandhi wrote that it was "the duty of the Indian soldiers to refuse to assist the British Government." Thereafter, *Swaraj*—Home Rule—would become the prerequisite for Indian cooperation in the empire's endeavors. Therefore, British racism and Indian soldiers' willingness to participate in racist violence against Indian civilians placed Indian national aspirations and British colonial rule at loggerheads at war's end. In this way Indian soldiers spearheaded both the high tide and the beginning of the end of British colonial rule in South Asia.

India and the War

When people spoke in 1914 of the "Great War," they were trying to capture something of its intensity and reach. All the war's major combatants were imperial powers, and the British, French, Belgians, and Germans had overseas possessions. War between the European powers therefore meant a war of global dimensions—one that invariably favored Britain and its allies, or so the London press boasted. "When the illimitable resources of the British Empire, our grand Fleet, our unconquerable Army, the flower of the manhood of these islands, our heroic kinsmen from overseas, our chivalrous Indian troops, are all placed in the scale in this mighty struggle from which we will never flinch nor falter, who can doubt what the end will be?" newspapers such as the *Times* liked to boast.[2] And while the German Army spent most of the war proving that economic determinism is a poor predictor of battlefield outcomes, Britain's and France's reservoir of imperial resources (when combined with the industrial capacity of the United States) did help their armies outlast those of the enemy. Franz Schauwecker, darling of Germany's postwar radical Right, described the situation just one month before his country's defeat in 1918: "More than six and a half million French, English, American, Belgian and Italian soldiers now stand along the front. Every month, three hundred thousand fresh Americans arrive in France, as do nearly as many colored soldiers from France's colonies. Along with these men arrive seven thousand tanks and countless guns, mortars, machineguns, planes, balloons, and grenades."[3] World War I ended with the sudden and stunning collapse of three great empires—those of the Hohenzollerns, Habsburgs, and the Ottoman sultans (the empire of the Romanovs, Britain's ally, fell in 1917). The peace settlements secured for the British and French the expansion of their empires into the Middle East and Africa.[4]

It may be helpful to clarify that when people talked about "India" in 1914, they were referring to a landmass much greater than what we would today point to on the map. They had in mind an entire subcontinent, represented now by independent India, Pakistan, Bangladesh, and Myanmar (formerly Burma). Two-thirds of this massive landmass and its three hundred million people comprised British India, a sprawling colonial holding. British India's subjects lived under the direct rule of the British autocracy, known as the Raj. The one-third of India not under direct British rule was governed by hereditary monarchs, called "princes" for ease of reference. Great Britain's King George V was also India's king-emperor in 1914, but real power rested with the prime minister (Herbert Asquith from 1908 to 1916, and David Lloyd George from 1916 until 1922) and his cabinet at 10 Downing Street. The prime minister delegated the tasks of governing British India to his secretary of state for India, a cabinet-level post (which meant he did the job of governing India from London), and the governor-general in British India, known as the viceroy, who headed the Government of India (he did this work from his office in Delhi).

The Indian Army was the (British) Government of India's professional, all-volunteer garrison, paid for by the Indian taxpayer. In 1914 it comprised South Asians—drawn mainly from British India with a share of Gurkhas from Nepal, and Pashtuns, or Pathans, from the volatile North-West Frontier Province, what is now the border of Pakistan and Afghanistan—and British Army regulars on rotation from the Home Army of the British Isles. The Indian Army's units were of two kinds, combatant and noncombatant. Combat-

Introduction

ant Indian infantrymen (foot soldiers) were spoken of as "sepoys" and Indian cavalrymen (horse soldiers) as "sowars." Sepoys served in all-Indian battalions of anywhere from 750 to 1,000 men, led exclusively by British officers. An infantry brigade in 1914 typically comprised three battalions of Indian infantry and one British. An Indian division might have anywhere from 10,000 to 12,000 combatant soldiers, divided between three brigades. There were 159,134 Indians serving in the ranks of the Indian Army as combatants in August 1914. There were 34,767 more in the reserves. Another 45,660 Indians served as noncombatants, sometimes called "followers." Altogether, these 239,561 men served alongside 76,953 British soldiers. Between 1914 and 1919 another 1,440,437 Indians joined the Indian Army, 877,068 as combatants and 563,369 as noncombatants, a contribution in manpower exceeding those made by any and all of Britain's other colonies or dominions to the imperial war effort.[5] Indian soldiers deployed to three continents and at any given time belonged to one of the seven expeditionary forces India sent overseas during the war—to France and Belgium (Indian Expeditionary Force A, or IEFA); to East Africa (IEFB and IEFC); to Mesopotamia (IEFD); to the Sinai and Palestine (IEFE and IEFF); to Gallipoli (IEFG); and other theaters.

Just before the outbreak of war in August 1914, the Government of India had warned that any overseas deployment of Indian Army soldiers (Indian and British) above and beyond three infantry divisions and a cavalry brigade might precipitate domestic turbulence and instability. Nevertheless, the army had sent some 23,500 British and 78,000 Indian ranks abroad by Christmas 1914—far beyond the recommended limit. By that date Indian soldiers had already secured oil interests in Basra in the Persian Gulf, assaulted beachheads in East Africa, participated in the capture of Tsingtao in China, and helped absorb the brunt of the German attack on the Western Front.[6] Between October 1914 and the close of 1915, when commanders redeployed the infantry for the growing war in the Middle East, Indian soldiers belonging to IEFA fought for control of villages and towns up and down the British sector of the Western Front: Ypres, Festubert, Givenchy, Neuve Chapelle, Sec-

Introduction

ond Ypres, and Loos. In the Middle East, Indian Army operations began in earnest in November 1914 when the Indian 6th Division deployed to Basra in the Persian Gulf to secure the oil fields in nearby Abadan, in neutral Persia. Some 4,700 soldiers readily overwhelmed the Ottoman shore battery and garrison. At the same time, an Indian force gathered in Egypt to protect the Suez Canal, Britain's lifeline to Asia. In January 1915 well-entrenched and well-provisioned Indian troops repulsed a Turkish attack on the Canal. They then assisted a slow and careful advance into the Sinai desert, improving rail lines, digging wells, and laying water pipes to ensure that any offensives launched from the region would enjoy reliable access to drinking water. Additional brigades of infantry from India and another from Egypt joined the 6th Division in Basra in March 1915, where reports of an approaching Ottoman force alarmed Indian Army Command. General John Nixon took command of a force now 20,000 strong. In April his men repulsed an Ottoman attack at Shaiba, ensuring the British war machine's uninterrupted access to the oil upon which it relied. Then in 1916 Turkey redoubled its efforts to capture the Suez Canal. Empire soldiers fought a series of back-and-forth battles in the Sinai desert. Otherwise very little territory changed hands, and the Suez Canal remained safely guarded.[7]

Indian Army operations in Mesopotamia ultimately proved to be the army's most tortuous and tragic. In late summer 1915 IEFD began a slow advance up the Tigris and Euphrates Rivers into the heart of Mesopotamia. General Nixon's victory against Turkish forces at Kut on the Tigris in late September opened the hundred-mile road to Baghdad. At a time in the war when very little was going the Allies' way (the Germans remained lodged in France; the Turks held the high ground at Gallipoli), the capture and occupation of the city became a pressing priority. The viceroy of India, Lord Hardinge—who had exclaimed when he learned of Nixon's victory at Kut, "I hope to be the Pasha of Baghdad before I leave India!"—persuaded the British cabinet that the two Indian divisions fighting in France were needed more in the Middle East.[8] Yet British ambitions met reality when Turkish forces checked the advancing Indian 6th Division south of Baghdad at Ctesiphon in November 1915, and the division's commander, General Charles Townshend, ordered a hasty retreat to Kut. About thirteen thousand Indian and British soldiers dug in and withstood a siege until starvation forced their surrender in April 1916, a defeat, in Townsend's own estimation, comparable to Cornwallis's at Yorktown in 1781.[9] Hastily conceived rescue operations that winter produced thousands of additional casualties unnecessarily.

Fortune smiled brighter on Indian Army soldiers in the Middle East in the war's final two years, when the Indian Army became a formidable army of conquest.[10] Reorganized, reequipped, and under new leadership, IEFD punched its way through the Turkish lines and captured Baghdad in March 1917. An empire force under the command of the hard-fighting Edmund Allenby set out from Egypt to commence the invasion of Palestine. In November his soldiers took Gaza. In December, empire soldiers captured Jerusalem, a victory heralded by one Indian newspaper as "the greatest event in the history of the world."[11] IEFD mopped up remaining Turkish forces in what is now northern Iraq. Meanwhile, when the Allied Supreme War Council convened at the start of 1918, it tasked the Indian Army with knocking Turkey out of the war before the close of the year. Command set its sights on Aleppo in Syria, a distance of some three hundred miles from the empire force in Palestine. Indian soldiers fought that summer for control of the Jordan Valley. In September they broke through Turkish defenses at Megiddo. Indian cavalry soldiers, who had spent more time in France in the trenches than in the saddle, now put their mounts to good effect and exploited the breach. Allenby's pursuit led to the capture of Damascus, Beirut, and Aleppo in rapid succession. The Turks agreed to an armistice on October 30, 1918.

At war's end more than half a million men were serving overseas with the Indian Army. Between 1914 and 1918, the Indian Army sent some 1,096,013 soldiers overseas, 621,224 of them in a combat role.[12] Bullets and exploding shells claimed the lives of 53,486 men; 64,350 Indians came home wounded.[13] Indian soldiers collected more than twelve thousand decorations. A dozen men received the Victoria Cross, the British Empire's highest military honor for "gallantry of the highest order."[14] But not every soldier had remained loyal throughout—"true to his salt," to use an expression common among the troops. When Turkey joined the war in October 1914, the Ottoman sultan proclaimed a jihad and called on Britain's Muslim subjects to cast off the yoke of British rule. Backed by the German government, Indian radicals and propagandists headquartered in Berlin had, from the earliest months of the war, extolled Indian soldiers to murder their English officers. A global network of Indian revolutionaries inspired some soldiers stationed in South Asia in 1915 to munity.[15] Some soldiers participated in a rebellion by tribesmen in the North-West Frontier Province, a region seething under the yoke of racial violence and colonial rule.[16] Two dozen soldiers serving in France in 1915 deserted to the German lines, hoping that Turkey's ally, the kaiser, might provide them safe passage home to the North-West Frontier Province. A few actually made it, by way of a German-led expedition that sought to bribe the emir of Afghanistan into invading British India.[17] A dozen of these deserters only got as far as northern Persia before British agents caught up with them. One soldier, with his German wife and their infant son in tow, returned safely to Afghanistan in 1921 by way of civil war–torn Russia (the Indian Army, it is worth stating, recruited a limited number of men from Afghanistan). Another small batch of Indian soldiers, captured by the Germans in France, reenlisted in the Ottoman Army in 1916 and deployed to the Middle East to fight against the Indian Army.

Most Indian soldiers demobilized peaceably after the war. Those that remained in uniform reequipped and redeployed for the tried-and-tested prewar practice of policing the empire's volatile holdings east of the Suez Canal—to Iraq, for example, or the Afghan border. Others deployed to cities and towns in India where they suppressed Gandhi's first nationwide campaign of civil disobedience, or *satyagraha*, in March and April 1919. Indian soldiers fired on crowds in Delhi on March 30. Two weeks later troops fired on demonstrators in Amritsar and Lahore in the Punjab, and in Ahmedabad in the presidency of Bombay. Indian troops also gunned down Indian civilians in Calcutta and Bombay. At the Jallianwala Bagh in Amritsar, Brigadier-General Reginald Dyer, commander of the Jullundur Brigade of the Indian Army, ordered a detachment of Indian soldiers under his command to fire into a crowd of 20,000 people. The soldiers fired more than 1,600 rounds, killing 379 people and wounding more than 1,000 others. The events of March and April 1919 were decisive.[18] At the start of the war Gandhi had been a supporter of the empire. He wrote a letter to the *Times* in 1914 in which he urged Indians to support the war effort in any way they could, that they "share the responsibilities of membership of this great Empire, if we would share its privileges."[19] After Amritsar Gandhi considered it "the duty of every Indian soldier . . . to sever his connection with the Government," and that it was "contrary to national dignity" for any Indian to serve as a soldier for a government "which has brought about India's economic, moral and political degradation and which has used the soldiery . . . for repressing national aspirations."[20] Indian troops, who safeguarded British imperial holdings and spearheaded British imperial ambitions overseas during the war, squashed Indian national aspirations at home in the immediate aftermath of the war. The events of March and April 1919, more than anything else, propelled Gandhi to the forefront of Indian national politics. In 1920 the Indian National Congress abandoned its long-standing position as Britain's "loyal opponent" in favor of a stance intended to undermine British rule by means of non-cooperation and extralegal resistance.[21]

In both Great Britain and India the topic of "India and the War" became an industry unto itself during the war years. In 1914 and 1915 newspapers in England regaled readers with the exploits of the Indian troops fighting just across the English Channel. Headlines like "Indian Troops in Action," "Dash of the Indian Troops," and "Valour of the Indian Troops" gave audiences reason for optimism at a time when the war's outcome remained uncertain. Penny pamphlets written by members of the Indian National Congress reassured people that India was with Britain "Heart and Soul." Propaganda films taught schoolchildren that those were *their*

Indian soldiers fighting in the trenches. In Madras, G. A. Natesan & Co. offered India's newly emerging professional and educated classes *The Indian Review War Book*. Avowedly nationalist in its bent, Natesan's collection of essays and speeches were nonetheless pro-war and pro-empire.[22] The war's first histories appeared on bookshelves even as the war raged. Official histories hit the market in the 1920s.[23] British officers who served in the Indian Army on various fronts produced one account after another, many of them self-serving.[24] General James Willcocks said of the accomplishments of the Indian troops under his command in IEFA, "No one knows better than I do how utterly impossible it would have been for them to do what they did, without the help and example of their illustrious comrades of the Scottish, Irish, and English battalions which formed part of each brigade."[25] Indian Army veteran and historian Rana Chhina recently described this first generation of histories as narratives "shaped by the victors in the metropole and passed on to the colonies for uncritical adoption. These hollow narratives endured for as long as the colonial powers that generated them held sway."[26]

In the wake of a second and far more destructive world war and the end of British rule in India, the subject of "India and the [First World] War" was all but "consigned to the dustbins of history," forgotten in England and forgotten in the newly independent South Asian nations.[27] Students of World War I lost sight of the war's global and imperial dimensions. Where World War II generated an official Indian history, World War I did not. At the time of the war's eightieth anniversary in the 1990s, only a handful of titles had been added to the corpus. De Witt C. Ellinwood and S. D. Pradhan added a very important title in the 1970s, *India and World War I*, which explored some of the war's social, political, and economic impacts in India.[28] In the 1980s military historian Jeffrey Greenhut ruled that from the first shock of combat, Indian soldiers proved they were not up to the task of fighting a modern war.[29] Books by Byron Farwell echoed the conclusion.[30] Others such as those since written by Gordon Corrigan, Robert McLain, and George Morton-Jack have provided a reappraisal of the Indian soldiers who fought in

Introduction

France, finding that despite the material weaknesses of the Indian Corps, its Indian soldiers performed well.[31] David Omissi's published works have proven to be some of the most enduring. Drawing extensively on letters from Indian sepoys and sowars, Omissi provides readers with a previously unexplored perspective on the experiences of the Indian soldiers.[32]

Since the advent of the war's centennial, we have witnessed a growing interest among scholars generally to write the colonial presence into histories of the conflict. We now enjoy a richer appreciation for the fact that between 1914 and 1918, World War I involved not only British Pals, German *Frontschwein*, and French *poilus* but members of the Australian and New Zealand Army Corps (ANZAC) and Maoris, Sikhs and Muslims from South Asia, Moroccans, Algerians, and Tunisians, West Africans, Springboks, First Nation Canadians, Japanese, African Americans, Irish, Scottish, Italians, Magyars, Poles, Czechs, Russians, Mongolians, Indochinese, and Jamaicans. These soldiers shared canteens and shell holes. They haggled over the price of bread and cigarettes. Santanu Das writes, "The global reverberations of what at the time Germany alone, among the European nations, called the '*world war*' (Weltkrieg) become apparent as we substitute people, processes and effects of the war for places and events."[33] Battles and place-names no doubt serve as one marker of the war's "globality." The innumerable cross-cultural and interracial encounters engendered by the wartime mobilization of millions of human beings from almost every corner of the globe, the discursive representations of those encounters, and the implications of these on peoples near and far—these encompassed a second and no-less-important aspect of the war's global and imperial dimensions. Important works on the experiences of Caribbean, African, and Asian participants have challenged dominant Eurocentric narratives.[34] Another line of work better integrates the experiences of colonial subjects alongside those of Europeans.[35] Works of this sort—such as those of Richard Fogarty, Rozina Visram, and Heike Liebau—allow us to better capture the pre-1918 world "in all its integrated and multifarious complexity."[36] Books by Heather

Introduction

Streets-Salter, Leila Fawaz, Nikolas Gardner, and Charles Townshend (among others) underscore the point that it will no longer do to treat the protracted campaigns in Africa and Asia offhandedly as "sideshows."[37] Vedica Kant, Shrabani Basu, Kaushik Roy, and George Morton-Jack offer valuable reappraisals of Indian Army operations across the various battlefronts of World War I.[38] Santanu Das and Kate Imy bring to light the war's impacts on Indian colonial society and culture.[39] Gajendra Singh spans both World War I and World War II as he uncovers some of the ways Indian soldiers navigated multiple and sometimes competing identities.[40] At a 2014 conference coinciding with the centennial of the outbreak of the war hosted by Queen Mary University of London there was an entire strand devoted to Indian perspectives. There have also been a number of conferences in India. Alan Jeffreys has recently published a volume called *The Indian Army in the First World War*, part of a growing series in association with the Centre of Armed Forces Historical Research at the United Service Institution of India.[41]

Bearing Witness: Indian Soldiers in the Historical Record

What emerges in the pages that follow here is a story that captures something of the "globality" of India's war, of the interconnectedness of seemingly disparate events and distant places between 1914 and 1918. Drawing on a wide variety of sources, I draw comparisons and tease out long-overlooked connections that were (or were not) readily apparent not just to soldiers engaged on fronts spanning Europe, Africa, and Asia but to their contemporaries in Britain and India as well. The wartime experiences of the sepoys and the sowars are best revealed in the letters they wrote from the front to friends and family in India or to comrades deployed to other fronts. In late September 1914, as soldiers from India began arriving in France, British Army authorities decided to subject the soldiers' correspondence to systematic examination. Lieutenant E. B. Howell, a member of the Political Department of the Indian Civil Service attached to a regiment of Indian cavalry, was appointed censor of Indian mail and set up his offices in

Rouen at the Indian Base Post Office in November 1914. The station later moved to Boulogne. Through 1918 the Censor's Office provided military authorities with reports (of varying frequency and length) summarizing the contents and the tenor of Indian soldier letters postmarked from France or sent to soldiers in France from India or the Middle East. The office also included a large selection of translated excerpts with each report. When we read Indian soldier letters, we must not imagine that we are somehow eavesdropping on the innermost thoughts of the soldiers, as David Omissi has pointed out. Many of the soldiers did not pen their own letters but dictated them to a literate friend or officer. This dynamic alone may have changed what the soldier was prepared to say. Despite efforts to conceal the working of the Censor's Office from the troops, by April 1915 soldiers stationed on the Western Front knew that their letters were passing through the hands of men who were not their immediate superior officers.[42] The other real issue we have to bear in mind when working with this source material is that the censors excerpted what they wanted, what interested them. Soldiers exchanged tens of thousands of letters that we will never see. We only have access to the soldiers whose letters caught the eyes of the censor. "The fact that the sources exist only or largely in English complicates the situation further," Gajendra Singh reminds us in his book *The Testimonies of Indian Soldiers and the Two World Wars: Between Self and Sepoy*. "It is impossible to know if there were mistranslations in the texts or whether surrogates were found for untranslatable or indecipherable concepts."[43]

Be that as it may, these letters—housed in and freely available in digital format through the British Library—constitute an invaluable source, for even if the soldiers sometimes composed their letters in guarded language (or encoded, to keep the British censors guessing), their letters speak to the everyday anxieties, fears, hopes, prayers, courage, and sacrifice of men at war. I supplement these soldier letters with soldier testimonies, interviews, and witness statements—some collected by the British, some collected by the Germans; some collected during the war, some collected after the war. Just like any European who marched off to war in August 1914 to cheers of "To Berlin!" or "Nach Paris!" the severity of the fighting—regardless of where it took place—was far beyond anything the Indians expected. Indian soldiers fighting in France or the Dardanelles, Mesopotamia, East Africa, or Palestine experienced loss and learned to cope with industrial war as well as anybody else. They suffered through artillery bombardments, mass destruction, and prolonged exposure to the elements. In France they complained bitterly about the rain and the cold, just like French, German, and English soldiers did.[44] In Iraq soldiers endured debilitating heat. The Indians' hastily scratched prayers and poems, like those so finely polished by Wilfred Owen, reveal men profoundly affected by war. "The state of things is indescribable," so many of the soldier letters read. "What more can I write?" Historian Santanu Das writes, "The unprecedented violence of the First World War pushed men to the very edge of language. Yet, paradoxically, the war also produced an extraordinary outpouring of words, images and songs."[45] In some ways Indian soldier letters are evidence of what the German veteran-turned-novelist Erich Maria Remarque later wrote in *All Quiet on the Western Front*. War can destroy even those lucky enough to have escaped the shells.

The existence of so many Indian soldier letters, neatly catalogued and annotated in British archives, is itself a reminder that deploying colonial subjects to fight the king's enemies caused the British considerable unease. "There was nothing marginal about the existence of [Indian soldiers] under the British Raj," historian Gajendra Singh writes. Their voices "were not to be repressed or ignored, but censored; privileged in the sense that they were to be recorded, listened to, and stored for posterity."[46] The empire needed soldiers. And Indians fulfilled that need. At the same time, soldiering provided Indians with innumerable opportunities and previously unimaginable experiences, some of which the colonial state frowned upon.[47] The censor did not permit letters detailing sexual encounters with French women to ship to their intended recipients in India, for example. He worried that such letters might

Introduction

undermine white prestige and British colonial rule. Some soldiers complained in their letters that it was unfair to send wounded men back to the front after their convalescence. Partly in response to this, hospital administrators in England permitted hundreds of soldiers to return home. Repeated protest won Indian cavalry in France home leave starting in 1917. Men were needed at the front, to be sure, but sometimes it was best to give in to the soldiers' protests. Other sepoys complained that the British treated Indian lives as cheap. "There is no hope that I shall see you again for we are as grain that is flung a second time into the oven," one soldier wrote. Despite the hardships of the war or the deprivations of overseas service, despite the injustices soldiers experienced or the myriad ways their commanders made them feel their subordinate status, despite the sheer (at times) incompetence of their battlefield commanders or the reckless disregard with which their lives were sometimes held by the men conducting the war from 10 Downing Street or Delhi, the vast majority of Indian soldiers went "over the top" every time their officers gave the command. But when the Indian soldier complained about service conditions, his letter became a vehicle by which he could spread discord and discontent in and beyond the ranks of the Indian Army.[48] And the British worried that if they failed to keep soldier discontent in check, otherwise loyal Indian soldiers might turn on their colonial masters. That's why the British censored the Indian mail. Therefore, Indian soldier letters can teach us as much about British priorities as they can teach about Indian perspectives.

Soldier letters also serve as an important reminder that audiences in India were awash in war news. No matter where they served, soldiers found the space and time to write to folks back home, becoming, in fact, a main supplier of war news to Indian communities. At the time of the Battle of Neuve Chapelle in March 1915, soldiers at the front in France and Belgium sent upward of twenty thousand letters a week to friends, family, and fellow soldiers in India.[49] Punjabis had a particular interest in the fortunes of India's soldiers. Their province provided nearly half of the combatant soldiers India sent abroad during the war. The stories soldiers told were the stories for which people in India waited with baited breath. Theirs were the stories that could move a young man to enlist or move a mother to stand defiantly between the recruiting officer and her son. Peasants tilling their fields in the Punjab countryside cared a lot more about what their sons and brothers and husbands reported than what the *Times* had to say. And rightly so. One Punjabi Muslim serving as a recruiter in India observed of those at home, "Everyone's thoughts are always with their soldier sons across the sea, and they are in ceaseless anxiety." "From this war lasting so long uneasiness is caused in the whole of India," another man wrote to a soldier serving in France in 1915. "There is no one who has not some friends or relatives engaged in this campaign. When the telegrams announcing the casualties arrive in all the districts, near and far, great grief and trouble is caused; because each one is connected with the other by the chain of friendship or relationship." News of the war stoked the fears and anxieties of those at home. In other cases no news from the front was the worst thing imaginable. After suffering a debilitating defeat at the Battle of Ctesiphon, south of Baghdad, in November 1915, Indian soldiers belonging to the 6th Division did not have the opportunity to write. A soldier in the 22nd Punjabis in Hyderabad wrote to a cavalry soldier in France in early January 1916, "We have no news from the regiment, how they fared [at Ctesiphon]."

Beyond soldier letters what we might call official military and political documents—parliamentary speeches, correspondence between battlefield commanders and the viceroy or cabinet-level secretaries, and government-sponsored reports (just to name some of these)—take us beyond the frontlines and the Indian home front to the halls and offices of those who determined wartime strategy and policy. We learn from these, for instance, that British statesmen and army commanders had deep misgivings about the deployment of Indian soldiers to Europe, rooted in their empire's longstanding commitment to racial inequality and white supremacy, their public pronouncements notwithstanding. Official correspondence reveals that Indian soldiers were sent on a hastily conceived and inadequately supplied campaign to capture Bagh-

Introduction

dad in 1915 not because it was militarily expedient, but because Britain's war was then otherwise going badly in France and the Dardanelles, and a win, anywhere, before the close of the year might play well for Indian audiences. Two studies released by Parliament in 1917 on Indian Army operations in Mesopotamia reveal the gross incompetence of the commanders orchestrating operations in that theater. The findings of a Government of India–sponsored investigation into the causes of the 1919 disturbances that rocked the Punjab, and another sponsored by the Indian National Congress, reveal that although the war raised expectations in India for political change, four years of fighting had done next to nothing to uproot British racial prejudice. I find these documents important for they add layers and context to the decisions soldiers confronted on and off the battlefield.

Documents unearthed in German archives also have a story to tell. The German Foreign Office spearheaded an ambitious propaganda campaign targeting Indian soldiers captured on the Western Front. At a prisoner-of-war camp south of Berlin, expatriate Indian radicals belonging to the Ghadar Party tried to "convert" Indian sepoys to their cause—bringing anticolonial revolution to India. Ultimately the propaganda campaign did not bear much fruit, but tucked away in the files of the German Foreign Office are anecdotes about Indian soldiers in captivity or recollections of conversations between Ghadar agents and Indian sepoys, written in reports filed by Ghadar agents for the eyes of German Foreign Office officials. These documents add a rich perspective on the experiences of Indian soldiers, one to which we are not privy from a seat in the British Library or the British National Archives in Kew, London. We see from these documents, for example, that soldiers exhibited a range of responses to anticolonial propaganda. Some soldiers were sympathetic. A few renounced their allegiance to the British Raj, enlisted in the Ottoman Army, and disappeared from the historical record. One young man appears in the German archives and the British archives. Captured on the Western Front in late 1914, sepoy Mahomed Arifan told his German captors that he was eager to participate in their anti-British crusade, just as soon as he recovered from the wounds he sustained in battle. But by the end of the war, he'd passed through one punishment camp after another, having refused every attempt by the Germans and by Ghadar agents to win him over to their cause. A British officer who served with Arifan in captivity called him "a credit to the Indian Army." Arifan's case is a reminder that we must always approach our sources with humility, that we never have access to the "full story." Sepoys did not compose letters for our eyes. Sometimes soldiers told their captors one thing, their comrades another, and their commanders something else entirely. Testimony, giving interviews, letter writing—these are performative acts, crafted within a particular context for a specific audience. Soldiers like Arifan could not choose the terrain to which they were deployed, but they sometimes navigated war-torn landscapes in ways the authorities had not anticipated. Comparing what we find in German archives with what appears in British archives occasionally offers us glimpses of things the British or the Germans were unable or unwilling to see themselves.

British and Indian newspapers constitute a final corpus of sources. The wartime press in both Britain and India was not what we might think of as a free press. In Britain the 1914 Defense of the Realm Act banned reports that might undermine loyalty to the king or deter recruitment. Law barred newspapers from publishing military information that could be of potential value to the enemy. India's wartime government enjoyed comparable powers under the 1915 Defense of India Act. In Punjab, India, Lieutenant Governor Michael O'Dwyer wielded this law as a cudgel to shut down newspapers he deemed too critical of how the British handled the war, as well as newspapers that he believed showed too much empathy toward the Turks. Indian nationalists and the Indian press were free to criticize the government and its handling of the war to a point. But newspaper editors knew that if they took their criticisms too far, the Punjabi state might shut them down. Zafar Ali, the editor of the *Zamindar*, was confined to house arrest for much of the war. His newspaper was in and out of print per order of the state. In 1916 the Lahore *Panjabee* complained of "a hard-

Introduction

ening of the official attitude" of the state, "which is more surprising because the press all over the country has nobly responded to the call of duty and has eschewed much of the criticism in which it indulges in ordinary times."[50]

Above and beyond anything else since the invention of moveable type, newspapers have enabled people near and far "to think about themselves, and to relate themselves to others, in profoundly new ways," to quote the scholar Benedict Anderson.[51] Newspapers make it possible for people to imagine themselves as belonging to communities of people, most of whom they might never meet. The engines of print capitalism were very busy during the war years. It was through a subscription to the *Times*, for example, that people might have *felt* their Britishness during the war. It was in the newspapers that they followed the fortunes of their local "pals battalion" at the front. It was from the headlines that they might learn to cheer German setbacks and lament Russian retreats. When people in England learned about the exploits of Indian troops on battlefields in France or distant Mesopotamia, they were reminded again and again that those were *their* Indian troops in action. "An important success has been achieved by the British [at Neuve Chapelle]," one newspaper reported in the aftermath of that battle in March 1915. "The victory is due to the valour of *our* Indian troops, who first figured as soldiers on European soil near the village they have now captured."[52] In this way newspapers functioned as a form of imperial propaganda. Their headlines fueled the colonial imagination. A watchful British press also had very real impacts on the lives of Indian soldiers. When newspapers paid attention to Indian soldiers—as they did when Indian troops were deployed to France and Belgium, for example—Indian soldiers received better health care. When newspapers did not pay attention to Indian soldiers, civil and military authorities deprioritized soldier health care. This happened in the Middle East in 1915 and 1916 with disastrous results. When newspapers at last turned their attention to conditions in the region, sepoy health care improved. British media coverage therefore in two instances led to better healthcare outcomes for soldiers.

Introduction

India had a robust and energetic press at the outbreak of the war. Indian readers in cities such as Calcutta and Bombay, Lahore or Amritsar, had a number of newspapers in a variety of languages from which to choose. From the pages of these, India's college-educated middle-classes—sometimes referred to a "babus"—were able to articulate a host of reforms and, in so doing, position themselves against India's traditional ruling princes and the majority of Indians, the peasants and the urban poor.[53] I am particularly interested in how Punjabi newspapers reported the war, in no small part because Punjab Province provided more combatants for the Indian Army than any other province in the British Raj. Appropriately, newspaper readers in the Punjab wanted war news. One soldier stationed in India wrote to a friend fighting in France, "It is a great pity that you have not got the Victoria Cross. I have quite tired my eyes over the newspapers looking for your name but have not found it.... Well, I at any rate have spent 20 rupees on newspapers!" Punjab's urban centers—Lahore, Amritsar, Kapurthala, Jullundur, Ludhiana, and Rawalpindi—hosted a variety of English, Urdu, and Gurmukhi language newspapers, published by Indians for an Indian readership. Lahore was the epicenter of the industry, where readers could choose from more than seventy titles in August 1914. Most newspapers had a modest circulation of fewer than one thousand copies. Some, like the English-language *Tribune*, printed in Lahore, had a more robust daily run of two thousand copies. The largest daily was the Urdu-language *Zamindar*, with a circulation of fifteen thousand copies. The Government of India's Criminal Investigation Department routinely collected and translated samples of the Indian nationalist press. During World War I, the department issued weekly reports on the tenor of the Indian press, along with a collection of translated newspaper articles. Like the Indian soldier letters, these reports and translated extracts are readily accessible in the records of the India Office, housed at the British Library in London. In 2016 I published an edited collection of five hundred of these extracts in a book, *War News in India*. Here I expand on the findings of that work.

Introduction

Between 1914 and 1918 some Punjabi newspapers that were mostly in line with Indian nationalist organizations such as the INC or the Home Rule League made the case for a host of reforms, including changes in army recruitment policy, Indian eligibility for officer's commissions, and political rights. The future of India's place within the British Empire inspired some of the most heated editorializing. When Britain declared war on Germany in August 1914, Indian nationalists and nationalist newspapers lined up behind the empire's cause. "Let Indians assist Government during the present crisis," urged the editors of one Amritsar newspaper in September 1914. "Then we feel sure that Government will feel more disposed to grant self-government to India in the future."[54] Sentiments like these were consistent with the stance of the moderate politicians who then dominated the INC. Many newspapers of various shades and stripes—those catering to Sikh, Muslim, or Hindu readerships, for example—advanced this logic. For Indian nationalists, the services of Indian troops stood as proof positive that India deserved self-government and its own representative institutions modeled after those enjoyed by white Canadians or Australians. "There can be no doubt but that our soldiers, by their undaunted bravery, have won for themselves and for India an imperishable fame," another Punjabi newspaper recorded. "Their casualties [on the Western Front] may be heavy; but the reward is rich.... [The soldiers' deeds] will win for India the honour she deserves among the nations of the world."[55] As the war dragged on, Indian nationalists became more organized and nationalist newspapers grew bolder. Local politics and reform campaigns were infused with a more "national" flavor. Bal Gangadhar Tilak and Annie Besant founded the Home Rule League. In 1917 Besant served as president on the INC. The *Kisan* editorialized for its majority Muslim readership in Lahore in September 1917, "the services of Indians in the war have extorted the love and sympathy of British statesmen and even members of Parliament have been interested in the subject of Indian self-government. The question of Home Rule, which we are anxious to obtain but which we never expected to obtain for an indefinite period, has entered within the

Introduction

range of practical politics."⁵⁶ In the end the war left as many new questions in its wake as it had resolved. In 1918 and 1919 all eyes turned to the peace talks in Paris, where the American president, Woodrow Wilson, was preaching national self-determination. But when the Government of India decided to extend its wartime suspension of civil liberties into peacetime and subsequently deployed Indian troops to Indian cities to impose law and order, many Indian nationalists renounced their loyalty to the British Empire.⁵⁷

Scope and Sequence

This book is broken into eight chapters (plus a conclusion), organized chronologically and spatially, reflecting two of the work's underlying premises. The first of these is that human beings encountered empire and rehearsed (or resisted) racist ideologies and policies in everyday spaces. The second premise is that even though the stalemate and trenches of the Western Front continue to dominate popular imagination and memory of the conflict (and most especially in American and British cinema), World War I was in fact a period of intense (albeit temporary) intercontinental human migration. Chapter 1 is about the racial politics of the British Empire from the 1857 Indian Rebellion through 1914. It explores why Indian peasants from Punjab made careers as soldiers in the Indian Army, why recruiters barred most Indians from the army's ranks, and how members of India's emerging nationalist movement responded to racial prejudice. Chapter 2 explores the range of responses Indians offered to news of the outbreak of war in 1914. As rumor shot through the countryside, the INC rallied to the imperial standard. Ghadarites, on the other hand, incited soldiers to mutiny. The advent of World War I was a complicated moment in India, far beyond what British newspaper readers appreciated at the time.

Chapters 3 through 6 follow Indian soldiers to battlefields in Europe, Africa, and the Middle East. Among other things, we explore in these chapters the ways race and racial prejudice clouded the perceptions and decisions of battlefield commanders, and the choices soldiers made as they navigated the terrains to which they had been deployed. Chapter 3 is about the fourteen months the Indian Corps spent on the Western Front from late October 1914 through the close of 1915, how soldiers responded to the conditions they encountered there, and what the wartime press relayed to British and Indian audiences about the troops across the English Channel. Chapters 4 and 5 perform comparative work. Chapter 4 contrasts the experiences of soldiers wounded in combat in France to those of soldiers wounded in combat in the Middle East. Where soldiers fighting in Belgium and France in 1914 and 1915 had access to life-saving health care, their comrades fighting in the Middle East did not. Chapter 5 looks to things on the other side of no-man's-land, to the experiences of Indian soldiers captured by the Germans or the Ottomans. Where Indian soldiers captured on the Western Front found a ready-made prisoner-of-war camp waiting for them south of Berlin, complete with a Mosque paid for by the German kaiser, Indian soldiers captured at Kut in Iraq in April 1916 found that nothing had been done by the Ottomans to prepare for their care and comfort. Thousands of Indian soldiers died on forced marches into the Syrian dessert. Chapter 6 looks principally to Indian Army operations in the Middle East in 1917 and 1918, the closing years of the war. Amply equipped and well led, Indian soldiers enjoyed one success after another on the battlefield against a stubborn albeit outmatched Turkish opponent. On October 30, 1918, the Indian Army knocked Turkey out of the war.

The book's final two chapters shift the gaze to wartime and postwar India, where Indian national aspirations increasingly ran counter to British colonial ambition. Chapter 7 is about wartime recruitment in India. In order to meet the demand for manpower, the Government of India ramped up recruiting efforts considerably in 1917 and 1918. In the final summer of the war Gandhi emerged as one of India's most enthusiastic pro-war and pro-empire propagandists. He toured the countryside, extolling Indians to join the army. All the while, the Government of India orchestrated a brutal and coercive campaign to secure manpower for the war. Chapter 8 looks to the closing months of the war and the immediate post-

Introduction

war period. Between November 1918 and February 1919 all eyes turned to the peace conference in Paris where Indian hopes for self-government were dashed by the Allies' commitment to making the world safe for white supremacy. In March and April 1919, events in India claimed the spotlight when Indian troops deployed to Indian cities to gun down Indian demonstrators participating in Gandhi's first nationwide general strike, or *hartal*. The events of the immediate postwar months were decisive. They were when Gandhi and the Indian National Congress abandoned their earlier stance of unconditional support for the empire. In the conclusion I consider some of the legacies of the war on South Asian communities as well as the racial politics that went into commemorating India's dead after the war.

This book follows the fortunes of the Indian soldiers who fought in World War I, as well as the destinies of those who followed the fates of the sepoys. In the chapters that follow, we'll trace the movements of men from remote rural villages in the Punjab who joined the ranks of the Indian Army to the trenches of Belgium and France, to the beaches at Gallipoli, and to the walls of Baghdad and Jerusalem. We'll read accounts of Indian soldiers in action penned by their British commanders and comrades-in-arms as well as by their German opponents. We'll hear from the soldiers who recovered from wounds at hospitals in southern England and in the Persian Gulf; who endured starvation at Kut, death marches across Syria, or the loneliness of captivity in a prison camp outside Berlin. We'll uncover what Indian soldiers said to their king, to comrades serving on other fronts, and to family back home. We'll unpack the assumptions of people in wartime Britain and India and Germany who wrote about Indian soldiers in newspapers and propaganda pamphlets. We'll trace Gandhi's development during the war, as he went from a cheerleader of the British Empire to one of its most outspoken critics. And we'll hear from some of the Indian soldiers and Indian Army officers who participated in the violent suppression of Indian demonstrators in places such as Delhi and Amritsar in 1919. It is to those stories that we now turn.

1

Peasants into Sepoys

> Brother, this is the opportunity to show your worth. To give help to your family and render aid to Government, fight well, kill your enemy and do not let him attain his object. If you die, you will make a name up to seven forefathers and will go straight to Paradise. You will become as famous as the sun. Bravo. Bravo.
>
> —Letter from an Indian soldier to his comrade fighting in France, February 1915

One cannot help but wonder what parting words Indian soldiers shared with each other and with their families when war broke out in 1914. Reading the letter above, one is led to the conclusion that some Indian soldiers must have looked forward to the opportunity to "show [their] worth" in battle during World War I. Likely just as many thought the war an inconvenience. For the Indian soldier who deployed to France, or to East Africa, or the Persian Gulf in the opening months of the war, overseas deployment was what he had come to expect from the job. Indeed, Great Britain had a long history of recruiting Indian colonial subjects into its armed forces by the start of the twentieth century. The Indian Army recruited young men mainly from the British-controlled Punjab and North-West Frontier Province. Soldiers also hailed from independent Nepal and Afghanistan. These men had gained considerable experience in the field before 1914, in places such as China, Tibet, and Somalia, or along the Indian border with Afghanistan. The British Empire also had a long and ugly track record of racism and racial exclusion. Where a white man might be free to emigrate from one corner of the empire to another in 1900, an Indian man was not. Separate policies governed the conduct and treatment of Indian soldiers and British soldiers serving in the Indian

Army. The Indian Army, therefore, was itself a racist institution whose soldiers—British and Indian alike—fought on behalf of a deeply racist empire. This chapter is about the Indian Army and the British Empire's racial politics between 1857 and 1914. Why did Indian men from Punjab or North-West Frontier Province serve in Britain's armed forces? What did India's emerging nationalist movement make of the Indian Army and its sepoys? What ideas or prejudices about Indian soldiers did British audiences harbor? Some answers to these questions—knowing something of the Indian Army's history prior to 1914 alongside the British Empire's racist history—will help us better understand the choices people made when the world went to war in 1914.

"Martial Races" and the Long Shadow of 1857

Indians had been serving in British colonial militaries since the eighteenth century when the East India Company began employing an irregular force of a few hundred Indian troops who guarded four to five company-owned factories. By 1856 the body had grown to a force of 214,985 native troops supplemented by 39,375 Europeans. This army comprised three distinct presidency armies, each with its own commander-in-chief and each with its own distinct recruiting areas. Of these, the Bengal Army—which drew its recruits mainly from high-caste Rajputs and Brahmins from the Purabiya region of Awadh and Bihar—was the largest, boasting 137,000 regulars and 20,000 cavalry. In 1857 about three-quarters of the soldiers belonging to the Bengal Native Infantry were high-caste men from Awadh.[1] In 1858 British rule changed from East India Company hands to rule by the Crown. Thereafter the Indian Army answered to the British monarch. By 1914 the Indian Army was the largest employer in British India. There were 159,134 Indians serving in the ranks as combatants, mostly as infantrymen (sepoys) or as cavalrymen (sowars), supported by 34,767 Indian reservists. Another 45,660 Indians served as non-combatants. The British maintained a regular garrison of British troops in India as well, men on rotation from the Home Army.

The Indian Army was an institution born of political crisis. In

1857, a little more than half a century before sepoys deployed to the battlefields of World War I, Indian soldiers serving the East India Company very nearly drove the British from the subcontinent. On May 10, 1857, the 11th and 20th Bengal Native Infantry Regiments as well as the 3rd Light Cavalry stationed in Meerut mutinied, murdered their European officers, and began marching southwards to Delhi. Sepoy grievances had been mounting over the previous decade, caused largely by growing dissatisfaction with service conditions. In 1850 the 66th Native Infantry Regiment stationed outside Calcutta mutinied when military authorities decided to withdraw compensatory allowances for services in the recently annexed territory of Punjab. The General Service Act of 1856 stipulated that all sepoys, irrespective of caste, would be deemed eligible for overseas service. For many high-caste Rajputs and Brahmins, crossing the "black waters" of the Indian Ocean meant a loss of caste. When authorities further decided to open the Punjab to Sikh recruitment, these soldiers felt their monopoly on military service (crucial to their economic well-being) under threat. British authorities at last pushed their own soldiers to the breaking point when they issued cartridges greased with cow and pig fat—an insult to Muslim and Hindu soldiers alike (or so the story sometimes goes, when, in fact, the British never issued greased cartridges to their sepoys). Be that as it may, the mutinous soldiers marched on Delhi on May 10, rumor spread far and wide that the city had already fallen to the soldiers and that Bahadur Shah II had been proclaimed emperor of Hindustan. What began as a localized mutiny then exploded into a full-scale military and civil rebellion, one that quickly consumed most of north-central India. The rebellion lasted until June 1858, when the last of the rebel strongholds in Gwalior finally fell to the British.[2]

We need not here revisit the events of 1857 in greater detail. The lessons the British took to heart—and to be sure, they oversimplified what really was a very complicated moment—became the drivers of policy. English audiences read that the loyalty of Indian sepoys should not be taken for granted. Newspapers told one story after another about this or that plot. Every week uncovered a new sepoy conspiracy. The *Sheffield Daily Telegraph* reported "a Mohammedan conspiracy," in one instance, "aiming at the utter destruction of the English rule in India, and making the Hindu sepoys ... the tools for accomplishing it."[3] Another article reported that the sepoys of a Sikh regiment, "which was much trusted," had fired at their own officers, "who had been speaking in such high terms of them." Routed in short order by well-disciplined white soldiers, the rebels retreated and proceeded to terrorize the nearby cantonments, "maddened by defeat and thirsting for blood."[4] One August 1857 letter to the editor of the *Times* pinned blame for the "Mutiny of 1857" on

> the system introduced within the last 10 years of pampering, humbugging, toadying, and educating the 'high caste' natives to such an extent as to give them the idea that they are equal to Englishmen. For all useful purposes the low caste men are infinitely superior—they are the best soldiers and the best servants, while the others are insolent, lazy, and insubordinate. It is vain to suppose that a native is to be treated the same as an Englishman. It is only by keeping him completely subordinate that we can hope to keep the country. Once elevate him and make him think that he is an Englishman's equal, and good-bye to all power over him.[5]

Again, the point here is not to reproduce British colonial assessments of things, but to analyze British assumptions. To be sure, some people became more skeptical of the empire. John Stuart Mill comes to mind. But 1857 failed to shake Britain's commitment to colonialism.[6] Instead observers and policymakers blamed the East India Company for poor governance. Or they blamed the whole thing on a few bad officers—"bad apples"—rather than looking for something more deep-seated, more systematic, more inherently unjust in the social system they had imposed. Thus a British policymaker might reason, where some sepoys readily mutinied against officers lacking in sympathy or command of the language, others remained loyal thanks to the presence of "good officers" who had long ago earned the trust of the men. All that was needed to hold on to India were better officers, our imagined policymaker might conclude. When British newspapers sold their readers lurid accounts of Indian violence, these stories buried for English audiences whatever legitimate grievances the sepoys had. As scholar Arjun Chowdhury puts it, "the very idea that the peasants might desire something other than what the British intended for them, and thus could perceive the British as enemies, was inconceivable."[7] The British imperialist could denounce the violence committed by Indians as obviously "savage," while dismissing the violence perpetrated by British soldiers as "rational" and "limited."[8] British newspaper readers in 1857 read, for instance, that English soldiers in Calcutta showed "dauntless bravery" and "dogged endurance."[9] The wave of insurrectionary violence indicated only that India had "relapsed to . . . the brutish state which British intervention had rescued her from."[10]

All of this is to say that the British failed to take a good honest look in the mirror. They failed to call their own colonial enterprise into question. The *Brighton Gazette* reassured its readership, "The history of British annexation in India, although here and there disfigured by acts of questionable morality, has been, upon the whole, one in which both our military glory and our character for benevolence and humanity have been considerably advanced." The newspaper continued, "If we do not take timely steps to reconquer India, it will pass away from beneath our sceptre and become the victim of some more grasping power."[11] The Crown assumed command in 1858. Thereafter public discourse minimized the scope and significance of the rebellion. Discounting 1857–58 for what it really was, it became just "The Sepoy Mutiny." In his 1911 book, *The Armies of India*, army major and popular commentator on Indian military affairs George MacMunn dismissed 1857 as an "unreasoned and uncalled-for mutiny."[12] He called it an episode of "madness," an exception to two centuries during which, "come rain come shine, the sepoy has followed and trusted" his British officer, his "sahib," "chanting the old chant of the patient East . . . 'Sometimes pleasure, sometimes pain, the servant of the English.'"[13]

The year 1857 set in motion a shift in recruitment practices in India, one that took several decades to develop fully. The exigencies of the rebellion had already prompted significant (ad hoc) changes in the composition of the Bengal army. Grateful to the nearly thirty thousand Punjabis who helped put down the rebellion, the British began immediately to replace "disgraced" Bengal units with soldiers mustered in the Punjab. By June 1858 about seventy-five thousand of the eighty thousand native troops in the Bengal army were Punjabis, with Sikhs alone numbering twenty-three thousand.[14] In July 1858 the British government appointed a commission under Secretary of State for War Major-General Peel to recommend changes to the organization of the Indian Army. Beyond rejecting outright two ideas—garrisoning India with an all-European army, on the grounds that such a measure was expensive to the extreme; and importing soldiers from other colonial holdings, on the grounds that they might inflame Indian racial feeling—the Peel Commission recommended little more than that the Indian Army was to remain Indian.[15] Recruitment in India remained largely haphazard and accidental for some time after that, but Russian expansion into Central Asia in the 1880s combined with the disappointing performance of the Indian Army in various border wars left key British observers doubting whether the Indian Army could take on a Western power. From then on, the search for the best fighting material, the "martial races," became an imperial obsession.[16]

The idea that certain "races" in India—just as readily referred to as "classes"—had a natural proclivity to military service first gained currency in the opening decades of the nineteenth century when the British started referring to Nepal's "martial tribes."[17] During the Second Sikh War (1848-49), a British general wrote that the Sikhs were "naturally brave." Newspapers were quick to reassure readers at the height of the 1857 Rebellion that these men—Nepalese Gurkhas and Punjabi Sikhs—had remained loyal. The *Times* billed Sikhs as the Punjab's "hereditary soldiers" in one article titled "How the Punjab Was Saved."[18] Following the explosion of social Darwinist racial theories at the end of the nineteenth century, the idea that some groups of people were more martial than others found the pseudo-scientific justification it required.[19] Thereafter, racism—coupled with a wary eye on Russian encroachment on Central Asia—dictated that the British shift their recruiting biases in India consistently in favor of the Punjab, the North-West Frontier, and Nepal. In January 1893 these three regions provided 44 percent of the Indian Army's manpower. By 1914 nearly 75 percent of the Indian Army came from these regions.[20]

This was an army, by British thinking, "based on a systematic grouping of men by race and sept and clan, with a view to the full development of race thinking."[21] Europeans, Major George MacMunn asserted, innately had the stuff to be soldiers whereas Indians did not. "It is one of the essential differences between the East and the West," wrote MacMunn, "with certain exceptions, only certain clans and classes can bear arms; the others have not the physical courage necessary for the warrior." In Europe, he claimed, "every able-bodied man, given food and arms, is a fighting man of some sort." The same could not be said of Asia. "In the East, or certainly in India, this is not so," MacMunn believed. "The existence of this condition, therefore, much complicates the whole question of enlistment in India. It renders any form of levy *en masse* impossible."[22]

Owing to martial race theory, the British relied on only a very narrow segment of the Indian population to fill the ranks of the Indian Army. And within the Punjab, North-West Frontier Province, and Nepal, recruitment doctrine narrowed the pool of candidates even further. The emphasis was on securing the bulk of the army's manpower from certain groups—Sikhs, Punjabi Muslims, Dogras, and Hindu Jats from the Punjab; Pathans from the North-West Frontier; Gurkhas from Nepal.[23] Lord Roberts, onetime commander-in-chief in India, stressed "the necessity of carefully studying the varying characteristics of the several Indian races" that served in the army, a bias rooted in his experience in the Second Anglo-Afghan War and 1857 (more on him in a moment). Recruiting handbooks in the late nineteenth and early twentieth centuries instructed recruiters to seek out "races" of people characterized by self-sufficiency, physical and moral resilience, orderliness, fighting prowess, and a sense of courage and loyalty.[24] One recruiting handbook described Gujars of Ferozepore as "a manly type," marked by a "love of fighting" and "the character for manly independence."[25] The British in India were obsessed with getting what they believed to be the right sort of men into the army and keeping the wrong sort out. This, they convinced themselves, was essential to maintaining the cohesion and loyalty of Indian battalions. "It must always be remembered that in India, military service is a source of much honour and prestige, so that pretenders will often try to pass themselves off as better born than they are," MacMunn commented in his 1911 book.[26]

The British segregated battalions and companies within battalions by nationality, or creed, or tribe, maintaining that the "solidarity and morale of the regiment often hinged on the shared values and traditions of the men who made up the regiment."[27] The 15th Sikhs, for example, was a "class regiment," made up of eight companies of Sikhs. The 58th Rifles, on the other hand, segregated different classes into different companies. The battalion deployed to France in 1914 comprised three companies of Sikhs, one of Dogras, three of Pathans, and one of Punjabi Muslims. The 59th Rifles consisted of three companies of Pathans, one of Punjabi Muslims, two of Sikhs, and two of Dogras. If a company of Punjabi Muslims took casualties during an expedition, recruiting parties looked for their replacements among a select few socially dominant Muslim tribes such as the Gakkhars, Januas and Awans, and a few Rajput tribes from the Rawalpindi and Jhelum districts in the northern Salt Range of the Punjab.[28] "Recruiters should always be of the same class as the required recruits as it is useless to send out a Shekh to enlist Rajputs, and *vice versa*," read one recruiting handbook.[29] The social structure of the village was typically replicated within the company or battalion. The authority of a subedar-major (sergeant) was generally reinforced by his position as a village elder. The localization of recruitment had a political purpose too. By recruiting evenly among different populations who (the British believed) harbored traditional or historical animosities, the British prevented any single group from becoming dominant within the military. It was an example of "divide and rule."[30]

Indian Soldiers in the British Colonial Imagination

Martial race doctrine received wide currency in Europe where newspapers, periodicals, and books brought the ideologies of colonial rule home for popular consumption. In Britain popular ethnography traced the origins of India's martial races to the age of Alexander the Great.[31] Frederick Roberts, commander-in-chief in India during the heyday of Victorian imperialism (1885–93), had been deeply conditioned by his experiences in the 1857 Rebellion and believed that the soldiers who had proven their worth during that episode—especially Scottish Highlanders, Sikhs, and Nepalese Gurkhas—embodied the physical and masculine qualities of ideal soldiers. Roberts used his celebrity status (acquired during the Second Afghan War in 1880 when he successfully commanded a 320-mile march from Kabul to Kandahar to rescue a beleaguered British garrison) and his political connections to publish a series of magazine and newspaper articles in order to buoy metropolitan support for martial race doctrine and British expansion into Northwest India and Central Asia.[32] Just before World War I, the aging commander passed the torch to Major George MacMunn, penning the foreword to MacMunn's book on the Indian Army. "No one is better able than myself to esteem that Army at its proper value," he said, "as regards to what it has—with the help of British training and example—achieved in the past, or to appreciate what it is capable of doing in the future under the same conditions."[33]

MacMunn's 1911 book brought home to British readers the orientalist tropes and racialized thinking then at the heart of recruitment policy in South Asia. His book advanced the stuff of colonial fantasy as fact for English readers.[34] The British liked to imagine that they and India's martial races shared a common—albeit somewhat stretched—Aryan lineage. The men who served in the ranks of the Indian Army were, like themselves, "of the northern races, whom a cold winter, and a lesser period of the enjoyment of peace, have for the present preserved from military deterioration."[35] One could even be forgiven for mistaking some of India's soldiers with those who marched in the armies of Alexander the

Great. Afridi Pathans, MacMunn wrote, "some of them, with close-cropped fair hair and blue eyes, have a distinctly European appearance" with "traces of the Greek soldiers" visible.[36] "European" in appearance or not, the thinking was that India's "martial races" possessed the characteristics the British sought in a soldier, the very same traits—so they told themselves—Britain's elite boys acquired at the country's prestigious public schools. Mazbi Sikhs were "faithful," MacMunn declared.[37] Since the Mutiny, he continued, "the Sikh" "has become a world-wide adventurer."[38] They were "tall, well-knit men." As a fighting man, the Sikh's "slow wit and dogged courage give him many of the characteristics of the British soldier at his best."[39] Dogras, MacMunn observed, were "among the most valued of all the soldier races of Northern India." He added, "Their good behavior, courtly manners, high courage, and physical endurance, make the Dogra a valued soldier by all who know him."[40] In Pathans the British saw some of the finer qualities they hoped for themselves too. Pathans were "hardy, active, alert, and inured to war. . . . To the best type of Englishman their open, irresponsible manner and delight in all exercise and sport, with their constant high spirits, appeal greatly, and certain types of Englishmen appeal greatly to them also."[41] Afridis especially were "famous as good soldiers, and, of course, excel as skirmishers."[42] Garhwalis of Nepal, "though not such soldiers by instinct as the Gurkha, they are a courageous hill-race who make active and obedient soldiers of considerable fighting value."[43]

But MacMunn was just as quick with a racist put-down, reminding (reassuring, one might say) his readers that South Asia's "martial races" remained nonetheless dependent upon the British for tutelage and leadership. Jats, he wrote, were "proverbially thick in the uptake."[44] Pathans were "imbued with considerable courage *when well led*, and capable of much *élan*."[45] In fact, whatever feats of daring or martial accomplishments Indians might achieve, MacMunn accredited to "some love of service, some power of the white man for attracting faithful service and admiration."[46] Absent a firm white hand to lead the way, there was little one could expect from the sepoys, in other words. Despite the best efforts of the British to "civilize" the native, there was only so much that could be done. One recruiting handbook from 1915 read, "In matters pertaining to his superstitions, the Punjabi Musalman does not appear to advance with the general rise in education. He is as superstitious as ever, and as prone to believe any fabulous tale."[47]

And the memory of 1857—fear of another mutiny—continued to plague British perception right through the eve of World War I. Certain Indian soldiers, the British worried, possessed a tendency for indiscipline. MacMunn wrote that Afridi Afghans of the Khyber Pass "are intensely republican or, more accurately, democratic, at times even paying no heed to their counsels of elders, every man a law unto himself."[48] Further south in Waziristan the British recruited from the Mahsud clans, the Darwesh Khel, and other Wazir clans. "They give us immense trouble, but make remarkably fine soldiers, especially when, as in the case of the Irish, they serve away from their own land." MacMunn asserted, "The clans are all, with the exception perhaps of the Afridis, intensely fanatical when stirred by the roll of the drum ecclesiastic."[49] Sayads, read one recruiting handbook, "if of good physique and extraction make excellent soldiers. A drawback to their enlistment is that being of a priestly class, they may use their influence in the wrong direction if they become discontented."[50] "It is not profitable to consider at any time the question of [the Indian Army's] faithfulness," MacMunn concluded, "since the measure of the fidelity of this great force is the measure of the fidelity of all mercenary armies, that is to say, of all armies that serve voluntarily for a wage."[51]

Peasant Soldiers

Decades after World War I, Mulk Raj Anand interviewed a number of the war's survivors as he prepared to write his novel about the sepoys deployed to France, *Across the Black Waters* (1939). "When they first joined the army," he wrote, "these legionaries did so because, as the second, third or fourth sons of a peasant family, overburdened with debt, they had to go and earn a little ready cash to pay off the interest on the mortgage of the few acres of land, the only thing which stood between the family and its fate." Of course, young Punjabi men who had known only the "confined life of small interests" in their "remote villages" were sensitive to the "elegant cut" of the sepoy uniform and the "well-oiled soft shoes which the Sarkar [the king-emperor] gave as regulation mufti." That uniform earned its wearer some esteem and prestige back home—it kept the local policemen at bay. And though the soldier's pay was not enough to "feed the insatiable greed" of the landlord or the moneylender, it might be enough keep the family fed, or "make up the gaps in the arrears in rent for five years ago due to the Sarkar." A promotion or a sudden award for conspicuous bravery might help the peasant family "pay off all arrears and start clear of all the misery once again with full possession of the land."[52] Upon retirement, a man who made his career in the military won for his family a pension and a grant of up to fifty acres of canal-irrigated land.

In 1914 the Indian Army was Britain's only professional overseas army. Its soldiers were volunteers, like those who served in the Home Army, drawn almost exclusively from the rural peasantry. Why might a young man from Punjab volunteer to serve in the armed forces of his colonial masters? The allure of reliable pay was always forefront in the young recruit's mind. Sikhs, Dogras, Pathans, and Gurkhas did not join the military because they loved it, historian Heather Streets-Salter argues. They joined the military because they had to.[53] For many of the Indian peasant families whose sons became soldiers, the Indian Army was all that stood between them and ruin. India's largest pool of recruits, the Punjab, experienced dramatic social and economic changes in the nineteenth century as a result of its annexation by the British Empire in 1849 and subsequent integration into global markets. An already impoverished region became increasingly dependent on fluctuations in the global wheat market and ready access to cash. Debt-ridden peasant families supplemented the family income through military service, and young Punjabi men became soldiers to secure the financial solvency of their families in response to a seemingly unpredictable and remorseless global market. An infantry private drew a base salary of 11 rupees a month in 1914. Active service earned the soldier one bonus or another.

So economics mattered, but as Anand's description of the sepoys in *Across the Black Waters* makes clear, pay and pension alone do not sufficiently explain the relationship between the Indian soldier and the British Raj. "It is becoming increasingly obvious that colonialism—as we have come to know it during the last two hundred years—cannot be identified with only economic gain and political power," Ashis Nandy wrote more than three decades ago in *The Intimate Enemy: Loss and Recovery of Self under Colonialism* (1983). Nandy's purpose was not to deny the importance of the political economy of colonialism, rather to redirect our gaze to what he termed the "psychological contours of colonialism in the rulers and the ruled," to define colonialism as "a shared culture which may not always begin with the establishment of alien rule in a society and end with the departure of the alien rulers from the colony."[54] The key here for our purposes is that understanding why a Punjabi peasant might choose to join the Indian Army requires that we examine more than just his family's finances. We must try to locate the social or cultural rewards that man believed he might gain from fighting for the very men who wished to use Indian peasants in order to extend British rule, to perpetuate Britain's "search for political and economic advantage" (again, Nandy's words) in South Asia. In a fascinating article centered on two retired British military officers who embraced fascism and yoga in the decades between the two world wars, historian Kate Imy points out that British soldiers serving in India "increasingly came face to face with their own physical inadequacies compared to South Asian men."[55] Indian soldiers enjoyed wrestling. They liked to "show off" by swinging clubs far too big for British soldiers to handle. The presence of these athletes in the ranks of the Indian Army in the interwar period stemmed from a growing trend in India at the turn of the century to cultivate "cultures of strength and martial masculinity." Imy writes, "Believing that South Asian bodies had been emasculated through years of colonialism, several late nineteenth- and early twentieth-century South Asian activists promoted physical culture."[56] They saw in the gymnasium, the playing field, and the recruitment office a space in which to restore their masculine virility.

Peasants into Sepoys

So, some combination of pay and prestige lured men to the military. And military service, in turn, functioned as a vehicle by which young Indian men improved their standing at home, reinforcing an ideal of manliness held by those who made their careers serving in the ranks.[57] One Indian wrote to his brother deployed to France in 1914: "We all hope that you will enlight the names of your ancestors by performing your duties to the utmost satisfaction. Be always brave as your ancestors, who were tiger-like warriors to spare their lives for the honor of Great Britain, & were called Bahadurs. If you want to face this side again, face as Bahadur. We all pray for your success & our daily devotion for the success of Great Britain."[58] One woman wrote to her three brothers serving with a mountain battery in Egypt during World War I: "God grant victory to our King, & bring you home from your wars in safety, my brother. War is the task of young men, to sport with death upon the field of battle, to be as a tiger & to draw the sword of valour & daring."[59] A Rajput in India wrote to his brother serving in France: "I am delighted to hear that you are going to the war.... There is no room for doubt. A Rajput could not find in all his life a better opportunity than this in displaying the virtue of the sword."[60] Letters such as these suggest that martial exploits garnered a young man his reputation; heroics won him and his family greater standing in the pecking order of the Punjabi village.

Indeed, Indian families sometimes wrote to their soldiers, describing the social advantages they hoped to accrue when their young men fought bravely on the battlefield. One Indian soldier deployed to France in 1914 received this from his father: "I have heard with much pleasure about your welfare and about the excellence of your work. If you are worthy you will render good service and secure a name (reputation). My father (your grandfather) was a soldier. I have reached the rank of Kot-Dafadar, now let us see what rank you can attain by exertion and bravery."[61] Letters like this abound in the reports filed by the censor of Indian mail in France. Families exhorted their soldiers to fight to defend their honor, reputation, and prestige—in a word, *izzat*.[62] Wartime service in the king's Indian Army, therefore, was something to which entire

Indian peasant families were prepared to rally by 1914. "You are very lucky, my brother to get such a chance," one man wrote to his brother deployed to France. "With heart and soul do your duty and you and your family will be highly honored. We unlucky ones are left behind in India and can do nothing for our illustrious Government nor can we gain reputation for our families."[63] "I shall be well pleased with you, if you do not turn your back on the enemy, so that our neighbors may not taunt us," wrote a woman from Jhelum to her son serving in France. "I have no other son to send to the war, therefore on no account whatever turn your back on the enemy."[64]

When an Indian peasant joined the army, he was subject to a code of conduct prescribed by the Indian Army Act of 1911, passed by the viceroy and his council. Although modeled after the statutes of the (British) Army Act of 1881, a careful read reveals that Indian soldiers and British soldiers were not equals in the eyes of military law. Because an Indian officer's commission came from the viceroy and not the king, he was automatically of lower rank than any British officer he met in the service, for example. His inferior status also guaranteed that an Indian officer had no chance of drawing a salary commensurate with that of a British officer serving in the Indian Army. Indian soldiers and Indian officers were subjected to harsher punishments that white soldiers and white officers, furthermore. If his crime was anything short of mutiny, a British officer could expect nothing worse than three years imprisonment or a dishonorable dismissal from the king's service. An Indian officer could be sentenced to death, to transportation, or to imprisonment for up to fourteen years.[65] Where flogging fell out of favor in the late nineteenth century as a form of punishment for British soldiers, the 1911 Indian Army Act permitted the use of the lash as a method of punishment for Indian soldiers. The Indian soldier may have been an imperial soldier. But the language of the law that governed his employment made clear that he was not to be treated as a white soldier might be treated. He was to be treated as distinctly Indian.[66]

Unequal in the British Empire's racial hierarchy, military service nonetheless made Indian peasants into some of the British

Empire's most formidable killers. Between 1900 and 1913 some seventy-five thousand Indian soldiers were sent overseas. In 1900 the Indian Army deployed soldiers to China to suppress the Boxer Rebellion. As part of an international coalition featuring soldiers from Britain, France, Russia, Germany, the United States, and Japan, Indian soldiers burned villages, looted temples, and executed Chinese civilians.[67] In Tibet in 1903 and 1904 Gurkhas threw terrified noncombatants from cliffs. That same year in Somalia, Indian troops fought Somali and Arab jihadists. In 1911 Indian troops burned Iranian villages and crops in the Persian Gulf, all to deter the smuggling of European rifles to tribesmen along the Afghanistan-India border. In 1913 Hindu soldiers of the 7th Rajputs massacred unarmed Hindu men, women, and children who were peaceably assembled to protest British colonial rule. Most of the experience that Indian soldiers acquired on campaign had been gained fighting in the independent tribal areas on the border of independent Afghanistan and the North-West Frontier Province. From these campaigns, such as the 1908 month-long war against Afridi and Mohmand tribesmen, Indians earned decoration, promotion, and all-around accolade from their British commanders. In the decades before World War I the Indian Army had earned a reputation in Britain and India for effectiveness and efficiency in the empire's service. In an interview with the *Natal Advertiser* (South Africa) in 1897, Gandhi said that India "furnishes some of the bravest soldiers to fight the wars of Great Britain in almost all parts of the world."[68] One prominent Indian politician said in a 1905 speech in London, "some of the best troops that fight the battles of the Empire today are drawn from the Indians themselves."[69]

Racial Discrimination and Immigration in the British Empire

The priorities of Indian Army commanders reflected the larger priorities that shaped policy across the British Empire. When the Indian soldier deployed overseas or to the North-West Frontier, he fought on behalf of a racist empire. This had been made plain just fifteen years before the start of World War I, when the British found themselves embroiled in a larger-than-expected war against Boer settlers in South Africa. Defeats early on taught the British that dominating the region would not come easy.⁷⁰ Accordingly some 448,435 imperial soldiers fought for the British Empire between 1899 and 1902, against a stubborn enemy adept at humiliating the highly touted British Army. The White Dominions of Australia, New Zealand, and Canada supplied more than 30,000 imperial troops. But when the viceroy of India, Lord Curzon, offered the services of the Indian Army in December 1899, policymakers turned him down. At a time when the secretary of state for war thought about 100,000 more men would be needed to fight, Conservative statesman A. J. Balfour, then in charge of the Foreign Office, assured Parliament that the war would remain a "white man's war." The secretary of state for India, George Hamilton, explained that deploying Indian troops to South Africa "would be dangerous in the extreme. It would probably raise the whole Dutch population up against us," because of the racial affront such a deployment would represent. The secretary also worried that sepoy victories against a white enemy in the Natal might inspire subjugated populations in India and elsewhere to defy the racist policies that were part of everyday British rule. The emboldened Indian Army might be willing to risk open mutiny.⁷¹ The specter of mutiny always hung over the British when it came to the Indian Army, a product of the 1857 Indian Rebellion. And racial discrimination was, after all, woven into the very fabric of the armed forces. Recall that only white officers could command Indian units, for example. During the South African War—a mere fifteen years before the outbreak of World War I—racism and a commitment to protecting white prestige overrode Britain's need for troops.

The South African war took place at a time when the world's racial boundaries were hardening, as countries such as the United States, Canada, South Africa, and Australia all implemented policies designed to establish themselves firmly as "white men's countries." Indians were then traveling throughout the empire, some pursuing education, others pursuing work. Tens of thousands of Indians lived abroad as indentured laborers. What worried the white settler governments were the Indians who immigrated freely, intending to stay. British Natal stripped the colony's forty-one thousand Indians of voting rights in the 1890s.[72] "These Indians were brought here for the purpose of supplying labor for development of local industries and were not intended to form a portion of the South African nation," said the attorney-general of the colony of Natal.[73] Gandhi—then working in the country as a lawyer—had never experienced racial discrimination like what he experienced in South Africa. "I think it will be readily granted that the Indian is bitterly hated in the Colony," he wrote in an 1894 pamphlet. "The man in the street hates him, curses him, spits upon him, and often pushes him off the footpath." The white settler press was unsparing in its venom and vitriol. "These parasites"; "Wily, wretched, semi-barbarous Asiatics"; and "a thing black and lean and a long way from clean, which they call the accursed Hindoo" were just some of the things an Indian might read about himself in a press that, in Gandhi's estimation, was unable to find "a sufficiently strong word in the best English dictionary to damn him with."[74] By 1910 Indians in South Africa had seen their voting rights stripped away, their marriages nullified, their schools shuttered, their right to work and own property restricted, and their movements carefully watched.

Gandhi would have encountered similar prejudices and conditions in Australia and New Zealand. One of the first laws Australia's newly minted government enacted in 1901 was a law effectively banning Asian immigration by means of a literacy test. In the debates leading up to passage of the Immigration Restriction Act, members of the Australian Parliament talked about their fears of "racial contamination," that immigration restriction was "a matter of life and death to the purity of our [white] race."[75] An editorial in the *Sydney Morning Herald* in March 1901 expressed its support for excluding Chinese, "Hindoos," and "men of other Eastern races" from Australia. "The experience of all countries shows the danger or unrestricted coloured immigration," the newspaper's editorialists warned, "and if we are to have 'a white Australia,' the Federal Parliament must devote its attention to the matter at an early stage."[76] The secretary of state for the colonies, Joseph Chamberlain, did not object to racial discrimination. He merely urged that Australian lawmakers discriminate tactfully, that they eschew explicit racial discrimination in favor of a literacy test modeled after that adopted in Natal. Legislation imposed in New Zealand in 1881, 1888, and 1896 restricted Chinese immigration. A dictation test of a hundred words in English was added to the arsenal in 1907 in order to have "the purity of our race maintained," in the words of successive prime ministers.[77]

At the same time, a similar story played out in North America. Responding to rising nativism among its white West Coast population, the United States banned immigration from China in the 1880s. Congress passed legislation in 1896 that would have severely curtailed immigration from Eastern Europe had President Grover Cleveland not vetoed it. In 1908 Canada enacted its own discriminatory immigration policy. Effectively closing Canada's borders to Indian immigrants, the Canadian governor-general stipulated that only those who had sailed directly to Canada from their port of departure and could afford the exorbitant entry fee of $200 per head would be allowed to enter the country. This was a thinly veiled attempt to defend the whiteness of Canada, one that the Indian viceroy, Lord Minto, applauded for its "elegance," for "keeping out Indians without needing to be clumsily direct in acknowledging the awkward two-tiered status of the dominions separating the white-settler colonies of Canada and Australia from His Majesty's Asian and African possessions."[78]

The racial discrimination Indians encountered abroad was the focus of considerable criticism in Indian newspapers. Calling attention to "the wretched condition of Indians in the colonies," the editorial staff at the *Hindu* opined to its Lahore readership in 1914, "We would be quite justified in saying that a dog would receive better treatment in South Africa than the Indians do at the hands of the Europeans there."[79] The Indian press hammered on the fact that white settlers in Great Britain's self-governing dominions—South Africa, Australia, New Zealand, and Canada—had the authority to determine their own immigration policies and that Indians did not. "The exercise by the self-governing colonies of the right to control immigration can in the present circumstances only mean that while they can exclude Indians, India cannot exclude their citizens," the *Panjabee* reminded its Indian readership. "This is absolutely unjust and is utterly inconsistent with the existence of common Imperial citizenship."[80] The newspaper hammered on this point in a scathing piece.

> The vital fact . . . is that no Englishman has ever been excluded on the ground that he is an Englishman. He is excluded either on the ground that he is physically unfit, or because the labour market in some particular department is overstocked or for some equally intelligible reason. What distinguishes the case of the Indian is that he is excluded because he is an Indian. Not that this is always openly avowed, but there is no manner of doubt that, in the majority of cases, this and nothing else is the reason. [Canada's continuous journey clause is] only a hypocritical device for excluding Indians.[81]

Imperial Brotherhood, the Aryan Connection, and the Indian Army

Mohandas Karamchand Gandhi was a struggling lawyer in Bombay when, in 1893, the firm of Dada Abdulla & Co. offered him a one-year contract to assist with a legal matter in the British colony of Natal, in South Africa (then not yet a country). He decided to remain in Natal, however, when Indian merchants asked him to assist them in resisting a bill abolishing Asian enfranchisement, then working its way through the Natal Parliament. "Providence has put the English and the Indians together," he wrote in a December 1894 open letter to the colony's lawmakers, "and has placed in the hands of the former the destinies of the latter."

Between 1893 and 1914—during his time in South Africa—Gandhi began formulating a semicoherent vision of what he would sometimes call "imperial brotherhood." In his 1894 open letter, Gandhi pleaded his case that "India is not Africa." Rather, he said, "It is a civilized country in the truest sense of the term *civilization*." Gandhi's appeal coincided with what some historians have called "the Aryan moment," a time when British imperialists and Indian elites alike appealed to an imagined, shared Anglo-Indian lineage. "The English and the Indians spring from a common stock, called the Indo-Aryan," Gandhi's letter asserted. It was for these reasons he opposed racial discrimination against his fellow Indians. He sought to "unify the hearts of the two races [Indian and English], which are, legally and outwardly, bound together under a common flag."[82] And here we begin to see that what Gandhi sought was his own integration, not that of all of the colony's inhabitants. His appeal was rooted in racism. Ashwin Desai and Goolam Vahed write in their book, *The South African Gandhi*, "Gandhi carried the idea of a hierarchy of civilizations to South Africa."[83] Gandhi denounced what he called "a general belief" among the colony's white settlers "that the Indians are little better, if at all, than savages or the Natives of Africa. Even the children are taught to believe in that manner, with the result that the Indian is being dragged down to the position of a raw Kaffir." When it came to black Africans, Gandhi could be just as contemptuous as Natal's white settlers.

Gandhi fervently hoped, even believed—despite mounting evidence to the contrary—that proffers of Indian loyalty might win the hearts and minds of British statesmen and secure for Indians redress under British rule.[84] During the South Africa War he urged his countrymen to support the British war effort unconditionally, "in any capacity in which they could be useful, in order to show the Colonists that they were worthy subjects of the Queen."[85] In 1899 Gandhi formed an Indian ambulance corps of some six hundred stretcher-bearers who, foregoing pay, tended to the war's British wounded. Speaking before a large gathering in Durban in 1901, he articulated his aims: "What was wanted in South Africa was not a white man's country; not a white brotherhood, but an Imperial brotherhood. Everyone who was the friend of the Empire should aim at that."[86] Gandhi did not extend the affections of brotherhood to black Africans. At the close of 1903, when the Johannesburg Municipality permitted a number of Africans to live alongside Indians, Gandhi protested the decision. He wrote to the city's medical officer of health, "About this mixing of the Kaffirs with the Indians, I must confess I feel most strongly. I think it is very unfair to the Indian population and it is an undue tax on even the proverbial patience of my countrymen."[87] When the plague hit Durban in 1905, Gandhi complained that "at the plague hospital, no distinction is made between Indians and Kaffirs, all being herded together indiscriminately."[88] And when the Zulu nation rose in rebellion against white settler colonialism in 1906, Gandhi again rushed to the defense of the British Empire, volunteering his services once more as a stretcher-bearer. While British machineguns and dumdum bullets ripped apart African bodies, Gandhi wrote in his newspaper, *Indian Opinion*, "Indians have now a splendid opportunity for showing that they are capable of appreciating the duties of citizenship."[89]

Gandhi's appeal to an "imperial brotherhood" of Indian and English was quite typical of the moderates who dominated the Indian National Congress (INC) at the dawn of the twentieth century. Founded in 1885, the INC was India's first nationalist organization. Its membership was largely drawn from a narrow stratum of university-educated Indian bourgeoisie. Moderate nationalists saw a greater role for themselves in helping govern the British Raj, and for India within the framework of the British Empire. They were reformers. In the words of their most recognized spokesman, Gopal Krishna Gokhale (Gandhi's close mentor, a member of the INC since 1889, president of the INC in 1905), the moderates wanted "to secure for the people of [India] a system of administration in India itself similar to that enjoyed by the self-governing members of the British Empire; and, secondly, a participation for [Indians] not only in the burdens and responsibilities of the Empire but also in its privileges on equal terms with those other members." The moderates were not anti-imperialists. Neither were they anti-racist. Speaking at the National Liberal Club in London in 1905, Gokhale stressed for his English listeners that Indians were not "some savage or semi-civilized people whom you have subjugated. The people of India are an ancient race who had attained a high degree of civilization long before the ancestors of European nations understood what civilization was."[90]

Indian nationalists were not all of one mind, of course. For the better part of three decades leading up to World War I, educator-turned-politician Bal Gangadhar Tilak had preached the doctrine of swaraj ("self-rule") and independence. "If thieves enter our house," he said, referring to the British in India, "and we have not strength to drive them out, should we not without hesitation shut them in and burn them alive?"[91] Britain's decision to partition Bengal in 1905 outraged and emboldened Tilak and led to a fissure within the Indian National Congress between his followers and the moderates, and to a wave of antigovernment demonstrations that did not abate until the government reversed its decision in 1911, relocating the seat of government to Delhi. In 1907 Tilak organized his supporters and articulated the position of the so-called extremists. "This government does not suit us," he said that January in a speech outlining the tenets of India's extremist politicians. "Pax Britannica has been established in this country in order that a foreign Government may exploit the country."[92] Where Gokhale expressed confidence that resurgent Liberalism in England would usher in more enlightened colonial rule, Tilak cautioned, "I have seen Liberals in England come out to India to get into Conservative ways."[93] Where Gokhale and the moderates hoped to win for Indians a greater stake in colonial governance by means of persuasion and petition, Tilak wanted "self-government" and control of the "administrative machinery," won by means of direct action and the boycott. "The future rests entirely in your own hands," Tilak told his supporters. "We shall not give [the British] assistance to collect revenue and keep peace. We shall not assist them in fighting beyond the frontiers or outside India with Indian blood and money. We shall not assist them in carrying on the administration of justice."[94] Tilak's position made him a target. In 1909 he was tried for sedition and imprisoned in Burma, where he remained until his release in June 1914.

What did Indian nationalists have to say about the Indian Army? During the South Africa War Gandhi lamented Britain's decision to prohibit the Indian Army from participating in the fighting. "If the Ghoorkas [sic] or the Sikhs had been there, they would have shown what they could do in the way of fighting," he said in a speech in Johannesburg in December 1899.[95] With this comment Gandhi was pushing back on a colonial narrative that said Englishmen were "manly" and that Indians were "effeminate." In the late nineteenth century, as members of India's educated bourgeoisie began demanding a share in the privileges hitherto reserved for the British Empire's white citizens, Britain's colonial rulers increasingly deployed ideas about gender and masculinity in order to defend white privileges. When it looked like Britain and Russia might go to war in March 1885, for instance, the Government of India flirted briefly with raising a volunteer reserve force (effectively a militia or national guard) comprised of educated Indians. The viceroy scrapped the idea, but soon petitions from volunteers flooded his office from all over India. Newspapers in Calcutta, Madras, Bombay, Poona, Allahabad, Meerut, Lahore, and Bengal kept up a steady drumroll all summer. For Indian politicians, this was about the redemption of Indian manhood. The Anglo-Indian press (newspapers read by India's white British residents) attacked the idea as preposterous. One such newspaper in Lahore offered, "The *babu* although a valiant wielder of the pen, is not so handy with the sword."[96] But educated Indians were coming of age, and their politics pitted them against the traditional landed elite—the princes. India's princes ruled India jointly with the Raj, and they enjoyed participation in as well as access to the benefits that accrued from the colonial state's martial traditions. Indian volunteering represented the vehicle by which the Indian bourgeoisie could reassert their own masculinity and, with that, claim a greater share of the Empire's privileges. British colonialism had "de-militarized" them, so the argument went in 1885. Indians "have not the same taste for warlike pursuits as before," said Ashutosh Biswas at a meeting of the Indian National Conference held that year at Calcutta.[97] Speaking at the second meeting of the Indian National Congress in 1886, Raja Rampal Singh criticized the colonial government for "converting a race of soldiers and heroes into a timid flock of quill-driving sheep," but he reassured that if Indians were given the chance, they would willingly give their lives "for the support and maintenance of that Government to which we owe so much."[98] In March 1886 the viceroy put the issue to rest. At a public gathering in Madras, he formally rejected the demands for Indian volunteering.[99]

Barred from the ranks of the military, members of India's burgeoning nationalist movement nonetheless remained outwardly supportive of the Indian Army, its soldiers, and its operations overseas. When Gandhi told the South African *Natal Advertiser* in 1897 that his mother country "furnishes some of the bravest soldiers to fight the wars of Great Britain in almost all parts of the world," he did so because he saw in the Indian soldier a vehicle to advance his cause.[100] "All over the world, whenever necessary, Indian soldiers have been fighting the battles of Great Britain," he reminded Joseph Chamberlain, secretary of state for the colonies, in an 1898 letter. "Can it be that the fellow-countrymen of these soldiers . . . are not to be allowed to earn an honest living in a portion of Her Majesty's dominions?"[101] In 1903 Gandhi reminded readers of his newspaper, *Indian Opinion*, that Indian soldiers had performed "heroically" in one campaign after another: Indians fought "uncomplainingly" for the British in Afghanistan; they had stubbornly endured privations in Somaliland; deployed to China to put down the Boxer Rebellion, "the Indian soldiers fought just as bravely as their other comrades, and commanded the admiration, by their bearing, of all the composite troops." The slights and prejudices Indians encountered in the White Dominions was therefore unconscionable. "Is it an equable bargain that, while India is expected to bear the burden of the Empire, she may not get the benefits of that Empire?" Gandhi asked.[102] "Quite in keeping with the traditions of the Indian army," he wrote the following year, the "great courage" of the Indian soldiers deployed to Tibet in 1904 saved Britain's military campaign "from disaster." He continued:

> The news, however, gives rise to many a thought. The Colonies would be prepared as part of the British Empire to appropriate the results of the Sikh bravery, and if it were found that the great plateaus of Tibet

were filled with gold, there would be a mad rush to the land. But it is a sad fact that they are not at all prepared either to welcome the Sikh soldiers themselves or their compatriots as settlers in the Colonies. It is to be wished that such an inconsistent attitude will strike the Colonial leaders as something to be rectified.[103]

Right up through the start of World War I, Indian nationalists never abandoned their campaign to secure for themselves the right to serve in the military. One Lahore newspaper claimed in August 1914 that it would be folly to pit India's peasant soldiers against the German Army. "It must be remembered that Indians are divided into two distinct classes—the educated and the illiterate," offered an editorial in the *Prabhat*. "To pit the latter against German soldiers who are fighting with a spirit of patriotism is ridiculous. What Government should do is to enlist the services of educated Indians. Such men have a conception of the meaning of patriotism and would thus be fit to meet Germans in the battlefield."[104] The *Panjabee*, a tri-weekly newspaper circulated in Lahore, under surveillance in 1914 by the Criminal Intelligence Department of the Government of India for advancing a "Hindu, advanced nationalist" agenda, called on government and army authorities to abandon martial race doctrine in favor of mass enlistment much like that then underway across Europe. "The distinction that has hitherto been made in this respect between Indians and other classes of the King's subjects is galling to the self-respect of the Indian and is a great hindrance in the way of his thinking 'imperially' and having that Imperial patriotism which he has been asked by friends and foes alike to cultivate."[105] Another editorial offered, "Apart from the exhibition of moral sympathy there is one and but one way which the citizens of an Empire can support it in a crisis like the present, and that is by taking up arms to fight for her. Will the people of India be permitted to do so if need be?" The editorial stated: "We remember that some years ago when a war was about to break out between England and Russia a number of educated young men in India offered their services as volunteers. The offer was not accepted. The present crisis is much graver and India itself is now far more self-conscious and far abler to give effective help to England than she was a quarter of a century ago. Will British statesmanship rise to the height of the occasion and permit India to do her duty to the Empire?"[106]

The key so far is that Indian nationalists wanted the chance for India's middle classes to serve in the army. Barred from the ranks as "un-martial," they nevertheless cheered Indian soldiers, men drawn mainly from the rural peasantry, whenever those soldiers deployed to fight the empire's battles overseas.[107] When war broke out in 1914, British and Indian audiences alike would find plenty more to read about Indian soldiers. But 1914 most certainly was not the first time Indian soldiers entered the collective conscious of British audiences, much less that of Indian nationalists. A lot of ink had already been spilled on the subject of Indian soldiers.

2

India's Splendid Rally

> All that is noblest, purest, best, the stainless honour of an ancient and mighty people, impels India forward to the battlefield.... But this does not mean that she is careless of her own honour, of her right to breathe the liberty which is the breath of England's life.
>
> —Annie Besant, "India's Loyalty and England's Duty," 1914

Irish theosophist Annie Besant had lived in India for two decades when World War I began. A member of the Indian National Congress and champion of self-government for India, Besant—like so many members of the INC—rallied "to the defense of the Empire" in its hour of need. But as Besant made clear in her remarks above, her support for the imperial war effort was predicated upon her earnest belief—shared alike by many in the INC—that Britain would fulfill its duty at war's end, and "pin upon [India's] breast the jeweled medal of Self-Government within the Empire." But of course, hers was not the only viewpoint expressed at the start of the war. This chapter is about the outbreak of war in 1914 and the range of ways people responded to the war's commencement and to the mobilization and deployment of the Indian Army to theaters in the Middle East, Africa, and Europe. Most Indian soldiers called to overseas service in 1914 obeyed orders. They boarded ships in Karachi or Bombay, bound for battlefields in France, or Egypt, or the Persian Gulf. Indian nationalists and members of the INC such as Annie Besant rallied to the empire. Some people went in the other direction. Indian revolutionaries flocked to the halls of the German Foreign Office in Berlin to prepare the groundwork for an anti-British crusade. Anticolonial and pan-Islamic propaganda reached Indian soldiers stationed in Southeast Asia, inspir-

India's Splendid Rally

ing some sepoys to mutiny. There was a lot at stake that year—1914 was a complicated, multilayered imperial moment.

Outbreak

In July 1914 Vera Brittain—who was then living out her otherwise privileged if provincial late adolescence in Buxton, England—recalled that people were paying little attention to events on the European continent. "To those of us who, wrapped up in our careers or our games or our love-affairs, had paid no attention to the newspapers, the direction from which the storm was rolling was quite unexpected."[1] But then the storm broke in August, and everything changed. "Wild rumours circulated from mouth to mouth; they were more plentiful than the newspapers, over which a free fight broke out on the station platform every time a batch came by train from London or Manchester."[2] One rumor held that a hundred thousand Russian troops had passed through Manchester. Young lovers hurried to marry. Parents hurried to shops to stock up on cheese and bacon and butter and anything else they might need "under the generally shared impression that by [the end of the week] we might all be besieged by the Germans." As people on holiday "wrestled with one another for the *Daily Mail*," Brittain devoured the daily *Times*. Her diary entries for those few days in late July and the start of August 1914 reflected what she later called "the pontifical mood" of the London newspaper. "Germany has broken treaty after treaty," she wrote, "disregarded every honourable tie with other nations. . . . If we at this critical juncture refuse to help our friend France, we should be guilty of the grossest treachery."[3]

Indians were caught just as unawares by the suddenness of the maelstrom of war in 1914 as Europeans. Sisir Sarbadhikari, a Bengali who would go on to serve as a doctor with the Indian Army in Mesopotamia, reacted to news of the murder of the Austrian archduke, Franz Ferdinand. "When we first heard the news none of us were particularly interested," he recorded in his memoirs. "Who cared where Sarajevo was and which Archduke had been assassinated there?"[4] But when Britain declared war on Germany on August 4, then everybody cared. People wondered, "Was India in any danger?" and "Would the army deploy overseas?" War news was suddenly in demand. The cities and bazaars were fertile ground for rumor, and just like in England much of what people in India consumed in the war's opening months was the stuff of false reporting. One rumor held that the German Army was preparing to storm Karachi. Another held that German airships had been spotted in the skies above Multan. "People should be warned of these unfounded rumours in order that they may not be deceived," advised one Punjabi newspaper.[5] Rumors such as these reveal the extent to which communities in India felt connected to events half a world away. People were frightened, worried that the war might come to their doorsteps. At a fair in early November 1914 at a temple in Mohan Lal Ganj Tahsil, Lucknow District, a sowar proclaimed that the Germans had massed on the Indian frontier. The news so frightened the assembled crowds "that the villagers ran away in great haste, and the women were so overcome by fear that they ran away leaving behind them their children, their ornaments and good deal of other property."[6] Newspaper reporters were beside themselves to get ahead of such rumors. But the official accounts about the war they received from the Government of India were too inconsistent. One minute the government reported a great victory, the next a tragic defeat. "The ordinary man is thrown into a state of confusion," lamented one Indian newspaperman in Lahore. "He is at a loss to know what to believe."[7]

One thing was clear—the British Empire needed soldiers. Ten years prior to the outbreak of World War I, planners in the War Office in London predicted that any conflict between Britain and Germany would be "a struggle between an elephant and a whale in which each, although supreme in its own element, would find it difficult to bring its strength to bear on its antagonist."[8] Britain was chiefly a sea power, its worldwide empire held together by the guns of the imperial navy (and those of its Indian Army, to be sure, a professional fighting force with extensive overseas experience). When the long-anticipated conflict did erupt in August 1914, the numerical weight of land forces rested with Britain's empire and its allies (France and Russia), but Germany's troops were among the best trained, best led, and best equipped in the world. Britain had only two army corps immediately available at the start of the war (armies are composed of corps, which are composed of divisions, which are composed of brigades, which are composed of battalions). Those two British corps and their French allies went up against Germany's twenty-six active and thirteen reserve corps. German soldiers went into battle backed by more heavy artillery than their opponents. Each German corps possessed 144 field guns and light howitzers, supplemented by modern heavy field artillery. A French corps had only 120 field guns, and a Russian corps only 108.[9] As of August 12, when Britain's single cavalry division and four infantry divisions belonging to the British Expeditionary Force began landing at Le Havre, Boulogne, and Rouen—a force numbering some one hundred thousand men—the only additional regular troops immediately available to the empire were those of the Indian Army. And although Britain's all-regular force very quickly proved at the Mons-Condé Canal on August 23 that a well-trained, professional British soldier, adept at firing fifteen well-aimed shots a minute with his Lee-Enfield rifle, could wreak havoc on advancing German troops, the fact remained that Tommy Atkins needed more men at his side.

Accordingly the London War Office decided that things necessitated abandoning the previously clung to "white man's war" policy. Lord Kitchener, as secretary for war, and Douglas Haig, as commander of the British Expeditionary Force's I Corps, envisioned a war of several years—provided of course that something could be done to halt the German Army's advance. Both Kitchener and Haig were also avowed critics of the 1899 "white man's war" policy. Kitchener had pressed unsuccessfully for the deployment of Indian cavalry to South Africa at the start of the Boer War. Then, with a watchful eye on Russian expansion into Central Asia, he pointed out that the Indian Army would have to fight white men at some point. Haig, during his tenure as chief of staff in India from 1910 to 1912, believed that a continental war against Germany lay in the near future. Concerned that England's security relied too heavily on the Royal Navy, he wanted to reorganize the Indian Army to fight in Europe and drew up the original plans for it to do so in 1912. So, at an ad hoc war council meeting at 10 Downing Street on August 6, 1914, Kitchener and Haig convinced the council to deploy the 3rd and 7th Indian divisions to Egypt for eventual use in Europe.[10] The viceroy of India threw his weight behind Kitchener's and Haig's scheme, pleading with Home authorities to use Indian troops in the European war. Not to do so, he said, would be seen as a slight to Indian loyalty, "pointing out the slur that would be imposed on India by the presence of Algerian and Senegalese troops in the French Army in France," he wrote years later.[11]

With that, Britain's Indian war machine set in motion. On August 7 the king issued a formal pardon to all personnel of the Indian Army who were in a state of desertion at the start of the war, giving them until the start of October to report for duty.[12] Commanders in the Indian 3rd and 7th Divisions received their mobilization orders the following day. Indian soldiers and British officers on leave began making their way to base camps. It took some weeks for Gurkhas on leave in Nepal and Afridis home in remote villages in the North-West Frontier to receive their orders. But these were veteran soldiers. They had done this business before. Husbands said goodbye to their wives. Sons said goodbye to their mothers. Sisters prayed for the safe return of their brothers. The 1st/4th (the 1st battalion, 4th regiment) Gurkhas boarded the SS *Baroda* bound for Suez and then France on August 24 despite being short nearly half of its British officers.[13] Made up mostly of men from India's North-West Frontier Province, the Punjab, and Afghanistan, the elite 58th Rifles received its mobilization orders on August 12. Two days later, roughly 250 on-leave and furloughed men rejoined the regiment. In September the elite battalion joined the rest of the 7th Division in Karachi and boarded ships bound for Marseilles.[14]

"Loyal India"

Standing before the House of Lords in early August 1914, the secretary of state for India, Lord Crewe, expressed "the desire of the Indian people that Indian soldiers should stand side by side with their comrades of the British Army in repelling the invasion of our friends' territory." To the applause of his audience, the secretary asserted, "It would be a disappointment to our loyal Indian fellow subjects if they were debarred from taking part."[15] A cursory review of some of the headlines and editorials that appeared that month in Indian newspapers might indeed confirm the secretary's assertions. In Punjab the staff at the *Observer* urged its Indian readers to table political discussions until after the war.

> In the light of the knowledge that war between England and Germany has commenced and the first shot has been fired, we deem it a sacred duty to the Great Empire of which we are proud to be the subjects and which has beyond doubt given to India a new, better and a higher life, to cease discussing questions of a political hue, likely to embarrass and cause anxiety to the authorities out here, and to concentrate all our energies in giving such support and assistance as is but the adequate expression of that splendid loyalty and devotion which has ever been the proud boast of His Majesty's humble Indian subject.[16]

Statements of loyalty poured into the viceroy's office in the months that followed. India's native princes, who still ruled about one-third of India in partnership with the Raj, enthusiastically offered troops, money, and other supplies.[17] The Indian National Congress pledged its support for the imperial war effort, as did the All India Moslem League, Madras Provincial Congress, Hindus of Punjab, and the Parsee community of Bombay. "Let not the world mistake us," said Sir Gangadar Chitnavis in a September session of the viceroy's Imperial Legislative Council, "should any outside danger threaten us we stand shoulder to shoulder round our mighty mother, England, and her enemies will find us arrayed in solid phalanx by her side, ready to meet any danger and render any sacrifices for the sake of the great and glorious Empire of which we are proud to call ourselves citizens."[18] Gandhi was ready to forgive the racism he'd so recently experienced in South Africa, proclaiming in 1914 his intention to, "for the sake of the Motherland and the Empire," place his services "at the disposal of the Authorities."[19] Arriving in London on August 4, he told Indian students studying in England that they should support the war effort in any way they could, that they had to demonstrate their readiness to "share the responsibilities of membership of this great Empire, if we would share its privileges."[20] Even Tilak got in line. "At such a crisis as this," he said, "I firmly hold, the duty of every Indian, be he great or small, rich or poor, to support and assist His Majesty's Government, to the best of his ability."[21]

The Indian nationalist press was of the same opinion. "Behind the serried ranks of one of the finest armies in the world, there stand the multitudinous peoples of India, ready to cooperate with the Government in the defense of the Empire, which for them, means, in its ultimate evolution, the complete recognition of their rights as citizens of the freest State in the world," read one article in the *Bengalee*, a newspaper from Calcutta. "We may have our differences with the Government," the article continued, "but in the presence of a common enemy, be it Germany or any other Power, we sink our differences, we forget our little quarrels and close our ranks, and offer all that we possess in defense of the great Empire, to which we are all so proud to belong, and with which the future prosperity and advancement of our people are bound up."[22] In Bombay, the *Jam-e-Jamshad* proffered for its readers, "This is the time when India should feel it to be her duty to show to the world—to England's foes and allies alike—how greatly she is attached to her, how staunch and resolute is her devotion to her interests, how ready and willing she is to make any sacrifice she can in men and treasure, for the defense of her possessions and the assertion of her honor and dignity."[23] In Madras the publishing house of G. A. Natesan & Co. released a hefty volume of English-language pro-war and pro-empire articles and speeches by prominent Indian nationalists.[24]

For Indian nationalists, wartime loyalty represented a springboard from which they hoped to lobby more effectively for reform and reward within the British Empire. British audiences readily overlooked the fact in the war's opening months that many of the assertions of loyalty that poured into the offices of the Government of India (then reprinted in pamphlets, books, and newspapers in

Britain) stipulated that Indians expected to receive self-government in exchange. "Let Indians assist Government during the present crisis," urged the *Khalsa Sowar* (Amritsar) in September 1914. "Then we feel sure that Government will feel more disposed to grant self-government to India in the future."[25] In Lahore the *Zamindar* chimed the following month, "The war has its advantages and disadvantages. Its disadvantages consist in the terrible loss of life and the consequent suffering which inevitably ensues. Its advantages will be seen in the benefits which it will bring to India. We are convinced that self-government will be granted to this country."[26] Prominent Indian politicians struck the same chord. "We are not blind to the fact there are many defects in the existing system of administration, that there are many grievances which require to be addressed," stipulated Madan Mohan Malaviya, a prominent educator and member of the Indian National Congress, in a 1914 speech in Allahabad. "But making allowance for that, I believe that no foreign nation that I can think of, would have governed India better, than on the whole the British have done. It is also our settled conviction that our progress under British rule will be far greater in the future than it has been in the past, and that a day will come, distant thought it be at present, when India will under the aegis of the British Crown, attain self-government such as the Dominion of Canada and the other self-governing colonies of Britain enjoy."[27]

The nationalist press likewise cheered Britain's decision to deploy Indian troops to the Western Front. This was exactly the policy the nationalists had championed. In August 1914, the Lahore *Tribune* urged, "If any troops are to leave this country for active warfare in Europe, let Indian as well as British soldiers be sent without distinction of race and creed to serve side by side in defence of our united cause." France "would not refrain from employing her Algerian troops against a European enemy," the newspaper offered. "India expects at least as much from Great Britain."[28] One month later, as it became apparent that the 3rd and 7th Divisions of the Indian Army were bound for the Western Front, the *Panjabee* rejoiced. "The employment of Indian troops in the present war is to be commended principally for the reason that it is a step towards the eventual obliteration of existing racial prejudice, so essential to India's self-fulfillment as a nation and an integral part of the Empire."[29] The *Jhang Sial* proclaimed in September, "In the present war all colour distinctions have been removed. Three Divisions of 'our' Indian army have been sent to France where they will fight side by side with the French and English soldiers against Germany."[30]

This was all good news from the point of view of the British government. In early September Prime Minister Herbert Henry Asquith spoke before Parliament on some of the war's early developments, impressing upon his audience the urgency with which men were needed for the army. "It would be a criminal mistake to underestimate either the magnitude, the fighting quality, or the staying power of the forces which are arrayed against us," he emphasized. The prime minister applauded the men from Canada, Australia, New Zealand, South Africa, and Newfoundland—"the children of the Empire," he called them—who "assert, not as an obligation, but as a privilege, their right, and their willingness to contribute . . . [the] lives of their best manhood." Then to cheers from the members of Parliament, Asquith spoke of India's ready and willing support for the war effort. "India, too, with not less alacrity, has claimed her share in the common task," he said. "Every class and creed, British and native, princes and people, Hindoos and Mohammedans, vie with one another in a noble and emulous rivalry." Two divisions of "our magnificent Indian Army" were already on their way. This aid was welcomed, he said, "in an Empire which knows no distinction of race or class, where all alike, as subjects of the King Emperor, are joint and equal custodians of our common interests and fortunes." Asquith hailed the sepoys' "association side by side and shoulder to shoulder with our home and Dominion troops, under the flag which is a symbol to all of a unity that the world in arms cannot dissever or dissolve."[31]

Komagata Maru

Just as the prime minister was concluding his remarks about "an Empire which knows no distinction of race or class," whose subjects were "joint and equal custodians" of the empire's "interests and fortunes," a gross racial injustice was then underway on the other side of the globe. It involved the Government of India and a band of Indian emigrants who had chartered a passenger ship called the *Komagata Maru* earlier that year. The *Komagata Maru* sailed from Hong Kong in April 1914 bound for Vancouver, Canada. The ship's 376 Punjabi passengers, mostly adult male Sikhs, were deliberately challenging Canada's thinly disguised Indian immigration ban. When the ship arrived at Vancouver in late May, authorities denied the ship docking rights, and the ship sat in the harbor—all its Indian passengers effectively trapped on board—for two months before finally sailing back to India. When the *Komagata Maru* arrived at Calcutta in September 1914, the angry and frustrated passengers were met by police, who insisted they board a waiting train to Punjab, where the government intended to detain them indefinitely without trial. A majority of the Sikh passengers refused to board the train. The police panicked and opened fire, gunning down nineteen of the passengers in what the press called the Budge Budge Riot.[32]

So at a time when British prime minister Herbert Asquith was hailing the decision to deploy soldiers belonging to the Indian Army as "joint and equal custodians of our common interests and fortunes," the *Komagata Maru* and Budge Budge incidents reminded Indians that they remained anything but equals in the empire. The prime minister's lofty pronouncement—that the British Empire was one "which knows no distinction of race or class"—did not reflect the lived experience of Indian people. The Indian press was quick off the block, its own pronouncements of loyalty notwithstanding. The editorial staff at the *Azadi* affirmed for its Urdu readership in Lahore: "Our loyalty is undoubted; yet we venture to disagree with Mr. Asquith's statement that there is no distinction of race or creed in the British Empire. The treatment of Indians in British colonies refutes such an assertion."[33] In September 1914 one Lahore newspaper, the *Panth Sewak*, discussed the *Komagata Maru* affair in light of the pending deployment of Indian soldiers to France.

India's Splendid Rally

If our thoughts are occupied with the hardships of our brethren, who are about to take part in the (European) war, they are in no less degree concentrated on the harsh treatment of which our brethren have recently been the victims in Canada. Even as our clansmen are now going to do battle with the injustice of Germany, so did they go to Canada to fight against the unjust laws of that country. The only difference is that now they go armed with weapons of war, while in the Canadian instance their only weapon was legal right. . . . O Government of Canada! We are subjects of the same Empire as you. We are to fight side by side with you against a common foe. . . . In this Canadian affair it is not only a few individuals that have suffered, the whole of India has suffered; it is not a mere four hundred who have been dishonoured, the whole 300 millions of the peoples of India have been dishonoured and it is essential, absolutely essential, that justice should now be done.[34]

The viceroy, Charles Hardinge—who had impressed upon Asquith's cabinet in August "the slur that would be imposed on India" if Indian troops were not allowed to take part in the war against Germany—was otherwise unmoved by the *Komagata Maru* incident. In a speech delivered at the opening of the Legislative Council in Simla on September 8, the viceroy said: "We must all regret the discomfort suffered by the 400 Indians on board the *Komagata Maru* for which the organizers of the expedition were, in my opinion, culpably responsible. They must have known perfectly well that entry would be refused."[35] Some minutes earlier Hardinge began his speech by reading aloud a message from the king reaffirming "that the destinies of Great Britain and India are indissolubly linked." Hardinge said that it was "with confidence and pride that I was able to offer to His Majesty the finest and largest military force of British and Indian troops for service in Europe that has ever left the shores of India." Then he transitioned to "another question which has seriously occupied the attention of the Government of India . . . a subject to which we attach the very highest importance." Of course he meant only one thing, "the question of migration from one part of our Empire to another."

"It is being commonly asserted," Hardinge began, "that the full rights of citizenship of the British Empire include the right to settle in any part of that Empire, irrespective of the existence of local legislation barring or limiting access to the Dominion to which access is sought." But no such right existed, he claimed. "Our Empire is largely composed of self-governing units. The Dominions have been given their own legislatures by the Imperial Government in order that they may regulate the management of their internal affairs as may seem best to them." And that the control of immigration was an internal matter was beyond question, Hardinge said, "for each self-governing unit must know best from what materials it desires to provide its future citizens." Considering that matter settled, Hardinge then tried "to correct any misapprehension that may exist in this country regarding the attitude of the Governments of the Dominions towards Indians as a whole." He did not believe that countries like Canada or Australia were motivated by "feelings of animosity towards Indians." It simply was not true, he said, that the White Dominions proffered an open door to all white migrants. "Some years ago, three English hatters were turned back from Australia on the ground that the local labor market for hatters was overstocked." Canada had an ordinance barring any laborer from any country from landing on its shores. In light of such evidence, the viceroy said, "it is out of place to assert that the policy of exclusion is directed against Indians alone."

One can only imagine what the viceroy's audience thought of Hardinge's speech. It was thin gruel, a smokescreen to hide racial discrimination. Still, what could Indians do? Hardinge's answer was simple. Wait, he said. Let the war follow its course. Let India do its part. Forego any resort to political stunts, he advised, and let the Government of India handle any and all negotiations with the dominions. In the meantime, Hardinge maintained, it was the burden of Indians to accommodate white supremacy and the discriminatory policies of the empire's member nations. Effectively lending racial discrimination his unwavering endorsement, the viceroy reassured his listeners that the dominions might be willing to revisit their policies, "provided that we on our side show our readiness to meet them half-way." He never elaborated as to what it might look like to meet racism "half-way." Instead, he asserted that the contributions of Indian soldiers to the war effort might do more than anything else to "secure for our Indian fellow-subjects any of the advantages that are now denied." He optimistically stated:

> There is, I believe, nothing like comradeship in arms before the enemy, and joint participation in the dangers and hardships of war to level all distinctions, to inspire mutual respect, and to foster friendships. This I regard as the bright side of the dispatch of our troops to Europe and of the heavy and material sacrifices that are being made by India for the sake of the Empire. I cannot help feeling that as a consequence better relations will be promoted amongst the component parts of the British Empire, many misunderstandings will be removed, and outstanding grievances will be settled in an amicable and generous manner. In this sense out of evil good may come to India, and this is the desire of us all.[36]

Determined to Help Win Their Emperor's Battles or Die

Just as Indian police were gunning down Indian emigrants in Calcutta, Indian soldiers began to disembark from steamers at Marseilles. The first ships to berth on the morning of September 26, 1914, belonged to the British India Company, the *Mongara* and the *Castilia*. These ships carried between them a battery of Royal Horse Artillery, a signal company, a field ambulance, and part of a mule corps. The next day two ships weighed down by the 15th Lancers, a cavalry battalion, took their place at the docks. Indian infantry arrived over the next several days. Author Mulk Raj Anand captured the moment Indians first disembarked from the troop ships into the welcoming arms of a delirious French crowd in his 1939 novel about sepoy Lal Singh and his comrades in the 69th Rifles, *Across the Black Waters*. "'*Vivonlesindu!* Something, something . . .' the cry rang out, above the 'lef right lef' of the N.C.O.s, from the crowd, which stood five deep under the awnings of tall, white-shuttered houses under the shadow of the harbor walls."[37] As the soldiers proceeded through the streets of Marseilles to their camp on the outskirts of town, "the long pageant, touched by the warmth of French greetings, inflamed by the exuberance of tropical hearts marched through this air, electric with the whipped-up frenzy, past churches, monuments, past rows of shuttered houses ... till, tired and strained with the intoxication of glory, it reached the race-course of Parc Borely ... to rest."[38] Indian Army officer J. W. B. Merewether recalled vividly the "remarkable reception" the Indian soldiers received. "Our warm-hearted Allies, men, women, and children, vied with each other in showing honor and kindness to the men who had traversed so many weary miles by land and sea to play their part in the World War at its most critical period."[39]

The arrival of Indian troops in France sparked a flurry of headlines in the British press. "The races of Asia are among the most warlike in the world," readers enjoyed in the *Birmingham Mail*, "and the vast community of Eastern creeds will respond in heart to the honourable place given to their representatives by the British Raj."[40] For a halfpenny, readers of the *Daily Mirror* poured over page after page of photographs of the pageantry and excitement that accompanied the arrival of India's "dusky warriors" on the streets of Marseilles. "Enjoying liberty under Britain's enlightened rule, these men have no cause to [love] Germany or her tyrannous system of government, and they themselves asked to be allowed to take their share in the fight for freedom." Towering Sikhs smiled good-naturedly at French youngsters who gleefully ran alongside the columns of soldiers. The *Manchester Guardian* littered its pages with photographs of maharajas atop mighty war horses, or barefoot Indian troops preparing food in French camps. When Indian troops paraded through the streets of Marseilles on their way to trains to take them to the front, the *Birmingham Daily Mail* commented that the soldiers' "fine appearance evoked great admiration from dense crowds, who cheered them heartily."[41] As the troops hurried to the front, the *Daily Mirror* kept readers abreast of their movements, eagerly anticipating the moment

India's Splendid Rally

India's soldiers would meet the Hun in the lines. "The French not only admire the men themselves, but are full of praise for the manner in which they are equipped. It is felt that such magnificent fighting men will be a pillar of strength to the Allied Forces."[42]

The ephemera followed sure enough. Postcards depicting Indian soldiers engaging in the trivialities of camp life or enjoying the sunshine on hospital grounds became bestsellers in France and England. European audiences wanted to have something of the Indian Corps' experience in Europe that they could keep for themselves. The *Times* called the Indian camps in New Forest a "Gypsie-like spectacle."[43] Tourists thronged at the camp perimeter and jostled for a better view of the soldiers. Massia Bibikoff, a Russian artist and expat, visited the Indian camps outside Marseilles shortly after the soldiers disembarked in October 1914, where she produced sketch after sketch of the men. She was especially taken with Maharajah Sher Singh, who, she wrote, "realised the dreams of beauty in which I loved to wrap the heroes and princes of the Arabian Nights."[44]

All of this was the stuff of colonial self-congratulation. "India has thrown herself enthusiastically into preparation for war, and a wave of ardent loyalty is sweeping over the country," the *Times* declared.[45] The presence of Indian troops in France was itself a rebuttal of "all the foul slanders which have been circulated in the past years regarding British rule in India."[46] The *Manchester Guardian* reflected on the pride an Englishman must feel at seeing his hard work in India pay dividends. "The remarkable, spontaneous, and practical way in which the princes and people have shown their loyalty to the empire at a time of grave danger is a testimony to every Englishman who has assisted in the development and consolidation of India."[47] In a penny pamphlet titled *India and the War*, Sir Ernest Trevelyan asserted that Britain's loyal Indian troops fought on the behalf of the entire (loyal) Indian nation. Never, he wrote, "has there been an occasion when India has been more united than at the present time. . . . Every class and every race have shown their loyalty and their anxiety to take their share of the burdens and duties of citizens of the Empire."[48]

Indian nationalists were as much a part of the chorus in Britain as anybody. Bhupendranath Basu, president of the Indian National Congress, assured British audiences that despite some of the disappointments and shortcomings of British imperial rule, India was "heart and soul" with its colonial master in the present crisis. His 1914 pamphlet, *Why India Is Heart and Soul with Great Britain*, provided English audiences with an Indian's reassurances that the war had swept away all doubt, all hesitation, and all question. "In all of India," he asserted, "there was but one feeling—to stand by England in the hour of danger."[49] The war represented a great opportunity for India and Britain, he told his English readers. "The Indian princes are eager to show that they are in fact, as they have been in name, pillars of the Empire." The people of India, Basu continued, "who have so thoroughly identified themselves with the British people . . . are prepared to lay down their lives on the field." Basu claimed that the war heralded "an era brighter and happier than any in the past—the East and the West, India and England, marching onwards in comradeship, united in bonds forged on the field of battle and tempered in their common blood."[50]

After disembarking in Marseilles, the newly minted Indian Corps boarded trains and raced across France, bound for the Western Front. Newspaper after newspaper reprinted the king's message to the Indian troops. "I look to all my Indian soldiers to uphold the izzat of the British Raj against an aggressive and relentless enemy," the king said. "I know with what readiness my brave and loyal Indian soldiers are prepared to fulfil this sacred trust on the field of battle shoulder to shoulder with their comrades from all parts of the Empire."[51] "You are the descendants of men who have been mighty rulers and great warriors for many centuries," the newly appointed commander of the Indian Corps, General James Willcocks, reminded the soldiers as they prepared to take up their positions in the lines. Newspapers reprinted the commander's remarks. "You will be the first Indian soldiers of the King-Emperor who will have the honor of showing Europe that the sons of India have lost none of their ancient martial instincts and are worthy of the confidence reposed in them."[52] For the moment, Allied commanders could only wait and hope the general was correct.

Unholy Alliance

Opposite the Indian and British soldiers taking up their positions on the battlefield were German soldiers whose government was then hatching a plot to topple British rule in India. On July 30, when it became apparent to Berlin that "perfidious Albion" would intervene in the unfolding conflict on the continent, the kaiser—always one for bluster and bombast—furiously scribbled a note in the margins of a telegram from the German ambassador in St. Petersburg. England must "have the mask of Christian peaceableness torn publicly from her face," he wrote. "Our consuls in Turkey and India, agents, etc., must fire the whole Mohammedan world to fierce rebellion against this hated, lying, conscienceless people of hagglers; for if we are to be bled to death, at least England shall lose India."[53] The chief of the army's General Staff, Helmuth von Moltke, sent a secret dispatch to the foreign minister, Gottlieb von Jagow, three days later. "England's neutrality is of such importance to us," he wrote. In the event that England did take a stand "as our opponent," he pressed, "attempts must be made to instigate an uprising in India."[54]

England's declaration of war on Germany on August 4, 1914, meant that Germany would have to contend with the world's foremost imperial power. Germany had already lost the naval arms race of the previous decade, so there was little hope of taking on and defeating the British fleet.[55] The shortcomings of the German Army's plans—the so-named Schlieffen Plan—were plain to see by early September. His forces checked at the Battle of the Marne, the commanding general, Helmuth von Molkte, suffered a nervous breakdown and then allowed a subordinate to make the decision that ordered a general retreat to the River Aisne. Now Germany had to contend with the frightening prospects of a long war, something its commanders had wanted to avoid. In this context, the German government decided to widen the scope of the war, go global, and strike at its enemies on the cheap by fomenting anticolonial rebellion in Africa and Asia.[56]

How to do that? Turkey was one solution. The Ottoman capacity to lend military assistance to Germany in Europe was certainly limited, but Turkey could interrupt Britain's ability to deliver imperial resources to European battlefields.[57] Ottoman forces could attack Egypt and the Suez Canal in an attempt to block Britain's link with India. The Ottomans could close the Dardanelles, impeding Russia's ability to coordinate with its allies. Turkish forces could strike into the Caucasus, diverting Russian troops from Germany's Eastern Front. If Germany could persuade a high Muslim authority in Turkey to proclaim a jihad, or holy war, it might improve Germany's chances. Britain was the world's foremost "Muslim Power." In India alone, the Muslim population exceeded sixty million. British and German officials took seriously the appeal of pan-Islam, and the British feared the revolutionary potential of anticolonial revolt.[58] There was a lot one could hope for, clearly. For Baron Max von Oppenheim, an influential orientalist with the ear of the kaiser, the prospects of such a coup were too tantalizing to ignore. "A great European war," he wrote, "especially if Turkey participates in it against England, one may certainly expect an overall revolt of the Muslims in the British colonies." In such a war, England's colonies would prove "the most dangerous enemy of an England strong on the seas."[59]

The German government had been laying the groundwork for an alliance with Turkey since the 1890s. Timed to coincide with the one-hundred-year anniversary of Napoleon's invasion of Egypt, the kaiser's 1898 visit to Constantinople produced some of the wildest speculation in European newspapers. Was the kaiser trying to shore up the Sultan's rule and frustrate Russian, British, and French designs on the Ottoman domains? Was Wilhelm staking his own claim to the Ottoman inheritance?[60] No one could say for sure. In October 1898 the German emperor visited Jerusalem clad in a Prussian field marshal's uniform. At the site of the Assumption of the Virgin Mary, he "placed himself, his army, and his Empire in the service of the Mother of Christ."[61] Then in Damascus the kaiser paid tribute to the Muslim warrior Saladin, and at a banquet he saluted the current sultan, pledging, "May the Sultan and his 300 million Muslim subjects scattered across the earth, who venerate him as their Caliph, be assured that the German Kaiser will be their friend for all time."[62]

In the closing days of July 1914, the Kaiser's ministers worked furiously to ensure Turkish allegiance in the coming war. On August 2 they secured the signature of the Ottoman grand vizier, and on November 14 the Ottoman sultan proclaimed the anticipated jihad. On the Wilhemstrasse the German Foreign Office had the green light it wanted to set the world aflame. At the epicenter of this effort was Baron Max von Oppenheim, a onetime diplomat and the prodigal son of the Oppenheim banking dynasty, recalled to the Foreign Ministry on August 2. His plan was grandiose. Berlin would be the headquarters of a "qualified" global jihad—"qualified in the sense that it was to be fought against Britain, France, and Russia, not against all *kafirs*."[63] Fronting his own fortune for the scheme, Oppenheim founded the Nachrichtenstelle für den Orient (Intelligence Office for the East).[64] This organization would function as a pan-Islamic clearinghouse in Berlin responsible for distributing anti-Allied pamphlets in every conceivable language. It would also coordinate the activities of agents and expeditions to the far corners of the globe intended to provide the spark—as well as guns—for revolution.[65] Germany, Oppenheim wrote, must arm the Muslim brotherhoods of Libya, Sudan, and Yemen and support anticolonial rebellion in French North Africa.[66] He had India in his sights too. The baron wanted the German government to incite Habibullah Khan, the emir of Afghanistan, to invade British India at the head of an Islamic army. This, he believed, would inspire India's Muslim population to a revolt that would in turn, he assured Chancellor Bethmann Hollweg, "force England to [agree] to peace terms favorable to us."[67]

The Germans quickly found a ready and willing band of Indian revolutionaries to participate in their scheme.[68] These radicals included students such as Virendranath Chattophadhyaya and scholars such as Dr. Abinaschchandra Bhattacharyya, both of whom were already in Europe. Other important participants who flocked to Berlin from British India were Champakaraman Pillai, Bhupendranath Dutt, and the aristocrat Mahendra Pratap. Muhammed Barakatullah, Taraknath Das, Bhagwan Singh, and Har Dayal also made it to Berlin and joined what Oppenheim called the Indian Independence Committee.[69] Germans who had some prewar experience in India worked in collaboration with the Independence Committee. This small group was directed by the missionary Ferdinand Graetsch and included among its ranks Dr. Helmut von Glasenapp, the businessman Ernst Neuenhofer, and the missionary Paul Walter.[70]

Among the Independence Committee's members were a few who already belonged to a larger confederate network of revolutionaries known as Ghadar. Founded by Indian immigrants in California in 1913, Ghadar was committed to the violent overthrow of the British Empire in India. Its program was among the most radical in the world at the time, its members' frame of reference coming out of two places—their experiences with racial discrimination in the United States, and their experiences with colonialism in the British Empire. Where moderate politicians in the INC called for Indian inclusion in Britain's existing imperial framework, members of Ghadar sought a revolutionary program, one that would overthrow hierarchies of not just race and colonialism but class and religion too. Ghadarites envisioned "a comprehensive social and economic restructuring for postcolonial India rather than a mere handover of the existing governmental structure."[71] Speaking on the "scope and aim of Indian nationalism" at the University of California in October 1912, Taraknath Das said that Young India "must demand a revolution in social ideals so that humanity and liberty would be valued over property, special privilege would not overshadow equal opportunity, and women would not be kept under subjection."[72] Ghadar's vision was global, as were its activities. Speaking at the same University of California event, Har Dayal, Ghadar's most outspoken early theorist and propagandist, declared himself an internationalist. From its wellspring in San Francisco, Ghadar cells soon dotted the globe where its members became involved in a number of revolutionary networks—anticolonial nationalist, pan-Islamic, Marxist, and combinations thereof. To be sure, Germany's aims for the Indian Independence Committee were not those of the committee members themselves. The German government wanted to destabilize and topple British rule in India because that outcome advanced Germany's war aims. The Indian Independence Committee wanted to topple British rule in India in order to establish in India a republican system of government. Germany's aims were self-serving. Members of Ghadar sought the emancipation of Indians from despotic colonial control.[73]

His team assembled, Oppenheim and his Independence Committee envisioned various plots in order to topple the British Empire in India, combining interchangeably the revolutionary elements of nationalism and pan-Islam. Before joining the Independence Committee in Berlin in October 1914, Dayal traveled to Constantinople, where he hoped to spread propaganda among Indians in Turkey and Persia in cooperation with the Germans. His goal was to establish a "revolutionary center" in Kabul, Afghanistan. "As India is a vast plain, and England holds the seas, and the semi-independent Indian states have no modern armies, an effective military movement against England can be started only with the help of Afghanistan, a mountainous country of brave soldiers, numbering 5,000,000, who hate England & Russia," Dayal wrote in September. "A non-official group of priests and notables, bearing letters from the Shaikh-ul-islam (Head of Islam) at Constantinople should visit Kabul and persuade the Court to attack the English forces in Beluchistan."[74] Paul Walter wanted to spark a mutiny in the Indian Army. He proposed printing Hindi-language newspapers and leaflets for distribution, propaganda aimed at harnessing the memories of 1857.[75] The great Indian Mutiny of 1857 was one of the belated consequences of the Crimean War, he believed. Had the mutiny taken place in 1854 or 1855, England surely would have lost India. As it was, in 1857, England's hands were free to deal with the crisis without distraction. In the uprising, "Hindus and Muslims united against the hated foreign ruler." Although the English managed at long last to suppress the rebellion, "the course of the war revealed to the Indians the inherent military weakness of the hated foreign rulers, and this revelation kindled hope for the possibility of freedom."[76] Shackled in their "boundless ignorance and poverty," Walter argued, the people of India were unfit to act as one for their own political liberation. The same did not hold true, however, for the priests and princes of India, the landowners, merchant guilds and civil service, "and above all the native regiments." "These priests and nobility of the sword," he wrote, "nourish and cherish the hope of national liberation as a religious ideal." In them, "the self-sacrificing will to freedom is still alive." It was these men, he maintained, who could put the "deep-rooted religious prejudices of the masses" into action, just as they had in 1857 when the English issued greased cartridges to the sepoys. "The conditions necessary for an uprising are the same today as they were in 1857," he concluded. "The tinder is there. All it needs is for us to throw the torch."[77]

The mobilization of the Indian Army and its preliminary deployment to Egypt caused a flurry of excitement in Berlin. "How many Indian troops have [the English] deployed to Egypt?" Undersecretary Zimmerman wanted to know. "What languages do they speak?" If Oppenheim's Intelligence Office could deliver pamphlets to these troops by way of Constantinople, he believed, the soldiers might be incited to fight against England.[78] In Constantinople the German ambassador, Hans Freiherr von Wangenheim, found a willing printer and distributor. "It is preferable that the leaflets are produced here," he noted, "because [the leaflets] will have a greater influence on the Indians if the font and layout do not bear the mark of European work." The ambassador added that a Turkish army officer, Halil Sami Bey, was departing for Syria shortly and was willing, for a fee, to transport the leaflets.[79] By September it appeared to Oppenheim that the British were massing an army of Indian soldiers in Egypt. German agents verified that the Jodhpur Lancers and two Gurkha battalions, along with the 15th, 34th and 47th Sikhs, were all in Egypt.[80] Urdu-language pamphlets alone would not suffice, he realized, and he wired the ambassador in Constantinople, asking him to make sure to print pamphlets in Hindi and "other important Indian languages" as well.[81] Owing to the sectarian diversity of the Indian Army, pan-Islamic appeals would not suffice. "If the Afghan army should invade India, the British Empire in India would be overthrown," stated Mahendra Pratap of the Indian Committee. "In case of an Afghan invasion of India, it will be necessary to secure the hearty cooperation of the Hindus, who may oppose it, if they look upon it as a raid of foreign Mussalman adventurers." Pratap proposed that the German government make every effort to "convert" not just Muslim but Hindu, Sikh, and Gurkha sepoys fighting in France so that they could send them to Kabul to join the Afghan army.[82]

Mutiny

The German-Ottoman-Ghadar alliance was perhaps bound to cause the British considerable unease. Indian newspapers lamented Turkey's decision to enter the war in November 1914. "The one big contingency, which the Muslims of India had long been dreading ... has at last happened," the *Observer* reflected for its Indian readers in the Punjab. "Turkey, despite the entreaties of the whole Muslim world to stand aloof and against her own best interests, has succumbed to the chauvinistic influences which were ruling her and has decided to plunge her people into a blood war."[83] Subscribers to the *Prabhat* read, "Turkey's participation in the war will undoubtedly be followed by trouble in Egypt and Tripoli. The war spirit with eventually spread throughout the Muslim World." What might this mean for India? "Frontier Pathans will immediately fall on India. And then we shall have to see whether Indian Muhammadans will pray in their mosques for the victory of the Union Jack!"[84]

After the Sultan declared the jihad in November, British authorities hurried to get ahead of public opinion. The viceroy distributed a proclamation guaranteeing the Holy Places of Islam in Arabia and the Middle East against any attack or molestation by Britain or its allies. He telegrammed to the secretary of state for India, Austen Chamberlain, "His Highness the Aga Khan has given a complete statement of his attitude, which has been published in India, and I am daily receiving telegrams from his followers giving assurances of their entire accord with those views, and of their devotion to the British Empire."⁸⁵ India's ruling princes outdid one another in displays of loyalty. The Nizam of Hyderabad, the Begum of Bhopal, the Nawab of Rampur, and the Nawab of Tonk impressed upon their Muslim subjects that it was their "duty at this critical juncture to adhere firmly to their old and tried loyalty to the British government." The Begum of Bhopal, for example, in an address to her people, explained that Great Britain had been unwillingly drawn into the war in order to protect a small state against "the rapacity of Germany." She hoped that all Muslims "will show that they are as staunch as ever in their loyalty, and will not allow themselves to be led away by hostile influences." According to the viceroy's account of the address, Her Highness called attention to the "many occasions upon which Great Britain had shown herself a true friend to the Ottoman Empire."⁸⁶ Resolutions poured into the viceroy's office assuring him of the "steadfast loyalty" of Indian Muslims. The All Indian Moslem League, the Bombay Presidency Moslem League, the United Provinces Moslem League, the Punjab Moslem League, the Behar Provincial Moslem League, and the All India Sufi Conference—all promised their unwavering commitment to British rule. The All India Moslem League resolved that the "participation of Turkey in the present war does not and cannot affect [Muslim] loyalty in the least degree." The Council declared, "[No] Mussalman in India will swerve a hairs breadth from his paramount duty to his Sovereign."⁸⁷

But some soldiers were already unsettled by the prospect of fighting the Turks. A number of soldiers deserted the 130th Baluchis in August 1914 when the regiment was ordered into service. Seventy-nine Afghan Mahsuds of the regiment were convicted by court-martial and imprisoned for insubordination. On November 20, 1914, the 130th were preparing to embark at Bombay. Owing to recent reports that Pathans of the 20th Infantry fighting in the Persian Gulf had demonstrated a disinclination to fight Arabs and Turks, the destination of the Baluchis had been changed at the last minute from Force D (Mesopotamia) to Force B (East Africa). But as the soldiers of the regiment boarded the ship, an

India's Splendid Rally

Afghan sepoy killed a British major with his bayonet.[88] Embarkation for the war in East Africa halted immediately. The murderer was quickly tried and executed, and other Mahsud tribesmen in the regiment were disarmed and jailed on suspicion of complicity. "It was considered politically inexpedient to allow them to return to Waziristan during the war," the viceroy reported. The remainder of the regiment deployed instead to Rangoon, where it remained until January 1915, when it received orders to embark again, this time for Mombasa. On January 19, however, authorities learned that the battalion's Pathans would refuse to embark on the pretext that "there were now many people dependent upon them." The following evening, three companies of Pathans were arrested. Two of the mutiny's suspected ringleaders were tried and sentenced to death, and 202 remaining soldiers were sentenced to transportation.[89]

The remaining 447 men of the 130th Baluchis left Rangoon for East Africa without incident on January 26, but the viceroy remained troubled by the regiment's recent difficulties. "There is no doubt that there is a strong disinclination among certain classes of Pathans especially Afridis to fight against the Turks or their allies," he wrote in late January.[90] Secretary Chamberlain asked that he be kept informed in the event of similar incidents, adding that it was important to keep abreast "of the temper of the Native Army," and especially of its Muslim companies. "Please wire if desertions are abnormal amongst Pathans generally or only in certain regiments," he added.[91] Soon enough, Indian soldiers were talking about the mutiny. One sepoy deployed to France in 1914 wrote to a friend serving with the 129th Baluchis, "We are very anxious. The 130th refused to go the war. Subedar-Major Sultan Mir has been court martialed, and all the Afridi sepoys have been put into custody. Ninety sepoys are in custody. But our *maliks* have gone to Peshawar to make a representation."[92] People in India were talking about it, also. In Peshawar one man wrote to a friend in the 129th Baluchis in France, "As for the 130th Baluchis . . . there is great excitement . . . in Peshawar. Among the Afridi people there is hope that their object with regard to them may be effected. That hope is this, that they may come back and be released."[93] The censor of Indian mail in France observed that among Pathan sepoys, "the Afridis in particular are much concerned to know the truth of what has happened to their fellow tribesmen in the 130th."[94]

Meanwhile, Ghadar agents in the United States set to work, selling their land and pooling resources in order to pay for passage to India. "Your duty is clear," Ghadar leadership instructed. "Go to India and stir up rebellion in every corner of the country."[95] Preferring Japanese vessels to American or British, some 579 Indians embarked from North America and 470 from East Asia. The unusually high number of emigrants returning to India after years abroad attracted the attention of the Government of India, whose police received instructions to treat every Indian arrival with suspicion. A number of Ghadar agents also traveled to Hong Kong and Manila, to the Malay States, Singapore, and Burma. The authorities apprehended and jailed many Ghadar agents immediately upon their arrival, but a few slipped past the grasp of the police, smuggling guns and ammunition. They set to work spreading anticolonial propaganda by word of mouth or by pamphlet in India's rural districts. Some of the Ghadarites were themselves veterans of the Indian Army, so they visited the army cantonments in northern India, in the hope of securing recruits to their cause among uniformed sepoys. Between January and February 1915, Ghadar agents talked to soldiers stationed in Ferozepore, Jhelum, Rawalpindi, and Hoti Mardan. Ghadarites talked to Afridis on the North-West Frontier. They found that some soldiers stationed in Lahore, Ferozepore, and Meerut harbored grievances that made the troops especially receptive to Ghadar propaganda. A few troops said they were ready to mutiny. Ghadar agents set a date of February 21, 1915, for troops of the 23rd Cavalry stationed in Lahore and the 26th Punjabis stationed in Ferozepore to mutiny. These soldiers would provide the spark that set the Indian powder keg alight, or so the revolutionaries hoped.[96]

But it would not be so. A Punjab Criminal Investigation Department officer infiltrated the conspiracy's inner circle and betrayed its plans to the authorities. On February 19, Punjabi police raided Ghadar's Lahore headquarters and arrested the ringleaders. The Government of India rushed as many white soldiers as were available to Lahore, Delhi, and Ferozepore to round up as many rebel leaders as they could find. Ghadar's plan collapsed. When soldiers of the 23rd Cavalry and 26th Punjabis got wise that the plot had been compromised, they stood down. Over the next several weeks Punjabi police swept up other conspirators. Eighteen sowars were court-martialed later that summer for co-conspiracy and sentenced to death. Some 175 people were tried under the Defense of India Act between April and September 1915, netting 136 convictions. As a striking testament to the persuasiveness of Ghadar agents, historian Maia Ramnath observes, a majority of the defendants tried in Punjab were local residents, not returned emigrants. By the start of 1916 the Ghadarite threat to Punjab had been neutralized, but between late 1914 and early 1915 the Indian government had only narrowly averted a potential disaster.[97]

In Singapore, however, where Ghadarites established communication with sepoys in the decorated 5th Light Infantry, their efforts did bear fruit.[98] On the afternoon of February 15, 1915, some four hundred Rajput Muslims of the 5th Light Infantry stationed outside Singapore killed their commanding officers. One party of the soldiers then went to a compound three miles away housing three hundred German prisoners under guard. The mutineers easily overwhelmed the guard and then opened the gates to the compound, handing out rifles and ammunition to the German prisoners. A second party of mutineers attempted to surprise a detachment of eighty British soldiers of the Malay States Volunteer Rifles at another nearby camp. The British soldiers held out through the night and were rescued the following day by a force made up of Singapore Volunteers and armed civilians. The mutineers scattered. British authorities regained control with the aid of Japanese, Russian, and British troops. In the wake of the Singapore mutiny, British authorities were at pains to downplay the soldiers' anticolonial motivations. The official report pinned the mutiny on "petty jealousy and dissatisfaction concerning recent promotions." One mutineer, Jellal Khan, told his captors that the men had been told at Mosque that they could not fight against the "head" of their religion, the Sultan in Istanbul. Though he had no desire to fight against the British, he refused to fight for the British Empire in Asia. The secretary of state for India said in Parliament that what happened in Singapore was not a mutiny at all, but a "regimental riot." But the soldiers of the 5th Light Infantry had been in contact with Ghadarites. They had read revolutionary propaganda. Some of the men had been in communication with the German prisoners they freed, from whom they learned about the Ottoman Sultan's declaration of jihad. The truth of the matter, therefore, is that the Singapore mutiny wove together Ghadarite and pan-Islamic ideologies.[99] In the end, 41 men were executed by firing squad and 126 were sentenced to transportation or imprisonment.[100]

Into the Breach

Most sepoys were willing to fight the Turks, whatever their misgivings. At the Censor's Office in France, E. B. Howell contented himself that the Turkish-German alliance meant little to the soldiers. One letter he intercepted from a Muslim officer serving in France to his brother in India read: "What better occasion can I find than this to prove the loyalty of my family to the British Government? Turkey, it is true, is a Muhammadan power, but what has it to do with us? Turkey is nothing to us."[101] Letters from India to the soldiers in France offered similar reassurances. A father wrote to his son in a Garhwal battalion, "From the news received from the west it appears that the Turks have got ready an army near the Suez Canal to attack our Government. Our Muhammadan brothers however are quite unmoved & all it quiet here."[102] Inspiring soldiers to mutiny was a tall order. "In order to win people over," historian Heather Streets-Salter explains, "anti-Allied propaganda and pro-German activists not only had to target issues that spoke to actual grievances of colonized subjects, but they also had to convince people that acting against colonial rule was worth the risk."[103] The latter ultimately proved far more difficult than the former.

India's Splendid Rally

And so within months of the outbreak of war in Europe in August 1914, tens of thousands of Indian soldiers had deployed to practically every theater. In October Indian soldiers prepared for their debut against the German Army in France. In November, as another expeditionary force of Indian soldiers secured the Persian Gulf, their comrades stormed the beaches of East Africa. British audiences applauded the deployment of "their" Indian soldiers to the war's battlefields. So did Indian nationalists, albeit for different reasons. In Berlin and Constantinople propagandists lay the groundwork for the end of the British Raj. Indian radicals established contact with Indian soldiers in Singapore and Punjab and North-West Frontier Province. The stakes were certainly high in 1914. But a speedy conclusion to the war, one way or another, might limit or contain its impacts. What might come out the other side of a long war remained anybody's guess. Be that as it may, where things went next in 1914 depended in large part on the rapidly unfolding situation on the Western Front. Accordingly, it is to Belgium and France that our focus now turns.

3

In Flanders Fields

[The war] is a manifestation of divine wrath. There is no counting the number of lives lost. We have to deal with a terrible and powerful enemy, who is completely equipped with every sort of contrivance.

—From a Punjabi Muslim to a sepoy in Egypt, May 28, 1915

Indian infantry and cavalry arrived on the Western Front in October 1914, at a time when the British were desperate for manpower. The Indian Corps remained in France through the close of 1915, when commanders redeployed the sepoys to Mesopotamia (Indian cavalry soldiers remained in France until the war's final year, when they redeployed to Palestine). How well did these soldiers perform? That's the question we consider here. An Indian soldier's ability to fight well depended in no small part on variables beyond his control—the terrain, the strength of the enemy, the resources his commanders placed at his disposal. In 1914 the timely arrival of the Indian Corps may have saved the British Expeditionary Force from annihilation. In 1915, when stalemate set in on the Western Front, Indian soldiers adapted to the horrors of industrial war as well as anybody. Throughout, a good many demonstrated exemplary courage under fire. Of the twelve Indian soldiers to receive a Victoria Cross during World War I for valor "in the face of the enemy," six earned the honor for their performance on the Western Front. But let us take none of this to mean that Indian soldiers were determined to win their "King-Emperor's battles or die," as British newspapers reported. Soldiers had their limits. They wanted to return home intact. How might one do that in the midst of what some soldiers described as a "war of machines"? How was one to hold on to any hope at all when his comrades and commanders were being killed in an industrial fashion? "It is just like the grinding of corn in a mill," one soldier said of his time in France. Lured by Indian Independence Committee propaganda, a small number of men deserted to the German trenches, hoping to secure a second lease on life.

Into the Trenches

Awaiting the soldiers who deployed to the Western Front in 1914 was a war quite unlike anything anybody had ever faced. Between 1871, when Germany defeated France and proclaimed the unification of the Second Reich, and 1914 there had not been a single war in Western Europe. The only fighting experienced by British, French and German soldiers had taken place overseas in colonial frontiers.[1] In these so-called small wars, soldiers deployed many of the killing technologies and methods made possible by the second wave of industrialization in the late-nineteenth century.[2] The wanton murder of Africans and wholesale destruction of African communities with machine guns was common practice by 1914, and no European soldier could have been wholly unaware of the murderous capacity of the weapons he carried to war.[3] And yet the reality of industrial warfare still caught many by surprise. "The merry, fresh war which we were all looking forward to for years has turned out to be quite different from what we thought!" wrote a British cavalry officer on the Western Front in December 1914. What happened in France was not war, but the "murder of troops by machines."[4] Indian soldiers quickly reached the same conclusion. In their letters home they deployed metaphors that might help their agrarian kin grasp what was unfolding half a world away. "Here the people are being butchered as a butcher slaughters goats," wrote one sepoy deployed to France. "The man who will return to his own country will be a man of very exceptional fate."[5] A soldier described an attack on Christmas Eve, 1914: "The whole line advanced & the enemy's guns roasted our regiments even as grain is parched."[6] "My brother, this is no war," wrote a third. "It is the 'Parlo' (the final destruction of the world). A whole world is being killed."[7]

Although Indian soldiers deployed to various theaters, the war against Germany on the Western Front was where Britain might win or lose the world war. The German government's "September Program" called vaguely for a German Empire in Africa, but all that would have been a moot point if Germany's armies in Europe could not secure victory. By the same token, the largess of Britain's global empire allowed it to exploit the military situation to enlarge the Empire overseas, but all that would have been for naught if German armies won the war in Flanders and France. From the outset the Western Front was bound to be the epicenter of the British Empire's war.[8] Between 1914 and 1918 no other place on earth consumed more men, materiel, and money per square mile than that narrow patch of ground housing the opposing armies. And no place claimed a greater share of the total number of Indians killed and wounded than the battlefields of France and Belgium.[9] A total of 89,335 Indian combatants deployed to France and Belgium during the war. Of those, 22,619 ended up killed, wounded, or missing—25.3 percent of all combatants deployed. In Mesopotamia the casualty rate among combatants was much smaller. Of 326,656 Indian combatants who served in Mesopotamia, 51,017—or 15.6 percent—were reported killed, wounded, or missing. Between 1914 and the close of 1919 a total of 621,219 Indian combatants deployed overseas, with 14.4 percent serving in France. Yet France's 22,619 Indians killed, wounded, or missing represent 22 percent of the 102,254 Indian combatants killed, wounded, or missing in World War I.[10] And most of these 22,619 Indian casualties came prior to the close of 1915.

Owing to the grave manpower deficit British commanders faced at the war's outset, Indian troops played a crucial role in British strategy between 1914 and 1915. The sepoys arrived on the Western Front just in time for the Battle of Ypres in late October 1914, which swelled as both sides rushed men and materiel headlong to one of the "dreariest landscapes in Western Europe."[11] The outcome of the war remained anybody's guess. Soldiers struggled to find the words to describe their first encounters on the Western Front. "Our brothers who are in the trenches have endured sufferings beyond the power of words to describe," wrote one non-commissioned officer of the 47th Sikhs. "When God grants me to see you again, I will tell you the whole story. I think you will not believe what I tell you."[12] Holding trenches that were really nothing more than "a thin scrawl of more or less detached posts," the Indians fought against an enemy superior in manpower and virtually every aspect of materiel.[13] Communication trenches were still a rarity at this point, as was barbed wire.[14] Everywhere the Germans held the high ground. "Our men had to face mortars, hand-grenades, high explosive shell, and a hundred other engines or contrivances of war, with which they themselves were not provided," their commander, General Willcocks later wrote of the situation.[15] The Germans outgunned their enemies in artillery two to one, and in heavy artillery ten to one.[16] Indian soldiers did not have hand grenades, but their enemies did.[17] Inexperienced British officers commanding Indian units did not know how to properly deploy their troops. Throughout late October, officers consistently overloaded frontline trenches, exposing the men to unnecessary dangers while also failing to keep sufficient numbers out of harm's way in reserve to respond to German breakthroughs.[18]

It is difficult to fathom how the British Expeditionary Force might have held out through early winter 1914 without the timely arrival of the Indian Corps. Frederick Smith and John Merewether, the Indian Corps' official recording officers, wrote of the situation at the dawn of Ypres, "The resistant power of the British Army, cruelly outnumbered, and exhausted by constant fighting against superior artillery and a more numerous equipment of machine guns, was almost overcome. And except for the Indian Army there were no other trained regular soldiers in the Empire available at that moment for service."[19] "The length of the trenches held was far greater than the numbers available warranted," General Willcocks wrote of it later. "It appears incredible that the Germans did not now, and for eight weeks to follow, break through our attenuated line on the Indian front. It was nothing but the dogged pluck of the men, with occasional bits of good luck thrown in, that prevented it."[20] In late November the Germans resumed their search for a breakthrough, this time around the village of Festubert. The battle turned into a back-and-forth slugfest. Soldiers were easily separated from their officers and their units.[21] The snow-covered ground slowed troop movements and made the men easy targets for rifle, machine gun, and artillery fire. Willcocks insisted to his superiors that the officers and men of the Indian Corps fought well.[22] One noncommissioned officer of the 47th Sikhs wrote to a friend in Amritsar, "Our troops have proved their fidelity to Government, so that our renown was very great."[23] German soldiers belonging to the 112th Regiment captured at Festubert in November said that the Indian soldiers who counterattacked "showed great determination" and that the advance was "well conducted."[24] Other captured German soldiers "spoke highly of the gallant attack made upon them [by Indian troops] and explained that further resistance on their part would have been futile."[25]

In December fighting focused on the town of Givenchy. "There was a very fierce fight," wrote one Sikh. "The whole line advanced & the enemy's guns roasted our regiments even as grain is parched. On all sides men were fighting with sword & bayonet."[26] One British officer serving with the Indian Corps wrote to his mother in December 1914 that his men had performed "splendidly" in recent fighting. "We rushed from our trenches across the open into a German sap about 30 yards ahead, just before dawn. We did this in two places. Both the first rushes succeeded," he said, "but then dawn broke and *every single man* who tried to cross those fatal 30 yards after that was shot. It was sickening. They were absolutely fearless & have gained the admiration of everyone who saw or heard of them."[27] Between November and December, the Meerut Division served twenty-five consecutive days in the trenches.[28] At the height of the fighting, Sir John French turned to the commander of French Army Group North, Ferdinand Foch, and said, "There is nothing left for me to do but go up and be killed with the I Corps."[29] Seventy-five of the eighty-four battalions in the seven British Expeditionary Force (BEF) infantry divisions had fewer than 300 men, a third of their strength at the start of the war in August. Eighteen of those battalions had fewer than 100 men.[30]

Those first months of grizzly combat left the Indian Corps exhausted and scrambling to replenish its depleted ranks. Indian regiments first went to the front at a full strength of 764 men. At the start of November the average strength of the committed Indian regiments stood at less than 550. The 47th Sikhs were down to 385 men, the 15th Sikhs to 392, the 9th Bhopals to 469, and the 58th Rifles to 461. On a single day in late October, the 2nd/8th Gurkhas broke after losing 600 men while trying to repulse a German assault.[31] In the fighting around Givenchy on December 19 and 20, the 1st/4th Gurkhas lost 302 men from their ranks, including 7 British and 10 Gurkha officers.[32] The Indian Corps lost more than 2,600 men the week just before Christmas.[33] By Christmas the average strength of the Indian regiments had fallen to 450.[34] All told, the Indian Corps had suffered 1,397 dead, 5,860 wounded, and 2,322 missing by the close of the year out of an original contingent of 24,000 men.[35] Almost one in four sepoys who landed at Marseilles had sustained some form of physical trauma.[36] Popular perception held that the actual figures were even higher.[37] Even Indian soldiers with years of experience under their belts before deploying to France in 1914 had never experienced loss on such a scale. "I have no confidence in being able to escape death," one soldier wrote. "In the space of a few months how many men have fallen & how many have been wounded."[38] "Many of the men show a tendency to break into poetry which I am inclined to regard as a rather ominous sign of mental disquietude," the censor of Indian mails reported. "The number of letters written by men who have obviously given way to despair has also increased both absolutely & relatively."[39]

It could be argued that what was asked of the soldiers in late 1914 went above and beyond the call of duty. Most of the men rose to the occasion. A few soldiers demonstrated exemplary courage and leadership under fire. The 129th Baluchis reached the front in Belgium on October 23 and was engaged in heavy fighting practically nonstop through early November. On October 31, at Hollebeke, a wounded twenty-six-year-old sepoy named Khudadad Khan continued to man his machine gun throughout the day even though his British officer and the rest of his crew had been killed.[40]

His stubborn resolve kept the Germans at bay and bought the British the time they needed to bring up reinforcements and prevent a breakthrough. For his gallantry he became the first Indian ever awarded the Victoria Cross.[41] Others followed in short order. The 39th Garhwal Rifles entered frontline trenches for the first time on the night of October 29 near Richebourg, France, where they immediately came under heavy German shellfire. On November 4 a bayonet charge by sixteen Garhwal sepoys sent an approaching party of eighty Germans running for their lives. On the night of November 9 Garhwal sepoys used their prewar frontier training to pull off the first successful trench raid of the war, capturing six Germans. On November 23 the Garhwals were at it again, ordered to recapture a frontline trench recently lost to the Germans. When the sepoys entered the German trench, they fought traverse to traverse, with bomb and bayonet, until all of the Germans were either dead, taken prisoner, or put to rout. Naik Darwan Singh was in the thick of things every bloody step of the way. He fought tenaciously—the first to round each traverse—despite two wounds to the head and one to the arm. For his conspicuous gallantry he was awarded the Victoria Cross.[42]

Onto the Front Page

"People are constantly asking for news of the Indian soldiers in France," offered a correspondent of the *Newcastle Daily Journal* on October 21, 1914, "and curiosity about their movements has undoubtedly been stimulated by illustrations which have appeared in some of the newspapers showing Indian troops on the march. We shall doubtless hear more about these stalwart and swarthy soldiers of the Empire in due time, and when we do they will assuredly be found to have given a good account of themselves against the enemy."[43] This kind of reporting came at a time when industrialized societies were at last coming face-to-face with their own killing potential. Amid the back-and-forth of battles won and lost, or the advances and retreats of 1914, newspaper accounts about the exploits of Indian soldiers lent to the war something for which British audiences might cheer and applaud. "The newspapers consider the prospects of the success of the Allies are becoming clearer every day," noted the *Observer* in October. "The entry of the magnificent Indian troops, which was a colossal triumph, must have caused considerable astonishment in the enemy's ranks."[44] As Indians took up their positions outside Ypres, newspapers had plenty to say about their exploits. "One of the first [Indian] regiments to go into action was badly shelled while entrenching," reported the *Times* in November 1914. "An officer who was present particularly observed the indifference of the men to this—to them—novel experience. It was noticed that after the first few shells they hardly troubled to look around."[45] "Magnificent Indians," ran one headline in the *Aberdeen Evening Express*. "Great Charge by Bengal Lancers"; "Irresistible Onslaught"; "Village Streets Covered with German Dead!" Five thousand dismounted Indian cavalry, sent to rescue beleaguered Allied forces at the battle of Yser, charged fortified German positions "lance in hand." "At this magnificent sight a loud hurrah burst from the ranks of the Allied infantry, who in their turn dashed forward with fixed bayonets."[46] "Our Indian troops are doing splendid work and the enemy fear them," reported the *Western Daily Press*.[47] The *Daily Mirror* reported that at a battle outside Lille in October 1914, "Indian troops have delivered their first blow at the Germans and have left their mark." Things had not gone well that morning, the newspaper reported.

> A great column of Germans poured down upon the English trenches and with a great rush swept through a heavy fire, causing the British to evacuate the position. Then, cheering and singing in triumph, the Germans went on and came face to face with the British reserves—the Indian troops. The Sikhs and Gurkhas had been waiting for this chance, and they took it. With terrific force they charged. The Germans wavered, then turned and ran pell mell, while the pursuing Indians wrought terrible slaughter. No fewer than 20,000 dead and wounded Germans were, it is stated, left on the field.[48]

This outlandish episode must have generated considerable talk among the *Mirror*'s readership. "Everyone in London yesterday seemed to be talking about the glorious charge of the Indian troops," the *Mirror* reported the next day. One wonders if English readers imagined Indian troops cutting their way clear through the German Army all the way to Berlin. "The Germans are now beginning to understand why the Gurkhas never draw their 'kukris' without drawing blood," the *Mirror* reported. "Yet only a few weeks ago the Huns' Press was sneering at these troops as 'Eastern Cripples.'"[49] Throughout late 1914 even the most otherwise insignificant of skirmishes in which the Indian Corps participated were worthy of a few lines in columns devoted to the most sensational war news. Amid cluttered headlines anticipating the imminent collapse of the Central Power on the Eastern Front—there the Germans were purportedly surrendering in thousands to the "Victorious Russians" who doggedly pursued their "broken foe"—the *Mirror* treated its readers to the dash and exploits of Indians on the Western Front. "The Indian Corps has gallantly retaken some trenches which were lost yesterday, and has captured three German officers and more than 100 men, together with one mortar and three machine-guns."[50]

Newspapers returned to tried-and-tested orientalist tropes to describe the Indian Corps in action. The exploits of Nepalese Gurkhas quickly became a favorite topic for British (and French) reporters. "In battle, the Indian troops were once again covered in glory with the *kukri* of the Gurkhas playing, as always, its terrible role," reported one French newspaper in November 1914.[51] If events on the Western Front as reported by the *Times* were to be believed, then Gurkhas made a habit of "discarding their rifles and kit" at nightfall and, "armed only with their kukris, stealthily set out from the trenches, spreading out in open formation and adopting a system of signaling known only to themselves" to cut down German sentries. "It is with such night attacks that openings are made for the British troops."[52] No need for rifles, in fact, according to one timely book, *Famous Fights of Indian Native Regiments* (1914). "Given a human mark—let us say in the shape of a German—[the Gurkha] can take off his nose and ear, or pierce his eye with deadly precision."[53] In late November the *Times* captured what it called a "characteristic exploit by Gurkas":

In Flanders Fields

> The Indian divisions have been engaged. For several days they had to face a terrific assault, and their ranks were daily thinned by a most murderous fire from heavy artillery and machine guns, against which they had little opportunity of showing their prowess in the kind of warfare in which they are most useful—the charge and the stealthy night attack.
>
> Occasionally, however, they have done wonders in this way. A company of Gurkhas had been terribly worried one day by the fire from a certain German trench about 200 yards from their own, at each end of which a [machine gun] was posted. At nightfall they determined to have done with it. Secretly and silently four men left their trench and crept away into the darkness. An hour passed, two hours, three, and nothing happened. Then, just before dawn, came the alarm. There was a sudden cry of terror from the German lines, then mingled shouts and shots. After a minute's struggle in the dark against an invisible foe, who slashed and stabbed without being seen, the Germans were seized with panic and bolted to the rear. Rifle fire blazed out along the whole front, but the four happy Gurkhas slunk back to their comrades unscathed. When dawn broke the German trench lay untenanted save by the two silent [machine guns] and the gashed and bleeding bodies of 15 of its defenders.[54]

Newspapers and the wartime press also peddled to Home audiences the racist myth that Indian troops proved unable to acclimate to the Western European climate. The white European medical establishment had long held by the time of World War I that climate affected different peoples differently. To be "out-of-place" was a medical problem, doctors believed, one that produced or prolonged ill-health.[55] The British public believed it too. In simplest terms, racial pseudoscience instructed that white people had the stuff to endure a French winter. Black people and Asian people—absent abundant preparation—did not. British newspapers told their readers that "climatic considerations" merited careful study when it came to deploying Indian troops.[56] On leave in England at the end of February and the start of March 1915, General Willcocks was struck by "the note of something approaching pity" held by prominent politicians. "What I and many others of the seniors in the Corps felt was that people in England believed that the Indians could not stand the severe climate," he wrote.[57] In his popular history of the war on the Western Front, Sir Arthur Conan Doyle said that the Indians troops in France were fighting at an enormous disadvantage. "As well turn a tiger loose upon an ice-floe and expect that he will show all his wonted fierceness and activity," wrote the acclaimed author. "There are inexorable axioms of Nature which no human valour nor constancy can change. The bravest of the brave, our Indian troops were none the less children of the sun, dependent upon warmth for their vitality and numbed by the cold wet life of the trenches."[58] In time, wartime racial prejudice and popular perception became the stuff of historical consensus. The historian A. J. P. Taylor wrote of the Indian Corps in France in his 1964 *Illustrated History of the First World War* only that "Indian troops were used in France, where the climate hampered them."[59] In his 1998 book the eminent historian John Keegan wrote of the Indian soldiers who served in France: "Though they included a high proportion of hardy Gurkhas, [they] were scarcely suitable for warfare in a European winter climate against a German army." Echoing racist stereotypes prevalent during the war, Keegan said Indian troops offered nothing more than "barbaric flurries of slash and stab."[60]

Contrary to popular opinion, however, Indian Corps headquarters reported in the winter of 1914 and 1915 that "the Indians have stood the climate better than the British." To no small extent, this was because relieving the Indians of any and all weather-related discomfort had become a cause célèbre in England. Since October 1914 the Indian Soldiers' Fund (ISF) had coordinated a massive charity relief drive, providing food, clothing, and comforts of every kind to Indian soldiers at the front as well as to their wounded comrades recovering in hospitals in England and France.[61] By late November 1914 the ISF had already raised £151,762 and had started to send to France socks, gloves, mittens, balaclavas and winter jackets.[62] In December Willcocks wrote to the Fund that his men were "over-clothed."[63] In his postwar memoirs he recalled, "As for clothing and necessaries; beginning with somewhat scanty garments, the sepoys were gradually supplied with an outfit in which it became an impossibility to move." Vests, balaclava caps, warm coats, goatskin overcoats, flannel shirts, socks, underwear, wool mufflers, and gloves "poured into their wardrobes or kit-bags until a man could neither put on nor even stagger under the burden." Some units—"chiefly Departmental ones"—complained about shortages of warm clothes, Willcocks noted. "But though this may have been the case during the first month or so in France, the exact contrary was the case later on."[64] By November 1915 the ISF had supplied 78,000 socks and 12,000 balaclava caps. Other items reached the sepoys too: 22,000,000 cigarettes, 40 gramophones, 7,000 religious books, 85,000 handkerchiefs, 125,000 pounds of sweets, 850,000 envelopes, 2,000 periscopes, and 130 footballs.[65] Combined with frontline medical care from doctors employed by the Indian Medical Service, warm winter clothing helped keep sickness among the Indian ranks to a minimum. Indians reported sick at a rate less than half that of the BEF's British soldiers.[66]

The proximity of the Western Front to major centers of industrial production—as compared to other fronts in Africa or Asia—made ameliorating the misery of the troops comparatively easy. And British audiences wanted to *do something* for the troops in France. "The truth is that the health of the Indian troops in France is better than it is in India," the *Evening Dispatch* reported in March 1915. "If the Indians have found the weather this winter often trying and always disgusting, it has not affected their health. Their officers have seen to that."[67] General Willcocks wrote that the Indian soldiers "were, of course, undergoing great hardships, but so were others, and if the ordeal was harder for them to bear it was only the luck of war." Willcocks said that he "was always very careful to keep my lips closed as to this phase of the situation when the native officers and men asked me (as they always did) what I had heard about them in England."[68] None of this is to say that the men enjoyed squatting in trenches in the bitter cold. But then, nobody did. "The Government makes the most excellent arrangements against the cold," wrote one sepoy. "It gives us warm clothes. If it did not do so, everyone would die of the cold, & what kind of battle would they fight then?"[69]

Life-Saving Measures

Warm winter clothing mattered. But for some soldiers, the Western Front was more than they had bargained for. In late 1914 British commanders began to suspect that Indians were self-inflicting wounds. At the start of November more than half of the 1,848 Indians admitted to hospital had sustained gunshot wounds to the hand.[70] Authorities acted quickly to reduce the number of sepoys they believed were trying to escape frontline duty. General Willcocks had five of the men shot for cowardice and assured Lord Kitchener that the matter had been dealt with.[71] Cases of hand wounds dropped off afterward, but Indian soldier letters suggest the tactic never went away entirely. "I was hit on my trigger finger, & the third part of it is cut off," admitted a wounded Sikh to his brother in Amritsar. "So I hope that I shall return neither to the battle nor to the trench."[72] The number of hand wounds spiked again in May 1915 among troops freshly arrived from India. Willcocks made another example of some offenders, and rates once again fell.[73]

One shouldn't make too much of incidents when Indian soldiers wounded themselves to escape frontline duty. Lord Asquith had learned by Christmas Eve 1914, "There have been quite a number of cases lately of [British] privates being tried and sentenced for mutilating their left hands, so as to make them incapable of handling a rifle. I knew this had happened with the Indians; that it should have spread to our men shows what a shattering thing the trenches must be."[74] Self-inflicted wounds also became a problem in 1914 in the French and German armies.[75] Commanders in every army, maintaining their rigid monopoly over the right to deploy the bodies of soldiers, responded in draconian fashion.[76] The British Army went to great lengths to maintain military discipline, sentencing more than three thousand of its own soldiers to death for desertion, cowardice, mutiny and other offences.[77] Executions and punishments were always public spectacles, grim reminders to soldiers to follow orders and respect the military hierarchy. The Indian mail censor worried nonetheless that drastic punitive measures might not be enough to keep the men at their posts. "Despair of survival ... continues to be very prevalent, and one is tempted to hazard the prediction that this feeling must sooner or later culminate in a regrettable incident unless some fairly definite and clearly perceptible measure of relief can be accorded."[78]

Then there was the matter of desertion, a potentially life-saving stunt to which a small number of soldiers resorted when all other options appeared exhausted. Going over the top to seek refuge among the Germans was a very high risk gamble. A German lieutenant stationed opposite the Indian Corps wrote that on the night of November 10, 1914, a number of Indians tried to desert to the German trenches. "It was dark out and as our men had no way of knowing whether the Indians meant to attack us instead, we shot them all down." In the morning, the Germans found the Indian soldiers, "dead, lying in front of our trench, without any weapons."[79] British authorities concluded that the men deserted "not due to disloyalty or a desire to join the enemy," but because desertion to the German lines appeared to offer "a short cut to India and home."[80] During the Indian Corps' fourteen-month deployment in France, some thirty-eight soldiers deserted successfully to the Germans.[81]

At the start of March 1915, just prior to the start of British spring offensive operations on the Western Front, twenty-four Pathan sepoys in the 58th Rifles abandoned their posts.[82] The elite 58th Rifles had been involved in some of the worst fighting on the Western Front since arriving outside Ypres in late October 1914. The twenty-three men who deserted had been in some of the unit's most harrowing situations. Two of the deserters, Jemadar Mir Mast and Sepoy Azam Khan, were due to receive the Indian Distinguished Medal for exemplary conduct under fire. Part of the Bareilly Brigade, Meerut Division, the regiment repulsed a strong German attack at Givenchy on October 30. At 2:30 a.m. the following day, the 58th Rifles rushed German trenches, capturing them with minimal casualties. For the remainder of that day, however, the men could do nothing more than huddle in their trenches and endure a murderous bombardment of artillery and trench mortars from nearby German troops. At this early point in the war, soldiers were not yet digging traverses into trenches. If an explosive devise landed squarely in one of them, there was nothing to stop the blast and shrapnel but human bodies. Casualties in the 58th were three British officers and five other ranks killed, in addition to four Indian officers and seventy-nine other ranks wounded.[83] Bombardments became something of a routine for the regiment. On the morning of November 22 as many as sixty projectiles fell on their trenches. The regiment was in the very thick of the fighting two days later at Festubert. Although the men held most of their positions, they did so at a terrible loss of life. One company lost 75 percent of its strength, including the commanding officer.[84] Ordered later that day to retake a line of trenches that had been lost, some of the men hesitated before attacking. Casualties for the regiment were three British officers, an Indian officer, and forty-two other ranks killed; two British officers, an Indian officer, and sixty-one other ranks wounded; eleven missing.[85] The regiment fought without pause in mid-December in heavy rain and mud. Casualties were a British officer, an Indian officer, and twenty-four other ranks killed; thirty-two others wounded.[86] The regiment spent most of January and February in billets behind the lines, recuperating and training with hand grenades.

By the start of March it was clear to soldiers up and down the line that another major offensive was just around the bend. A Dogra in hospital wrote to a friend in India, "For a month the fighting was stopped on account of the snow. Now it has begun again. . . . It will be at its height in March and April and after that there will be an advance from 260 miles of trench."[87] For many sepoys in early 1915—not just those in the 58th Rifles—the prospects of an offensive were too much to bear. If desertion offered them any hope of surviving the war, they had to act fast. Some sepoys spoke openly about deserting to the German lines. In February the censor uncovered a planned desertion among trans-border

Pathans in the 129th Baluchis and called attention to the matter. Eight letters in total, all written "in very guarded language" by a Pathan recovering from wounds in a hospital, were "full of injunctions to obey the behest of the Almighty by using the eyes, ears, hands, and feet which God have for the preservation of man's life." Alluding to various conversations held between the soldiers in the trenches, the writer added, "What you suggested to me one day in the support trenches I now approve of."[88] No desertions took place from the 129th Baluchis, but the intended recipients of those letters belonged to the same class and tribe as the twenty-four Afridis from the 58th Rifles who deserted only a few weeks later. The censor read only a tiny fraction of the letters to and from the soldiers in France. While he did not intercept any letters of this nature addressed to the men in the 58th Rifles, we do know that Pathan soldiers in the 129th and 58th wrote to one another. Hence this interesting letter, written by a Pathan of the 58th Rifles in a hospital in England to a Jemadar in the 129th Baluchis serving in France from March 3: "Do not be distressed, our people, the Afridis, the Mohmands, the Swatis and the Kabulis have begun a great fight with the English. They say to the English, 'Bring back our Indians.' We all hope to go back to our country, India."[89] Stationed in an advance position on the night of March 2–3, the twenty-four Afridis had to know that this was as good a chance as they might ever have to use their "eyes, ears, hands and feet" to save their own lives.

The evening of March 2 was clear and crisp. Along a small section of the front outside Vielle Chapelle in France, the 58th Rifles Frontier Force relieved the 1st/9th Gurkhas, taking up positions in advance of the rest of the army in pickets. Except for the occasional crack of a sniper's rifle, the night was mostly quiet and the calm undisturbed. At 1 a.m. the commanding officer of the regiment's 4th Company, which occupied a small orchard and scattered pickets, discovered that one post had been deserted by the Indian noncommissioned officer and seven other men occupying it. Patrols went out at regular intervals through the night to find the missing soldiers with no luck. It was as if they had just vanished. Another Indian officer and fifteen sepoys moved forward and occupied the position.⁹⁰ With no further information forthcoming, all signs hinted at desertion. The 58th Rifles spent a rainy March 3 building up traverses and repairing the brick flooring of their redoubts, all while dodging sporadic snipers' rounds. Around 6 p.m. a party of soldiers sent out to check on the sixteen Indian soldiers who had taken the place of the deserted men in the forward picket found the position empty yet again. Then events moved quickly. Scottish soldiers of the Black Watch moved into the forward position. The 4th Suffolk Regiment relieved the 58th Rifles from the frontlines. The Seaforth Highlanders disarmed all 120 men in the discredited 4th Company and escorted the men to a separate location.⁹¹ The men spent most of month under guard as authorities tried to figure out what to do. On March 26 Willcocks ordered that seven Afridis from the Regiment—all relatives of the deserters, save one—return to India under guard. Two others returned to India, deemed "undesirables." The remaining men rejoined the regiment. Willcocks did not recommend any sort of special punishment beyond removal of service. The secretary of state for India was reluctant to grant such leniency. "I am doubtful if it would be expedient to follow such a course; on the return to their homes they will spread injurious report and be centers for propagating grievances." The secretary preferred to attach the men to some unit in India "where they would do no mischief."⁹²

The horrors of frontline service certainly offered soldiers a compelling "push" reason to desert, but these alone are not sufficient enough to explain the phenomenon. Indian soldiers had to believe that their chances were better with the enemy than they were with the British. The German Army had been trying to cultivate this very notion since learning of the arrival of Indian troops in France. In November 1914 German airplanes dropped leaflets over the British and Indian trenches in France. One of these called Indian Muslim soldiers to jihad.⁹³ More leaflets dropped into the Indian trenches in early 1915 called on Hindus to fight against English rule in India. "You brave Indian soldiers," read one, "do not follow the common English. These English tyrants suck the blood of your veins like vampires."[94] In February the Germans planted incitements to disloyalty written in Urdu and Gurmukhi in glass bottles in front of the Indian lines.[95] These efforts won the Germans some converts and sympathies within the ranks of the Indian Army. An Afridi serving in France wrote to his father in Peshawar in February 1915: "A letter has come from those of our men whom the Germans took prisoner, and from the men of our regiment, saying 'We are now under the German king. You can please yourselves. We are well and happy.'"[96] The Indian soldiers also received letters from comrades serving in uniform on other fronts extolling the virtues of Germany and Turkey. "Be not anxious," wrote a Pathan Afridi sepoy stationed in Hong Kong to a friend in the 57th Rifles in France. "Man dies by God's command, not by order of the German Badshah or of Anwar Beg (Enver Bey)."[97] A Pathan sepoy in the 55th Rifles, stationed at Kohat, wrote to a friend in the 58th Rifles in France on February 15: "Remember this one thing, that the Sultan Badshah is one of us. We hear that the German Badshah has become a Mussulman. You are a wise man, understand and think over this. Then draw your own conclusion. Islam is a good thing. You are out of reach nor can we help you. But we pray much."[98]

From the evidence available in British archives, all we can really do is speculate. A visit to the archives of the German Foreign Office reveals that the twenty-four men who deserted from the 58th Rifles gave testimony to their German captors shortly after deserting their trenches. The sepoys told an agent of the German Foreign Office that they had planned for some time to desert to the German lines. Although they were aware of the German-Ottoman alliance and had heard that the Germans treated Indian prisoners well, many still had their doubts. On the night of March 2, their jemadar (corporal), Mir Mast, sent one of the men across no-man's-land alone to the German trenches with one of the German leaflets in hand to verify the rumors. When he was satisfied, he whistled three times, the signal for the other men waiting in the picket to desert. He repeated the system through the night until the remaining twenty-three men had all deserted safely.[99] The sepoys had grievances born of their experiences in the trenches. They told their German captors that the 58th Rifles had already suffered 507 casualties, not counting the sick. They resented the meager 11 rupees they were paid each month. From the Germans they said they wanted rifles, money, and safe passage through the Middle East to Afghanistan. "They are under English rule and do not know when English rule will come to an end," their German interrogator penned in his notes. When he asked the men how the Germans might compel other Afridis to desert, Mir Mast replied, "If you want to do something, just write: 'We will give you a Mauser and a good German rifle.' That is enough. Then they will all come."[100]

Enduring Stalemate

In 1915 Indian infantry and cavalry continued to fight for control of villages and towns up and down the British sector of the Western Front: Neuve Chapelle, Ypres, Festubert, and Loos. "We are busy every moment in the trenches," wrote one soldier at the front in May.[101] Soldiers readily adapted skirmish tactics learned on the North-West Frontier Province. They received training in new weapons and equipment.[102] Combined British and French strategy from that year forward was focused on one thing: driving the Germans out of Belgium and France.[103] Each offensive yielded the kind of results that haunted both sides for most of the war—little strategic gain in exchange for a horrific loss of life. A sepoy in the 69th Punjabis described the fighting at Loos in late September 1915: "Our brigade took six trenches from the Germans, but afterwards the support did not reach us and we had to retire. In our two companies we lost 25 killed and 60 wounded."[104] David Lloyd George later wrote of Allied strategy that year:

> Whilst the Germans were engaged in . . . tremendous operations to rout and wreck the great armies of Russia, the military authorities in France, Britain and Italy could think of no more effective means of coming to their aid than to hurl great masses of their troops against impregnable positions in France, Flanders, and the Austrian Alps. No decision on the part of their enemies could have suited the Central

Powers better than this course, pursued with an obstinate and senseless determination which sacrificed the flower of the Allied armies in vain efforts to break through defenses bristling with cannon and machine-guns, and with two or three equally powerful positions to fall back upon in the event of the first being carried.[105]

The battle of Neuve Chapelle in March 1915 had all the elements that contributed to disaster after disaster that year on the Western Front. Field Marshal French's plan for the attack was simple. Neuve Chapelle, a ruined village twenty miles south of Ypres, was to be attacked on March 10 by the British 7th and 8th Divisions as well as both divisions belonging to the Indian Corps. The front of attack extended eight thousand yards, behind which the British assembled five hundred guns and a stock of two hundred thousand shells. As light caliber shells dropped into the German trenches, a barrage of heavier explosives would drop behind the German frontline trenches to prevent reinforcements from advancing.[106] The bombardment opened at 7:00 a.m., taking the Germans completely by surprise. At 8:05 a.m., the 1st/39th Garhwal Rifles, 2nd Leicestershires, 2nd/3rd Gurkha Rifles, and 2nd/39th Garhwal Rifles went over the top, reaching and capturing the German frontline trenches by 8:30.[107] One Garhwali wrote of his experience in the battle: "As we advanced we lost a lot of men ... no one could endure the firing of bullets and shells which fell thicker than drops of rain. We lost a great many men and so did the Germans." But the man reached the German lives intact. "When we reached their trenches we used the bayonet and the kukri to such an extent that we were all covered with blood but I did not fall."[108] The advancing British and Indian troops quickly overran the defenders, two infantry regiments and a Jäger battalion. Before 9:00 a.m. the British had all the makings of a victory, local but nonetheless significant.[109]

But then the wheels came off, as they would time and time again. German troops abandoned the village and retreated toward strongpoints built precisely to prevent any enemy breakthroughs. British infantry then received orders to hold their positions momentarily before advancing. This afforded German machine gunners the precious time they needed to get ready for action. Wave after wave of soldiers fell when thousands of British and Indian troops tried to squeeze through a narrow corridor. As German junior officers hurried reserves to the flanks and responded to events on the ground as they were happening, British junior officers passed their observations of the local situation back up the chain of command and waited for permission from the corps commander, five miles behind the lines, to alter the pre-battle plans. The Dehra Dun Brigade, supported by two battalions of the Jullundur Brigade, sat waiting for orders to advance until after 3:00 p.m. The troops were not deployed and ready to attack until 4:30 p.m. When the brigade advanced, German rifles and machine guns opened up on its left flank, and the attackers were forced to withdraw and dig in along the banks of a river.[110] Along the length of the British and Indian lines, the advance ground to a halt.[111]

Nor did it continue the following day. A thick mist enveloped the field, preventing artillery from locating targets. Both sides spent the day consolidating positions. The Indian troops received orders that they would continue the attack the next day. As the mist cleared that night, German artillery opened fire on Neuve Chapelle. The Jullundur Brigade took three hundred casualties before dawn the next morning when it received orders to advance through the thick of the bombardment to the village.[112] The following day (March 12) the Germans launched a counterattack that was quickly halted by twenty machine guns the British had placed at well-chosen positions along their new front lines. At the northern portion of the front held by the Indian Corps, units belonging to the 6th Bavarian Reserve Division and the XIX Corps took very heavy casualties. "The Germans attacked in three lines," one sepoy remembered. "Two lines were blown away."[113] Another soldier wrote home, "The German dead lay like corn after reaping."[114] By the early afternoon commanders were satisfied that the German attack had been halted and ordered the Jullundur and the Sirhind Brigades to advance. A murderous enfilade fire raked the ranks of the Indian troops, who had to withdraw after heavy casualties. Later that night the Indian Corps received orders to halt all further operations and consolidate positions.

Though the exchange ratio of casualties favored the Germans—there were in total 11,652 British killed, wounded, or missing (including 2,188 Indians) to 8,600 German—British Command judged the seesaw battle a partial success.[115] "I desire to express to all ranks of the 1st Army my great appreciation of the task accomplished by them in the past four days of severe fighting," Douglas Haig wrote in his *Special Order to the Army* on March 14. The 1st Army, he reported, had captured German trenches along a two-mile front, inflicting "very serious" losses on the enemy: 2,000 prisoners and 16,000 killed and wounded. The organization of the German forces from Ypres to La Bassée "has been thrown into a state of confusion," he asserted, and the British soldier "has once more given the Germans a proof of his superiority in a fight, as well of his pluck and determination to conquer."[116] Survivors of the battle had plenty to say about Neuve Chapelle. "We have taken many [of the German] trenches," wrote one to a friend in India. "We have had a good victory."[117] The censor of Indian mail noted in his post-battle report, "The letters written by infantry soldiers at the front show [a marked improvement of spirits due to the recent successes gained against the Germans], but it is tempered by the reflection of the severity of the loss which has been sustained."[118] An Indian officer in the 15th Sikhs wrote to a fellow soldier: "The Native Army worked valiantly and took two miles of the enemy's lines. The enemy suffered severely but our native Army's losses were beyond measure. It is finished—vanished."[119]

But it wasn't. Indians participated in offensive operations later that summer and fall. The sepoys had no choice therefore but to acclimate to the conditions on the Western Front as best they could, where constant exposure to the elements—both natural and material—were quickly turning the frontlines into a troglodyte world. Soldiers in all the armies underwent this process of acclimating to frontline conditions. The German soldier Otto Dix described the front as an infernal landscape, plagued by "lice, rats, barbed wire, fleas, shells, bombs, underground caves, corpses, blood, liquor, mice, cats, artillery, filth, bullets, mortars, fire, steel." Paul Nash called the Ypres Salient "unspeakable, godless, hopeless," while the French *poilu* (soldier), Henri Barbusse, in a letter to his wife, referred to the trenches as "an extraordinary topsy-turvy world, a chaos of weapons, bullets, grenades, fuses, equipment mixed with bodies." Indians described the front much in the same way. "Bullets and shells fly around and from both sides bombs are thrown," wrote one sowar; "clouds of gas and sheets of fire, showers of burning acid."[120] "Thousands & hundreds of thousands of soldiers have been killed," wrote a wounded sepoy. "If you go onto the field of battle, you will see corpses piled upon corpses so that there is no place to put hand or foot."[121] A Gurkha sepoy said, "It is like being between the devil and the deep sea."[122]

Long spells in the trenches could be a special agony. One had to be vigilant to protect against trench foot in the spring and autumn whether one was Indian, French, German, or English. French soldiers complained more about the rain than they complained about German artillery.[123] Indian sepoys were no exception. Frostbite stalked the trenches in the winter on both sides of the battlefield. A Sikh wrote to his brother in January 1915: "It rains without ceasing every day, & many men have been killed by the cold. Many have lost the half of a foot from the frost."[124] "In this country rain falls every day," another soldier echoed. "There is great hardship."[125] As summer turned to fall in 1915 and soldiers faced the prospect of another winter in the lines, one soldier wrote home: "It remains to be seen who will catch cold and die of pneumonia and who is to live. Last year more people from Hindustan died of pneumonia than as a consequence of the war."[126] One wounded soldier of the 40th Pathans wrote from his hospital bed in England in September to his friend still serving at the front that he had "heard that the 40th is not going into the trenches again. I was delighted to hear this."[127] And if battling the elements could prove a daily grind, the suddenness and violence of an artillery bombardment might produce abject terror. "Days seem like years, but I have no confidence for five minutes of what will happen," wrote a Dogra to his brother.[128] The main business of the men in the trenches in such moments was to exercise self-control. "We are trapped here like animals," wrote one Punjabi.[129] Soldiers in all the combatant armies coped as best they could, pooling whatever material and cultural resources were available. Some turned to their religion. "Pray for us who are fallen into this trouble that the Almighty may be pleased to bring our people home again out of the affliction into which they have fallen," wrote one Punjabi Muslim. "Pray always."[130]

Soldiers also had to contend with the racist attitudes of their white allies. "I knew these troops would be no good," one Home Army staff officer recalled hearing people say as they shook their heads when Indian troops retreated at Givenchy in December 1914.[131] When Indian troops broke and ran at Loos in September 1915, British soldiers also serving in the line shouted racist epithets at them. Sifting through the Indian mail, the censor noted in one report: "It may not be out of place to remark that several men of the 2nd Black Watch, whether rightly or wrongly, ascribe the misadventures which their regiment experienced during the recent attack, to the behavior of the Indian troops who were co-operating with them. Expressions such as 'At this point the niggers began to run' were found in one or two letters (and were of course deleted)."[132]

As if exploding German shells were insufficient danger, Indian soldiers also had to dodge a steady barrage of racist epithets hurled by their own British comrades. Indian officer Amar Singh served with the Sirhind Brigade during his 1914–15 deployment to France, spending more time at brigade HQ than in harm's way in the trenches. The Rajput aristocrat endured innumerable harangues from British officers on the supposedly inferior fighting qualities of the Indian troops as compared to the British.[133] "A great trouble under which we have labored is that whenever we fail in the slightest degree anywhere people raise a hue & cry whereas if a British troop fails under the same circumstances no one mentions it," Amar Singh recalled. Indian troops performed admirably through November and December 1914, "but when we had the reverse at Givenchy & Festubert there was hue and cry. However no one at that time said that there were British troops in it as well."[134] During a visit to the India Office in London in January 1915, he overheard talk that the Indian soldiers were poorly acclimated to the cold climate.[135] And in the immediate wake of Neuve Chapelle, one British officer told Amar Singh "that the Indians ought to be withdrawn.... He said that they cannot fight against the Germans."[136] Racial prejudice placed Indian soldiers in an impossible position. The daily grind of racist abuse left Amar Singh exasperated and angry. "I do not know what is expected of the Indians," he wrote. "After all a man can give his life up & no one can say that the Indians have been sparing themselves in any way."[137]

The vast majority of the Indian sepoys who served in France performed their duty to the end. "Be very bold in the performance of your duty," Habib Khan, a Pathan with the 59th Rifles, read in a letter sent to him from Wana in the North-West Frontier. "Do your duty well. Let no one say 'He ran away from his duty.'"[138] Another Pathan serving with the 59th Rifles in France discouraged a comrade serving in India from deserting his regiment. "Do your duty in the regiment and take pains with your drill. Do your duty well," he said. "In every letter you write [that you are thinking of deserting]. I do not like it. Do your duty well and do not do any such evil action."[139] In September 1915 the Indians participated in their last major offensive operation of the year, the Battle of Loos. "Much has happened," sepoy Lal Khan wrote after the battle. "If God grants me life I shall meet you again. What has happened took place on the great battle on the 25th September. God defend even the enemy from such a day."[140] Soldiers in the 33rd Punjabis described the battle as "a terrible storm," one that "came and uprooted and carried off several trees." To their friends and families in the Punjab, they wrote, "We are not cleaning buckets like you. We are doing our duty (as soldiers)."[141] A sepoy in the 47th Sikhs described how his regiment captured several German trenches during the battle. "Then violent rains came on and the mud prevented any further advance. But for this we should have got a long way."[142]

The ferocity of the fighting in 1915 coupled with the year's disappointing outcomes sobered newspaper accounts to some extent. No one honestly believed by that summer that kukris might break the stalemate. As Home audiences gradually came to terms with the fact that lots of people were going to be dead before it was all over, many longed for something familiar to which they might cling, for some assurance that the war had not shattered everything they once took for granted. And their newspapers continued to make sense of the war and to make meaning out of the carnage by drawing on prewar ideas and symbols. Absent a breakthrough or decisive victory, newspapers provided reassurance in such words as "heroism," "gallantry," and "honor." British casualties at Neuve Chapelle in 1915 were heavy, but newspapers reminded readers that "our troops have shown in attack, as they have already shown in defence, that they can endure the highest test of all great losses; and the cheerfulness of the survivors and their readiness for another fight are proofs that their comrades have not died in vain." As for the sepoys, "[they] are especially elated by the result of the action, and continually ask when they are going to have another fight."[143] Indian troops had their chance one week later when they apparently wreaked such havoc on advancing Germans that, "in their picturesque phraseology, some of our Sepoys said that 'shooting the enemy was like cutting grain.'"[144] By late 1915 "Thrilling Deeds by Indian Warriors" could still make headlines. "The Indian troops yield to none in staunch and heroic tenacity," offered the *Mirror* that August.[145]

By the time the Indian Corps withdrew from France for the Middle East at the end of 1915, the appetite of British newspaper readers for stories about the Indian soldiers had declined considerably from its peak in the heady months of late 1914. A quick search for the term "Indian troops" in the digitized British Newspaper Archive (home to over ten million searchable pages from more than two hundred newspaper titles from the United Kingdom and Ireland), available on the website of the British Library, returns more than 21,700 hits. So we might conclude that Indian troops made the news a lot. But what is so interesting is that Indian troops made the news more in the war's opening two years than they did in the remaining three years combined. The search term "Indian troops" appears 7,136 times in a search of newspapers from the year 1914. It appears 6,911 times in a search of news-

Table 1. Total mentions of "Indian troops" in UK and Irish newspapers, 1914–18

	1914	1915	1916	1917	1918
January		983			
February		781			
March		771			
April		630			
May		571			
June		412			
July		504			
August	409	406			
September	801	456			
October	1,470	428			
November	2,373	422			
December	1,312	547			
Total	7,136	6,911	3,284	2,557	1,854

Source: From the digital British Newspaper Archive, British Library, accessed January 23, 2016.

papers from 1915. But then "Indian troops" made the news just 3,284 times in 1916; 2,557 times in 1917; and 1,854 times in 1918. This means that the Indian soldiers who fought in France and Belgium in 1914 and 1915 made the news more than their comrades who fought in the Middle East, or East Africa, or Gallipoli, or Palestine. And fighting in October, November, and December 1914 produced more news than the years 1917 and 1918 combined. We might put it another way. From the perspective of the British press, the exploits of Indian troops were newsworthy when Indian troops were fighting in Europe. When Indian troops fought in the Middle East, their exploits were less newsworthy.

At Home among the French

French civilians were especially welcoming of the Indian troops when the Indian Corps arrived at Marseilles in September and October 1914. When they weren't in the trenches fighting, Indian soldiers billeted with French families. During their fourteen-month deployment, to varying degrees Indian sepoys wove themselves into the fabric of daily life of the French communities in which they were housed and billeted. Many worked to overcome barriers of language and custom, integrating themselves in local economies. By January 1915 a "good many" of the men had acquired some French.[146] At times sepoys went in and out of shops and cafés seemingly like regulars. Others went in and out of French homes. That's why the Indian soldiers had very good things to say about the French in their letters home.[147] "The people freely opened their doors to us," Victoria Cross recipient Mir Dast (brother of the deserter Mir Mast) recalled. "They treated us as if we were so many members of their families." Older French women "adopted" Indians as surrogate sons.[148] "You tell us that near the place where you are a French Madam lives, who . . . treats you in every way like a mother," one sowar read in a letter from home. "We, your parents and relatives are very much indebted to her for her kindness to you. . . . May God bless her and all her family."[149] Soldiers reciprocated with kindness of their own. Soldiers resting behind the lines provided unpaid childcare from time to time for French children whose fathers were away at the front. "It was very noticeable how well the Indians got on with the French children," one British officer associated with the Indian Corps wrote. Regimental bands put on concerts for French villagers with Punjabi drums. Other sepoys helped out around the farm, chopping wood or harvesting wheat for French families.[150] Thrown together amid the war, Indian soldiers and French villagers quickly discovered how much they had in common.

This frightened racist army commanders. Philippa Levine has demonstrated that the deployment of Indian soldiers to Europe "brought about an increasingly alarmist link between racial mistrust and a vision of sexual disorder in which 'unruly' women and potentially disloyal colonials were subject to far more rigorous controls than other groups."[151] In India, women were foundational to the construction of whiteness and the policing of racial borders.[152] Imperial states tended to matters of intimacy—both sexual and affective—because it was precisely within this realm that the imperial project, with all policies designed to protect white prestige, was at its most vulnerable.¹⁵³ Indian soldiers and French civilians frequently transgressed the empire's racial boundaries. Plenty of letters from Indian soldiers at the front to friends and family in India make mention of sexual liaisons with French women—although, to be sure, it is nearly impossible to disentangle fantasy from fact in letters from soldiers boasting about their own sexual exploits.¹⁵⁴ "The people [French women] are very affectionate and our men are being ruined," wrote one soldier at the Kitchener Indian Hospital in southern England.¹⁵⁵ "The English ladies ('meman') love me," bragged one Sikh recovering from wounds at Milford.¹⁵⁶ For other soldiers the ordinary conduct of European women and European men shocked their sense of propriety. "Every evening the youths one and all go to the town where women meet them. The women have no modesty but walk with the men who please them most."¹⁵⁷ What is clear, however, is that some Indians overcame whatever initial culture shock they may have experienced to form romantic relationships with French women. By 1917 several Indian cavalrymen had fathered French children of their own. One soldier, Mahomed Khan, married a French woman in April 1917 despite the vehement disapproval of his family.¹⁵⁸ Another Indian artillery soldier remained in France after the war, settling down as a newlywed with his French wife.¹⁵⁹

At the Censor's Office, E. B. Howell worried that these kinds of encounters and experiences "cannot but be very prejudicial to good discipline."¹⁶⁰ The sepoys, he wrote in a June 1915 report, "cannot understand the freedom with which the [European] sexes mingle. Hence, when they are allowed unlimited freedom from hospitals etc. to go where they please, they are liable to gain many wrong ideas and impressions which might be difficult afterwards to eliminate."¹⁶¹ Indian Corps commanders and officers went to great lengths to prevent intimate encounters, freely resorting to corporal punishment between 1914 and 1915. Disciplinary regulations as they applied to Indian soldiers in 1914 were already considerably more stringent than those governing the behavior of British soldiers, and corporal punishment comprised a routine and important ingredient in the exercise of (white) authority.¹⁶² Indian soldiers deployed to France could suffer flogging for any number of loosely demarcated offenses, including "housebreaking or plunder," "serious offenses against the person or property of inhabitants of the country," and "disgraceful conduct."¹⁶³ Officers imposed an 11 p.m. curfew on Indian troops encamped near Marseilles. Those caught out past curfew, officers told their men, were assumed to be "seeking romance" and would be punished with a dozen lashes.¹⁶⁴ "We are not allowed to go into the villages, and are forbidden to speak to anyone, so what could I have to tell you?" grumbled one Havildar.¹⁶⁵ General Willcocks worried officers were not applying his regulations evenly. Accordingly he distributed instructions to subordinate officers in which he advocated for the severe punishment of Indians convicted of rape "in this country." Willcocks also changed disciplinary regulations to allow corporal punishment of troops found absent without leave, "when there is reason to believe that the offence was due to immoral relations, actual or intended, with a European woman."¹⁶⁶ Henceforth sepoys need not have been "caught in the act" to receive punishment. The suspicion of intent was enough. Historian Nikolas Gardner relates the account of one British officer serving in the Indian Cavalry Division upon witnessing the punishment of an Indian soldier convicted of propositioning a local woman.

> A Sowar, Hazura Singh, of the 6th [Native Cavalry] was publicly flogged before the 4 native regiments for making indecent overtures to a French girl in Olivet. After a careful inquiry & court martial he was let off with the mild sentence of 20 lashes. However, these were well administered by a sturdy corporal in the 17th, a former sailor & well versed in the art of flogging. We all wished the fellow had got more, but he will have plenty of bare-back riding and fatigue duty for the future to remind him to behave better in Europe.¹⁶⁷

At the Censor's Office E. B. Howell took what measures he could to disrupt attempts by Indians and French women to form ongoing friendships or amorous relationships. The censor described in one of his reports the steps he had taken to prevent soldiers from securing the postal addresses of French women, "as it is understood that it is especially desired to prevent this practice from becoming common."[168] Howell worried that despite his effort, by the time he examined letters to and from the Indian troops, the damage had already been done. Hence his colorful commentary from an August 1915 report that he had found nothing "worthy of note [in the soldiers' letters] except a fair number of letters addressed by French women residing in the neighborhood where the Indian Cavalry Corps spent the winter to Indian members of the Corps, which has now been moved elsewhere." The censor was gobsmacked. "Some of the letters were of a violently amatory nature."[169]

In his postwar memoirs General Willcocks conveniently overlooked the considerable efforts he made during his tenure in command to disrupt the formation of too-congenial ties between the troops and the French. The commander had not been entirely insensitive to the needs of his men at the front, of course, but he remained nonetheless a staunch defender of white supremacy throughout. Willcocks commented at some length on relations between the French and the Indians in his book *With the Indians in France*.

> Take a look at the race-course by the sea. Leaning on the rails are twenty or thirty French, men, women, and children, watching our Indian soldiers cooking their evening meal; these have doffed their khaki uniform and are now clothed in the scantiest of garments. They exchange words, French and Hindustani; a French child offers one of them a sweet, the Indian gives a chapatti in return; cigarettes are offered by a passer-by; a Mahomedan pulls out from his haversack a bamboo flute and plays a ditty; all laugh heartily. The West has already conquered the East; the East has sown a seed which gradually grew until within a few months Indians in Flanders were entering shops, bargaining and buying as if they were to the manner born, and the vendors were even more civil to them than to Europeans, and that is saying much for those fine people the French.

In Flanders Fields

What may eventually be the result of all the friendliness and *camaraderie* between the French and Indians is hard to say. It will have its advantages; it will assuredly have its disadvantages. "East is East and West is West": the Ganges and the Seine flow in different directions; the artificial meeting of these waters may not be an unmixed blessing. The Hindu on his return to Kashi (Benares) or the Mahomedan at his prayers at the Jumma Musjid at Delhi may think differently of the white races across the sea to what he thought before the transports bore him across the *kala-pani*, the black water.[170]

It remains markedly difficult to pin down how exactly wartime service in France altered attitudes or patterns of behavior once the Indian soldiers returned home. To be sure, wartime service in Europe led many soldiers to question previously held ideas and assumptions. "Our minds have been opened up," a Hindu Jat said of his experience in Western Europe. Another veteran went home ready to reject the "absurd prejudices of castes and religions" to which he had previously adhered. Some Sikh veterans began growing vegetables with their own hands, a task they thought fit only for their inferiors before the war. A good many letters from soldiers at the front exhorted friends and family to treat women better and to permit women access to an education. In the village of Beri in Punjab's Rohtak district, veterans led postwar efforts to reform marriage practices. Among other things, the village council agreed that fathers could no longer sell their daughters. The same village relieved women of the burden of cutting thorn bushes for fuel and shifted the responsibility to its menfolk. Other soldiers pooled their resources in order to send their sons and daughters to school after the war. In Waziristan, a veteran of the 127th Baluchis named Mir Badshah founded a primary school. Despite an attempt by local tribesman to burn his school to the ground as a symbol of British control, Mir Badshah's school not only survived—it thrived, launching the military career of his son, the future general of the Army of Pakistan, Alam Jan Mahsud. Gurkha veterans of the Western Front also established schools for their children in Nepal.[171]

Bound for the Middle East

Between October 1914 and November 1915 the Indian Corps sustained more than thirty-four thousand British and Indian casualties—killed, wounded, and missing. On October 31, 1915, the Indian infantry received notice that they would leave France for good. The Indian 6th Division in Mesopotamia had advanced to within a hundred miles of Baghdad earlier that summer, an opportunity too tantalizing to ignore. The year 1915 had been bleak for the Allies, and the government was desperate for a win someplace. The Gallipoli operation appeared doomed to failure, and the Franco-British offensives in Champagne and Loos had ground to a halt. The Central Powers, meanwhile, had crushed Serbia and seemed poised to welcome Bulgaria to their roster. On October 8 Secretary Austen Chamberlain asked the commander of IEFD, John Nixon, what additional forces he would require to occupy and hold Baghdad.[172] Nixon replied that he would require one additional division if the British meant to hold Baghdad permanently. Viceroy Hardinge, eyeing Baghdad as a prize—one that might, if captured, bring the war in Mesopotamia to a speedy and successful conclusion—now changed his mind on IEFA. He found a ready and willing champion for the operation in the secretary of state for India, who pressed the British government to provide the required reinforcements.[173] At last, on October 24, the cabinet gave the capture of Baghdad its formal sanction, overruling strong objections from Lord Kitchener, promising two more divisions "as soon as possible," and earmarking the Lahore and Meerut divisions for the job.[174]

Thus it was on November 4 that the Lahore and Meerut Divisions left the trenches for the last time, relieved by the British 11th Corps. Imperial ambition dictated that they were required elsewhere. None of this is to say that the Indian soldiers harbored any desire to fight the war in France and Belgium a moment longer than required. The censor's reports confirmed that with the onset of cold weather in late 1915, prayers for "deliverance" in sepoy letters had once again become widespread. One soldier wrote

In Flanders Fields

from the front at the end of September: "My heart is sadly failing. There is no sign of the end of the war.... The cold is beginning to increase once more and the rain has begun again. And yet there has been no relief from the trenches."[175] Redeployment to Egypt was a prospect many of the men welcomed. One sepoy wrote to a comrade in the Punjab of Egypt: "There is nothing but ease there, the warmth and the cold in fact everything is like our own country. Even the water is just like that of my own village, and the fighting there is nothing, the Turks are not able to fight against our Government soldiers."[176] Time and experience would prove the soldier's impressions about the Turks wrong. For the moment, Indian infantry left France with the words of the BEF's commander, Sir John French, who assured them they had done their work for the empire admirably. "On the departure of the Indian Corps from my command, under which you have fought for more than a year, I wish to send a message of thanks to all officers, non-commissioned officers and men for the work you have done for the Empire," the commander said. "You have done your work here well, and are now being sent to another place where an unscrupulous enemy has stirred up strife against the King-Emperor."[177]

4

Healing the Empire

> I was standing on the bridge in the evening when [the wounded from Ctesiphon (Iraq) arrived on board a ship and two steel barges].... [The men] were covered with dysentery and dejecta generally from head to foot.... I found men with their limbs splinted with wood strips from "Johnny Walker" whisky boxes.
>
> —Report from a major with the Indian Medical Service, stationed in Basra, Persian Gulf, 1915

Access to life-saving health care can make or break any army. An Indian soldier needed and deserved access to good hospitals as much as any other soldier did in World War I. At the start of 1917, according to one cabinet memo, the Indian units deployed to France, East Africa, Mesopotamia, Egypt, the Dardanelles, Aden, Tsingtao, and the North-West Frontier had already sustained a combined 67,213 casualties (killed, wounded, or missing), roughly 30 percent of the total number of Indians deployed to battlefronts by that time.[1] Just how many tens of thousands more fell sick and had to visit a doctor at some point is anybody's guess. Did Indian soldiers serving overseas have access to life-saving health care? As this chapter reveals, the experience of being wounded or getting sick on campaign was different from one theater to the next, depending upon the extent to which commanders prioritized sepoy health care. On the Western Front, the lives of sick and wounded Indian soldiers mattered to commanders and to the Home Government. Military and Home authorities responsible for the welfare of sick and wounded Indian troops bent over backward to guarantee the men live-saving medical care. In fact, Indian soldiers in France enjoyed access to health care far surpassing anything they had come to expect from the Government of India before the war. Indian soldiers who got sick or wounded fighting in the trenches in France or Belgium very often survived. In Mesopotamia, however, the lives of sick and wounded Indian soldiers mattered comparatively less to those in command of the region's military operation. (What happened to the Indian Corps was the purview of the government in England; what happened to IEFD was the purview of the Government of India.) The commander of IEFD in 1915, General John Nixon, cared a good deal more about capturing Baghdad before the end of the year than he cared about ensuring his soldiers the health care such an operation necessarily required. Sometimes Indian soldiers in the Middle East didn't even have access to health care. When this state of things caused an altogether predictable and preventable breakdown of the Expeditionary Force's already deficient healthcare systems in late 1915, IEFD command took a crisis of its own making and pushed things to their complete and utter collapse. In January 1916 the Indian troops who had fought in France arrived in the Middle East. Tasked with rescuing the Indian 6th Division—then surrounded and under siege more than two hundred miles upriver at Kut—the Indian 3rd and 7th Divisions went into action before their medical equipment had a chance to be unloaded from the transport ships that brought them all the way from Europe. "The medical provision for the Mesopotamia Campaign was from the beginning insufficient," read the findings of a government investigation. "By reason of the continuance of this insufficiency there was a lamentable breakdown in the care of the sick and wounded [in November 1915]." Ill-conceived and hastily attempted rescue operations in January 1916 resulted in "the most complete breakdown of all."[2]

"Economy" and Sepoy Health Care

At the turn of the twentieth century, infected wounds and communicable diseases were the greatest scourge of armies, taking the lives of more soldiers than explosives or steel. In the American Civil War (1861–65) sickness claimed approximately two-thirds of the estimated 620,000 soldier deaths. Two-thirds of all British deaths in the Boer War (1899–1902) were attributed to disease. Across much of the planet during World War I, germs continued their deadly work. Seven times as many Turkish soldiers died of disease as from wounds, and in the protracted campaigns ranging across East Africa, disease was the major killer of Europeans, Indians, and Africans.[3] At the start of August 1915 the Indian force in East Africa numbered some seventeen thousand men. But disease had so ravaged the men that only four thousand were fit for duty. One member of the British cabinet lamented at a meeting to discuss future operations in East Africa, "One Indian Regiment, the 13th Rajputs, is suffering to such an extent from malaria and debility that they will never be of any more use in the field."[4] The sudden onset of extreme temperatures also presented a very real danger to armies. During the Carpathian Winter Campaign, between January and April 1915, temperatures routinely hit minus 30 degrees Celsius (minus 22 degrees Fahrenheit). Entire Russian and Habsburg armies—hundreds of thousands of men—quite literally froze to death.

The Russo-Japanese War and the Western Front were the first major conflicts in world history in which soldiers had a better chance of being killed by high explosives and bullets than by disease and exposure to the elements. This is not to say that the soldiers in Belgium and France did not get sick. And this does not mean that they did not suffer from exposure to rain, wind, and snow. But owing to recent and remarkable advances in medicine, wounded and sick soldiers stood a decent chance of surviving and returning to active duty at the front where their commanders wanted them. From a medical standpoint, one of the great ironies of the war on the Western Front may very well have been the fact that the modern medicine soldiers accessed in France (when combined with the insatiable demand for manpower) contributed to innumerable cases of repeated bodily trauma. Conditions were so bad in Mesopotamia in 1915 and early 1916 that IEFD's operations became the topic of official inquiry and opprobrium. The secretary of state for India, Austen Chamberlain, had called some attention to conditions in the Middle East in 1915. In the wake of that year's disastrous operations and an outcry in the British press in 1916, command of IEFD passed from the hands of the Government of India to the British government, and two commissions were appointed to investigate things—the Vincent-Bingley Commission (created in March 1916) and the Mesopotamia Commission (created in July 1916). The publication of the findings of these investigations in 1916 and 1917 exposed the gross deficiencies Indian soldiers had long endured in the employ of the Government of India.

When World War I began in 1914, Indian soldiers still received medical care under what was called the "regimental system." Regimental hospitals were based on the principal of bringing "the hospital to the patient rather than the patient to the hospital."[5] Under this system in South Asia, hospitals and equipment were transported with the regiment to which they were attached when that regiment moved. Surgical equipment and facilities were quite naturally subpar; comforts and amenities otherwise absent. Patients generally provided their own bedding and clothing (contributing to the spread of contagion) and relied on healthy comrades to provide them with food and nursing. The shortcomings of the regimental system were too much for authorities to stomach when it came to treating British soldiers employed by the Indian Army. British soldiers in South Asia had enjoyed the perks of "station hospitals" since 1882.[6] But until 1914 military authorities had rejected any attempt at reforming the way Indian soldiers were treated. "The salient rationale behind the system," historian Samiksha Sehrawat points out, "was the spirit of nonintervention in indigenous customs and the principle of managing sepoy health care as economically as possible."[7] We might put it this way. The Indian Army's healthcare system was separate and unequal.

Since "economy" was the rule by which Indian Army Command made decisions affecting the health and welfare of the sepoys, cutting costs was the modus vivendi of its underlings. "Under a policy so rigorously defined," read the Mesopotamia Commission, "it is not unnatural that military and medical officers thought that they were best discharging their duty to the Government by keeping down demands, by carrying on as best they could without incurring fresh expenditure, and by discouraging their subordinates from pressing new ideas or ideals which... would entail... additional expenditure."[8] The life of an Indian soldier was cheap, in other words. Better to keep quiet and permit conditions to deteriorate for the men than stick one's neck out and call attention to the inadequacies of a healthcare system the army had already deemed inadequate for its white soldiers. Witnesses interviewed by the Vincent-Bingley Commission testified that this "Indian system," as they called it, did more than anything else to contribute to the breakdown of the medical arrangements in the Mesopotamia campaign in 1915 and 1916. According to the Vincent-Bingley Commission's witnesses, it was "a system which allows officers to think, whether rightly or wrongly,"

a. That there is more merit to be obtained by keeping quiet and not worrying the higher authorities than by asking for what is necessary;

b. That keeping down expenditure is more meritorious than efficiency;

c. That nothing new is likely to be sanctioned unless a corresponding saving in something else can be shown; and

d. That even in small matters anything asked for will be cut down by half... A system of this nature will possibly be good and economical in peace time, but is bound to break down in war.[9]

It was no secret to the doctors and medical personnel employed by the Indian Medical Service (IMS) that they were not adequately supported by the government in the work they had to perform. "I doubt whether you gentlemen would consider that the Sepoys' hospitals in peace time in India are hospitals at all," one officer with the IMS recalled.[10] Havelock Charles called India's peacetime medical hospitals "a disgrace to the Government of India."

Another witness told the Mesopotamia Commission of the Indian Army's peacetime hospitals: "They are so bad that I think it would be necessary to reform them *ab initio*."[11] Alfred Keogh, who would have a hand in overseeing the operation of Indian hospitals in France and England during the war in his role at the War Office as director-general, Army Medical Services, said in 1916 of India's prewar military hospitals: "I have no hesitation whatever in saying that the medical arrangements connected with the Army in India have been for years and years most disgraceful. I say that with a full sense of responsibility. I have served many years in India. I have not been there for some time now, but in my opinion things are not better than they were. Anything more disgraceful than the carelessness and want of attention with regard to the sick soldier in India it is impossible to imagine."[12]

This was the system to which Indian soldiers had long been subjected in the years prior to World War I.

Repairing Bodies for the Battlefield: Indian Hospitals in England and France, 1914–15

Jeffrey S. Reznick demonstrates convincingly in the British case that hospitals were critical parts of the war machine. They sustained manpower by repairing damaged bodies and returning soldiers to the front. Hospitals also serviced as a form of propaganda. They sustained popular support for the war by masking some of the horrors of war from audiences at home while also providing a place where those who remained at home could contribute to their country's war effort.[13] When the Indian Corps reached the trenches in France and Belgium in 1914, there was no reason at all to continue treating the men to business as usual. Walter Lawrence, Lord Kitchener's hand-picked commissioner of Indian hospitals, laid out in 1914 that the challenge "was to get the Indians quickly into warm and dry buildings, as they suffer greatly from a wet and cold climate, and it was essential to concentrate in one or two localities." Wounded British soldiers, he held, "could be sent to any part of the kingdom." Indian soldiers presented a unique logistical challenge, "owing to their special requirements," and Lawrence insisted they "must be kept together."[14] Lawrence rejected outright the "Indian system." He personally scoured the countryside in France to find locations that would be suitable to treating Indian patients. In France large hospitals were established at Boulogne in a converted Jesuit college and at Marseilles in a large camp and at the adjacent Chateau Mussôt. Smaller hospitals included a converted hotel overlooking the sea near Hardelot and a military school at Montreuil that took in an especially large number of wounded Indians during the fighting at Festubert in December 1914. There was also a large camp for wounded Indians at Rouen attached to the military depot, although it closed in the spring of 1915. Authorities set up a clearing hospital in Lillers. At St. Venant, the British acquired a women's mental asylum and converted it to a convalescent depot where soldiers spent at most a fortnight before going back to the fighting line.[15]

Prompted by French protests in late 1914 that the railways could not accommodate the large number of Indian wounded, Lawrence scoured southern England for any location with the infrastructure to house large numbers of wounded men. In Brighton he obtained the Royal Pavilion, the York Place Schools, and a block of buildings that became known as the Kitchener Hospital. The Lady Hardinge and the Forest Park Hotel opened as hospitals at Brockenhurst. Lawrence also secured sites for hospitals in Netley, Bournemouth, and Milford-on-Sea, and a site for a convalescent home at Barton-on-Sea, New Milton.[16]

The flow of mangled Indian bodies to surgeons' tents and hospital beds behind the lines in France began in earnest as soon as the Indian Corps reached the front in late October 1914. In just two days stretcher bearers carried 240 men of the 15th Sikhs to the rear with nasty shrapnel wounds received before the regiment had the opportunity to entrench. Their comrades in the Jullundur Brigade fared no better the last week of October. In the span of eight days, the 59th Rifles lost 189 men to wounds, and the 47th Sikhs lost 120.[17] The Indian Corps fought through the month of November without relief. By the start of December, 3,915 Indian and British soldiers of the Meerut and Lahore Divisions had been removed from the lines wounded. By the start of 1915, that number had risen to 5,860. Nearly one out of every four sepoys who landed at Marseilles in late September and October had sustained some manner of physical trauma in just three months of fighting.[18] At Neuve Chapelle 38 Indian officers and 1,720 sepoys suffered wounds in three days of fighting in March 1915.[19] By the close of 1915, total casualties among the Indian Corps numbered 34,252.[20] Fourteen months in Europe had left some Indian regiments almost entirely depleted of their original contingent. Fighting at First and Second Ypres, Givenchy, and Festubert reduced the 129th Baluchis to four British officers, five Indian officers, and fewer than two dozen men of the ranks. During that time, 2,547 Indian soldiers had cycled through the regiment. Of those, 944 sustained wounds.[21] A wounded Punjabi Muslim wrote to a relative serving with his regiment in France:

> Well, my brother stood fighting the enemy on three sides with the bayonet. My eyes were filled with mud & we were not allowed to move hither & thither in the trench. But by the decree of God the first bullet hit me in the forehead above the left eye. For this reason I came out of the trench. When I had gone a little way I found that there were about twenty of the enemy in the support trench who fired at me & hit me in the thigh, breaking the leg. Being without assistance I lay still thinking what to do. After a little time I began to push myself along on my back, & I left my great coat there because it prevented me from moving. I struggled along on my back for about fifty yards.[22]

The war on the Western Front churned up human bodies at previously unimaginable rates. Like those hospitals that repaired the bodies of British soldiers, the Indian hospitals were part and parcel of a whole industry of mass healing helping to perpetuate total war by repairing bodies and returning soldiers to the front as efficiently as possible. "The great preoccupation of the officers [working at the Indian hospitals] was to heal and render the men fit for the fighting line," Lawrence wrote to Kitchener.[23] Lawrence had designed a system that would send the worst cases to England while lighter cases would remain in France, but the system never worked perfectly. "When the rush comes—and in the case of Indians it has always been a rush—they [the French] put them on ship because they have no provision for sifting them at Boulogne."[24] Hospital personnel hailed from every corner of the empire. Most Royal Army Medical Corps officers who controlled the administration of the Indian hospitals had served in India earlier in their careers. Additional staffers came from as far away as Peshawar, Bombay, and Poona. In London Gandhi organized the Indian Field Ambulance Training Corps and recruited 198 Indian students studying in England at the outbreak of the war to work as orderlies, dressers, and interpreters in the hospitals.[25] "In my humble opinion it ought to be our proud privilege to nurse the Indian soldiers back to health," Gandhi wrote in the *Times*.[26] Lawrence boasted in his letters to Kitchener that by March 1915 the convalescent depot in England had returned 57.48 percent of its Indian patients to the fighting line.[27] The commander of the Kitchener Hospital assured the India Office later in June, "Out of 2600 cases treated here I have already returned 900 to duty; and every effort is made to get men out as quickly as possible."[28]

There can be no doubt that the medical care Indians received in France and Britain was far superior to anything they might have received previously. The converted Jesuit college in France admitted 19,858 patients, of whom only 223 died, or 1.16 percent of all those admitted. The Kitchener Hospital in Brighton admitted 3,890. Only 26 soldiers died from wounds, a mortality rate of 0.75 percent.[29] "It is correct to say that the same care which is given to the British wounded has been extended to their Indian comrades," Lawrence remarked. "The arrangements are the same as those made in British Military Hospitals, which are of course very superior to those obtaining in Military Hospitals in India for Indian troops."[30] An Indian surgeon working at one of the hospitals wrote to a relative in India: "There are about 1,000 patients, all quite happy, & seeing the arrangements there, I think every one of them must be thanking God for having a bullet in their body. I really envied them."[31] A Sikh wrote to his brother in Amritsar, "If any of us is wounded, or is otherwise ill, Government or someone else always treats him very kindly. Our Government takes great care of us."[32] The British also excelled at getting wounded men to hospital beds quickly. During the three days of fighting at Neuve Chapelle in March 1915, the hospital at Boulogne received 750 serious cases in the span of twenty-four hours.[33] Four days after the battle, 474 of those cases arrived at the Kitchener Hospital in Brighton, England.[34] Once there, administrators treated convalescent troops to various comforts the soldiers had never expected while undergoing treatment in South Asia. Repairing bodies for the Western Front, Lawrence insisted, depended in no small measure "on the mentality of the Sepoys."[35] "Every effort was made to keep them cheerful and to provide the simple comforts, which mean so much to the Indians... the Indians knew that every precaution had been taken to insure that his caste scruples would be respected. Caste committees were appointed in each hospital.... Every facility was given for religious observances.... The fast of Ramazán was duly kept."[36]

Lawrence was attentive to the wants and needs of the men in his care. In December 1914 he arranged with the India Office that the letters sent from India to the wounded men would arrive and for the distribution of a vernacular newspaper to the patients.[37] At the Kitchener Hospital soldiers enjoyed a large recreation room where hospital personnel projected scenes of Punjab life on a screen "to a delighted audience of soldiers from the north of India." At the Pavilion Hospital nine different kitchens catered to the dietary requirements of the Indian soldiers. At the convalescent depots gramophones played "the native airs of India."[38] After repeated outbreaks of disease at the convalescent depot in Rouen sent many recently healed sepoys back to hospital beds, Lawrence ordered the hospital closed. "I am convinced from what I have seen and from what I have heard from the Sepoys that Rouen is not the place for Indians," he wrote to a colleague in March 1915. "They speak of it as a 'shaitan ka jagah' and a place of ill luck." Marseilles, by contrast, offered a much more accommodating climate. "The one thing needed to bring the Indians round, and to turn a convalescent man into a cheerful fighting man, is sunshine," Lawrence maintained.[39] Marseilles was ideally suited to this end. "The atmosphere is Indian—there is sunshine—the supply depot is close at hand, and they cost less to feed here than at Rouen."[40]

The preoccupation of hospital administrators with the "mentality" of the sepoys was part and parcel of the Indian hospitals' propaganda function. The empire required more than just soldiers with healthy bodies and tethered nerves. The empire needed soldiers who were loyal and wanted to fight. Lawrence coordinated propaganda efforts at each of the Indian hospitals in the hope of reinspiring wounded sepoys. News of important victories, he believed, was just the thing convalescent men required. "The result of the Neuve Chapelle fighting has been very remarkable," he noted in late March 1915. "When I communicated the news to the patients at Brighton they received it with delight and it had a marked effect on their spirit. I have never seen a greater change in my life, and now that the wounded and sick have arrived, the change is still greater."[41] Elaborately staged visits from imperial notables became a common feature at the hospitals. In August 1915 King George visited the Royal Pavilion Hospital, and in an elaborate investiture ceremony on the lawn of the hospital, a thousand wounded Indians gathered to witness eleven of their comrades receive decoration for gallantry in the field.[42]

Ever since the 1857 Rebellion very nearly drove the British out of India, British policy vis-à-vis the Indian Army had been deeply rooted in suspicion and paranoia. Hospital administrators believed they had to monitor the sepoys closely. "There are so many political agitators, Indians and English, that one has to walk warily," Lawrence observed in December 1914.[43] When the Raja of Kapurthala paid a surprise visit to the hospital at Marseilles, hospital authorities made sure that he remained accompanied by a British officer at all times. "He asked many questions about the food of the Sikhs," Lawrence reported. "The answers to these questions were satisfactory, but if he had been allowed to go round the Camp unescorted, his questions might have led to trouble. Strict orders have now been given ... and any visitors of this character, if allowed in the Camp, will be very carefully watched."[44] After Lawrence discovered in late 1914 "that in the absence of ghee, margarine was being supplied" to the wounded soldiers, the India Office worked quickly to ensure that regular supplies of ghee came to England and France from India. "This is a matter that must be very closely watched," ordered Alfred Keogh at the War Office. "If it got about that we were using margarine, there might be an explosion similar to the old cartridge trouble of the Mutiny."[45]

But there might not have been. Soldiers on campaign allowed themselves exceptions all the time.[46] Soldiers ate butter served by the hands of their French host families, for example. "I regard our existing customs and rules are useless, as it is quite true that the only result which comes from their observance is expense," one sowar fighting in France explained to his family in Gujranwala, Punjab.[47] British fears were not rooted in the reality of the lived soldier experience. Nevertheless paranoia informed policy at every turn. The British also believed that Christian missionaries had contributed significantly to the explosion of popular unrest in the 1857 Indian Rebellion.[48] Walter Lawrence therefore ordered that hospital authorities in France, where the YMCA was in close contact with the Indians, "keep a very sharp eye on the proceedings" of the organization "and to prevent Sepoys using Y.M.C.A. paper with the inscription 'Christian Anjuman' for their letters home. Many such letters have gone, and great capital will be made in India by agitators who are doing their utmost to cause disaffection in our Army."[49] In February 1915 at the Pavilion, Lawrence discovered that a wounded Indian soldier had a vernacular translation of the Gospel of St. Mark. "I asked him where he had got it, and he said a lady had given it to him. Everybody who visits the Hospitals is supposed to write their name in a book, and they will be shown a notice begging them not to take any books of a religious nature." Lawrence stressed, "We cannot be too careful, as if it got abroad that any attempt has been made to proselytize men who are sick or wounded, there would be great trouble."[50]

The Press and Indian Hospitals

The British press was especially taken with Lawrence's efforts and accomplishments at the hospitals in France and England. When the *Times* learned in October 1914 that batches of wounded Indians were due to arrive in England, it hailed the development. "It will give us added opportunities of showing in practical form our appreciation of India's enthusiastic cooperation."[51] When King George visited an Indian hospital in December 1914, he spent forty minutes in the wards talking with the wounded. "A visit from their Padshah and personal talk with him is the greatest event that could happen in the lives of these loyal men," reported the *Times*. This was all the stuff of self-congratulations. The *Times* reported that the staff at the Kitchener Indian Hospital in Brighton "has had strenuous days and nights, and this body of men of the IMS has accomplished a remarkable feat since its arrival in England about the middle of January." Faced with the task of renovating buildings intended for a union, the IMS had, "in very short time . . . made a hospital, ready for military patients and equipped in the latest and completest fashion." At the Kitchener Hospital, over a thousand bullet and shell wounds had been examined by X-rays. "Naturally," the article went on, "the conduct of a hospital for Indian wounded is a much more complicated business than the conduct of a hospital for Europeans." The hospital had to meet demand for two supplies of drinking water, two ways of preparing meat, and three kitchens. "The results are worth the trouble," the *Times* concluded. The sepoys "seem a cheerful and kindly set, these dark-skinned patients of many races and creeds, as, clothed in the same hospital kit as is issued to the British wounded, but clinging always to their turbans or their long hair, they sit in the sunny gardens, or wait their turn for a 'joy-ride' and a visit to a cinematograph, or get their strength back in light fatigue duty."[52]

In an effort to spread the good news throughout Great Britain and India, the Brighton Corporation issued a propaganda booklet in 1915 in English, Gurmurkhi, and Urdu on the history of the Royal Pavilion and its time in service as a hospital for Indian soldiers. More than a hundred pages long, the booklet contained some thirty photographs. The curious reader would come across scenes of convalescent soldiers playing cards on the lawn, Sikhs preparing meals in their kitchens, or sepoys shaking hands with grateful British statesmen. The uncritical reader couldn't help but be impressed at the lengths to which the sepoys' British hosts accommodated the needs and wants of India's wounded men. Hospital administrators went to pains to ensure that hospital personnel respected soldiers' caste rules—not an easy task, the booklet asserted, but an important one. "In the arrangements of such a Hospital the complicated Indian question of caste dominated everything," the booklet informed its readers. "A mistake or omission in connection with caste might have serious political consequences."[53] Soldiers prepared food in nine different kitchens.[54] "There is ample evidence to show that the Indians greatly appreciate the care and hospitality which they have received in England," the booklet gushed. "The Mayor and the citizens of Brighton, who have given up much for the sake of India, have earned so well the gratitude of her people that Brighton will now be a sacred name in India for many generations."[55]

But where British propaganda told stories about happy soldiers, many of the letters wounded soldiers sent home reveal deep dissatisfaction with hospital policy. Soldiers resented their close surveillance. "The supervision over us is very strict," one soldier complained. "We have no freedom," said another.[56] And when the press uncovered that Indian hospitals employed white women as nurses, praise for the work performed in hospitals quickly turned to shock and horror. Images of "the nurse" were everywhere in Britain during World War I. "To a large extent," Alison S. Fell and Christine E. Hallett point out, "an idealized version of the nurse—as devoted, caring, virtuous, and pure—was adopted in the Allied nations as the female equivalent of the mobilized man."[57] But at the Indian hospitals authorities worried somehow that this ideal might not be able to hold up. In October 1914 General Willcocks protested against the employment of women at the Indian hospitals in any capacity. Lord Crewe concurred, and in November the War Office decided that women would not be posted to military hospitals for Indian troops. Hospitals did not adhere to the policy uniformly. The Kitchener Hospital never had any female nurses, its commander reported. "Women as nurses are out of place in an Indian unit."[58] Women did continue to work at the Pavilion, York Place, and Lady Hardinge Hospitals without any further comment from the authorities. The matter only erupted into scandal when the *Daily Mail* published a photograph on May 24, 1915, showing an English nurse standing at the bedside of a wounded sepoy at the Lady Hardinge Hospital in Brockenhurst. Sir Alfred Keogh in the War Office promptly "condemned absolutely and totally the employment of nurses with Indian troops" and ordered the withdrawal of all nurses from the Indian hospitals, adding, "Anyone who knew anything about Indian customs would have prevented this scandal by forbidding the services of women nurses with Indian troops."[59]

Sir Havelock Charles, the commanding officer at the Lady Hardinge Hospital, and J. P. Hewett, chairman of the Indian Soldiers' Fund, protested. They insisted that nurses there "merely look to the cleanliness of the wards, see to the distribution of linen, give all medicines and supervise the food and help in the training of orderlies." Upon further investigation Hewett determined that the offending photograph had not even been taken at the Lady Hardinge Hospital. The soldier, Khudadad Khan, had received the Victoria Cross, and the Lady Hardinge Hospital had never housed a Victoria Cross winner. By comparing the uniform of the nurse in the picture with that worn by the nurses at the Lady Hardinge, it was clear that they were not the same. "So in this case we are totally innocent," Hewett concluded. "If this has occurred at Brighton then it is very hard that the Lady Hardinge Hospital should be made to suffer by it." He closed, "We started this Hospital to do our best for the Indian wounded committed to our charge . . . so that our fellow subjects returning to India should carry with them the kindliest memories of England. . . . If you desire to keep our standard of efficiency you may close the Hospital if you give up the nurses."[60] Excluding those employed at the Lady Hardinge Hospital, women nurses were removed from all Indian hospitals in England in June 1915.

As Alison Fell makes clear in her study of British and French nurse memoirs, most nurses' texts reveal ambiguous attitudes toward colonial soldiers in their care. But in many cases women employed in healing wounded African or Indian men "simply realigned the real-life encounters to fit in with their preconceptions and slipped into available vocabularies or colonial clichés."[61] Negative stereotypes of African soldiers abound in the letters and memoirs published by nurses during the early years of the war. One letter written by a British nurse published in the *British Journal of Nursing* in 1915 reproduced lurid rumors about Senegalese men routinely resorting to cannibalism on battlefields back in Africa. The letter's author, Edla R. Wortabet, questioned the perceived wisdom behind French republicanism and egalitarianism, which had resulted in integrated hospitals that housed both Africans and French. "It is nice of the French to do it," she wrote, "but one wonders whether the British plan of giving the Indian troops their separate hospitals, and meeting their customs and requirements, is not wiser and more comfortable for both sides."[62] Other British nurses were just as quick "to delight in the 'novelty' of nursing ethnically diverse patients."[63] Americans had, of course, read about the deployment of Indian and African soldiers to the Western Front. As the first American soldiers and nurses reached France in late 1917, the encounters they recorded with colonial soldiers reinforced—or just as likely, initiated—admiration for the "genius" of imperial rule. In mid-1917, Marian Baldwin set out on a steamship from New York City bound for Paris, where she would join the ranks of the American Fund for French Wounded. Passing through Normandy in September, she came upon a camp of Indian soldiers ("Hindus"). "You can't imagine how strange it seemed to see those black people camping in the quiet Normandy landscape," she wrote. "As one of the young officers told us how they had left their warmth and beloved tropics to come into a strange land, I found a respect in me growing, not only for these weird black boys—but for the English and their great genius in colonization." She continued:

> Surely if England has become the great and powerful nation that she is to-day, there must be some fine, human influence behind it. Her colonies have come to her rescue *en masse* and many of them have not

waited to be drafted. As I saw the friendly relationship—the human bond—between these husky Indian lads and their Anglo-Saxon officers, I felt that the reason why England is the biggest colonizing nation and the most successful is because she has made herself stand in her far off possessions of equity, ethics, and a fair standard of morals. Those are things even half breeds can comprehend, and they have answered the call and come to do their bit, for a country and a master whom they have learned to trust!⁶⁴

The bald-faced racism of hospital administrators and personnel was not so easily lost on Indian audiences as it was on the American. By 1915 the Punjab and other provinces were rife with rumor that "the Indian soldiers serving in the war are not well treated."⁶⁵ Lawrence received two letters from Sir Shapurji Broacha "urging that Sepoys were entitled to the ministration of Nurses." Another Indian working with the Indian Medical Service in the hospitals complained, "You take our men and money and yet deny us good nursing." Racism was proving itself a double-edged sword: protecting white prestige undermined British prestige. Lawrence tried to smooth over any ruffled feathers by lying outright to those who complained. "I have explained to Sir Shapurji Broacha that the removal of the Nurses from Brighton was due to the fact that their services were more urgently required elsewhere," he wrote to Kitchener in August 1915.⁶⁶

"When a Man Has Once Been Wounded, It Is Not Well to Take Him Back Again to the Trench"

Despite their efforts, doctors and hospital personnel could not mend all wounds. Many of the sepoys who fought on the Western Front suffered crippling psychological traumas for which doctors had no remedy. The censor of Indian mail warned in January 1915 that many of the soldier letters written from hospital beds "show a tendency to break into poetry," which he regarded "as a rather ominous sign of mental disquietude."⁶⁷ The first cases of "shell shock"—the crude name given to what was, in all likelihood, undiagnosed post-traumatic stress disorder (PTSD)—appeared early in the war in every army. By 1918, 5 percent of all beds at base hospitals in Germany were reserved for men suffering from shell shock.[68] Soldiers suffering from PTSD exhibited a range of symptoms, which military authorities sometimes dealt with in the harshest terms.[69] Many doctors considered shell shock a sign of social insubordination and congenital weakness. Others advocated that it was a serious injury requiring evacuation and treatment. Along the length of the Western Front, it remained nearly impossible to verify the difference between cases of "real" shell shock and simulation or malingering.[70] Behind the lines doctors struggled to prescribe a reliable cure.

In February 1915 the India Office instructed the censor of Indian mail to provide some "analysis of the classes and regiments" serving in the Indian Corps "from which the more despondent view emanated." The India Office stipulated, "We are all aware of the great differences that exist in the soldierly qualities of the various classes composing the Indian Army, not only in courage, which is common to most of them, but in grit and endurance."[71] Try as he might, E. B. Howell struggled to provide his superiors with a neat profile of the Indian Army's different groups. Trauma, it turns out, defied British colonial categories and racial assumptions.[72] Lawrence never settled on a clear policy for diagnosing and treating mental trauma among the patients. When he noticed that wounded men of the 15th and 47th Sikhs arriving in England in December 1914 appeared "somewhat morose," the best the commissioner could do was divide the men "as much as possible among the various Hospitals" in the hope that their mood might improve in different company.[73] The India Office outfitted the Indian hospitals in England with wards for patients requiring psychological care. The Kitchener Hospital devoted an entire building for its "mental cases."[74] By May 1915 Lawrence noted what he called "a very large number of . . . trench cases where men have been crushed by the falling in of the trench dugouts." The experience "seems to crush them physically and morally. They are very difficult cases to treat."[75] Lawrence and his colleagues conceded there was nothing they could do but provide the men with a bed on board a hospital ship to India. "The medical view is there is only one thing to do for a trench back, and that is to invalid the man to India."[76]

No doubt many of those cases Lawrence deemed "trench cases" were genuine. Lawrence's willingness to concede as much and his attempts to provide the men some manner of treatment are notable when one discovers that British soldiers suffering from shell shock did not begin receiving treatment until much later in the war. The British Army did not open its first hospitals for treating shell shock until October 1916, and those first hospitals were for officers alone. It was still assumed at the time that the rank and file of the British Army were too simpleminded to suffer from emotional trauma.[77] In a way, therefore, Indian sepoys fighting in France in 1915 were receiving better health care than British Tommies, whose psychological wounds remained unacknowledged. Scholar Gajendra Singh explains: "The speed with which the Indian Army acted to create a support structure for the diagnosis and treatment of military shell shock victims was due to the belief that the Indian psyche was particularly susceptible to war trauma."[78] Doctors in prewar India had kept watch for signs that a sepoy might snap and begin "running amok," for instance. So racism guided British medical thinking. And of course the long shadow of 1857 hovered overhead. Authorities worried that traumatized sepoys might forget their oaths of loyalty. Walter Lawrence also had to consider the possibility that just as many sepoys were feigning illness (be it physical or mental) to avoid returning to frontline service. One soldier was caught putting red pigment in his urine. "Unless I am forced by an order I will do my very best to get out of [returning to the front]," another wrote to his friend still serving at the front. "I said that I had the pain of heat (i.e. venereal disease) in my groin. If you . . . are in trouble certainly say that you are ill and have the pain in your groin. So you will come (here). Those who are ill in this way are certainly sent back to the Punjab."[79]

Letters like this abound in the reports of the censor of Indian mail. They reveal that convalescent Indian soldiers engaged in a variety of subtle—and sometimes not so subtle—acts of resistance in order to avoid returning to the front. Generally these stopped well short of outright collective defiance or direct confrontation with authority and were more of the form typically practiced by powerless groups—foot dragging, faking illness, false compliance, sabotage, and so forth—requiring little in the way of coordination or planning, often representing a form of self-help.[80] Sometimes sepoys came to the rescue of comrades who had been found out. One Pathan of the 58th Rifles recuperating in a hospital in England in March 1915 wrote to his friend still with the regiment in France: "Sikandar Shah has come here too. I have made thorough enquiry from him. He told me that a man of the 57th came & our people asked how Inzar Gul was. He replied that Inzar Gul himself had hit his own hand. Then the Doctor caused him to be arrested, saying 'You have caused your own injury.' There was another sepoy with him who said 'I saw him hit,' i.e. he gave evidence in his favor. Then the Doctor let him go."[81]

There was plenty of good reason to want to avoid returning to the front. But what some soldiers did in hospital went beyond foot dragging. They organized and protested against what they saw as exploitative army policy. Returning wounded men to the front was outrageous, they claimed. This was too exploitative, even for the British, they added. At the convalescent depot at Milford-on-Sea, sepoys confronted Walter Lawrence. They complained "that it was not fair to send them back to the trenches until other fresh regiments from India had been sent to the front."[82] Soldiers lamented the injustice of army policy in letters to their families back home. "I am now about to return to the trenches," one soldier wrote to his father. "There is no hope that I shall see you again for we are as grain that is flung a second time into the oven, and life does not come from it."[83] "Grain flung a second time into the oven"—the idiom of a peasant farmer who knows that his life has been taken as cheap, who sees that his employer means to extract from him everything that he can. The soldiers were not incorrect. Army command had changed the terms of their service without any notice, much less without the soldiers' consent. "Briefly," Lawrence wrote, "I think that the Indian point of view

Healing the Empire

is that if an Indian is wounded or falls sick on campaign, then it is his right to go back home." Indeed, Lawrence knew that to be the army's policy. "My impression is that in the Afghan War, when I saw something of operations on the Kurram and the Khyber lines, a wounded man usually found his way back to India, and there was no question of his returning to his regiment."[84]

Talk that the sepoys were being unfairly exploited permeated the hospital wards in France and Britain. In February 1915 the commissioner noted a growing consensus among the soldiers that "the pay of the Indian Sepoy is not sufficient remuneration for the work which they have been called upon to do in France."[85] At the Pavilion Hospital authorities removed an Indian medical student when they discovered he had been telling the soldiers "that it was a wicked thing to send them back to the fighting line, and that they were fools to go on their present pay."[86] A soldier at the hospital in Milford-at-Sea drafted a letter "to the King." The sepoy wrote, "Your majesty's order was that a man who had been wounded once should be allowed to return to India or that if he had recovered should not be made to serve again." He concluded, "Any man who comes here wounded is returned three or four times to the trenches. Only that man goes to India who has lost an arm or leg or an eye."[87] Lawrence recommended that the Government of India increase the monthly salary of all Indian soldiers fighting overseas. Authorities agreed, and increased the soldiers' monthly pay from 11 to 19 rupees. Then in June 1915 Lawrence was alarmed to discover that "in the Sepoys' letters there is constant mention of the fact that the 'black pepper' is being used up and the 'red pepper' is being saved; in other words that the Indian troops are being deliberately sacrificed and the British troops preserved." He attributed this phenomenon to the fact that "the Indians in Hospitals only see the Indian wounded and never see the British Hospitals; and in England, in towns like Brighton and Bournemouth, they see a large number of Civilians whom they all regard as young men of military age."[88] But the hypothesis that commanders were sacrificing the lives of their Indian soldiers to spare those of their British soldiers had currency in the trenches too. One sepoy serving at the front with the 107th Pioneers wrote to another soldier in India after the battle of Neuve Chapelle. The English, he said, "put the black men in front and the second line is of white soldiers. Of complete regiments only 400 or 200 are left. We black men suffered heavily. They put us in front."[89] The same man wrote in another letter, "When the brigade attacks, the Gurkhas and Sikhs go first and the white troops are put in the second line."[90] Lawrence did what he could in the hospitals to dispel the notion. "From some rough figures which I got regarding the affair at Neuve Chapelle I am of the opinion that it could be shown that the British have suffered more heavily than the Indians. I have not yet received the statement which I asked for, but it would be very valuable to obtain figures showing the proportions of casualties in the British Army and the Indian Army."[91]

To be clear, the complaints of the wounded sepoys in the hospital were not the complaints of disloyal men. Quite the opposite. These were the grievances of men who had done their duty and now expected the British to uphold their end of the bargain. The story of Mir Dast—the brother of the deserter Mir Mast—is exemplary.[92] Mir Dast had served in the Indian Army since 1893. When the war began in 1914, he was stationed in India as a junior officer with the 55th Coke's Rifles—one of the Indian Army's elite frontier forces. He deployed to France in January 1915 with more than 350 men as reinforcements for the 57th Rifles. At the Battle of Second Ypres in April 1915 (recall that his brother had deserted to the German trenches the month prior), he participated in an abortive assault on German lines. Trapped in the middle of no-man's-land on April 26, it was then that the air around him began to turn yellow-green. Gas! He didn't know what to do. Nobody had been issued gas masks at this point in the war. Germany had only deployed the weapon for the first time a few days prior, and then against French and North African troops. But when Mir Dast's eyes and throat began to burn, he dashed back to the Indian trenches where another sepoy poured a bucket of water over his head.

When the burning subsided, Mir Dast made a fateful decision, one that saved the lives of dozens of his fellow sepoys. He returned to no-man's-land to help men who could not help themselves. All the British and Indian officers on the spot were killed or wounded. Seizing the initiative, Mir Dast collected panic-stricken soldiers belonging to assorted units, organized them, and shepherded them to safety back in the Indian lines. He then returned to no-man's-land under fire no less than eight times to carry wounded and gassed British and Indian officers to safety. For his gallantry Mir Dast was recommended for the Victoria Cross. He then chose to remain at the front where he continued to perform the duties expected of him, all while enduring lingering complications and pain caused by the gas he inhaled at Ypres. "This gas gives me no rest," he wrote. "It has done for me."[93] Mir Dast remained with his unit at the front until June when a painful shell wound landed him at the Brighton Pavilion.[94]

At the front Mir Dast had demonstrated exemplary courage. He behaved courageously again in August 1915, this time on the grounds of the Brighton Pavilion. On August 25, 1915, the king visited Mir Dast to present him his much-deserved Victoria Cross (VC). The event was headline news, just the kind of publicity Walter Lawrence hoped the Indian hospitals would garner. One soldier wrote home, "George V and Queen Mary came and visited all the sick, and they asked us about the arrangements made and how we were. At that time we subjects expressed our feelings of joy at their having visited us, and prayed to God. They praised us for the services we had rendered."[95] In advance of the ceremony, the India Office asked Mir Dast to draft a petition to present to the King for anything he wanted as an extra reward for his bravery. Rather than ask the king for personal reward—money, land, or a promotion—Mir Dast instead asked for justice for all of the Indian soldiers serving at the front. "I have no son that you might give him a Jemadari or a Hawaldari," his petition began. Then he spoke truth to power. "But this is my request, that when a man has once been wounded, it is not well to take him back again to the trenches. For no good work will be done by his hand, but he will spoil others also."[96] Two days after presenting this petition

Healing the Empire

at his VC ceremony, Mir Dast wrote to a comrade with the 55th Rifles stationed in Kohat:

> By the great great great kindness of God the King with his royal hand has given me the decoration of the Victoria Cross. God has been
> very gracious,
> very gracious,
> very gracious,
> very gracious,
> very,
> very,
> very,
> very,
> very gracious
>
> to me. Now I do not care. I want the kindness of God. If I go to Egypt, I do not regret it. The desire of my heart is accomplished. Show great zeal in your duty and be faithful and eat the salt of the government with loyalty.[97]

Mir Dast's bravery secured safe passage home for some of his comrades. But his was not the only protest to which hospital administrators submitted. "It is abundantly clear from letters written in all parts of the globe that Indian opinion is quite solid against the sending back to the trenches of men who have been wounded," Howell warned from his desk at the Censor's Office.[98] In May 1915 hospital personnel received secret orders that "no wounded sepoy would be sent back to his Regiment unless he volunteered to go." The origin of the order remains unclear. Lawrence himself did not hear of it until well after it had circulated the wards and reached the soldiers' ears. "The sepoys in the French hospitals know now that some such order has been given," he lamented, "and I am of the opinion that very few wounded men now will volunteer to return to the firing line." Lawrence went on, "There is a form of trades unionism in India, and any man who volunteers to go back will be regarded as a black-leg by his comrades who, for various reasons, do not want to go back."[99] The flow of recovered men from the hospitals to the front slowed to a trickle. At the advance

Healing the Empire

base in Boulogne on May 22, only 30 out of 249 wounded sepoys volunteered to return to their units. On June 2, just 4 soldiers from another batch of 71 recently healed men agreed to return to the front. The remainder returned to India.[100]

The Breakdown of Sepoy Health Care in Mesopotamia, 1915-16

The resources Home authorities devoted to healing the Indian soldiers fighting in France far surpassed anything the soldiers had previously experienced. Indian soldiers fighting in Europe had reliable access to life-saving health care. To be sure, the Indian hospitals in France and England were part and parcel of the war machine. Doctors repaired bodies so that the army could reoutfit and redeploy those bodies to the line of battle. The lengths to which authorities in France went to ensure that Indian soldiers enjoyed access to excellent health care stand in marked contrast to what awaited Indian soldiers deployed to the Middle East. Unlike the Indian Corps, amalgamated into the British Expeditionary Force and therefore under the aegis of Home authorities, IEFD remained under the exclusive purview of the Government of India and Indian Army command. Where the Indian Corps belonged to Whitehall, IEFD belonged to Delhi. This fact alone made a considerable difference for soldiers deployed to the Middle East in the war's opening years.

IEFD faced a formidable challenge in Mesopotamia— overcoming a tenacious opponent in a hostile climate, while also operating at the end of a very long and unreliable supply chain.[101] The negligence of commanders would prove to be of far greater significance to the fortunes of the Indian Army's Mesopotamia campaign than anything else, however.[102] Already at the campaign's early stage in early 1915, IEFD was woefully unprepared for the number of sick and wounded its operations in the region produced. Soldiers confronted "grave deficiencies" in medical personnel and material, shortages of rations, and a general lack of comforts. The base in Basra had a clearing hospital with 200 beds, a British general hospital with 250 beds, and 600 beds for Indian soldiers. Prior to the fighting at Shaiba 8,900 soldiers had already been treated for wounds or sickness. After the battle the hospitals were choked with more than 1,000 cases. All of these men were in the care of fewer than 35 medical personnel.[103] Operations in May produced 3,000 more cases of sickness in the 12th Division. In June, as temperatures approached 120 degrees, the British hospital with its 250 beds housed 635 sick patients, and the Indian hospital with its 600 beds housed 1,671 sick and wounded patients. Men had to make do in overcrowded and unventilated thatched sheds. There were no fans. Townshend's 6th Division admitted 4,200 more men to the hospital that summer, 1,300 sick from malaria. Personnel shortages prolonged sickness. There simply were not enough doctors and not enough hospital beds to treat the sick and wounded.[104] Not surprisingly, soldiers treated at the Basra military hospitals complained that they were not comfortable. "The heat was almost unbearable," doctors told investigators. One officer attached to the expeditionary force explained that the whole campaign "was believed to be a side-show and 'no man's child.'"[105] As a consequence, no one took charge to ensure that the soldiers had access to quality health care.

General Nixon ordered IEFD up the Tigris and Euphrates Rivers despite being unable to guarantee his men even a single dedicated hospital ship. The Mesopotamia Commission later found that the general's negligence had "more prejudicial results than almost any other defect in the organization."[106] Without a dedicated hospital ship, Nixon's soldiers competed for space on board ordinary steamers and barges that labored to evacuate the sick and wounded to hospitals in Basra. In late September 1915 IEFD hit Ottoman forces at Kut, securing the town easily enough. But the fight cost his force another 1,100 casualties—men who had to be evacuated and treated. Doctors had only limited supplies of drugs and dressings. The entire force only had two motorized ambulances. Troops wounded in battle relied instead on what were called army transport carts—small carts made of wood and iron, drawn by mules or ponies, ordinarily employed for the carriage of supplies. These rattled and shook violently under the best of circumstances. Men with shattered hips or broken femurs could only cry out and hope they might endure what must have been the utmost agony.

Nixon pressed his men up the river without adequate medical provisions because he had his sights firmly set on Baghdad. The general was a man of ambition. A successful advance on Baghdad might vault him from the Middle East to the Western Front, where he would have preferred to deploy in the first instance.[107] When the Indian 6th Division first secured Basra in the Persia Gulf in November 1914, government authorities had then rejected any talk of capturing Baghdad. "Unlike Basra, which is easy to capture from the south and very strong against any attack from the north, Baghdad has no advantages as a position against an attacking enemy," the viceroy concluded. Taking and holding Baghdad would require a significant increase in Indian manpower in the region. In a letter to the secretary of state, the viceroy stressed that the "political advantages" of taking and occupying the city, "which are really considerable . . . must be subordinated to the military objections that would be involved in such a course."[108] But General Nixon and his superiors in the Indian Army—among those, Chief of the General Staff Sir Percy Lake, and Commander-in-Chief Sir Beauchamp Duff—never abandoned the scheme. And when General Nixon's troops took Kut in September 1915, the viceroy lent the campaign his endorsement.[109] The viceroy made his case to the cabinet in October via telegram, arguing that the capture and occupation of the city had become a pressing priority, one that offered the British an opportunity to "inflict the maximum damage upon Turkey at the least cost to ourselves."[110] The viceroy stated:

> There can be little question that the occupation by British troops of the ancient seat of the Khalifate would produce an immense impression, not only in Persia, but throughout the Middle East. Orientals are impressed by tangible success, which can be measured in square miles and demonstrated on the map, much more than by negative results, however brilliant or important, such as our armies have achieved in the West. Thus the conquest of German South-West Africa, to judge

from the congratulatory messages and accounts of public rejoicing which have reached the India Office, caused much more stir in India, where it represented the first solid achievement of British arms after months of uncertainty, than it aroused in England where the relative unimportance of the event was better appreciated. During the present war, our enemies have achieved this kind of tangible success in many directions; we have done so in two theatres only, viz., Mesopotamia and South-West Africa, and have conspicuously failed in a third region where events have been watched with paramount interest in the Middle East.... In these circumstances it appears to be of primary importance for the maintenance of our prestige in the East, that we should get full value out of our military achievements wherever possible.[111]

With that, some fifteen thousand men of the Indian 6th Division under the command of Nixon's subordinate, General Charles Townshend, began the advance on Baghdad. Townshend did not share his superior's enthusiasm for the operation. In fact, he told Nixon's chief of staff that he thought the capture of Baghdad was a risky proposition.[112] Townshend's troops were optimistic, however. "We all assumed that Baghdad would be easily taken," recalled Sisir Sarbadhikari, a doctor in the Indian Medical Service (the medical wing of the Indian Army). "That any other result might be possible never so much as entered our minds. In many units, British officers began to say that they would celebrate Christmas 1915 in Baghdad."[113] Sarbadhikari kept a journal for the length of his deployment in the Middle East—a remarkable feat: he survived the 1915 campaign only to be taken prisoner when the 6th Division surrendered at Kut in April. His self-published memoir, *On to Baghdad*, describes his experiences in battle, on forced-marches, and in prisoner-of-war camps.[114] As Sarbadhikari and other soldiers advanced on Baghdad in November 1915, his commanders expected little resistance from the Turks. General Nixon hoped the 6th Division could pull off the whole operation on the cheap, with fewer than five hundred Indian and British casualties. But on the morning of November 22, Townshend's forces crashed into a superior and well-entrenched Turkish army at Ctesiphon, south of Baghdad.[115] Sarbadhikari watched troops of the Indian 6th Division advance on entrenched Turkish positions. "The boom of cannons could be heard continuously. Battalions were advancing one after another, right before us. In front of us were the 66th Punjabis; now they moved too. We understood that our turn was coming." When his turn to advance did come, Sarbadhikari and other Indian medical personnel advanced behind the infantry, "with the whine of bullets passing over our heads," Sarbadhikari remembered. "We had to advance with great care. After every few moves we would have to fall into a 'lie down' position. In the meantime shells and bullets were falling like hail, all around us. Many were killed and wounded."[116]

Things seemed to have gone well enough from a tactical perspective. Indian troops had captured two lines of Turkish trenches. They'd taken field guns and more than 1,300 prisoners. The Turkish forces had suffered heavy casualties, and their commanders worried they might not be able to repulse another sustained attacked by Townshend's men.[117] But then Turkish reinforcements counterattacked along the entire front. The exhausted Indians fought bravely, but as more and more of their comrades fell, their positions became increasingly untenable. "Around us were innumerable dead bodies," Sarbadhikari wrote. He described a gruesome scene:

> On all sides, the corpses of men and animals. In some places they seemed to be in each others' arms; in some places men had been pinned under animals and were lying there, groaning. In front of the trenches, along the lines of barbed wire, was where the greatest number of wounded lay. In some places men were hanging from the wires; some were dead (they were the lucky ones) and some were still alive. Here there was a severed hand hanging from the wire; there a foot. One man was hanging on the wires with all his entrails tumbling out. In some trenches four or five men had died with their limbs thrown over each other—Turkish, Hindustani, British, Gurkha, all mixed up together.[118]

By nightfall the situation appeared dire. "Everyone started to say that a great number had been killed," wrote Sarbadhikari. "Apart from our own brigade, wounded men from other brigades came to us too. Everyone was saying the same thing, that many had been killed and wounded." The darkness offered some relief. Soldiers scavenged the battlefield for water bottles and ammunition. Sarbadhikari's bottle was empty. His chest "was splitting in thirst." "There was a dead sepoy nearby, and his bottle had a little water. I used it to wet my lips and throat." In the morning General Townshend ordered his men to pull back to their original positions. "We left behind those who were badly wounded," Sarbadhikari wrote. "They couldn't stand let alone walk. When they saw that we were leaving they began to weep, and who could blame them?" Dead bodies littered the battlefield. "We tried to not step on them but it wasn't always possible. There was no space for one's feet."[119]

Ctesiphon need not have dashed any hope of capturing Baghdad that year. To be sure, Ottoman forces blocked the way, and Townshend's 6th Division had suffered 3,800 British and Indian casualties. Townshend's Indian battalions had advanced up the Tigris in the first instance with a shortage of British officers.[120] At Ctesiphon half of the Division's British officers and half of its Indian officers had been killed or wounded. But Turkish forces were also badly mauled. Townshend might yet have limited Ctesiphon to little more than a check had he greater faith in the Indian troops under his command.[121] The loss of so many white officers left Townshend unsettled. Indian soldiers were at the best of time unreliable, in his estimation. Absent white officers, he doubted anything could be done to keep the men "steady and in hand."[122] The racist lens through which Townshend gazed at the battlefield showed him only one open road—the one his men had just taken. Townshend gave the order to retreat. "Instead of taking Baghdad we were forced to retreat," Sarbadhikari recalled. "Marching beside me was a Muslim sepoy of the 66th Punjabis. He had taken his boots off his feet, and tied them together by their laces; with his rifle in hand he was limping along and saying to himself, 'Ya Allah, abhi le Baghdad,' meaning by this: 'On to Baghdad' you said; now enjoy this."[123] One week later, Sarbadhikari and the beleaguered men of the Indian 6th Division entered Kut, having fought rearguard battles every step along a ninety-mile retreat. "On the way many soldiers had been parted from their regiments and were marching alone. Not all of those who'd been separated made it to Kut," Sarbadhikari wrote. "Some had bandaged heads, some had their arms in slings, and many were limping."[124] The soldiers dug in and prepared to withstand a siege.

But what of the thousands of men wounded at Ctesiphon unable to make the retreat? Sarbadhikari wrote that many men had sustained multiple hits from bullets and shrapnel. Fighting during the second day of the battle took place right where many of the wounded had been collected. "Many of them were killed by bullets and many sustained new wounds. Those who weren't hit could see others being wounded around them and tried to get away—even though they were unable to move. They were seized by a kind of terror—and who can blame them?" Some of the wounded were loaded onto carts. "But the convoy did not have a large Red Cross flag," Sarbadhikari lamented, "so it was mistaken for an ammunition column and was heavily shelled by the Turkish artillery."[125] The Vincent-Bingley Commission reported the harrowing ordeal of soldiers too badly hurt at Ctesiphon to make the retreat with the rest of the 6th Division. Wounded men did not know where to go for medical attention, "and when field ambulances and collecting stations were found, the supply of food, tents, blankets, hot water and any kind of comfort was insufficient." There were only two motor ambulances available to transport thousands of broken men from the battlefield to the river. Men lay on the ground for days in agony, fully exposed to the elements as they awaited evacuation on board the only two barges available. "The lack of properly equipped river hospital steamers proved, as may be well understood, disastrous," the Vincent-Bingley Commission found. "The number of wounded at Ctesiphon was 3,852 and the accommodation, such as it was, which these two steamers afforded, was insufficient for a fraction of that number. The result was that as soon as they were filled with patients, the remainder of the wounded had to be crowded on to other river steamers which had not been prepared in any way for the reception of sick and wounded." Wounded were packed together as close as they could be packed on the decks, without beds or mattresses. Doctors did not have the space or the supplies they needed to save lives. "In some cases the vessels had, moreover, been used for the carriage of animals, and it was impossible, in the time available, to clean and disinfect them." Open flesh wounds were exposed to animal excrement. We can only imagine the suffering and discomfort unnecessarily caused by a journey in such conditions. "Patients suffered from cold, hunger, thirst and want of care," commissioners found. "Wounds which required dressing and re-dressing were not attended to, and the condition of many of the patients who travelled by these steamers was, when they reached Basra, deplorable. There the wounds of many were found to be in a septic condition, and in urgent need of re-dressing. In some cases bed-sores had developed, more than one patient arrived soaked in feces and urine, and in a few cases, wounds were found to contain maggots."[126]

The arrival of the men some weeks later in Basra overwhelmed medical personnel struggling to maintain already impoverished hospitals. Doctors did their best. But they needed more supplies and more personnel. Compounding these shortages, the 6th Division had been surrounded by Turkish forces at Kut and was in need of rescue. Indian Army HQ rushed troops to the region. In total, 139,000 troops deployed to the Middle East between December 1915 and April 1916. The 3rd (Lahore) and 7th (Meerut) Divisions arrived from France in January. Before their medical equipment had the chance to unload—an operation that could take weeks because "Basra was not a functioning port in any real sense of the word"—Nixon rushed the men into the field.[127] Again Nixon's haste produced disastrous results. The medical situation was already undergoing a "lamentable breakdown"—to use the words of the Mesopotamia Commission. Now it turned into "the most complete breakdown of all." The 7th Division encountered stubborn Turkish resistance. Casualties were numerous. The medical staff that was there on the ground—already stretched thin—ran out of drugs and bandages. Field ambulances were in such short supply and so overcrowded that patients passed through them without receiving any medical attention at all. Men wounded in battle massed on riverbanks where they sometimes waited for days without shelter or medical attention, hoping for evacuation by steamship. The sick relied on the kindness of officers. They huddled in makeshift camps where too-few doctors tried to perform one miracle after another. But wounds went untended. Nursing personnel were absent. One camp, "situated on filthy muddy ground," housed almost eight hundred wounded and sick Indian soldiers, supervised by a lone temporary IMS officer and two sub-assistant surgeons. The doctors had no supplies. The camp had no latrines, and two hundred of the patients had dysentery. In the middle of the camp there was a pile of ten days' rations, ruined by the rain.[128]

The Mesopotamia Commission summed up the entire operation, from the October 1915 decision to advance on Baghdad through January's abortive rescue operations. "The advance to Baghdad under the conditions existing in October, 1915, was an offensive movement based upon political and military miscalculations and attempted with tired and insufficient forces, and inadequate preparation. It resulted in the surrender of more than a division of our finest fighting troops and the casualties incurred in the ineffective attempts to relieve Kut amount to some 23,000 men."[129] The lion's share of responsibility rested with General Nixon. His "confident optimism was the main cause of the decision to advance," the report continued. The evidence collected "did not disclose an imperative need to advance without due preparation." The viceroy, Lord Hardinge, and the commander-in-chief, Beauchamp Duff, in India also shouldered blame. In England so did the military secretary of the India Office, Edmund Barrow, the secretary of state for India, Austen Chamberlain, and the War Committee of the cabinet. The Vincent-Bingley Commission found the senior medical officer of IEFD, Surgeon-General G. H. Hathaway, "failed to urge the necessity for adequate and suitable transport for the sick and wounded."[130] The Mesopotamia Commission said of Hathaway that he was "unfit for the high administrative office which he held." IEFD's administrators and commanders were the problem, the commission concluded. As for the soldiers of the expedition, the Mesopotamia Commission concluded most favorably:

> Our investigations show that what is in default is not the fighting capacity and efficiency of the combatant forces of the Indian Army, but the system of military administration in control of that Army. Rarely, if ever, have greater courage or pertinacity been shown by British and Indian troops than is recorded in the operations of the Expeditionary Force both during their successes and reverses. They had to operate under unfavorable conditions of climate, weather, flooded terrain, insufficient supplies and wholly inadequate transport, and they were surrounded by a hostile and marauding population. In our judgment, no praise can be too high for the gallantry and spirit evinced by the officers and men of all ranks of the British and Indian Armies under this accumulation of difficulties. It is most desirable that the governing machinery of the Indian Army should be so reformed as to enable it to be a help and not a drag on the fighting capacity of the armies it controls.[131]

Health Care and Imperial Prestige

Just as things were spinning out of control in the Middle East, Walter Lawrence sat down to draft his final report to Lord Kitchener. Under his supervision 14,514 Indian soldiers had received medical care at a hospital in England. "Looking back on the experiences of the last year and a half, I think that on the whole, from a political point of view, the decision to bring the Indians to English hospitals has done more good than harm." There had been doubters. Some said that "the hospitality and sympathy shown by England to the Indian sick and wounded may have a spoiling effect on Indian character." Caring for so many wounded Indians certainly required a great deal of labor, but Lawrence remained of the opinion that the labor "had not been in vain." He had received a letter from Lord Hardinge—the same viceroy of India then taking flak for the failures of the Mesopotamia campaign—who wrote "that the work done in the Indian hospitals in England and France 'tends to increase our prestige in this country and also the attachment that the lower classes have to the *Sircar* [King].'" Hardinge also wrote Lawrence, "We at this end can only judge of the manner in which the hospitals are managed in England by the results we see in the returned sick and wounded soldiers, and I hear from all accounts that the frame of mind in which these men return to this country, with very few exceptions, is quite admirable, and it reflects the highest credit upon the manner in which they have been looked after in the hospitals in France and in England."[132]

At a time when the war was going badly for the British Empire; when the Indian 6th Division remained under siege and thoroughly without hope of rescue at Kut; when thousands of soldiers in the Middle East remained without adequate medical care; when nobody knew how or when the war might end, much less who would win, Walter Lawrence offered this final assessment of the work he and his staff had performed in France and England:

> I think that the work has been of some use. It has shown to the sick and wounded Indians in very strange circumstances that there was a personal interest in them.... In some ways they are children, but intensely proud, shrewd and sensitive. They appreciated the message of goodwill.... Of one thing I am sure, that it was a wise policy considering the political condition of India to bring Indian troops to Europe. They have left France with a profound respect for the British soldier and for British resources. They go back deeply impressed with the mechanical side of warfare. They talk with insight about the various natures of guns and contrivances employed in trench fighting.... It has been an education to them ... and the lesson taught by the bold and wise policy of giving India a chance may be of enormous value to those who will soon be called upon to organize the real and actual British Empire.[133]

The Indian hospitals in France and England were designed with two purposes in mind: to return as many sick and wounded Indian soldiers to the trenches as quickly as possible and to reinvigorate the soldiers' commitment to the empire. In some ways

Healing the Empire

hospitals in France and England achieved these ends. But one wonders how much lasting goodwill the hospitals garnered, especially once the Vince-Bingley Commission and the Mesopotamia Commission released the findings of their investigations in 1916 and 1917. Austen Chamberlain wrote after the Mesopotamia Commission's report went public, "A perfect storm is raging in our papers in which all concerned come in for severe criticism."[134] On top of all that, a newly formed battalion of Indian soldiers was about to depart from its base of operations outside Berlin, Germany. These soldiers—onetime loyal sepoys in the Indian Army—now pledged allegiance to the Ottoman Sultan and the German Kaiser. In 1916 they set out on a campaign to bring about the end of British rule in India.

5

In the Hands of the Enemy

Those who passed along the route from Kut to Aleppo ... will never forget the sights they saw and the tales they heard. How our men were marched in the blazing heat sometimes for 30 hours and more across waterless stretches of desert land.... At every halting place one saw little bands of half starved, wholly miserable and dying men usually without medical attendance or care of any sort.

—Letter from Major Cree, IEFD, to the under secretary of state for India, January 8, 1919

Indian soldiers fought in Europe, Africa, and the Middle East. Thousands of them were taken prisoner during the war—perhaps a thousand in Europe; many thousands more in the Middle East in the war against Ottoman Turkey, notably those of the Indian 6th Division at Kut when it surrendered on April 29, 1916. The experiences of Indian prisoners of war were markedly different depending upon the captor. To the Germans, captured Indian soldiers represented a propaganda opportunity. Accordingly, the German government earmarked Indian prisoners for prison camps in Germany designed as propaganda camps to "convert" captured Indian (and French North African) soldiers. Some of the converts, the Germans hoped, might freely reenlist in the Ottoman Army. A small number of Indian soldiers received equipment, money, and guns from the Germans and safe passage to the Middle East to act as the vanguards of nationalist or pan-Islamic revolution in British India. This was Germany's version of world war on the cheap. Ottoman forces in the Middle East received Indian soldiers far less favorably. Likely thousands of Indian soldiers died on death marches into the Syrian wastes at the hands of their Turkish captors. Others wasted away in forced labor camps. The treatment the Turks meted out to British and Indian prisoners of war taken at Kut was thought to be so brutal that in 1918 the British government briefly toyed with threatening the Turkish government with reprisals. But one British survivor of Turkish captivity thought reprisals would do no good. "They [the Turks] care as little what becomes of their prisoners as of ours."[1]

The Crescent Moon Camp

Captivity was a central part of the war experience for millions of human beings during World War I. Between 1914 and 1918, between seven and nine million people saw the inside of a prisoner-of-war camp.[2] None of the combatant states were prepared in August 1914 for such a flood of prisoners. By one estimate Germany held 586,000 prisoners of war at the end of 1914: 310,000 Russians, 220,000 French, 40,000 Belgian, and 16,000 British. A little more than a month later, Germany held 700,000 captured enemy soldiers—about one percent of its prewar population.[3] The conflict also marked a watershed in the way European states and their militaries treated captured civilians and soldiers. At the turn of the century, Spanish general Valeriano Weyler used internment camps during the brutal war he waged in Cuba from 1896 to 1897. During the South African War, the British used crude concentration camps to segregate and supervise the Boers. World War I marked the first time Europeans deployed these colonial practices in Europe.[4] The majority of soldiers who fought in the war had been civilians prior to August 1914, and in the age of mass armies any civilian could just as readily become a soldier. The military powers fighting in Europe deposited civilians and soldiers in vast and complex labyrinths of concentration camps, prisoner-of-war camps, and forced labor battalions. All the major powers, Germany included, made some nominal effort to honor their prewar commitment to the liberal tradition and the stipulations of the 1899 and 1907 Hague Conventions.[5] But any lingering "benevolent captivity interpretation" fails to take into account the widespread brutalities and systematic violence forced upon combatant prisoners of war.[6] Perhaps as many as one million soldiers died in prisoner-of-war camps.

During the war nobody overlooked the profound tactical implications of soldiers surrendering to the enemy in large numbers. On August 8, 1918, the British Army attacked exhausted and badly outnumbered German troops near Amiens. Although the attack stalled out two days later, the German commander, General Erich Ludendorff, called August 8 "the black day of the German army," because nearly thirty thousand German soldiers surrendered. It was the clearest signal yet that the German army was beaten.[7] Captured enemy soldiers served far greater utility than killed soldiers. Captured soldiers could be used as sources of intelligence, labor, hostages, and even as propaganda. Treated well, a prisoner could induce his comrades to surrender.[8] Offered the right combination of carrot and stick, he might even be persuaded to take up arms in the cause of his captors.

The decentralized nature of Germany's network of prison camps, combined with poor record keeping, makes it nearly impossible to pin down the exact number of Indian soldiers taken prisoner on the Western Front. In all likelihood the Germans never pinned down the actual number of Indians in their care.[9] German soldiers captured a handful of Indian sepoys during the seesaw battles outside Ypres in the closing months of 1914. Havildar Ganga Ram of the 2nd/2nd Gurkhas told his German captors that he and his men had only been at the front eight days when a hail of German hand grenades forced them to surrender.[10] Two days of fighting in late December produced roughly a hundred more Indian prisoners of war from the 129th Baluchis, 59th Rifles, and 125th Napier Rifles.[11] Taken prisoner at Festubert on December 19, 1914, Subadar-Major Sher Singh Rana of the 1st/4th Gurkha Rifles spent the remainder of the war in captivity; first at a camp in Lille, where, he said, "the Indian soldiers were left behind, but the Gurkhas (who were treated as Europeans) were sent with the Turkish and French prisoners to Cologne"; a brief stint in Cologne; Osnabruck until April 1916; Zossen through August; Clausthal through much of 1917; a punishment camp in Strohen; and finally a hospital in Holland. The Germans repatriated the subadar-major to England in 1918.[12] Rana's case is exceptional. The English—and just as likely the Germans—rarely knew the whereabouts of individual soldiers. In August 1915 Field Marshal John French complained that the Germans never furnished him with an accurate list of Indian prisoners. The lists he did receive were "so incomplete in details that hitherto it has been impossible to identify more than sixty per cent of the individuals mentioned."[13] One list, for example, identified an Indian prisoner only as "Thapa." A beleaguered secretary at the Prisoners of War Department in London circled the name and scribbled in the margins, "In one Gurkha regt alone there are over 100 'Thapas' missing."[14] By November 1915 the Indian Soldiers' Fund had the names of nearly 500 South Asian prisoners in Germany to whom it sent care parcels.[15] At that time 3,247 Indian soldiers were still categorized on its rolls as missing.[16]

Families in India and Indian audiences knew even less than military officials about the fates of those captured by the Germans on the Western Front. The Germans delivered soldier letters only sporadically. In Lahore the newspaper *Akhbar-I'-Am* wrote in a February 1915 article, "We wonder what treatment [the enemy] is meting out to [Indian prisoners]. Some American commission should pay a visit to these poor people also, though they are not Christians."[17] In early 1915 the Maharaja of Rewa wrote to the Government of India: "I have read in the papers from time to time with pleasure the arrangements made by the British Government for the Indian soldiers, but I wish to know, if possible, whether the enemy respects scruples of the Hindus with regard to food. For example, a Hindu would rather die than take beef." The Government of India's political agent in Baghelkand replied that no reports had yet been received concerning Hindu prisoners of war, but that the British army would make enquiries.[18]

Starting in 1915 the German War Ministry concentrated Muslim and Indian prisoners of war in two camps located about thirty miles south of Berlin in Zossen. Nearly twelve thousand Russians lived in the Tatarenlager at Zossen-Weinberge. French Muslim prisoners and Indian prisoners were held at Wünsdorf, generally referred to as the Halbmondlager (Crescent Moon Camp). The Indians were later confined to their own section, the Inderlager, and then transferred to a camp in Romania in April 1917.[19] At its maximum occupancy Zossen housed approximately fourteen thousand Russian, African, and Indian troops. The kaiser provided the 45,000 marks required for the construction of a small mosque for the camp's Muslim inhabitants.[20] Muslim soldiers observed the fast of Ramadan, as most did in the British trenches and hospitals by 1915.[21] Indian soldiers prepared their own food and baked their own bread. North Africans had access to a coffee stand and gramophone.[22] After a January 1915 visit with a small number of Gurkhas, Rajputs, one Sikh, and one Pathan, the Indian Independence Committee reported that the soldiers wanted more bread, butter, rice, and vegetables. Tobacco and "something to read," the committee added, would also please the prisoners.[23] "It will likely serve our own interests to see to it that these small requests are met as soon as possible," Baron Oppenheim penned.[24] J. B. Jackson of the American Embassy in Berlin visited the Indian prisoner-of-war camp at Zossen in July 1915 and reported that the troops were satisfied with the arrangements. The soldiers' barracks were not overcrowded, there were no armed German guards in the camp itself, and the noncommissioned officers who attended to its administration were "very considerate of the feelings of the Indians and do not go into their kitchens or the prayer section of the Mahommedan barracks." The health of the camp appeared satisfactory, and "all in the camp seemed to be in good spirits."[25]

The propaganda campaign Germany deployed in the camp was relentless. "Everything should be done to impress upon the prisoners that we are not their enemies," Oppenheim stressed, "and that it is only because of circumstance that we find ourselves opposite one another." Captured in November 1914, sepoy Mahomed Arifan later recalled, "the camp [Zossen] was overrun with Mahommedan propagandists, Turks, Fakirs, and what not, who tried by every means to influence the Indian soldiers to break their allegiance to the British Empire." Oppenheim's revolutionaries and

Ottoman officials paid the camp frequent visits. They combined the appeals of anticolonialism and pan-Islamic jihad interchangeably. "It is in our interests to develop Muslim and Hindu elements together," Oppenheim instructed. "If handled delicately, cultivating both elements is possible."[26] Ottoman officials and religious leaders delivered frequent lectures focused on the glory of former Islamic empires, the history of various Islamic peoples, exchange and interaction between the Orient and the Occident, the political, economic, and intellectual strength of Germany, and wartime relationships between Germany and Muslim territories. In November 1915 a member of the Indian Committee delivered a lecture at Zossen for the Indian troops on the "political geography" of India, concluding on the subject of "the people of India, their essential unity in spite of apparent diversity of races and creeds." In September 1915 the Germans took a group of prisoners on a tour of Berlin to impress the men with German "order, authority, and power."[27] The Indian Committee published a newspaper in Urdu and Hindi for Indian prisoners called *Hindustan*. One edition of the paper touched on "English misrule in India," a general uprising in India, and actions taken by Indian soldiers to carry out anticolonial rebellion.[28] Cheaply and quickly printed leaflets reinforced the message. "Never forget about your oppression by the English," ran the headline of one. "The time for revenge is now."[29]

The Germans also hoped their activities at Zossen might win them converts among the Indian soldiers still stationed in front-line trenches. In December 1914 Paul Walter asked that a few captured Indians be allowed to work with him in Lille, where he saw to the needs of recently captured sepoys. "It is important to try and influence new arrivals from the very outset," he told Oppenheim. "Then when they are ready, they will return to their tribal brethren in the enemy lines at night, or in some other suitable way."[30] Airships and balloons dropped leaflets and propaganda over the lines occupied by Muslim troops.[31] At the Censor's Office E. B. Howell worried that German activities at Zossen might have some effect on troops at the front. Letters and postcards written by Indian prisoners of war in Germany revealed that the Germans were "anxious to impress upon the Indian troops in the field the good treatment which their fellows who have been taken prisoner are receiving in Germany." He also warned, "[The Germans] have lately been distributing over that part of the line held by Indian troops leaflets with pictures of the Indian prisoners' camps, and information about the number of prisoners, guns taken, and the extent of territory conquered by the German army."[32]

The Indian Volunteer Battalion

The pressure on Indian prisoners of war in Germany to "convert" intensified as joint German-Ottoman plans came together in late 1915 to form a battalion of North African and Indian soldiers. The idea was that these men would fight in the Middle East as part of the Turkish army. At the end of Ramadan in October 1915, Muslim soldiers in Zossen celebrated the Bairam Feast. As German camp authorities handed out cigarettes, sugar, and tea, the Turkish ambassador watched a procession of the first battalion of nine hundred North African Freiwilliger (Volunteers) for the Holy War march through the camp to the sound of drums and horns. "The course of the festival can be described as entirely successful," observed one German witness. "It should have a good influence on the mood of the prisoners."[33] The first detachments of the North African Volunteers left the prison for Constantinople the following month.[34] In January 1916 about 1,400 Russian Muslims departed for the Caucasus.[35] Amid the spectacle forty-four Indians pledged allegiance to the German-Ottoman–sponsored venture.[36] German guards moved them to their own barracks, "resulting from, as anticipated, complications between them and the other Indian Muslims."[37] They departed for Constantinople in April.

What about the holdouts? Camp authorities tried to isolate them and send them away to punishment camps. In August 1916 camp authorities transferred a handful of men to Clausthal and thereafter to Strohen, owing to their refusal "to accept German advances."[38] In mid-1916 the Indian Committee wrote to the Foreign Office, calling attention to what it called "the baneful influence that is being exercised on the prisoners in Wuensdorf by the Sikh Jamadar Suwai Singh and the Gurkha subedar-major Sher Singh Rana." From conversations with the prisoners, the Indian Committee concluded that these two men were not only "doing their best to resist the spread of patriotic ideas among the soldiers, but that they are secretly carrying on a strong anti-German and pro-English propaganda."[39]

What were the holdouts thinking? Why not just take the German money and guns and run? For many of the soldiers recruited in India, fighting for Turkey was completely out of the question. "They come from the British territory of Punjab, their land and their families are dependent upon [the British], and they want to go back to India once peace has been declared," camp authorities conceded.[40] Transborder Pathans from the North-West Frontier Province or from Afghanistan also worried that if they were recaptured while fighting for the Turks they would lose their pensions and suffer a lengthy prison sentence.[41] Some Indian officers used their position and influence among the men to keep sepoys loyal to the British.[42] "I did my best to dissuade Indian soldiers from listening to any advances," Sher Singh Rana recalled. "In my opinion the sedition propaganda had little effect on them 'going in at one ear and out at the other.'"[43] When persuasion did not work, some Indian prisoners relied on intimidation and violence to keep comrades in service to the British Empire. On January 10, 1916, a fight broke out in the camp among Sikhs. Three men were badly beaten. Soldiers told camp authorities, "the fight was the outcome of some foolish and petty jealousies." But the Indian Committee investigation revealed other reasons:

> About fifteen non-commissioned officers and Mr. Kartaram (whose word cannot be doubted) hold that the fight was brought about by the Sikh Jemadar and his faction to intimidate the patriotic Sikh prisoners, especially Mita Singh, who has been very active in carrying on propaganda among the Sikhs.
>
> Undoubtedly the Sikh Jemadar and the four Mohammadan officers have been using their influence (which is not a negligible quan-

tity) to counteract our work and to dissuade men from participating in our patriotic cause. There is also a rumor that some of the officers are spending money to win people to their side and keep them subservient.[44]

Sepoys interned at Zossen had a choice to make. They could renounce all allegiance to the British Empire, collaborate with their captors, and join the Indian Battalion; or they could refuse the overtures of the Germans and Indian Committee and wait out the war in captivity. Either option came with considerable risk. Collaborators risked ostracism or physical violence from a resentful peer group, death on another battlefront, or a lengthy prison sentence if recaptured by the British or if the Germans lost the war. Those who held out against the Germans might be sent to punishment camps, forced to perform life-threatening physical labor, or endure severe physical violence at the hands of vengeful camp guards.

In some ways, the lot of the Indian soldiers was unique to those of the other men held in Germany. France's North African soldiers very likely never had a choice. One Tunisian soldier, captured trying to desert from the Ottoman army, told his captors that he never wanted to fight for the Turks. German documents verify his claim. France's colonial subjects who traveled to Mesopotamia to fight for the Turks were forced to go.[45] Sepoys were not. The different treatment North Africans and Indians experienced reveals as much about the political priorities of the Germans and their allies as it does a shared, pan-European repertoire of racist attitudes. World War I coincided with the heyday of German (and American) racial science. Racial hygienists combined pseudoscience with social Darwinism, classified and isolated "desirable" and "undesirable" racial characteristics, and proscribed plans for improving the biology of the human species.[46] At times the Germans applied racial stereotypes to Indian and African prisoners of war indiscriminately. When authorities finished construction of the camp mosque in early 1915, the *Berliner Tageblatt* commented on the inauguration of the "strange looking [building] on the soil of Germany" for "our oriental enemies fighting for France and England."⁴⁷ In his 1916 book, *Unsere Feinde*, artist Otto Stiehl provided a number of portrait photographs of the different "races" interned in German prison camps. "The mixture of tribes and races mobilized by our enemies from all five continents to fight on the old soil of Europe is outrageous, far surpassing anything ever seen before in world history."⁴⁸ But visitors to the camp just as readily drew sharp distinctions between Indians and Africans. In early 1915 U.S. senator Albert Beveridge, a Republican and onetime ally of Theodore Roosevelt, toured Zossen and commented on the camp:

> In the barracks occupied by the prisoners from India there is an unusual feature: every Hindou [sic] cooks and in every way prepares his own food, for he will not eat anything touched by Christian hands. Many of them were observed at this private and religious culinary occupation. The Gourka [sic] sergeant in charge of this barrack, spoke English very well. He and his comrades were treated very well, he said—much better than they expected.
> Would he like to get back to India? He would—more than anything.
> Why had he come to the war?
> "Orders, sir"
> He good-naturedly interpreted for a group of tall, grave-faced Sikhs, statues of dignity and gravity.
> Why had they come so far to fight?
> "The service" was the answer; and the Gourkha sergeant tried to make their meaning clear by such expressions as "their duty[,]" ["]their profession," "their business." As to wanting to go home, we gathered that they were quite indifferent, that it was all the same to them, and that they took things as they happened.⁴⁹

Senator Beveridge had made a name for himself in the late 1890s for championing United States imperial expansion in the Philippines. He was a proponent of white supremacy and social Darwinism. When he toured the barracks housing Algerian soldiers, he contrasted the "gravity" and "dignity" of the Indian sepoys to the North African prisoners he met there:

In the barracks where the Turcos lived, came the one disagreeable, even shocking surprise of the day. It is impossible to imagine more villainous looking creatures. Nearly all of them are small men, and most of them have viciousness stamped on every feature. Their evil eyes follow you expressionless, unblinking, like those of a serpent. Some of these men undoubtedly are criminals—the forehead, jaw, mouth, back head, and above all the merciless, soulless eyes spell depravity. The Sikhs and Gourkas from India, many of whom have fine and even noble features, are infinitely superior to this scum of Northern Africa; for such at least most of these particular Turcos must be. There are some faces among them that are not bad; but, most of them justify the harshest description. It is not thinkable that these are fair samples of the inhabitants of northern Africa.[50]

After the small detachment of Indian Volunteers departed for Constantinople in April 1916, camp authorities abandoned their recruiting efforts. The Ottomans did not demonstrate a sustained interest in forming an Indian battalion.[51] India had never been part of the Ottoman Empire as North Africa had. Indians had never been Ottoman subjects. One January 1916 camp report read, "Future propaganda efforts... are unlikely to win over any more Muslims because the remaining are Punjabis who have little interest in the Holy War."[52] And try as they might, the Indian Committee never convinced the Germans to do more in Zossen to cultivate anticolonialism alongside pan-Islamism. Hindu prisoners of war told members of the Indian Committee that while they might be willing to fight for India, they did not want to take up arms for Turkey or Germany.[53] "We are, of course, aware that the Mohammedans are impatient to go to Turkey," offered one Indian Committee report, "but our object in our propaganda among the prisoners has been to get them to accept the idea of fighting their way through Persia to India."[54] By mid-1915, with Indians deployed in large numbers against the Turks in the Middle East, the Indian Committee argued that the only hope for convincing Indians to join the Volunteer Battalion was to cultivate national sentiment:

In the Hands of the Enemy

> From the Lager authorities I have come to know that they have instructions from the General Staff to carry on propaganda only among the Mohamedans, so as to make them willingly leave for Turkey. About the Rajputs, Sikhs and Gurkhas the Lager [camp] authorities are instructed to carry on such propaganda that these people will feel friendly to Germany and speak well of the German Government and people when they return to India.
>
> If we mean seriously to organize an Indian Corps (composed of these prisoners and other Indians available in Turkey and Persia) which will march towards the Indian frontier through Persia, and if the German Government sees the feasibility and immense political and moral value of the scheme, then the Lager authorities should be asked to carry on propaganda in co-operation with the representatives of the Indian National Party, among the Sikhs, Rajputs and Gurkhas also, so that these people will volunteer for our cause.[55]

It is not even altogether clear that the sepoys who did join the Indian Battalion harbored any fiery commitment to pan-Islamism, much less anticolonial nationalism. Granted, one group of recently captured soldiers told the Indian Committee that they "felt betrayed by the English." Upon reaching the Western Front, they said, "they were placed at the forefront of the battle and ruthlessly sacrificed."[56] Another group of Afridi Volunteers proclaimed they were "ready to be the champions of their religion and their land in order to end British rule in India."[57] But these were likely the words of soldiers trying to make something out of nothing, to secure some modicum of advantage—we might also say, to minimize their disadvantage—at a moment when no one else in the world was looking out for them. The Germans promised them a one-way ticket home. And there were simple, household economics to consider. The Germans promised Indian Volunteers regular pay and a pension. Every single one of the twenty-four soldiers who deserted from the 58th Rifles in March 1915 joined the Battalion. By leaving their trenches, each had forfeited any and all pay, pension, and social status guaranteed by the British, "& this ruined their future prospects entirely," read one Indian

Committee report.[58] Three Sikhs of the Punjab also joined the battalion. Of these, Mita Singh deserted his post at the front, and Hardas Singh shot his British officer and then deserted. The third, Shemir Singh, only told his captors that he feared what the British might do to him if he ever fell back into their hands.[59] One group of recently captured sepoys admitted to the Indian Committee that "they fought for England because of the money, and would, for the same reason, be willing to fight for the Germans."[60] The committee suspected that many of the Pathan Volunteers had no intention of bringing revolution and jihad all the way to the gates of India. "Unless [the Indians] were all persuaded to take part in a general patriotic scheme, the Mohammadans would merely wish to go to settle down in Turkey, which is not good for them and is not what we desire."[61]

All one really had to do was determine what the Germans wanted to hear, and then say that. The example of one soldier reveals how adept some of the sepoys must have been at this. Sepoy Mahomed Arifan convinced the Germans and Indian Committee beyond any reasonable doubt that as a devout Muslim, he would "be pleased to fight with the Turks against their enemies."[62] A native of Peshawar, near the Khyber Pass, Arifan joined the Indian Army fourteen years prior to the outbreak of World War I and served in the 127th Baluchis. He was a veteran of an operation in Somaliland, where he had been wounded. Shot through the knees and captured on the Western Front in late 1914, Arifan assured the Germans that Afghan soldiers had no particular fondness for the British Empire and that they joined the ranks of the Indian Army because it provided a reliable source of income. "The Indian Army is able to recruit a lot of Afghans," he told a German interrogator, "because they are paid well." At the Battle of La Bassée, he said, many of his fellow countrymen ran when they spotted the Germans, "because they did not want to fight against our friends, the Germans." He was eager to participate in the Sultan's jihad. "I am confident that when the Muslim soldiers fighting in the English army learn about the Holy War, they will no longer fight against the Germans but against their true enemies."[63]

Yet Arifan never joined the Indian Battalion. The severity of his wound certainly undid his candidacy somewhat. Finding little to gain from the Germans, Arifan threw his lot back in with the British. In November 1915 the Germans transferred him to Görlitz. "He was in a wretched state... and was nothing but a miserable bundle of filthy rage," recalled Sergeant J. P. Walsh of the 1st Gloucester Regiment. Walsh "took charge of [Arifan] from the moment of his arrival, and he became devoted to me during the 17 months we were together in Görlitz." Arifan told Walsh that Germany's attempts to convert the sepoys were a complete failure. "And as a result the Germans systematically persecuted them by every means, withdrew the sanction hitherto accorded to caste feeling, and finally sent away from Zossen those who stood out firmest, and were most influential among their fellows in preserving loyalty to the King-Emperor."[64] Sergeant Walsh said that Arifan "bore himself well" during his internment "and is a credit to the Indian Army." The British sergeant "always assured him that the British Government would not forget his loyalty and that of his comrades at Zossen." Walsh concluded, "[Arifan] was intensely proud of being a British subject. He was frequently placed in prison for refusing to work for the Germans, and the last I saw of him was when he was sent away in March 1917 to Königsbruck to look after an elephant, but he told me he would continue to refuse to do any work for the Germans."[65]

Bad health care—like that Arifan received while in German custody—also undermined Germany's propaganda campaign. Sick soldiers were certainly in no condition to fight in the armies of their captors. "[The prisoners] cough practically all the time," read one camp report. "Most of the diseases [in the camp] are of the lungs. Deaths are almost all caused by pulmonary tuberculosis."[66] By the close of 1915 there were some 650 Indian prisoners in Zossen. They complained frequently that the camp failed to provide them with warm-weather clothing and coal.[67] As repeated outbreaks of tuberculosis ravaged the inmate population in 1915 and in 1916, the Germans lost any of the goodwill they may have earned from their propaganda and from the "small requests" they had provided. "We regret very much to have to say that the prisoners have no faith in the efficacy of the medical treatment they receive," warned the Indian Committee in 1916. "The chief reason is undoubtedly the high rate of mortality among the prisoners."[68] Repatriated to Holland in 1918, Jemadar Suba Sing Gurung of the 2nd/2nd Gurkha Rifles told a British officer that in addition to a "persistent campaign of sedition,"

> the main complaint the Jemadar had against the camp . . . is that the water was bad, and that in consequence large numbers of men became ill, and had to go to hospital. No men were allowed to go with them as orderlies or nurses, and the result was that they rapidly became worse, and a very large percentage died. There were 52 men of the Jemadar's regiment, 2/2nd Gurkha Rifles, taken prisoner, and of these 18 had died by April, 1917, and he states that this was not a remarkable percentage, and that from 33 to 50% of the original prisoners had certainly died. There was a good deal of tuberculosis as well, and one Subadar Prem Sing Thapa, 1/4 Gurkha Rifles, died of the disease.[69]

The Indian Committee tried repeatedly to bring the seriousness of the situation to the attention of the Germans and repair the trust they feared had been broken. In February 1916 they advised that camp authorities transfer Gurkha subadar-major Prem Singh, "who has been ill for some time and who in our opinion should be removed as soon as possible to a hospital in or near Berlin. This officer is highly respected and influential among the soldiers, and, if the special consideration that we are now requesting be shown to him, it will have a very good effect among them." The committee offered various suggestions to improve health conditions in the camp, but conditions deteriorated markedly in mid-1916.

And one Anglo-Indian camp guard employed by the Germans at Zossen might have single-handedly undermined the propaganda campaign as much as anything else. The man's name has been lost to history, but his behavior was the subject of numerous complaints filed by the Indian Committee. The man first came to the attention of Indian Committee co-founder Bhupendranath Dutt during a December 1915 visit to the camp. Sepoys told Dutt,

Table 2. Deaths in the Indian camps

	Zossen, Germany			Romania	
	1915	1916	1917	1917	1918
January	1	7	5	1	
February	2	6	9		
March		8	12		
April	3	10	7		
May	2	13		16	
June	1	14		7	
July	11	16		1	
August	2	10		2	
September	6	8		2	
October	6	6		2	
November	4	8		6	
December	2	8		1	
Total	40	114	33	38	1

Source: Deaths in Indian Camps, TNA FO 383/406.

"They [the Germans] want us to believe they are good, but they are no better than the English." Dutt filed a complaint with camp authorities requesting that they transfer the man to another camp. "The conduct of the officer in question is not conducive to success in our propaganda."[70] German authorities did nothing. The Indian Committee filed another protest in March 1916:

> We find that [the guard] has in no way changed his brutal conduct nor his ... language in dealings with the sepoys and even with the officers. The following are some specimens of the highly insulting language used by him without any sort of provocation:
>
> "Badmâsh" (You scoundrel), "Jangli" (You savage), "Suar ka bachcha" (You son of a pig), "Sala" (Fellow whose sister I have ravished), "Mâdarchôd," "Bahanchôd" (You fellow who have committed incest with your mother, with your sister).
>
> We beg to express our desire that this Anglo-Indian be immediately removed from the Lager, and replaced by Mr. Walter who is

much liked by the soldiers by reason of his gentlemanly and sympathetic treatment of them.[71]

In April things reached the breaking point. Pending the man's removal, Dutt wrote, it would be useless for the committee to continue its work in the camp to "try to do anything among the prisoners to make them believe that the Germans are really more gentlemanly and more humane than the English."[72]

Besieged at Kut

Germany abandoned its propaganda campaign in 1917 and transferred most of the Indian troops at Zossen to a new camp in Romania. Nevertheless, for much of the war Indian soldiers represented a prize coveted by the German government. The Germans may never have had much chance in winning the soldiers' loyalty, but they tried. In the Middle East, Indian soldiers captured by the Turks had a markedly different experience. Turkish forces captured 16,583 British and Indian soldiers during the war. Alone among the countries at war, Turkey refused to allow the representatives of any neutral power to visit and inspect its prison camps. Turkey concentrated prisoners of war at camps in Asia Minor or in camps east of Aleppo, Syria. General Townshend's division represented the single largest windfall: 284 British officers and 222 Indian officers surrendered on April 29, 1916. These men still had another 2,680 British soldiers and 10,486 Indian soldiers under their command. By November 1918 the British government could confirm the deaths of 3,290 of the British and Indian soldiers captured by the Turks; 2,222 more remained untraced, believed dead.[73] More than 250 British and Indian soldiers died in the hospital in Baghdad in the months after being taken prisoner at Kut. They died of pneumonia, and they died of dysentery. They died of scurvy, and they died of enteritis. They died of gastroenteritis, and they died of diarrhea. Some died from gunshot wounds taken at the battle. Hundreds more died along the roadside during a forced march to Baghdad immediately following their surrender. Many hundreds more died along a five-hundred-mile forced march from Baghdad to the Mediterranean coast.

Table 3. British prisoners of war in Turkey

Soldiers believed captured	
British officers	472
Indian officers	231
British other ranks	4,932
Indian other ranks	10,948
Soldiers believed dead	
British	1,840
Indian	1,429
Soldiers whereabouts unknown, presumed dead	
British	449
Indian	1,773
Taken at Kut	
British officers	284
Indian officers	222
British other ranks	2,680
Indian other ranks	10,486
Soldiers believed dead	
British officers	10
Indian officers	5
British other ranks	1,306
Indian other ranks	1,290
Soldiers whereabouts unknown, presumed dead	
British other ranks	449
Indian other ranks	1,773

Source: Treatment of British Prisoners of War in Turkey, IOR L/MIL/7/18737.

After suffering a debilitating defeat at Ctesiphon in November, General Townshend decided that retreat was his only option. When his men reached Kut ninety miles down the Tigris River, he ordered them to hold their ground. "By holding Kut," Townshend later wrote, "I blocked the advance of the 6th Turkish Army, as it was as dependent on water transport as the British were."[74] His one hope was General Nixon. "Now, all history is at hand to show that a force should not shut itself up in an entrenched camp unless the commander can reckon with certainty on approaching reinforcements, or unless it is close to the base and can easily be supported."[75] Townshend gambled that history might be on his side despite a lack of preparation. "Not a single trench existed" when his men reached Kut in December 1915. "The sole defenses consisted of a line of three or four block-houses suitable for savage warfare on the left bank [of the Tigris River], about 2,000 yards north of the town of Kut, and a mud-walled enclosure called a 'fort' to the north-east of the river bank about 2,800 yards distant from the town, also only suitable for savage warfare." The site was far from ideal, but Townshend convinced himself that further retreat was impossible. "So exhausted were my troops that they lay down and could do nothing but sleep and eat for two days!"[76] Townshend informed his men that he intended to hold the town. "The honour of our country and whole Empire [demand] we should hold up the Turks here," he told them. They had enough food for sixty days. That might be enough for Nixon to organize a relief force. Each man had about eight hundred rounds. That might be enough to hold the Turks at arm's length. Everything depended on Nixon. Townshend wired his commander: "I have shut myself up in Kut reckoning with certainty on being relieved by large forces now arriving at Basra."

Townshend's decision to hold Kut was not his only option, historian Nikolas Gardner has concluded. Neither was it his best.[77] To be sure, Townshend's men were exhausted and depleted upon their arrival at Kut. "The great bulk of the Indian troops could not move at all," Townshend wrote, "though I got the British to work [preparing defenses] on 4th December."[78] Sisir Sarbadhikari recalled that there had been "many bandaged heads and many arms in slings" in November, before Ctesiphon, when the army was on its way north. "But those things didn't hurt as much then as they did now. These things weighed on our minds much more during the retreat." But after a few days' rest the men were more or less recovered physically from their retreat. Morale was low, but unbroken. "We had great faith in the British lion and we believed that victory would come in the end. We thought this was but a temporary setback, that the British would do everything possible to redeem their prestige," Sarbadhikari wrote.[79] But where the Indians retained faith in their commanders, their commanders did not have much faith in them. Townshend was no fan of Indian troops. He never even bothered to learn Urdu, the lingua franca of his army.[80] Townshend worried that he'd lost so many British officers at Ctesiphon that those who remained "could not keep the men in hand so much as was desirable."[81] His Indian battalions, he wrote, had also lost heavily in Indian officers, "and the Indian battalions as a result had practically become armed bands (with discipline, it is true) from want of British officers."[82] Townshend's memoirs contain one insult after another like this. As the siege dragged on—as the weeks turned to months; as food rations grew meager; as starvation and disease began taking a toll—Townshend observed that his Indian soldiers gave way to despair. The British, however, "were as tenacious and brave as ever." "Kut might have fallen at the end of March had it not been for the white troops," Townshend wrote.[83] "How easy the defense of Kut would have been had my division been an *all British one* instead of a composite one," he claimed.[84] One wonders what the soldiers made of the contempt with which they were esteemed by their racist commander. As the siege wore on, Townshend wrote, most of the British officers had lost confidence in the Indians. "Not their [the Indians'] fault. [Indians] are not constituted by nature to stand misfortune and reverse with the same stoicism as Europeans."[85] As if having to worry about Turkish bullets was not enough, sepoys would also have to survive somehow the bigotry of the man with whom their fates now rested.

British and Indian troops dug in. The Turkish attack began on December 7. Turkish artillery probed the 6th Division's scratch-work defenses, killing and wounding thirty soldiers on the first afternoon. "The walls crumbled under the shells," Townshend wrote.[86] Sarbadhikari was in an orchard where medical staff had pitched tents to house the wounded. "The orchard took so much fire that the hospital was moved to the bazaar. But before that some patients were killed by shells." One shell failed to explode. Instead, it tore off half a man's face. "The man rose to his feet as he was dying and then fell to the ground. His eyes, nose and mouth were all gone, there were only holes in his face, spouting blood. The sight was so ghastly that it created terror amongst the others in the tent."[87] On December 9 a double company of the 69th Punjabis got caught in a murderous rain of bullets from Turkish infantry. A heavy bombardment on December 11 claimed the lives of more than two hundred Indian and British soldiers. The following day, Indian soldiers repulsed a heavy Turkish assault. Now the Turks changed their approach. They dug in, determined to slowly grind Townshend's men into dust. Artillery lobbed explosive shells over the heads of the Indian troops. Snipers took a man here, a man there. Captured Turkish soldiers revealed to Townshend that his men faced four divisions. Two more Turkish divisions were on their way. "I did not like this news at all! It meant that about 40,000 men would be besieging me."[88] On Christmas Day Turkish infantry launched an ambitious and risky predawn attack. They broke through Indian trenches in some places. Soldiers fought tooth and nail. Men threw grenades at enemy soldiers no more than ten yards distant. Indian reinforcements secured the breach. The Turks withdrew to their lines. Another three hundred Indian soldiers had been killed or wounded.

The men endured the start of the New Year alternatively in hope and despair, Sarbadhikari remembered. "It was very cold. We had lost most of our things at Ctesiphon, blankets included."[89] The rain was incessant. The roads and lanes filled with mud and water. Driven to despair, some Indian soldiers took matters into their own hands. A soldier of the 22nd Punjabis deserted to the Turkish lines. A man from the 66th Punjabis followed him shortly. "Both were fired on, but, unfortunately, were not hit," Townshend wrote in his memoirs.[90] Turkish propaganda appeared in the barbed wire in front of the Indian positions, "Rise and murder the British officers!" it called. "Join your brothers, the Turks, who will pay you better and give you land." In January a sepoy of the 103rd Mahratta Light Infantry shot his Indian officer and tried to desert to the enemy. He was captured, tried by Summary General Court Martial, and shot. South of Kut, General Nixon threw together a hasty relief expedition, made up of men of the Indian 3rd and 7th Divisions recently arrived from France. A first attempt to rescue Townshend's men in late January sustained heavy casualties and ended in failure.[91] Townshend ordered his men on half rations. On February 9 Sarbadhikari recorded, "Today our ration of firewood was suspended—and why just firewood, much else too—and instead of that we were issued a cigarette-tin of crude oil, for eighteen of us."[92] Another relief force failed to break through the Turkish lines in late February. "No sign of the Relieving Force. All our hopes dashed." Another spattering of Indian soldiers decided their chances of survival were better with the Turks and made a break for it. All told, perhaps 147 soldiers deserted during the siege.[93] Sarbadhikari and the men were very hungry. Lice had become a daily agony. "We had to wear just one set of clothes. We couldn't change; nor could we bathe. Everybody was covered with lice. They would swarm all over us, under our clothes. The torment was indescribable."[94]

A third attempt on the Turkish lines by relief troops failed in early March, just as every other attempt had failed.[95] Townshend had more than a thousand animals slaughtered. His men survived on horse meat. Townshend wrote of the situation, "There was a distinct feeling of gloom and depression in the garrison.... Serious doubt was in the minds of many, and desertions among the Indian troops increased accordingly."[96] Sarbadhikari wrote, "In Kut desertions happened from time to time, because of hunger. Firstly there was suffering of hunger; on top of these sepoys were being made to fight those of their own faith; these were the reasons why Muslims deserted. I have to say that desertions were few; what is surprising is that there weren't more." Turkish airplanes flew low overhead, dropping bombs on the force. Sarbadhikari witnessed: "A Gurkha was standing outside his tent, smoking, and the bomb fell near him. For a while there was only smoke and dust. When it cleared we saw only chunks of flesh and bone; the earth around there had turned into blood-soaked mud."⁹⁷ By late March there were almost six hundred cases of scurvy among the Indian troops. One last relief attempt in early April ended just as every other attempt had.

Babylonian Captivity

On April 29 General Townshend submitted to the inevitable. He surrendered his entire force to the Turks. By his own account the surrender represented the worst defeat suffered by British forces since Cornwallis had surrendered to Washington at Yorktown in the War for American Independence in 1781.⁹⁸ Sisir Sarbadhikari remembered the day combined British and Indian troops under General Townshend's command at Kut surrendered as "a day not to be forgotten." "Orders were published that the Turks did not want to release us on parole or any other grounds; we would have to surrender unconditionally. We were ordered to destroy all our weapons."⁹⁹ When the Turks entered the town, Townshend learned that he would go under guard to Constantinople, "the honored guest of the Turkish nation." "My force would be sent to Asia Minor to be interned in places in a good climate near the sea."¹⁰⁰ Sarbadhikari and the soldiers remained in Kut under guard the next day. On May 1 batches of men marched forth, "for now to Camp Shamran," they knew, "from there to Baghdad, where we would go from there nobody could say."¹⁰¹

The inadequacies of the Ottoman Empire's industrial infrastructure had been obvious to its own statesmen and soldiers from the very start of the war. Soldiers fought in disparate environments—from the Arabian deserts to the Albanian mountains. They often did so without adequate uniforms and insufficient food and had to live off the land as best they could by necessity. In total, the Ottoman Empire possessed just 5,700 kilometers of railroad track—1 kilometer per 304 square kilometers (France at that time had 1 kilometer of track per 10 square kilometers of territory). Soldiers therefore marched wherever they went. Ottoman troops deployed to Iraq in 1915 and 1916, for example, endured a two-month walk before ever facing the enemy. This took its toll on the army's health. Serving with the British Army in the Hijaz, Kermit Roosevelt observed of thirty captured Ottoman prisoners, "The captives were all very hungry and state that they get only a water-bottle of water and one small loaf per day."[102] Mass conscription in 1914 strained an already impoverished medical support system. Only five thousand physicians and surgeons were available to care for almost three million Ottoman soldiers enrolled during the war.[103] Ottoman soldiers often went into battle without ambulances or stretcher-bearers. As a consequence, more soldiers died of disease than bullets. Between 1914 and 1918 the Ottoman army lost 325,000 soldiers killed in combat. But 400,000 soldiers died of disease. Malaria, typhus, and dysentery were the major killers of Ottoman soldiers, not Russian, Indian, or British rifles. The Ottoman medical system was simply no match for the scale and scope of suffering unleashed by the war.[104]

Now some thirteen thousand British and Indian soldiers were in the care of an Ottoman army woefully unprepared to care for such a windfall.[105] What happened to the men captured at Kut is described in a report called *Treatment of British Prisoners of War in Turkey*, presented to Parliament in November 1918. Culled from the testimony of survivors, the report chronicles the terrible fate of Townshend's men. (Recall that he enjoyed a very different experience.) Some 1,450 soldiers were hospitalized at the time of Townshend's surrender. More than 1,000 of those men were placed on barges and sent down the Tigris into the waiting arms of IEFD in Basra. "They alone escaped the experience of becoming—as Enver Pasha presently expressed it to those who remained—'The Honored guests of the Turkish Government,'" Parliament learned. Turkish soldiers looted the remaining soldiers, the fit as well as sick, claiming for themselves boots, food, water bottles, and medical supplies.

> During the night and the following day the greater part of the British force, officers and men, was marched about eight miles up the river to Shamran, where they were to encamp until they could be sent on to Baghdad. They found no preparations for them whatever at Sham-

ran, only a bare piece of the desert ringed by Turkish sentries. Here for a week the men lay about unsheltered in sun and rain. For two days no rations were issued by the Turks; there was nothing to eat but some dates and black bread which Arab soldiers peddled among the men in exchange for boots and clothing, thus bringing their destitution a stage further; the Turks also plied a traffic in their dry and stony-ration biscuits, quite indigestible fare for semi-starved men and probably one of the main causes of the large number of death from gastro-enteritis and dysentery which occurred at Shamran. Nearly 300 of the men were dead within a week from the surrender. The Turkish medical department gave no help at all: in fact they took from our own medical staff their most important drugs. It was in short very soon clear—and at the time this came as a surprise—that the Turks had neither the power nor the will to protect the lives of the prisoners they had taken.[106]

Turkish guards separated officers from the men. At the close of the first week of May, detachments of soldiers under guard set out for the hundred-mile march to Baghdad. Those deemed too sick to make the march waited on the riverbank for steamers to bring them to the city. Men marched eight miles on the first day. They marched eighteen more on the second. They marched twelve to fifteen miles each day thereafter, collapsing exhausted on the open ground at nightfall. "They were herded like sheep by mounted Arab troopers," survivors recalled, "who freely used sticks and whips to flog forward the stragglers. Food was very short, the heat was intense, the clouds of dust perpetual, and a great number of the men had now neither boots nor water-bottles." Guards stripped the men of their uniforms. "By the time of their arrival at Baghdad most of the Arab guard were dressed in odds and ends of British uniforms, stolen during the march. There was little or no control by the Turkish officers, who usually rode at the head of the column." On the fourth day the army rested in the town of Azizie, where 350 sick British and Indian troops were left behind in a cowshed. "The rest struggled on, many of them now half naked, all so near the limit of exhaustion that there were daily deaths by the roadside." One survivor recalled how "any unfortunate men who fell out were shot through the head.... A British soldier who fell out on the roadside exhausted asked for a drink of water. An Arab took up several handfuls of dust, with which he filled his mouth and nose. The man subsequently died."[107] On the ninth day, the column reached Baghdad, where it marched four more hours before being taken to makeshift prison camps.

Sarbadhikari's own road to Baghdad had offered a lesson in cruelty—less that of Turkish, mind you, but British. He had not himself experienced anything untoward from his captors. It was the British soldiers who behaved badly, forming gangs and attacking Indian soldiers. "They say that it is because of the Indians that they lost at Kut! It's unimaginably vile. The astonishing thing is that even when complaints are taken to the British officers, they do nothing," he recorded. Placed on board a steamer, Sarbadhikari noted how "the whites are sitting in comfort in the lower deck, every one of them has space to sleep. We're on the upper deck— there's no roof over our heads, and we scarcely have enough space to sit."[108] Turkish authorities made some effort to deposit the sick and wounded in hospitals throughout Baghdad, but mortality rates remained very high. Eleven British medical officers tended to the men, "and the officers had to wage an incessant war against the prevailing dirt and disorder, neglectful nursing and mediaeval sanitation." The Turks had ten to fifteen thousand of their own sick and wounded to tend to. "The fierce Mesopotamian summer was now reaching its height, and at the best the men were in no condition to endure it. Baghdad was very poorly stocked with the necessary drugs; and what was even more serious—owing to the nature of the chief epidemic—there was much scarcity of milk and suitable food. Add to this that most of the nursing was performed by slovenly and untrained (often ill-disposed) Turkish orderlies, and it is possible to picture something of the long trial of these weeks."

The aforementioned November 1918 report, *Treatment of British Prisoners of War in Turkey*, detailed what happened next. Parties of soldiers departed Baghdad throughout June and July. Crammed into cattle cars, they traveled by rail seventy miles to Samarra. From there they set out on foot for a five-hundred-mile march across the Syrian desert in the scorching summer heat. "The truth of what happened has only very gradually become known, and in all its details it will never be known, for those who could tell the worst are long ago dead," the report offered. Men collapsed dead along the roadside, or huddled together in ditches "in the miseries of dysentery," where they waited for death, "disregarded and deserted." Survivors of these death marches recounted meeting along the way parties of men who had proceeded before them, "lying exhausted under any shelter they could find, in all stages of dysentery and starvation; some dying, some dead; half clothed, without boots, having sold everything they could to buy a little milk." Corpses littered the trail. The dead lay unburied, their naked bodies "plundered and stripped of their last clothing," desiccating beneath the desert sun.

> All across the desert, at one place after another, these sights were repeated; starving and dying men, in tens and twenties, lay in any scrap of shade or mud-hovel that might be allowed them and waited their end. Many weeks later, at a desert village about three days' journey from Aleppo, there was found a group of six British soldiers and about a dozen Indians, who for three months had lain on the bare ground of a mud-walled enclosure, subsisting solely on a few scraps thrown to them by Arabs or passing caravans. The Englishmen had been fourteen; eight had died; and of the survivors only one was still able to crawl two or three hundred yards to a place where there was water. It begins to be evident how it came about that of the men who surrendered at Kut more than three thousand, British and Indian, have never been heard of at all.[109]

What ultimately was the purpose of these death marches if not systematic cruelty?[110] As they marched, British and Indian prisoners unwittingly uncovered the evidence of another crime—Turkey's attempted genocide of the Armenians. Major Cree, taken with the 6th Division at Kut, remembered the road from Mosul to Aleppo in 1916, where the men "saw many signs and heard the most fearful reports of the Armenia massacres." Rumor circulated among the British and Indian prisoners that "the Turks had been massacring the women and children who had been deported from up country places after their men folk had been slaughtered." Then these men stumbled upon the site of a massacre. "We saw in one place deep wells which a few weeks before our passage had been filled with the dead bodies of some hundreds of women and children who had been done to death in this ghastly spot." Not far away the soldiers met orphaned Armenian children, "waifs and strays who might have been happier had they shared the fate of their slaughtered kith and kin."[111] British and Indian soldiers wondered if these sites might be an omen of their own fates.

Some Armenians remembered vividly meeting the British and Indian prisoners from Kut. Grigoris Balakian, an Armenian priest and survivor of the genocide, encountered a vanguard of British and Indian prisoners from Kut outside Birejik in 1916. The soldiers were in a pitiable state. They had walked for more than two months, from Baghdad by way of Der Zor to Amanos, brought to the region to work on the railroads. The men were "humpbacked, in tatters, covered in dust and reduced to skeletons," he recalled in his memoir, *Armenian Golgotha*. "They wore short pants that came down to their knees; their legs were covered with wounds and sores; they were dirty and desiccated . . . their cheekbones were protruding, their eyes withdrawn deep into their sockets. The Indians were practically naked." The soldiers called out for bread. They had not eaten a thing for days, they said. Balakian spoke with some of the British officers. They told him about the scene they had witnessed in Der Zor: "Piles of human bones, crushed skulls, and skeletons stretched out everywhere." "The Turkish officers and soldiers had treated the British prisoners just as they had treated the many thousands of Armenian deportees," Balakian wrote, "without fear of any subsequent accountability."[112]

In July 1916 batches of British and Indian soldiers began arriving within sight of the Mediterranean Sea. Those who had survived the long journey now endured "a new stage of suffering." A German company organized between two thousand and three thousand of the men into forced-labor battalions and put them to work on the Baghdad railway, laying track and blasting tunnels through the mountains. The soldiers "were, of course, absolutely incapable of work of any kind, after all they had been through. Nevertheless, they were distributed among various working-camps... and were somehow driven to their task."[113] In September 1916 the German railroad company handed the men back over to the Turkish authorities, "deciding that it was hopeless to try to get work out of them for the present." The Turks sent one thousand of the remaining British prisoners by truck and by foot to camps in the interior of Asia Minor. Thereafter the survivors "were absorbed into the chaotic system of the Turkish Empire." The majority of Indian prisoners were largely permitted to recover their strength before being sent to continue work on the Berlin-Baghdad railway. Some went to Constantinople and its suburbs to work on the roads. At one prison camp men were subjected to routine beatings by its whip-wielding commandant. The Kut prisoners under his care arrived in late 1916, "some of them naked, many half out of their minds with exhaustion, most of them rotten with dysentery." At a work camp at Ras al-'Ain in northern Syria, about 1,300 Indian prisoners spent the closing months of 1916 "ravaged by sickness, ill-fed and over-driven. An officer of the Indian Medical Service was fortunately there from the first, but in the lack of medicines and proper food it was inevitable that the death-rate should be very high." In the winter of 1917–18, some 650 British and 5,390 Indians prisoners remained in the region.[114]

Nomads

Sarbadhikari set out from Mosul to Tell Kaaf in what is now northern Iraq in August 1916. On his way he encountered two Armenian boys. "From what they said to us in broken Arabic," he wrote, "we understood that the Turks had slaughtered their fathers and older brothers; where their mother was they did not know."[115] After forty more days spent on the march, Sarbadhikari reached the town of Nisibeen, on the border of Turkey and Syria. In early September he reached Ras al-'Ain. He had marched for forty-six days from

Samarra and covered some five hundred miles. Prisoners began work on the rail lines. Cold set in. Many of the men worked without proper footwear. "[The prisoners] would be taken to work barefoot on the line, in the snow. They would get frostbite at first and then the flesh would fall off and the wounds would turn gangrenous." In November typhus struck. Sarbadhikari was sent to Aleppo with the most serious patients, a transfer that may very well have saved his life. Sickness decimated the camp's inmate population that winter. Aleppo proved far more agreeable. Sarbadhikari worked in a hospital. In February 1917 an Ottoman official distributed money to the prisoners from a POW fund—five liras for each of the white prisoners, three liras for each of the Indian prisoners. "Not only are we a defeated race, we're black on top of that," he protested. Sarbadhikari learned some Turkish, enough to converse with the hospital's Turkish patients. "One thing they always said was this: What are you going to gain from this war? Why are we cutting each other's throats? You live in Hindustan, we live in Turkey, neither of us have ever met, we have no quarrel with each other, but at the behest of a couple of men we've become enemies overnight."[116] Sarbadhikari returned to Ras al-'Ain in 1917. He survived the war's closing years. In January 1919 he arrived back home in India.

Thus Indian prisoners of war captured in the Middle East and Germany had very different experiences in captivity. The German government endeavored to make Indian prisoners captured on the Western Front the targets of a propaganda campaign to win their allegiance. The Turkish government made no commensurate effort to win the loyalty of the Indian soldiers captured at Kut in April 1916. As the war entered its final year, thousands of Indian soldiers remained in captivity, in Germany and the Middle East. Indian prisoners in Syria and Asia Minor were scattered across the landscape where they labored on roads and railroads. But Baron Oppenheim's schemes had petered out. His Volunteer battalions amounted to nothing. A few of his Volunteers had made it back home to Afghanistan. Others dallied in Constantinople or Baghdad, disappearing from the archival record. When the Indian and British prisoners captured at Kut entered Baghdad in March 1916, they recalled seeing numerous Indian deserters. Survivors noted: "A party of Indian soldiers, 35 in number, were seen.... They had originally been captured in or were deserters from France, and had been sent to this front to fight for the Turks, but the latter mistrusted them, and ordered their return to custody."[117] A few Indian soldiers were seen in Baghdad wearing German uniforms. In 1917 British intelligence officers captured a party of Germans, Austrians, Turks, and Indians in a raid in Shiraz, Persia. Nine sepoys from the 58th Rifles and two soldiers formerly belonging to the 20th Punjabis—all of them Kambar Khel Afridis—were with the party. The soldiers told British agents that they had been captured by the Germans and had been forced to accompany their captors, but the British never believed the story. The men carried identical purses, and each had £100 in his possession. A Civil Intelligence officer in Kabul concluded, "It is an established fact ... that the deserters of the 58th Rifles were employed as secret agents of the enemy when arrested ... all were equipped and commissioned as secret agents by the same authority."[118] Instead of going home, the captured sepoys spent the remainder of the war in a prison in Karachi.

6

The Empire's Fighters

> India is famous. For the courage and bravery her soldiers have displayed during this terrible war. The soldiers are loyal to the Motherland, for all she has done for them, dating back far back, during the growth of the British Empire. They cannot repay her for all her help.
>
> —Essay by eleven-year-old student Constance Fletcher, Liverpool, 1917

In 1917 students in Liverpool, England, gathered in schoolwide assemblies to watch a propaganda film. The film, *With the Empire's Fighters*, was about Indian soldiers on the Western Front. As the response essay by an eleven-year-old makes evident, some children were rapt at the scenes they witnessed on the silver screen: sepoys going over the top; Gurkhas showing off their menacing kukris; Pathans heating food around a campfire. Watching these scenes of Indian soldiers on campaign taught Constance Fletcher and her classmates "a lesson" they would "not easily forget": "May all who saw the pictures, take to heart, and be impressed, by the loyalty and devotion of our soldiers," the child wrote in her response essay. The footage she watched was two years old, however. A lot had changed for Indian Army servicemen by the third year of the war. For one, France was no longer the focus of Indian Army operations. The Middle East now claimed that title. The Indian Army's disastrous Baghdad offensive in 1915 and the subsequent loss of thirteen thousand men under General Townshend's command at Kut in April 1916 was all the proof William Robertson needed to order a shakeup of the Indian Army's operations. Robertson became chief of the Imperial General Staff in December 1915. He was convinced that the root problem of IEFD's woes was a lack of centralized command. In mid-1916 Robertson put IEFD under the direct control of the War Office in London. Thereafter the Indian Army's campaign in Iraq was under his control, not that of the viceroy. Next Robertson appointed new commanders. He replaced Beauchamp Duff as India's commander-in-chief with Charles Monro. In August 1916 General Stanley Maude took command of IEFD. This chapter looks at Indian Army operations in 1917 and 1918, when IEFD, from the throes of defeat and humiliation in the Middle East in 1915 and 1916, reinvented itself and became an army of conquest. In March 1917 Indian soldiers captured Baghdad (although Lord Hardinge never got to call himself the city's "Pasha"—his term as viceroy ended in April 1916). That same year Indian cavalry captured German trenches in France. In 1918 Indian soldiers punched through Turkish defenses in Palestine. In October of that year the Indian Army knocked Turkey out of the war. What produced such a marked turnaround in the army's fortunes in the Middle East? What recognition did Indian soldiers receive for the part they played in Britain's war? If the actions taken by the Indian Corps in France served as a lesson for English schoolchildren that India was "loyal to the Motherland," what lessons had the soldiers learned from their prolonged deployment overseas on multiple fronts? These are the questions to which we turn in this chapter.

Globetrotters

In September 1915 a soldier in France replied to a letter he had received from a friend in India. Evidently folks at home were struggling to keep track of the war's events. Who was fighting? Where was the fighting taking place? These were the things the soldier's friend wanted to know. "As to what you wrote asking who has won the victory in Africa, the fact is that the English are fighting in Africa, and [in France] too, and everywhere against the German Emperor," the soldier explained. But Germany was not the only enemy against whom Britain's forces were arrayed. "The Sultan of Turkey, who is the sovereign of the Musalmans, is helping the German Emperor, and is fighting the English steadily. He is fighting the English Army in the neighborhood of the city Basra." That matter clarified, the soldier segued, dispelling an apparent rumor that the fighting in France had come to a close. "Whoever told you so is lying," the soldier wrote. "The fighting is going on with great vigor and thousands of mothers' sons perish daily. There does not seem to be any arrangement to bring the war to a decisive issue. The matter is in the hands of God."[1]

Between 1914 and 1918, Indian soldiers participated in a global war. Because of the expansive nature of the war and the Indian Army's operations, many Indian soldiers found themselves deployed to multiple fronts. Soldiers belonging to the 39th Garhwal Rifles first entered the trenches in France in late October 1914. In November they fought for command of no-man's-land against a tenacious German enemy. In March 1915 the Garhwalis captured German trenches at Neuve Chapelle. They fought at Festubert in May, at Loos in September. Fighting in France and Belgium cost the 39th Garhwal Rifles more than half its original contingent. The battalion redeployed to Egypt at the start of 1916 and thence to Mesopotamia. In September 1917 the 39th Garhwals lost nearly two hundred men taking Turkish trenches at Ramadi. In March 1918 the battalion mopped up Turkish forces north of Baghdad on the Euphrates River. After a brief respite the soldiers redeployed yet again, this time to Greece, where they remained until the end of the war. In 1919 the soldiers deployed to Iraq, where they took part in search-and-destroy missions against Kurdish insurgents.[2] The war likewise made globetrotters out of the men of the 129th Baluchis. Deployed from India to the Western Front at the start of the war, the 129th Baluchis participated in nearly every major action on that front from 1914 through the end of 1915. In January 1916 the Baluchis deployed to East Africa. They spent the next two years pursuing German forces under the command of Paul von Lettow-Vorbeck through the East African backcountry, a wilderness completely devoid of the kinds of infrastructure the men accessed in France—roads, shelter, and hospitals. The men returned to Karachi in February 1918.[3]

One reason Indian soldiers deployed to so many parts of the globe during the war was to free up as many white troops as possi-

Table 4. Number of combatants sent for service overseas from India, 1914 to December 31, 1919

Theater	British combatants		Indian combatants	
	Officers	Other ranks	Officers	Other ranks
France	2,395	18,353	1,923	87,412
East Africa	928	4,681	848	33,835
Mesopotamia	18,669	166,822	9,514	317,142
Egypt	3,188	17,067	2,204	107,742
Gallipoli	42	18	90	3,041
Salonika	86	85	132	6,545
Aden	952	7,267	480	19,936
Persian Gulf	991	1,059	967	29,408

Source: Statistics of the Military Effort of the British Empire, 777.

ble for the war in France. In November 1916 the War Office pleaded with the Government of India to find some method to recruit soldiers more speedily for service in Egypt and Mesopotamia. "No effort should be spared to release as many white troops as possible from those now employed in the minor theatres for service on the main British front [in Europe]," read one memo.[4] This policy reflected Britain's broader commitment to maintaining white supremacy, even when it undermined Britain's ability to win the war against Germany. The British West Indies raised some fifteen thousand soldiers for the war, for example. Although these men did see action in Palestine and the Middle East, commanders barred them from combat duty on the Western Front. Instead black West Indian men loaded ammunition, cleaned latrines, or "Danced the Rag" for the entertainment of white troops.[5] When the men requested that they be given the opportunity to fight, British commanders explained that it was "against British tradition to employ aboriginal troops against a European enemy."[6] Britain's wartime cabinet likewise rejected an offer from the Japanese government in 1917 to send Japanese troops to the Western Front. "The question is one to a large extent of racial ascendancy and international prestige," read the notes from a cabinet meeting held that October. British and French troops might be perfectly willing to fight alongside Japanese troops, just as they had once fought alongside Indians. "But in Asia itself the impetus that would be given to Japanese ambitions and to racial jealousies between East and West would be enormous," the cabinet concluded, "and no one who knows Asia and is anxious to maintain European influence there would lightly run the risk." The British government tried to limit Japan's contributions to theaters "where Japanese intervention cannot be regarded as derogatory to the valor or capacity of European troops."[7] The British were whitewashing the war on the Western Front even as they were trying to win it. In 1914 and 1915 one might have encountered in the British-held trenches in France a patchwork of white and brown faces—a mix of English and Scottish, Welsh and Irish, and Canadian, Punjabi, Nepalese, and Afghan soldiers. By 1918 Britain's frontline trenches had turned lily-white.

By the start of 1917 some Indian soldiers had not seen home in more than two years. In that time they might have served on multiple fronts. What lessons had they gleaned along the way? One thing that Indian soldiers quickly discovered (if they did not know it already) was that geography and climate determined to a not inconsiderable extent the conditions under which they did the dirty work of war. In France and Flanders sepoys acclimated to soggy trenches in the spring and autumn and snow and frostbite in the winter. "It rains without ceasing every day, & many men have been killed by the cold," wrote one sepoy of things on the Western Front. "Many [men] have lost half of a foot from the frost." Cold wasn't a problem in East Africa. On that front soldiers struggled to endure the heat and the insects. "Jungle and desert all round and no sleep to be got at nights," one soldier said of the conditions he encountered there in 1917. The kinds of comforts a soldier might find in France—cozy cottages, hot meals, warm beds—these things did not exist in East Africa. Instead soldiers lived in "magnificent palaces built of grass and mud," our trooper explained. They had nothing but "grass to eat" and "sandy and warm water from the river" to drink.[8] In Mesopotamia temperatures topped 120 degrees Fahrenheit in the summer. What else could a soldier do during those months other than swelter in his tent? In the winter men were up to their knees in mud. Soldiers in the Middle East sometimes went without clean drinking water. "The water is bad and there is much sickness," one soldier said of the situation around Basra in January 1916.

For men who fought in France, redeployment to the Middle East required a readjustment of their own expectations. Fighting the Germans in France was hard work, but soldiers deployed to the Western Front enjoyed access to things, the likes of which their comrades fighting in the Middle East or East Africa could only dream. "We get rations and clothing in abundance," wrote a sowar about conditions in France in 1917. "There is no lack of anything. The arrangements of our Government as regards rations are excellent."[9] One soldier serving with IEFD in Mesopotamia wrote to a friend in France, contrasting the conditions under which soldiers labored in the Middle East with those enjoyed by soldiers in France. "We have got a fine opportunity of fighting. No doubt you are right in thinking that you too are fighting but you are having a very different time from us for you have everything you can want while the country here is absolutely uninhabited and desolate." When a soldier in France asked a friend in Mesopotamia to send him cigarettes, the friend lamented, "If I were in India ... then I would send you cigarettes every month. But what am I to do? My regiment has also joined the war ... and nothing can be obtained here."[10] Many soldiers described the French countryside as a land ripe with abundance. A cavalry soldier fighting Ottoman forces in Persia in 1917 described the "terrible famine" he encountered there. "In every town 15 or 20 persons die of starvation each day. The poor are in a dreadful condition."[11] Some soldiers discovered that even Turkish soldiers struggled to secure their daily bread. A Gurkha deployed to Egypt described how the Turks "of their own accord come into our trenches and ask for clothes and food, saying that they get nothing."[12]

In some ways war proved a great leveler. Soldiers encountered a formidable enemy wherever they deployed. "Day and night we are in the saddle," wrote one cavalry soldier fighting in Mesopotamia in January 1916. Another soldier compared his experience fighting in the Middle East with the fighting he experienced in France. "The fighting here is very severe," he said. "It is much more severe than against the Germans."[13] Regardless of whether one was deployed to France, East Africa, or the Middle East, combat could exhilarate and it could terrify alternatively, from one moment to the next. "The war is very terrible. Men are dying in thousands," one soldier wrote of the Western Front. Another Punjabi recounted the harrowing experience that landed him in the hospital. Surrounded by Germans, blinded by mud, he fought until a bullet smacked into his forehead just above his left eye. Semiconscious, he felt his way to the rear, but another bullet ripped into his thigh. "Being without assistance I lay still thinking what to do. After a little time I began to push myself along on my back, and I left my great coat there because it prevented me from moving. I struggled along on my back for about fifty yards." But fighting to command the very same ground in 1917, Indian cavalry soldiers in France relished the opportunity to fight in the saddle. "We were the first to go into action," wrote a sowar of the 36th Jacob's Horse, describing events of late March that year. "We took five villages from the enemy," the man boasted. "This was the first engagement of the cavalry on horse-back, and was secured by the Lucknow Brigade who acquitted themselves right well."[14] Another cavalryman shared the exciting news with his relatives. "After 2½ years of waiting we have now had our chance," he wrote. "We, the Cavalry, going in advance of the infantry, engaged the enemy."[15] The Indian cavalry made it to the other side of the engagement with minimal casualties. "I am delighted that we got this opportunity of fighting the enemy," confessed a third sowar. "May God continue to give us similar opportunities."[16]

Swept up by events on the battlefield, soldiers also wished to stay abreast of news from home. Some men knew nothing of how their family had fared in their absence. "I am greatly troubled about my home as I get no letters," one soldier complained.[17] Those who did hear from home must have experienced an unnerving powerlessness at times, especially when they discovered that life in the village was proceeding along despite their absence. Some men worried about the fidelity of their wives. Some worried about the solvency of their farms. "For one year my brother Ali Khan has attended to your affairs and to the cultivation of your land," a man in North-West Frontier Province wrote to a soldier overseas. "But consider for how long can an outsider be expected to help in this way? You know well that your father is dead and that you have no near relation here to look after your affairs."[18] Some soldiers worried that whatever prewar plans they had might not survive their prolonged deployment overseas. "I am urgently wanted in India for my marriage," one cavalry soldier serving in France lamented. "But what can I do? All the strenuous efforts I have made to get back on leave to India are wasted and there is not the slightest chance of return."[19] Would his fiancée still have him when he returned? And what chance did he really have of returning home? Soldiers worried about that, of course. "Have the Holy Quran read through for me," a Pathan sepoy wrote to a friend back home. "I do not mind death, but this is a very evil place. No respect is paid to the dead. There is no release from death, and one day we must all die. But at least let us die in our own country."[20]

On every front soldiers looked forward to the end of the war and the opportunity to return home. The censor noted in one report from the summer of 1915, "The prevailing topics of correspondence in the letters [from the soldiers] are, as usual, despondency as to survival owing to the large number of casualties at the front and a keen desire to return to India."[21] He repeated the point at the close of that year, when another flurry of letters written by the Indian soldiers—these on the eve of their departure from France—revealed this was their desire, irrespective of caste or creed. "The Indian troops do not exactly know the destination to which they are proceeding," the censor reported. "Many of them think it is Egypt and most of them hope it is India.... If they could be allowed to return to India even for a short period ... it would be an act of grace which would be greatly appreciated by the Indian troops."[22] "I hope that we are shortly going back to our own country," a sepoy wrote from France. "Pray that God of His mercy may quench this burning fire."²³ By 1917 the topic of peace was a recurring theme in the censor's reports. Troops hoped the next offensive heralded the end of the war and a well-earned return home. Sowar Mahomed Yar Khan wrote the following verses from the trenches in France to a friend in India, with instructions that his words be learned by heart and sung.

> Oh perfidious sky! What have you done!
> You have torn me from Hindustan and planted me in Europe,
> Tyrant, you have separated me from my beloved family,
> You have brought grief to every house in India,
> Helpless orphans are loud in lamentation against you,
> What cruel perfidy have you practiced on them,
> You have taken the life of thousands of brave men.
> Alas! That even now tyrant, you show no pity.
> Those for whom Hind was the natural home and resting place,
> You have driven about from place to place, in Europe
> What terrible cruelty you have wrought on their bodies,
> By depriving them, killed, of bier and grave.
> They were caught firm in the whirlpool of your revolution,
> And you brought on them all the evil that you had power to do.
> I defy you still O Tyrant, since He who created you He will show no pity & mercy
> This is the constant prayer of Yar, the exile. O God be merciful and give Victory to the British.²⁴

Soldiers' families were just as anxious to see their sons or brothers or fathers or husbands again. The death of a son or husband could be devastating. The *Prabhat* reported in 1915 that the widow of a killed Rajput sepoy committed suicide. "It is not known how many more incidents like this will happen next."²⁵ A retired soldier in Punjab confessed to a soldier at the front, "Whenever the newspapers come I look at the casualties in the Indian Army." The man's three nephews were serving in the 56th Punjabis. Each had been wounded, returned home for a short while, and then returned to the front. "For this reason I am very anxious about you," he said, "and the eyes of all your relatives are fixed on you."²⁶ In February 1917 the wife of a sowar serving overseas in France wrote to her husband, "My heart feels that it could not sustain separation from you for a single minute; but it is now three years since I was last blessed with your presence, what then must my heart suffer!" The young woman described the loneliness she felt. "I am wandering alone in the wilderness of this world. I cannot realize when it was that I last looked on your face, and I would thankfully give my life as an offering to anyone who would bring me into your presence once more." Though her husband faithfully sent remittances of his pay home to his wife, she confessed it was not money she needed, but her companion. "I need you alone! I am in need of nothing else and I do not hanker after riches."²⁷ The mother of another soldier wrote, "Only a sight of you will relieve my anxiety."²⁸ Every parent knows that feeling.

Letters were the vital link between soldiers at the frontlines and their families in India. Soldiers made letter writing a matter of routine when they could. "I am always at prayer for you," wrote the brother of a cavalry soldier fighting in France. "To-day in an auspicious hour your kind letter dated the 16th October arrived. I read it & took great pleasure from it, to learn that you & all our brothers are well."²⁹ An Indian clerk wrote to his friend fighting in France in 1917, "Every week we get a letter from you and hear about your welfare. This is as it should be, because it is only through letters that we can get news of our friends who are in foreign lands. All praise to our Government who, even in the stress of this worldwide war, maintains an unbroken postal service."³⁰ When a soldier got from one side of a fight to another unhurt, he wrote about that. When a soldier was wounded in battle but still able to write, he told his family that. "While in the act of charging, I was wounded by the enemy's machine gun," reported a noncommissioned officer of the 47th Sikhs fighting in France. "When I was wounded I came to England & many men of the Indian troops have come to England. Now I am all right again. My wound healed very quickly."³¹ Soldiers who did not write home frequently got an earful from their wives and relatives. "You seem to forget that you have a wife and children," Serai Aurangabad wrote to her husband, serving with the Indian cavalry in France in 1917. She had recently received a letter from her husband, evidently the first he had written in a very long while.[32] One wonders if he wrote to his wife more faithfully thereafter.

Soldiers in regular communication with home tried to assuage their family's fears and anxieties. "Your servant is well & happy here," one soldier wrote to his family at home in India. "You may set your minds at rest."[33] But such reassurances must have rung hollow at times to the very men composing them. Machine-gun bullets slaughtered people wholesale, they knew. Shrapnel mangled exposed flesh indiscriminately. One thing that readily strikes the reader is that many of the letters soldiers composed recounted harrowing details about what it was like to be in the thick of battle. "As we advanced we lost a lot of men," one soldier reported after the Battle of Neuve Chapelle in 1915. "When we reached their trenches we used the bayonet and the kukri to such an extent that we were all covered with blood." Then the Germans counterattacked. "We fired so much with rifles and machine guns that we won and all of them were killed. The ground was covered so thickly with them that you could not put your feet down without going over the corpses."[34] A Gurkha wrote to his brother (also in the army but stationed in India), "About the state of affairs here I tell you that both sides are using machine guns & cannon. Rifles are not much used. Consider yourself very lucky that you have returned to India."[35] What might a parent or spouse think of such a report?

Letters like those just mentioned are worth keeping in mind for the story that follows. In March 1917 the family of an Indian cavalry soldier serving in France received a letter from the man's "host mother." The French woman with whom he lodged and took his meals wrote that as long as the soldier "remains in France he shall, so far as it rests with me, want for nothing since he is dear to me as a son." Upon reading the woman's letter, "great satisfaction was experienced by the whole family," the soldier's father reported. The family took the French woman's letter out into the street and read it aloud to "each individual man and woman, and indeed all the people of the street had it read to them." The soldier's son took the letter in his hand and "ran about all over the place and showing it to each one he met said, 'This letter is from my [French] grandmother.'" "All the members of the family have felt themselves to be under great obligation to this (French) lady for her kindness to you," the soldier's father wrote, "but since her letter was received all the people of the village are also loud in her praise, saying that people who show such great kindness and generosity to a poor exiled soldier, must indeed be very few in this world." The soldier's father instructed the young man to read the family's letter to his French host. We have no way of knowing for certain if he ever did. But the soldier's mother wrote a letter of her own, addressed to her son's French mother. "I am deeply grateful for your kindness, and am much touched by the words of affection contained in your letter," she began. Then she invited the French woman to visit the family's home in Sargodha, Punjab. "Thus shall I know that your motherly affection for him is of the most perfect kind," she wrote. "Come without fail. Your presence here will confer distinction and honor on me, and I shall be able to present you to the people as [my son's] adopted mother."[36]

Breakthrough

In November 1916, about 64,800 British and 156,350 Indian troops were ready to renew the advance on Baghdad.[37] General Nixon had relinquished his command of IEFD earlier that year in January due to sickness. During the summer the Government of India rushed supplies and materiel to Basra. George MacMunn arrived, charged with organizing a stockpile of provisions for the army, a task to which he proved well suited.[38] By the height of summer, IEFD and its medical personnel enjoyed access to things such as hospital barges and surgical equipment. Airplanes began mapping the region's topography as well as Turkish positions. New troops rushed to the region. Veterans received new uniforms, equipment, and weapons and then set to the task of teaching freshly arrived replacements everything they needed to know about soldiering. In

August IEFD received its new commander, General Stanley Maude. Maude was energetic, meticulous, and popular—his promotion from divisional command to the head of IEFD was applauded by the force's British officers.[39] Nothing was left to chance. An enthusiast of the offensive, General Maude wanted to take Baghdad, perhaps more than anybody else in the wake of General Townshend's disastrous 1915 campaign.[40] When the Indian Army's new commander-in-chief, General Charles Monro, visited the theater in October, he was satisfied that IEFD was ready to finish the job it had begun a year earlier. In December 1916 General Maude set his army on the move.[41]

Turkish forces held formidable defensive positions along the left bank of the Tigris River at Sannaiyat, a stretch of desert sandwiched between river and marsh, ideally suited to bottlenecking an enemy force superior in numbers. The Ottomans had dug three lines of trenches. The first two were a mere forty yards apart and lightly held. But machine-gun nests in the third line of trenches enjoyed command of the battlefield. Turkish gunners would be ideally suited to mow down attacking infantry.[42] Supply lines and a network of trenches and bunkers that stretched back fifteen miles to Kut ensured Ottoman troops ample food, equipment, and reinforcements. Rather than throw the mass of his men at the hornets' nest of barbed wire and bullets at Sannaiyat as so many other commanders might have done, General Maude decided instead to outflank it. While a smaller force of Indian infantry of the 7th Division (including men deployed to France in 1914) and artillery kept the Ottoman troops pinned down in their trenches through the better part of December and January, the bulk of Maude's force advanced up the right bank of the Tigris.[43] Airplanes now began dropping bombs on Turkish installations connecting Kut to Sannaiyat. Mounted Indian cavalry raided Turkish positions dotting the Tigris. In January Indian cavalry sacked Kut.[44] Amid December and January rains Indian and British infantry crossed the river and assaulted Turkish positions. The fighting was bitter, lasting through February. "There is plenty of fighting going on," one soldier wrote of things in the Middle East that January, boasting that his battalion had "got a great name" for the number of Turkish prisoners it had taken. "The regiment has done real good work."[45] Turkish soldiers doggedly held their positions and fought for every inch of ground. Rifle fire and artillery ripped into Maude's advancing troops every time they advanced across no-man's-land.[46] The 47th Sikhs earned special mention in the general's dispatches for its actions. So did the men of the 14th Lancers. "During these operations the fighting had been severe and mainly hand to hand, but the enemy, in spite of his tenacity, had more than met his match in the dash and resolution of our troops," Maude wrote. "The enemy's losses, judging from the number of dead found by us, were very heavy, and we captured many prisoners and a considerable quantity of war stores."[47] By mid-February IEFD was gaining ground, slowly but steadily.

Satisfied by things upriver, Maude decided the time was right to hit Sannaiyat and hit it hard. Indian troops went over the top on February 17 and quickly overwhelmed Turkish forces holding the first two lines of trenches. But steep casualties and a sustained Turkish counterattack sent Maude's men scrambling back to their original positions before sundown with nothing to show for the day's fighting. Artillery gunners and snipers spent the next few days exchanging salvos. Then on February 22, Punjabi sepoys and Scottish highlanders went over the top again, capturing the first two lines of Turkish trenches. Again Ottoman forces counterattacked. But this time Indian reinforcements rushed to the aid of their comrades. The British and Indian battalions held out for the rest of the day, stubbornly repulsing one Turkish counterattack after another. General Maude wrote of things, "Many trenches were choked with corpses, and the open ground, where counter-attacks had taken place, was strewn with them."[48] Upriver, Indian infantry continued their assault. At last the dam broke. Ottoman forces retreated. With the Indian cavalry in hot pursuit, some Turkish battalions abandoned their trenches, their equipment, and many of their wounded. Others fought desperate rearguard actions. By the end of February Maude's force was in complete command of the once-thought impregnable fortifications at Sannaiyat. IEFD had captured more than four thousand Turkish prisoners. With the Ottoman army in disarray and evidently disintegrating, the road to Baghdad appeared open once again.

Now Indian soldiers raced up the Tigris River, retracing the very steps Townshend's men had trod during their retreat from Ctesiphon in late 1915. On February 25 the Indian Army captured Kut.[49] Baghdad lay just ahead. It tantalized the men. "Now our forces are approaching Holy Baghdad and by the grace of God they will have the privilege of worshipping soon at the shrines there," a Muslim sepoy wrote.[50] On March 7 Indian cavalry accompanied by the Indian 3rd Corps encountered Turkish resistance while crossing the Dialah River, just eight miles below Baghdad. Although well-placed Turkish machine guns mowed down advancing Indian cavalry, Turkish command had already decided against a costly battle to hold the city.[51] Over the next several days Indian infantry engaged in the dirty work of clearing trenches and capturing Turkish bunkers at bayonet point. When word reached General Maude in the predawn hours of March 11 that Turkish forces were retiring, he ordered his men into Baghdad. By midday the Union Jack was flying above the ancient city.[52]

This was great news from the perspective of British statesmen. The new British prime minister, David Lloyd George, called the capture of Baghdad "a stroke which at once rehabilitated our prestige in the East and cheered our people at home, much in need just then of some bright news."[53] The Indian press was no less ebullient. "No more gratifying news has been received for a long time from any of the theatres of war than that of the capture of Baghdad," offered the *Panjabee* that March.[54] In Amritsar the *Vakil* reported, "The fall of Baghdad is a great blow to the Ottoman Empire and a blessing to the Allies." While British statesmen outdid themselves proclaiming this the "most important event" of the war, the Turks could only console themselves "by saying that they retreated for military reasons."[55] In Lahore the *Al-Asar* opined, "The capture of Baghdad [has washed] away the stain which General Townshend's surrender had cast on British arms."[56] Indian soldiers' friends and relatives also had plenty to cheer at the news. "The Turkish forces are thoroughly broken up and will soon make peace," wrote one sepoy fighting in the Middle East.[57] "The fall of Baghdad and Kut-el-Amara has caused the greatest joy here," wrote one man in Kashmir to a sowar fighting in France. "It is evident that the faces of the Germans will shortly be blackened and that God will give our Government the victory."[58]

Things were finally going IEFD's way. But for the Indian soldiers serving under General Maude's command, Baghdad was not the end of the road. Raising the flag over the city was one thing. Securing the country quite another. Maude's army now fanned out from Baghdad and fought to wrest towns and rail depots from entrenched Turkish forces. On March 14 Indian troops hit the railhead at Samarra, sixteen miles north of Baghdad.[59] On March 19 Indian forces captured Fallujah, thirty-five miles west of Baghdad on the Euphrates River. Fighting continued intermittently through late April, when the heat of the summer brought things to a standstill.[60] Between December 1916 and April 1917 Maude's army had fought practically nonstop. In that time, combined Indian and British soldiers advanced more than two hundred miles and took nearly ten thousand prisoners. "British and Indian troops working side by side have vied with each other in their efforts to close with the enemy and all ranks have been imbued throughout with that offensive spirit which is the soldier's finest jewel," Maude wrote in his final report of the operation.[61]

Backed by ample resources and a reliable supply line, soldiers under General Maude's command were able to accomplish what those under the command of Generals Nixon and Townshend could not.[62] Barges and hospital steamers evacuated the wounded. Well-equipped and well-staffed army hospitals saved lives. One cavalry soldier described the medical care he received in Mesopotamia in 1917. In the thick of the fighting in late March, a bullet ripped into the man's thigh. His commanding officer at once bandaged the wound and called for a stretcher-bearer. But the soldier was too proud to be carried off the field prostrate. "I said I would not go in a dooli but on my horse so I got on my horse." The sowar regretted the decision soon enough. By the time he reached the dressing station, he was in so much pain that he could not dismount. "The doctor Sahib helped me off and at once took out the bullet and then took down my name." Then a motor ambulance drove the man to the nearest railway station, where he was put on a hospital train that carried him in no time at all to a base hospital. His letter closed, "Just think of the wonderful bandobast [care] of the Sirkar to have everything ready before we arrived!"[63]

Maude suspended his offensive at the end of April just as temperatures began approaching 120 degrees Fahrenheit. It was simply too hot to campaign. Soldiers set to work consolidating their positions. Indian noncombatants stockpiled the vast stores of food and provisions arriving daily, brought up the Tigris River by a now-uninterrupted supply chain that stretched from Baghdad to Bombay. When the heat broke in September, IEFD took Ramadi. The Indian Army captured Tikrit in November. In 1917, therefore, the Indian Army achieved an enviable breakthrough in Mesopotamia, the kind of breakthrough Allied commanders had sought for years without success. IEFD had advanced hundreds of miles. It had smashed through formidable Turkish defensive works, taking some 10,000 Turkish prisoners in the process. At the close of 1917, IEFD's 420,000 soldiers occupied one hundred thousand square miles in the Middle East. General Maude did not survive the autumn campaign, taken down by cholera on November 18. But his force continued to enjoy success after success the following year. In May 1918 IEFD captured Kirkuk, and in September 1918 it seized Mosul.

Comrades-in-Arms

Army policy at the start of World War I barred Indians from receiving commissions as regular army officers, or King's Commissioned Officers (KCOs). Indians could only receive commissions as Viceroy's Officers (VCOs). A VCO was always subordinate to a KCO. Indian nationalists had hoped from the start that the war would convince British policymakers to eliminate barriers to racial equality between Indians and white Britons. "In the present war on the continent both Moslem and Hindu soldiers have won the much-coveted Victoria Cross and have inspired wholesome dread in German hearts," wrote the *Tribune* in April 1915. "It would seem a fitting reward if such Indian officers, as are considered well qualified, were given commission ranks in Indian regiments in France and Flanders.... This would be a most appropriate recognition of the merits of Indian soldiers."[64] Later that summer the newspaper emphasized that soldiers exposed to the European battlefields could not help but resent their exclusion from army commissions. "Indian soldiers who are to-day fighting shoulder to shoulder with their British and colonial comrades, facing common dangers, enduring common hardships, and sharing common glory will return to this country with a broader outlook, wider experience, greater knowledge, and higher aspirations." The *Tribune* maintained:

> Their services have admittedly been of the utmost value to the Empire in this hour of England's greatest need. Slow as they are they cannot fail to perceive with perfect clearness that their risks being equal, their prospects should also be equal. The invidious distinction was sufficiently galling already; it will become twice as galling after their return from Europe. Their intercourse with the citizens of European countries, their exchange of ideas with them under conditions of war which have the wonderful effect of levelling distinctions, their contact with the free institutions of Great Britain and other European countries, and the manner in which they have been received by foreigners and treated by their own officers cannot fail to instill into them a spirit which will resent the badge of inferiority which has hitherto been placed on them.[65]

Making Indians eligible for KCOs early on might have done as much to promote the Indian Army's combat effectiveness as it would have appeased Indian nationalist aspirations. In August 1914 the Indian Army only had forty British officers in reserve. This made it nearly impossible to officer the army properly as soon as major wartime operations got underway.[66] One report from a February 1917 meeting of the British cabinet read, "The Government of India are at their wits' end to provide British officers for the Indian Army."⁶⁷ That the issue had gone nowhere owed chiefly to objections raised by the War Office. But the new secretary of state for India, Edwin Montagu, held that "the time was ripe for" political and administrative reform. "It [is] impossible to tell an Indian that he may control the destinies of Englishmen if he became a Judge . . . but that if he fights for the Empire he can never expect to hold a position of authority," he stated at an August 2, 1917, meeting of the war cabinet. In the war "Indian troops had displayed the greatest gallantry on many battle-fields in different parts of the world, and the fact that they were still barred from obtaining King's commissions was causing the profoundest dissatisfaction, and was very gravely hampering recruiting."⁶⁸ The secretary of state for the colonies, Walter Long, agreed with Montagu's proposal but "felt bound . . . to tell the Cabinet that he was informed that there would be trouble if Indians were put in command of Australian or Canadian troops." The secretary of state for war, the Earl of Derby, strongly opposed the concession on the grounds that "the vast majority of the men in the British Service were absolutely opposed to it." "If natives were granted King's commissions, they would have to be treated exactly as British officers were," he said, "both in regard to promotion and other things, and, sooner or later, an Indian would be commanding a mixed force."⁶⁹ Far better that the Indian Army have no officers at all than weaken white prestige, according to the secretary for war.

Montagu won the cabinet's approval over the War Office's objections, and nine Indian officers, among them Amar Singh, received the King's Commission in 1917. In India the nationalist press applauded what it considered a long-overdue reform. "Obviously this is the first practical Army reform adopted by the Government of India of the many that have been ceaselessly urged by the Congress during the last 30 years," reported the *Tribune* in Lahore. Secretary Montagu had also announced in the House of Commons that in recognition of India's wartime contributions, the Royal Military College at Sandhurst would henceforth reserve ten seats for Indian cadets. "We hope that in adopting this reform the Government will not make any differentiation or create dif-

The Empire's Fighters

ferences in pay rank, status &c., of Indians, but will grant Commissions to Indian youths of required fitness on equal terms with those of non-Indian subjects of the King-Emperor."[70]

What of the secretary of state for war's warning that "the vast majority" of white soldiers remained opposed to racial equality? Hadn't Indian soldiers' participation in the war led to mutual respect and interracial friendships between Indians and white troops? When they had some downtime, Scottish highlanders and Punjabi Muslims fighting together in the Middle East enjoyed sporting exhibitions, such as footraces and boxing matches.[71] When combined British and French empire troops hit Turkish forces at Gallipoli in April 1915, they included among the ranks sixteen thousand Indians, a mix of Indian artillery and infantry. The Indian artillery gunners were reportedly so skilled that they won the respect of their New Zealand and Australian comrades in arms. The Australians "were always hanging around chatting to our fellows," a British officer with the 21st Kohat Battery remembered. The Anzacs (New Zealanders and Australians) started saying "salaam" when they greeted Indian Muslim troops. A few Australians learned enough Urdu "to yell at them to take cover when there was concentrated fire on the beach."[72] The British press picked up the story. "One of the most satisfactory pieces of news from the Dardanelles is the feeling of camaraderie that has been established between Indian and Australian troops serving in the Gallipoli peninsula," reported the *Daily Graphic* in August 1915. "For many years past the friction between Indian immigrants and white colonists, not in Australia only, but in every one of the self-governing Dominions, has been a cause of the greatest embarrassment to all the Governments concerned."

But mutual respect and camaraderie born of the experience of war did not mean racists were ready to grant Indians any meaningful change in imperial policy after the war. "Whether it will ever be possible or desirable for Indians to settle in large numbers in the midst of a white population is more than doubtful," posited the aforementioned article from the *Daily Graphic*. "It is not so much a question of color as of different ideals and different social habits due to long centuries of distinct civilizations. The wisest leaders of Indian thought are now beginning to recognize that in the common interest both of Europeans and of Asiatics no wholesale mixture of populations should be attempted."[73] In December 1915, when Gandhi addressed the Indian National Congress at its Bombay session, he observed that the war and India's contributions to the imperial war effort had not softened white settlers' "hostile attitude" toward Indians. "It is the fashion now-a-days to consider that because we have taken our humble share in the war by not being disloyal to the Government at the present juncture, we are entitled to rights which have been hitherto withheld from us as if those rights were withheld from us because our loyalty was suspected." No, he said. Indians were not denied rights by white settler governments because their loyalty was in doubt. South Africa, Canada, and the other White Dominions—these countries denied rights to Indians because of racial prejudice. And even as the war raged, even as Indian soldiers secured battlefield victories, even as South African Indians tended to the empire's battlefield wounded, Indians still encountered one roadblock after another in the dominions. "There are men enough from South Africa who would tell you . . . the difficulties that we have to go through even now," he said. In Canada "it is not possible for those brave Sikhs who are domiciled there to bring their wives and children." Above outcries of "Shame!" from his audience, Gandhi lamented, "I feel that this unequal administration will not be altered because of the splendid aid which India is said to have rendered to the Empire."[74] Sure enough, Canada all but banned Asian immigration in 1923. The United States followed suit in 1924.

In England, meanwhile, cinemagoers were packing the cinemas to watch a propaganda film about Indian soldiers, H. D. Girdwood's *With the Empire's Fighters*. In 1915 Girdwood requested and received permission from military authorities to take photos and film of the Indian Corps in action on the Western Front. After the infantry withdrew to the Middle East, Girdwood remained in England, where he began editing his reams of film into a single work. The final product, *With the Empire's Fighters*, offered a kaleidoscopic glimpse of India's contribution to the war effort in France and Belgium. From the safety of a dark and cozy cinema, audiences could enjoy watching such mundane things as the Prince of Wales reading dispatches and examining war photographs or Indians enjoying leisure time in billets. Audiences could also see soldiers engaged in some of the more deadly work of war, like Gurkhas charging a German trench or field artillery in action. "Frequently taken under fire, as the films were, heightens their thrilling interest, for they show us the troops in some of their most heroic moments, going over the top and storming the enemy trenches and otherwise engaged in tough and successful work against the enemy," gushed one review of the film in the *Rochdale Observer*.[75] "It is open to question whether any of its forerunners equal 'With the Empire's Fighters' ... in bringing the spectators face to face with the realities of actual warfare" proffered a review in the *Reading Mercury*.[76] In 1917 Girdwood took his film on tour throughout England. Cinemas offered multiple daily showings.[77] "Everywhere it has been shown it has drawn crowded houses, and thousands have been turned away," noted one newspaper on the eve of the film's April 1918 premier in Reading.[78]

Entertaining and enlightening as *With the Empire's Fighters* must have been, Girdwood's 1917 tour also offered home audiences a much-needed morale boost in what was an otherwise disastrous year on the Western Front. "In this part of England we need someone to stir our imaginations and give us some idea of what great things are being done for us and the future generation," wrote one Lancashire vicar upon seeing the film in November. "[Girdwood's] film has helped us all to realize these things."[79] As a propagandist, Girdwood was prolific. His articles on anything from "the fine work of the Gurkhas on the western front," the intimate comradeship of Gurkhas and Scottish highlanders "formed amid strenuous fighting on the historic ridge of Delhi, ... deepened by heroic struggles and mutual losses on the battlefields of France," or the "picturesque" scene of Indian soldiers squatting around campfires littered periodicals such as the *Windsor Magazine* or newspapers such as the *Nottingham Evening Post*.[80] Screenings of his film were an opportunity to celebrate the imperial war effort. "We say unhesitatingly that everyone should make a point of paying at least one visit [to see the film,]" offered one Derby daily, "for it is a film which will interest and enthrall, and while it shows the difficulties which have to be surmounted by our brave troops, it also stirs the pride of race, quickens the patriotism, and makes one realize the wonderful spirit, resolution and determination which binds all units of the British Empire."[81] At a September 1917 screening in London, Secretary Chamberlain took the stage and addressed the assembled crowd. He said that although they met in the heart of London, the occasion was really an Indian occasion. He spoke, according to the *Times*, on "the remarkable way in which, at the call of the King Emperor, the Government, the princes, and the people of India had responded with all they had to offer."[82] Hundreds of newspaper clippings, congratulatory letters, and other paraphernalia chronicling the reception of Girdwood's film screenings (saved for posterity by none other than Girdwood himself) are now collected in a single file housed in the records of the India Office. He was as prolific a self-promoter as he was a propagandist.

Children were not spared from this wartime propaganda. Picture books, nursery rhymes, toys, and games reinforced for Britain's "future generation" the very messages their parents received daily. In January 1917 Girdwood's film showed at the Cosy picture palace in Derby. The cinema offered special Saturday morning matinees for school children. "Valuable prizes are offered for the best essays on the film written by Derby children," reported the *Derby Daily Telegraph*.[83] About 3,000 schoolchildren were ushered to the Rochdale Hippodrome in August to catch matinee performances.[84] In September Girdwood showed his film to all 120,000 children in the Liverpool schools. Teachers instructed their students to write response essays. John Slater, an eleven-year-old student, wrote, "In pre-war days our Indian soldiers were looked upon merely as picturesque figures by the majority of the English people. This war has drawn East and West together more closely."[85] At the St. Paul's

The Empire's Fighters

Girls School eleven-year-old Constance Fletcher wrote: "India is famous. For the courage and bravery her soldiers have displayed throughout this terrible war. The soldiers are loyal to the Motherland, for all she has done for them, dating back far back, during the growth of the British Empire. They cannot repay her for all her help."[86] Students like little Ms. Fletcher seem to have been especially perceptive to what was going on around them. They heard what trusted grownups had to say about the war, about India, and about the empire. And Girdwood seems to have been as gifted a speaker as he was a writer and photographer. "We are none the less impressed by the lecture as by the pictures, which the kind doctor gave us," Constance Fletcher's essay concludes. "It taught us a lesson we will not easily forget. May all who saw the pictures, take to heart, and be impressed, by the loyalty and devotion of our soldiers, to the country, and may we all who are not fighting do our share, in helping to bring the war to a successful peace, by economy in food, and every man who is a true Briton, should fight to create in the minds of all the people in the world, a truer friendship, in liberty and Christianity."[87] Response essays like these make evident that Girdwood's message reached elite and non-elite audiences. His propaganda film reinforced the views of those who (like Chamberlain) already had a hand in conducting the day-to-day administration of the empire, as well as the views of those who might one day become the empire's next generation of imperial advocates and caretakers.

Knockout

Since the departure of the Indian infantry at the close of 1915, Indian and British cavalry in France had evolved into a combined arms force, integrating mobility and firepower with some effectiveness.[88] In November 1917 dismounted Indian cavalry participated in their final operations on the Western Front. In one action at Noyelles sowars held the line against wave after wave of German infantry. "On November 30 at noon the Germans made a sudden attack," one sowar wrote his comrade. "Great God, what do you expect one to say! The enemy opened up such an intense fire that men and horses were thrown on to each other."[89] A sowar of the 2nd Lancers wrote that his regiment "secured great success and reputation" in the fight. "But alas," he went on, "in fulfilling the obligations our gallant commander, several British officers and Sirdars and brave men, went and knocked at the Gates of Paradise."[90] In December dismounted sowars advanced beside British tanks and captured German trenches. Mounted cavalry hurtled German barbed wire and captured a sunken road, from which they poured murderous enfilade fire onto German positions. British cavalry soldiers were evidently so impressed by the skill of the 18th Lancers that they presented the men with a trophy in the battle's aftermath. For conspicuous gallantry in the face of the enemy, sowar Gobind Singh won the Victoria Cross.[91]

One might not have known any of this, however, from General Haig's reports. On Christmas Eve, 1917, the British commanding officer of the 16th Lancers protested on behalf of his officers and men that "the services of the Indian Cavalry during the operations near Cambrai have not been noticed in any communique sent out from G.H.Q., France." The omission, the officer warned, had been "much noticed and commented on in France and among the Indian troops themselves." A quick investigation by India Office staffers revealed not only that Douglas Haig had failed to make any explicit reference to the work performed by Indian cavalry, but that "the only mention of the Indian Cavalry as having been engaged in these operations was in a German wireless which announced that they had met and shot down a number of Indian Cavalry soldiers!"[92] The India Office responded speedily, urging General Haig to set the record straight. One of Secretary Montagu's subordinates wrote to General Haig, complaining that his communiqués from the front failed to reference adequately the "gallant and distinguished service" Indian cavalry performed that year on the Western Front. "You will realize that it is of great political importance not to lose the opportunity of praising the work of Indian troops whenever this can appropriately be done," the India Office staffer wrote. The political situation in India was delicate. Secretary Montagu feared "it may have a very bad effect out there when the part some of these Indian Cavalry Regiments played near Cambrai becomes known and it is realized that no recognition has been made of their work, especially when they see that [white] troops were mentioned by you [General Haig]." Our India Office subordinate concluded, articulating the desire of Secretary Montagu that in the future General Haig "let the country and especially India know what splendid work these [Indian] regiments have performed."[93]

But Indian Cavalry would not enjoy any further opportunities to fight in France. When the Allied Supreme War Council convened at the start of 1918, it concluded that the Allies should knock Turkey out of the war that year. At that point in the war, War Office policy stipulated that Indian troops ought to replace British troops in the Middle East and Egypt. Those British soldiers should then be redeployed to France. This was referred to at the time as "Indianization." An army whose British soldiers had been replaced by Indian soldiers was said to have been "Indianized." (In the interwar period "Indianization" came to refer to the replacing of British officers in the Indian Army with Indian officers.) The year 1917 had been grisly on the Western Front, and London anticipated a six-hundred-thousand-man shortfall going into 1918.[94] The War Office advised the Government of India at the time "that no effort should be spared to release as many white troops as possible from those now employed in the minor theatres for service on the main British front [in Europe]." The War Office continued, "The proportion of Indian units serving in Mesopotamia and Egypt might with advantage be considerably increased."[95] The modus operandi going into the war's final year was clear: white troops belonged in Europe fighting Germans; Indian troops belonged in the Middle East fighting Turks.

The road to knocking Turkey out of the war in 1918 did not run through Mesopotamia, however. It began in Egypt. It would run through Palestine. Approximately 95,000 Indian combatants and 135,000 noncombatants served in Egypt and Palestine during the war. In 1918 the Indian Army was well prepared for offensive operations in the region. In 1915 entrenched and well-provisioned empire troops repulsed a Turkish attack on the Suez Canal. They then began a slow and careful advance into the Sinai, improving rail lines, digging wells, and laying water pipes to ensure that any offensives launched from the region would have reliable access to drinking water. Turkey, meanwhile, flush from its victory at Gallipoli, redoubled its efforts to capture the Suez Canal. The year 1916 witnessed a series of back-and-forth battles in the Sinai desert. Otherwise very little territory changed hands, and the Suez Canal remained safely guarded.[96] In March 1917, as IEFD marched into Baghdad, the British attacked into Gaza unsuccessfully. In April 1917 the hard-fighting Edmund Allenby transferred to the region from France and took command of the Egyptian Expeditionary Force (he considered it a demotion).[97] The new prime minister, David Lloyd George, did not think Palestine was a sideshow, and he instructed his new commander to take Jerusalem. Allenby said to a colleague before leaving England that he would ensure that "1,335 years of Mohammedan rule [in Palestine] would end in 1917."[98] When Allenby hit the Turks that autumn, he hit them hard. His force was superior in manpower and materiel.[99] On October 31 he captured Beersheba. Gaza fell on November 7. The following week he took Jaffa, Jerusalem's main port. Through these engagements Allenby had reduced his Turkish opponent to one-third of its original strength.[100] Then he made his move on Jerusalem. When Turkish forces withdrew from the holy city, Allenby was able to enter it on foot at the head of a triumphant army on December 11. In the words of one historian, the moment "symbolized the end of the British Army's most successful major campaign to date in the Great War."[101]

Command now set its sights on Aleppo in Syria, a distance of some three hundred miles from Jerusalem. But when Germany launched its last, desperate offensive on the Western Front in March 1918, London rushed British troops to France. Allenby had to let go of sixty thousand frontline soldiers—British and Australian. Allenby's force therefore "Indianized" as quickly as possible—it replaced white troops with Indian troops. The Indian 3rd (Lahore) and 7th (Meerut) Divisions joined the Egyptian Expeditionary Force (EEF) from Mesopotamia (having started the war in France, the Lahore and Meerut Divisions would finish it in Palestine). Indian cavalry stationed on the Western Front—ten regiments in all—redeployed to the EEF in April. More Indian battalions joined Allenby's force fresh from India. By May, Allenby had an Indian army under his command, ready to spearhead what would become the army's last serious offensive operation of the war into the heart of Palestine. Turkey mustered thirty-two thousand infantry and four thousand cavalry in the region. When Allenby hit them, he hit them with a force superior in manpower (fifty-seven thousand infantry and twelve thousand cavalry) and morale. Turkish trenches ran through the heart of the Jordan Valley. Both sides spent the summer probing the other for weaknesses. Indian cavalry usually fought dismounted in the trenches in France. Now they had a chance to fight as they preferred, in the saddle, lance in hand.[102] Allenby's plan was to punch through the Turkish lines in September with his infantry at Megiddo and then drive the cavalry through the gap. The morning of September 19 began with a brief but furious artillery barrage. Indian infantry broke through the Turkish defenses before 7 a.m., the cavalry hot on their heels. By the close of the first day, Indian cavalry had advanced sixty miles. General Allenby's praise was effusive. "Indian Cavalry and infantry have taken a leading and brilliant part in the fighting," he reported. On the first day of the operation, sowars of the 2nd Lancers charged advancing Turkish infantry, killing 46 and capturing 460. The 36th Jacob's Horse and the 29th Lancers charged a fleeing Turkish column, "killing or capturing the lot." Confusion reigned at Turkish HQ. The German commander (the Turks often had German commanders in their armies) only narrowly escaped capture by car in his pajamas.[103] Allenby pressed his gains relentlessly, achieving at the Battle of Megiddo that September one of the most complete victories of the war. His EEF mopped things up in October, capturing Damascus, Beirut, and Aleppo in rapid succession. When the 18th Lancers conducted a midnight charge on the Turkish garrison holding Haifa, they routed the enemy and collected three hundred prisoners in the process. The following day, while their comrades in the Mysore Lancers cleared the rocky slopes overlooking the town of its Turkish defenders, "the Jodhpur Lancers charged through the defile and, riding over the enemy's machine guns, galloped into the town where a number of Turks were speared in the streets." Between September 19 and October 26 the Indian 5th Cavalry Division advanced some five hundred miles and captured more than eleven thousand prisoners and fifty-two heavy guns, losing 21 percent of its troopers in the process.[104] All told, Allenby's Indian army smashed three Turkish armies and took more than forty-seven thousand prisoners. Secretary of State for India Edwin Montagu reported to members of the government and to the press, "All accounts that I have seen testify to the courage, discipline, and endurance of all [Indian] ranks." The secretary said it was particularly gratifying to note "that the new Indian units which have replaced European troops sent for service to the Western Front rivalled the conduct of veteran troops and fought in a manner worthy of the high traditions of the Indian Army."[105] On October 30 Turkey agreed to an armistice. India's war against the Ottomans was at long last concluded.

Empire

The Indian Army's successes in the Middle East in the war's closing years reignited the conversation about Indian immigration. What if Indians could claim former Ottoman and German territories as their own? Indian Nationalists such as Gopal Gokhale had tied national aspirations to Indian colonialism since the very start of the war. "German East Africa, when conquered from the Germans, should be reserved for Indian colonization and should be handed over to the Government of India," he claimed in a 1914 document he prepared for the Indian National Congress outlining plans for constitutional reform.[106] The Indian press also discussed Indian colonization during the war. "Sikhs and the Punjabis do stand in great need of a colony where they may settle without let or hindrance," offered the *Sher-i-Punjab* (Lahore) in March 1915, eying German East Africa. "If the Sikhs are told that they will be allowed to settle in a certain colony after it has been conquered, they will fight all the more enthusiastically and complete the work of months in weeks."[107] "[The annexation of Mesopotamia and] its inclusion in the Empire will be of the very greatest benefit to India," argued the *Desh* (Lahore) just two months later in May 1915. "Not only will it provide an outlet for the surplus population of India, but it will furnish Indian traders with a new market at not too great a distance. The question for decision is what share India is to have in colonising the new country, and what reward Indians will get for their efforts."[108] The *Desh* returned to the scheme later that year in September: "Mesopotamia . . . has been conquered by the Indian troops. It seems likely that the administration of Mesopotamia will be handed over to India. This is as it should be. Mesopotamia is not only near India in . . . terms of distance, but resembles it in many ways. It is very suitable for Indian colonisation and it will be encouraging if the country is placed under the Indian administration."[109]

The idea of an Indian sub-empire along the rim of the Indian Ocean was not beyond the pale. The new secretary of state for India, Edwin Montagu, noted in October 1918, "We shall be guilty of grave dereliction of Imperial duty if we do not see that the Indian has some opportunity of colonization arising out of the Indian partnership in this war."[110] As it turns out, the prime minister's Committee of Imperial Defense—an ad hoc body charged with coordinating the empire's military strategy—was also considering seriously the matter of how to develop, dispense with, and perhaps even govern conquered territory in the Middle East. Everything depended on a favorable conclusion of the war, of course. But there was a lot to like about Mesopotamia. Baghdad was an important trade center and railhead. Control of the ancient city promised new trading opportunities in lucrative Persian markets. Yet the entire region—from Basra to Baghdad—was in desperate need of development. The construction of roads, railways, and irrigation would require considerable manpower. Arthur Hirtzel, political secretary for the India Office, insisted that the region's own labor supply could not possibly meet the demand. "Without foreign labor," he wrote, "which must almost necessarily be

Indian, the work cannot be done." Accordingly Hirtzel proposed that land in the Persian Gulf and Mesopotamia ought to be reserved for Indian colonization. Such a scheme, he imagined, would pay a host of dividends. Foremost among those, Indian colonization along the rim of the Indian Ocean would make it easier for the White Dominions to stay white. Hirtzel wrote:

> The arguments in favour of this course are:
>
> (1) that we should get from the Punjab and Sind colonists admirably suitable for the agricultural development which irrigation will make possible,
>
> (2) that we should be giving India a tangible reward for her services in the war, and by directly interesting her in the country remove some of the resentment which Indian Moslems may be expected to feel at the British share in the dismemberment of the Turkish Empire,
>
> (3) *that by creating an Indian colony the excuse for emigration to the white man's colonies would be removed*,
>
> (4) that an Indian, and especially a Punjab, colony would help to provide the army necessary for its own defence.[111]

The scheme came to nothing, a casualty of opportunism and diplomatic double-dealing. In order to win the war in the Middle East, the British made one promise after another to competing parties. In May 1916 diplomats Mark Sykes and François Georges-Picot concluded a secret agreement to split much of the Ottoman Empire into British and French spheres of influence. The British would get much of what is now southern Iraq and the French most of Syria and Lebanon. Meanwhile, Henry McMahon, the British high commissioner in Egypt, promised Hussein bin Ali, leader of the Hashemites, postwar "independence for the Arabs" in order to encourage a revolt against Ottoman rule. In late 1917 the Bolsheviks published the Allies' secret treaties, proving that the British had not negotiated with the Hashemites in good faith. Then in November 1917 Foreign Secretary Arthur Balfour pledged that the British government supported the establishment of a "national home" for the Jewish people in Palestine. "Palestine for the Jews," ran the headline in the *Times*. "The British had got themselves into a monumental mess in the Middle East," historian David Reynolds writes in his book on the legacies of World War I, *The Long Shadow*.[112] A new order emerged in the Middle East in the immediate postwar years. The Paris peace settlements initially installed Sharif Hussein's son Feisal, who led the Arab revolt against the Ottomans, as ruler of Syria. But then the British belatedly agreed to honor the terms of the Sykes-Picot agreement. The French evicted Feisal. The British reinstalled him as their client in Iraq, cobbled together from three diverse Ottoman provinces, Basra, Baghdad, and Mosul. Hussein's brother Abdullah, meanwhile, took the reins in the newly created state of Transjordan. To the west the narrow sliver of fertile land became Palestine. Indians found their own colonial ambitions squashed.

7

The War's Most Critical Phase

> A recruiting poster recently shown in London represents an angry lion surrounded by his cubs and bears the following legend: "The Empire needs men. Australia, Canada, India, New Zealand, all answer the call. Helped by the Young Lions, the Old Lion defies his foes. Enlist now!" Unfortunately ... nine out of every ten Indians are not permitted to do this.
>
> —*Bulletin* (Lahore, Punjab), April 15, 1915

When war broke out in August 1914, British secretary of state for war Horatio Kitchener put out the call in Britain for a mass, all-volunteer New Army. Wartime recruiting posters featuring the mustachioed secretary—his stern gaze fixed squarely on the passerby; "Your Country Needs You!" he declares—were too compelling for some young men to resist. By the end of the war almost every family in Great Britain knew somebody in uniform. The call for manpower also rang out across the empire. "The Empire needs men!" another poster declared, this one featuring the British Empire's member states, represented as a pride of lions. New Zealanders, Australians, and Canadians rallied to the Old Lion, volunteering for the armed forces at impressive rates. About 1.5 million Indians joined the Indian Army during the war. In sheer numbers, India's contribution in manpower dwarfed that of New Zealand, Australia, Canada, and South Africa combined. But this contribution represented only slightly greater than 1 percent of British India's available manpower. Why such a disparity? Was it that the call for manpower rang louder in the British Empire's self-governing White Dominions? Or was it, as the Indian staff at the *Bulletin* told readers in the Punjab in April 1915, that the Government of India and the Indian Army were unwilling to permit

The War's Most Critical Phase

a greater share of the Indian population to put on the uniform of the Indian soldier? This chapter places wartime recruitment in India within its imperial context. It unpacks some of the politics, racial priorities, and perceptions of the wartime (British-led) Indian government. What variables did the British believe merited their attention when it came to recruiting Indian men to the armed forces? Finally, it looks at how Indian peasant communities responded when they received the call from the army. What reasons did an Indian peasant have to fight in this war? And what avenues were open to young men who did not want to fight? These are the questions to which we seek answers here.

The Call to Arms

The British Isles responded to the outbreak of war in 1914 by building an army on the fly. Secretary of State for War Horatio Kitchener put out the call in Britain for an all-volunteer New Army. The British government hoped to enlist 100,000 men. In a single week (August 30–September 5), nearly 175,000 men volunteered. On September 3, on the eve of the Battle of the Marne, the daily total hit its highest peak at 33,000. To slow the rush, the War Office raised the minimum height for recruits from 5'3" to 5'6" but restored it again to its original level in November.[1] Before the close of 1914, about 1,186,000 men joined the colors. By the end of 1915, some 2,466,719 Britons had volunteered.[2] In 1916 Britain introduced the draft, but up until the Battle of the Somme in July 1916, "Britons mostly fought because they wanted to, not because they had to."[3] The willingness to volunteer—to heed that call of the empire—played out in not dissimilar fashion in Britain's self-governing White Dominions. Canadians, Australians, and New Zealanders served at an impressive rate: 13 percent of Australia's male population put on a uniform voluntarily, and by the time of the November 1918 armistice, more than 112,000 New Zealanders—19 percent of the country's manpower—had served in the military. This shouldn't come as too great a surprise. White Australians, New Zealanders, and Canadians still looked to England as the mother country. Although Australian

Table 5. Army enlistments and recruitments in the British Empire as a percentage of population

Country	Total enlistments from all sources to November 11, 1918	Estimated male population in July 1914	Enlistments as a percentage of male population
England	4,000,158	16,681,181	24.02
Wales	272,924	1,268,284	21.52
Scotland	557,618	2,351,843	23.71
Ireland	134,202	2,184,193	6.14
Country	Total sent overseas or undergoing training on November 11, 1918	Estimated total white male population in July 1911	Recruits as a percentage of total white male population
Canada	458,218	3,400,000	13.48
Australia	331,814	2,470,000	13.43
New Zealand	112,223	580,000	19.35
South Africa	76,184	685,000	11.12
Newfoundland	6,173		

Source: *Military Effort of the British Empire*, 363.

"diggers" and their commanders—and just as often their English counterparts—adhered to identities (and just as often regulations) separate from the English (ANZACS and Canadians fought in their own distinct units and divisions, commanded by fellow countrymen, at the insistence of their home governments), many felt the pull of king and country.[4] Enlistment rates in the White Dominions did not match those of England, Wales or Scotland but far surpassed those of Ireland.

So Britain and its white member states saw theirs as an imperial war effort. It was an effort shared by Indians. By the close of 1919, some 1.7 million men from what are now the countries of India, Pakistan, Bangladesh, Nepal, and Afghanistan (among others) had served in the Indian Army—a contribution in manpower surpassing that of all of Britain's White Dominions (Canada, South Africa, Australia, and New Zealand) combined. None of this would have been possible without a concerted reallocation of resources by the (British-led) Government of India and the Indian Army to building India's armed forces. In August 1914 the India Army—Britain's only overseas trained professional force then available—employed some 160,000 Indians. At the end of the war—the November 1918 armistice between the Allies and the Germans on the Western Front in France and Belgium—520,000 men were employed as infantrymen in the Indian Army. Another 52,410 Indian men were serving in the artillery; 33,650 in the cavalry; 17,518 in the engineers, sappers, and miners; and 7,733 in the signal service. Between 1914 and 1918 the army created 155 new infantry battalions, expanded the number of Indian cavalry squadrons it fielded from 155 to 199, and added its first-ever Indian machine-gun companies.

At first glance the numbers might suggest that India's wartime experience was not altogether dissimilar to that of the British Isles. Between 1914 and 1918 Britain and India turned their small, all-volunteer professional forces into massive armies capable of defeating their German and Ottoman enemies on the battlefield by war's end. Yet further inquiry reveals notable differences in how Britain and India made war. For example, England's became a mass army. India's did not. The Government of India never resorted to conscription (the British Isles did in 1916). Instead the Indian Army leaned on only a few provinces and communities to the very near exclusion of others. Between August 1914 and the November 1918 armistice in Europe, about 60 percent of all combat troops raised in India hailed from just a single province—Punjab.[5] And of those Punjabis who joined the army as combatants, the overwhelming majority hailed from the peasantry. Punjabi Sikhs, who made up less than 1 percent of the population of British India, supplied 90,000 combatant soldiers, or one-eighth of all Indian combatants deployed overseas during the war.[6]

Table 6. Enlistments in the Indian Army by province

Province	Combatant recruits enlisted	Noncombatant recruits enlisted	Total
Madras	51,223	41,117	92,340
Bombay	41,272	30,211	71,483
Bengal	7,117	51,935	59,052
United Provinces	163,578	117,565	281,143
Punjab	349,688	97,288	446,976
North-West Frontier	32,181	13,050	45,231
Baluchistan	1,761	327	2,088
Burma	14,094	4,579	18,673
Bihar and Orissa	8,576	32,976	41,552
Central Provinces	5,376	9,631	15,007
Ajmer-Merwara	7,341	1,632	8,973
Total	682,207	400,311	1,082,518

Note: The Indian Army also enlisted 58,904 recruits in Nepal; 115,891 recruits were provided by the Indian States directly under the Government of India. Total recruitment up to the armistice was 826,855 combatants and 445,582 noncombatants.

Source: *India's Contribution to the Great War*, 277.

"True to the Salt of Our Government": Joining the Indian Army during World War I

Joining the Indian Army in 1914 was—as it had been for quite a long time—a difficult thing to do. In the Punjab, recruiting depots were few and far apart, and the paucity of recruiting centers likely deterred many would-be recruits during the heady months of 1914. The province boasted only four recruiting centers at the start of the war. These served a predominantly rural population sprawled across roughly 137,000 square miles of territory, much of which remained underdeveloped. Muslims enlisted at Rawalpindi, Sikhs at Amritsar, Dogras at Jullundur, and Jats at Delhi.[7] Joining the army therefore entailed many difficulties for a young peasant who had likely never traveled far beyond his village. A Sikh from Rawalpindi who wanted to join the army could not go to the Rawalpindi depot, which recruited only Muslims. He had to travel at his own expense to Amritsar, a hundred miles away.[8] The mostly urban populations of England, Wales, and Scotland—connected by one of the most sophisticated railway networks in the world—inhabited just shy of 89,000 square miles by comparison. British men in 1914 (accompanied by their pals) could report to any recruiting depot they liked. So the contrast between India and Britain (and much of Western Europe) at the start of the war is clear. Britain had the infrastructure to enable recruiting on a mass scale. India did not. In 1914 Britons could rush to the colors. Indians could not.

The Home Government asked for 21,000 combatant recruits from India in the last four months of 1914; recruiters secured 28,000. In 1915 recruiters enlisted 93,000 more.[9] This might have made people blush before the war. But as things unfolded in 1914 and 1915, these numbers were not enough to maintain the fighting strength of the Indian battalions deployed to battlefronts in Europe, Africa, and the Middle East, where machine guns and artillery (and disease, especially in the Middle East) destroyed sepoys faster than commanders could secure their replacements. A few examples help illustrate the point. The 59th Rifles arrived in France in 1914 with 13 British officers, 18 Indian officers, and 810 other ranks. One year later, it had no British officers, 4 Indian officers, and 75 men. The 47th Sikhs had no British officers or Indian officers and only 28 men remaining from its original contingent.[10] "In a few days you will hear that in our country only women will be left. All the men will be finished here," one soldier fighting in France wrote home.[11] India's reserve system buckled under the strain. By the start of January 1915, one-sixth of all the reservists deployed to France had been found unfit for active duty.[12] "As regards the sepoys," wrote Walter Lawrence in March 1915 as he oversaw the transport of Indian wounded in France to hospitals, "I noticed boys who have had no musketry training, elderly men who could not stand winter at the front. I have seen men returned from the front, and men who have come as reinforcements from India who will never now be of any fighting value."[13] During that year on the

Western Front, the Indian Corps took on additional British units because Indian troops were too few and far between. When the Indian Corps participated in British offensive operations around Loos in September 1915, the corps was Indian in name only. The 3rd (Lahore) and 7th (Meerut) Indian Divisions (which had first arrived in France in October 1914) counted 36,420 British riflemen and only 11,230 Indian riflemen. Where the Indian regiments were once made up of "well-defined and exclusive castes and tribes," they were, according to Walter Lawrence, by summer 1915 composed of "miscellaneous and dissimilar elements." The 15th Sikhs, he cited as an example, was composed of men taken from nine different units. "This is no longer a regiment," Lawrence wrote. "It has no cohesion. In many Battalions the British officers have been twice obliterated. So that when a wounded Sepoy is asked whether he wishes to go back to his regiment, he knows that it is a regiment commanded by officers whom he does not know and composed of men with whom he has no caste or tribal affinity."[14]

Wounded soldiers who returned home sometimes became an impediment to recruitment efforts. In Jhelum, in the Punjab, *Siraj-ul-Akhbar* reported in March 1915 that "the wounded, who come to the hospitals of our country, narrate before the common people or their relatives strange stories of what they have witnessed with their own eyes . . . such rumors especially raise obstacles in the way of recruiting new men for the army."[15] Indian Army enlistments fell off considerably through the first half of 1915. The British recruited 14,201 Indian soldiers between February and March. Between April and May the number of new recruits dropped to 10,397. Although these numbers far exceeded anything the British had ever achieved before the war, they still could not match the combined manpower demand of the various fronts to which Indian troops were deployed. Viceroy Charles Hardinge worried, "If our Indian forces are to keep the field, we must recruit far more quickly than at present and we are doing all we can to encourage recruiting."[16] But at the Censor's Office in France, Captain Howell worried there was really very little that could be done. "Now that the accounts of the hardships which the Indian troops have had to undergo during the winter in France are circulating freely in India, it may be expected that there will be a marked drop in recruiting for the Indian Army."[17]

Some soldiers actively discouraged their friends and relatives from enlisting in the army. "I have heard that a second reinforcement is coming," one soldier wrote in February 1915 to a relative in India. "For God's sake do not come with it. Preserve your life."[18] A wounded Sikh wrote to his father in the Punjab, "Teja Singh and Sundar Singh have been killed by bullets. Ladda Singh has been wounded by a bullet in the leg. My advice to you is that you must not allow any of our people to enlist."[19] Another soldier serving in France with the 59th Rifles tried to talk a relative out of joining the ranks. "Stay and work on your land and do not go anywhere," he instructed. "Just at present it is not advisable that you should leave your home. Think over what I have said and be wary. I am having a hard time of it. A word to the wise is sufficient."[20] The censor noted in one of his reports the tendency of soldiers "in a very very large number of letters" to congratulate "those who have escaped this war altogether or have been sent back to India." Soldiers' families knew what to do when they received letters like these. In the Amritsar district, the heartland of Sikh recruitment, one recruiting officer had noted already in November 1914 that wives and mothers had taken to following recruiting parties for miles to dissuade their menfolk from enlisting.[21] One Indian Army recruiter in Jabalpur noted, "A large number of recruits come from our country and when they come here and find out all about the war, then I am deluged with letters from their wives and other relatives asking that their men shall not be sent to the war.... I am utterly at a loss what to do. Why do they not look into these things before they enlist?"[22] A Punjabi Muslim stationed in Colombo wrote to a soldier serving in France in late June 1915:

> I went home to get recruits. Everything is very quiet at home. Everyone's thoughts are always with their soldier sons across the sea, and they are in ceaseless anxiety.... I had got eleven recruits and was to produce them at Jhelum at 6 a.m. on the 25th June at the Recruiting

Officer's bungalow. On the 24th I had them all collected, when at 4 p.m. there came a telegram addressed to Ghakkar of Khilaspur to say that Sahibzada, the son of Shakir, of Khilaspur, had been killed in action. When they heard this the heart of the recruits was shaken. But they said nothing at the time. At 4:30 p.m. it began to rain and a dust storm came on. I went off to bring my kit indoors and all the recruits ran away. When I came back, there was not one! I hunted high and low for them, but I could not find them.[23]

All of this helps us understand better why, at a time when more than 2 million British men volunteered for the army in the first year of the war (August 1914–July 1915), recruiters in India netted only a fraction of that, adding just 78,232 Indian combatants to the ranks. Any Indian "rush to the colors" was impossible without a change in policy. When policy did change, as it did later in the war, the Indian Army was able to muster more troops. The British Isles yielded another 1.2 million men to the army in the second year of the war (August 1915–July 1916). Between August 1915 and July 31, 1916, recruiters in India added 110,315 Indians to the army's ranks as combatants. Another one million men joined the British Army in the third year of the war (most were conscripts at this point); the Indian Army added 128,509 combatants to the ranks. Army recruitment in the British Isles tapered off in the fourth year of the war, when 588,686 men joined the army. In India that was when things intensified. Between August 1917 and July 31, 1918, the Indian Army netted 292,174 combatant recruits. And in the war's closing months, when recruitment in the British Isles can only be described an anemic, recruiters in India netted their biggest returns to date. Between June 1918 and November 11, 1918, the Indian Army added some 130,708 Indian combatants to the ranks.

The task of keeping the Indian Army flush with manpower fell chiefly to the lieutenant-governor of Punjab, Michael O'Dwyer. Starting in 1915, he directed all of the province's energies toward supporting the war effort. "The Punjab, with its hardy and martial rural population of peasant proprietors, had, since its inclusion in the Empire, been rightly regarded as the 'Shield,' and 'Spear-

Table 7. Total enlistments for the British Army (and Territorial Force)

First year ending July 31, 1915	2,008,892
Second year ending July 31, 1916	1,229,189
Third year ending July 31, 1917	1,060,369
Fourth year ending July 31, 1918	588,686
August 1, 1918, to November 30, 1918	82,766

Source: *Military Effort of the British Empire*, 364.

Table 8. Total combatant enlistments for the Indian Army

First year ending July 31, 1915	78,232
Second year ending July 31, 1916	110,315
Third year ending July 31, 1917	128,509
Fourth year ending July 31, 1918	292,174
August 1, 1918, to November 30, 1918	130,708

Source: *India's Contribution to the Great War*, 276.

head,' and the 'Sword-hand' of India," O'Dwyer reflected in his postwar memoirs (omitting his own longstanding fear of anticolonial rebellion in the province).[24] "The necessity of removing every obstacle to the successful prosecution of the War, and to the rally of our man-power to the colours, was the key to the policy which I considered myself bound to pursue during the War," he wrote. By 1917, his efforts yielded a thorough reorganization of the colonial state such that "the whole administrative structure of the province was converted into a formidable and monolithic recruiting machine, utilized mainly for the purpose of supplying military manpower for the Indian Army."[25] By O'Dwyer's measure,

> the civil administration was directly associated with the military in the task of providing men and munitions; the recruiting organization was rapidly expanded by the appointment of experienced civilians, official and non-official, with a knowledge of the people, as assistants to the military recruiting officers; Indian officials or non-officials of influence were employed on recruiting work in nearly every district;

the territorial system of recruitment by which suitable men of every class could be enrolled in nearly every district was substituted for the old class system under which there were only four recruiting centers, Rawal Pindi for Mohammedans, Amritsar for Sikhs[,] Jullundur for Dogras, Delhi for Jats; while in the more backward districts, unaccustomed to military service, local depots were established for the training of the young recruits near their homes. Above all, assistance in raising men for the Army was made a duty of all executive and village officials and of all who were enjoying grants of land or other marks of consideration from Government.[26]

Thus by 1918 Punjabis who prior to the war otherwise had little or no contact with the Punjabi state or the Indian Army might then have dealt with both as facets of daily life. Joining the army did not require so much effort as it had previously. The army earmarked seventy-five new classes as eligible for recruitment during the war. "We did not wish to spur the willing horse or to denude the martial tribes completely of the flower of their manhood," O'Dwyer remarked.[27] The monetary rewards attached to military service also improved considerably. In 1915 Lord Hardinge arranged for wounded men to receive 50 rupees upon landing at Bombay. In Punjab the poor, predominantly Muslim districts of Jhelum and Rawalpindi each had over thirty thousand men in the army in 1918. Each was receiving between £15,000 and £20,000 monthly in remittances, "and this undoubtedly encouraged those at home to continue sending their young men to the Army."[28] O'Dwyer extended the revenue settlements of these two districts for ten years—effectively forgiving them for £20,000 to £30,000 in tax burden annually.[29] The Government of India increased soldier pensions and soldier family pensions. Soldiers secured better pay and field allowances. Starting in June 1918, soldiers received a bonus of 24 rupees for every six months' service completed.[30] "These had a wonderful effect in stimulating popular co-operation," O'Dwyer recalled.[31] He commented in his memoirs: "I put at the disposal of the Commander-in-Chief one hundred and eighty thousand acres of valuable canal-irrigated land for allotment later to Indian officers and men who had served with special distinction in the field. I also set aside some fifteen thousand acres for reward-grants to those who gave most effective help in raising recruits."[32] This, he said, "was the most effective of all inducements to the Punjab peasant."

O'Dwyer's story brings us here to the motivations of those who joined the ranks of the Indian Army during World War I. Wartime military service spelled upward mobility for Indian peasant communities. Punjabi communities that sent their sons to the war in 1918 did so with the expectation that the government would reward them with land and remittances. "Much depended on the military traditions of the race's localities; much, too, on economic conditions," O'Dwyer observed.[33] That's why the topic of a soldier's pay and his family's finances surfaces again and again in the reams of censored letters addressed to and from soldiers serving in France. Soldiers belonging to the Lahore and Meerut Divisions deployed to France in 1914 "were all eagerly looking forward to a rumor that the Government was going to increase their pay while they were in Europe," noted the censor.[34] A cavalry soldier serving in France wrote to an acquaintance in the Punjab in March 1916 concerning a relative who had recently enlisted. "I am very pleased to hear it," he chimed. "It is a very good thing indeed to serve in the Army. It [provides] employment."[35] Another soldier—presumably a seasoned veteran of the war in France—wrote to a friend back home who was then weighing whether he should enlist, urging that the pay was not worth the risk. "You say that you can get employment [in the army] on a salary of Rs. 15 [per month]. My advice to you is that it would be better for you to go into the jungle and live there in a shed."[36] In 1916 famine plagued the Punjab countryside. Eligible men scrambled for the chance to join the army. A soldier stationed in Allahabad wrote in March: "Risaldar Major Malik Dost Mahomed Khan has been out recruiting for four months. He has succeeded in getting 40 recruits up to date. The country is suffering from famine and heaps of recruits are to be got. Here all sorts of castes have been recruited in place of you all on foreign service."[37] Another letter postmarked from

Jhelum that same month to a soldier serving in France reported: "There is a tremendous amount of recruiting going on in this part of the country. Recruiting parties go from village to village, and the reason is that the famine is driving thousands to enlist."[38] As the war dragged on, army authorities introduced new inducements to lure men to the ranks such as free rations and improved pay and pensions. In late 1917 new combatant recruits received a bonus then and there of 50 rupees. "These measures did much to overcome the hesitation of the would-be recruit and the opposition of his family," O'Dwyer concluded. "The family was more willing to part with one of its bread-winners when he was able to remit, as nearly all recruits did, the whole or the greater part of the bonus, and later a considerable part of his pay."[39] Soldiers who failed to send home part or all of their pay got an earful from their relatives. A father in Jhelum, Punjab, wrote to his son serving in France: "After promising to send money, you have even ceased to write for three weeks. It is famine time and how are we going to manage. For two years you have sent nothing. Other servants get wages, perhaps you serve gratuitously? ... Your companions have received in wages over Rs. 1000 each. Yet you (apparently) get nothing! If you get no wages, then where is the benefit in service? It would be preferable to dig or to beg."[40]

India's martial communities were adept and savvy—they recognized an opportunity when they saw one, and in this light the economics of military service are impossible to overlook. One soldier serving in India wrote to a soldier in France, "Abdul Ghafur of Baliawala has brought in 35 recruits, and the Colonel Sahib in recognition of his services has made him a Dafadar [a noncommissioned officer in the Indian Cavalry]."[41] "You speak of getting recruits," wrote a cavalry soldier serving in France in 1916 to a friend in Lahore. "If you want to do any recruiting, you should get men for the 22nd Cavalry, for in that regiment our family and our caste fellows have always enlisted and the officers know us." He continued, "This is the time because any one who does such service to the British government however unimportant he may be ... has a note taken of his name in the Lord Sahib's [i.e., the

The War's Most Critical Phase

king's] office."⁴² Another cavalry soldier in France received a letter from home in 1916, urging that he "fulfill [his] duty towards the government with all [his] strength." "Let it not happen," he read, "that you disgrace your family. Do your duty to the very utmost of your ability, so that the name of your family may be illuminated. And may God give victory to our British Government."⁴³ A soldier in the 33rd Cavalry stationed in Poona wrote to his brother in the 26th Cavalry serving in France to "be ever mindful altogether to be true to the salt of our Government.... I hope that we shall gain a speedy victory & shall soon come home again. And I am profoundly grateful that this opportunity has come to us of proving our loyalty to our Government, whose praise is beyond telling."⁴⁴ Medals offered the chance to win both prestige and monetary reward. A clerk in India wrote to the subedar-major of a Garhwal battalion serving in France: "I hope you have by now joined the front line & you are trying your best to show great valour in the battlefield in the hope of getting V.C. This is the only occasion when one could show his bravery & obtain titles & good name. Being Subedar-Major of the Battalion you should try to give courage to everybody in the field & devote your heart & soul for the loyalty of Government."⁴⁵

Let's not take letters such as these to mean that Indian soldiers and their families would have had but one goal—"death or glory"—as the *Times* had assured its metropolitan readership at the war's advent. Soldiers and their families hoped for a speedy victory. They did not want their sons or husbands to get killed. "This is my prayer, if the God of mercy will accept it, that our noble King the Emperor of India may shortly be victorious & that you all may return home safe & sound," wrote the brother of one cavalryman.⁴⁶ And while plenty of letters from home speak to the anxieties that gripped those who had sent their loved ones overseas, just as many encouraged soldiers to do their duty. "It is the practice of brave men to engage in warfare," read one letter written in 1917. "Be a brave man therefore, and a loyal one, since you have eaten the salt of the Sircar. Do not be alarmed or disturbed, and when you go into battle call on the name of God."⁴⁷ Another family urged its soldier: "Strive to do each and every part of your work to the best of your ability, and fulfill your duty towards your King with all your heart and soul. Our descendants will then view your deeds with pride."[48]

Halting the German Menace

For Indian nationalists, wartime service in the army represented a golden opportunity to secure for themselves the racial equality they needed. Starting in 1916, the Indian Army did open the ranks to a very limited number of recruits from India's educated middle classes. Nearly four hundred Bengali college students joined the Bengali 49th Regiment. Celebrated by Indian poets for rejuvenating Bengali prestige and manhood, the Bengali 49th Regiment deployed to Mesopotamia in September 1917 but never saw combat.[49] That same year the Indian Army agreed to form a double company in the Punjab of some 250 men. "Educated Indians cannot obtain a better opportunity to display their loyalty to Government," urged the *Khalsa Samachar* in Amritsar. "It is hoped that educated Punjabis will readily respond to the call and maintain the honor of their province."[50] Here we see that military service could function as much as a vehicle for regional prestige as it could for masculine and national prestige. "What to say of a mere Double Company the forming of which can do credit only to the Bengali *babus* [India's urban professional bourgeoisie]," ran the *Khalsa Advocate*. "The Punjab should not rest till there is available a full regiment of matrics, under-graduates and graduates. In England educated young men as willingly take the sword as they do the pen; so will the brave Punjab, of whose warlike spirit and traditions the whole of India is so rightly proud."[51] In Amritsar the nationalist editors at *Vakil* tried to drum up recruits for the venture.

> O educated Punjabis! Dally not.
> O matriculates and graduates! Go the front.
> Show your bravery by raising a Double Company.
> Kill the wicked Germans and reach Berlin.[52]

As we have seen, military service was a springboard from which Indian nationalists hoped to secure a stronger standing within the empire. "If we demand self-government, we should be prepared to sacrifice ourselves in defending the Empire," ran an article in the *Hindustan*.[53] On March 21, 1918, forty-four divisions of the German Army attacked British soldiers of the Fifth Army as part of a massive offensive operation code-named Michael. This was the kaiser's final gamble, a last-ditch attempt to secure victory on the Western Front before the Americans arrived in force. Stormtrooper tactics, rehearsed the previous year in Italy and Russia, paid enormous dividends initially. In the first two weeks the Germans advanced fifty miles. The British lost 170,000 men, 1,000 heavy guns, and the entire Somme river area for which they had paid such a high price in 1916. In London the British government hastened reservists and raw recruits to France without delay. Though the British and French armies bent, they did not break. The Germans launched another offensive against the British in Flanders on April 9, and a third against the French along the Chemin des Dames in late May.

The timely arrival of the American Expeditionary Force on the Western Front in June ended the threat, but at the height of the crisis—late-March, April, and May—it looked as if the Germans just might win the war. On April 9 Prime Minister David Lloyd George went before the House of Commons and said that the Allies had entered the "most critical" phase of the war. "The fate of the Empire, the fate of Europe, and the fate of liberty throughout the world, may depend on the success with which the very last of these attacks is resisted and countered," he said. The fighting had lulled somewhat, "but it is clear that the Germans, having gained an initial success, are preparing another—perhaps even a greater—attack on the Allied Armies." White soldiers in Palestine and Mesopotamia, therefore, had received their transfer orders. "In Mesopotamia there is only one white division," Lloyd George noted. "In Egypt and Palestine together there are only three white divisions; the rest are either Indians or mixed with a very, very small proportion of British troops in those divisions." This fact was a credit to the "splendid quality" of the Indian troops fighting in those theaters, he continued, "many of whom volunteered since the War—and . . . have been more than a match for their Turkish adversaries on many a stricken field."[54]

But then Lloyd George said something that would cause a firestorm in the Indian press. The prime minister warned, "There is a menace to our Eastern Empire through Persia, because through Persia you approach Afghanistan, and through Afghanistan you menace the whole of India." Fail to stop the Germans in France, in other words, and nothing could stop the Hun from invading India next. In Lahore, Punjab, the *Panjabee* reported two days later, "The people of India . . . realize the gravity of the situation as nothing else . . . before." The newspaper urged that in response to the crisis, the Government of India and Indian Army authorities abandon their long-standing martial race recruitment doctrine—a policy that, in effect, barred most Indians from military service outright—in favor of mass recruitment. "They should confer with the Princes and Indian leaders and devise means for preventing [quoting David Lloyd George] 'the German menace from spreading to the East.' Indians will rise like one man to defend their country and to save the East from the aggression of Germany."[55] *Khalsa Advocate* wrote for its Sikh readership in Amritsar on April 13: "It may be feared that some danger in the East also may be ahead. . . . As for the Sikhs we beg to submit that we endorse every word of the Viceroy and assure the Prime Minister that of all the sections of the Indian nation Sikhs in particular will see that their response to his trumpet call beats all previous records of human devotion and sacrifice."[56] As rumor shot through the cities and countryside that the Germans were poised to invade India at the very next chance, *Akhbar-i-'Am* told its Muslim readership: "Indians [must] open their eyes and see the importance of the present times. They should show self-sacrifice and enthusiastically render military aid to Great Britain. The people of this country should enlist in large numbers."[57] In Rawalpindi *Shanti* offered this editorial on April 27 to its readers: "The Prime Minister's message and the Viceroy's appeal show that if the military power of Germany is not crushed, there is every possibility of Asia and, for that matter of India, being confronted with serious danger. Finding that he can gain no success in France, the enemy desires to turn his face towards the East and to deluge Asia with blood and devastation. Every Indian should consider it his duty to gird up his loins to save the countries of Asia generally and India particularly from the impending danger."[58]

In order to secure additional Indian manpower to meet the empire's crisis, Viceroy Chelmsford assembled a three-day war conference in Delhi at the end of April. Speaking to an audience of Indian princes and delegates representing British-controlled provinces (Gandhi was among those attending), the viceroy opened the assembly on April 27. "We are met together," he began, "to prove that India remains now as ever true to her salt. We are met here then with quiet purpose and stern resolve to answer the call which our King-Emperor makes to us." The threat to India from Germany was real, he stressed. What the hour demanded, therefore, was more Indian manpower. "I want to feel that I am carrying India herself along with the Empire at large," he said. "I want [India] to realize that this is her war; and that her sons who go forth to fight go to fight for their own Motherland." To be sure, the viceroy continued, "if the war were to stop tomorrow, the tale of India's share in the Great War would form no unworthy page in her glorious annals." India's sons had fought on every front. In East Africa, Palestine, and Mesopotamia, Indian troops had smashed the armies of the king's enemies. "But until victory is achieved we cannot relax our efforts. The eyes of the world are upon you," the viceroy said in closing. "I am sure you will quit yourselves like men."[59]

India's princes, politicians, and press responded in unison. The ruling princes outdid one another in proffers of loyalty. The Maharaja of Patiala said that the viceroy's appeal "has not failed to touch our loyal hearts." "If everyone will only try to realize what a successful invasion of India [by Germany] would mean in devastation of the country," the Maharaja of Bikaner asserted, "then there will be no fear of [Indians] failing to cooperate to their utmost with the British Government in preventing that danger from becoming a grim reality." At the conclusion of the war council three days later, its attendees pledged to help secure five hundred thousand more Indian recruits for the army, stipulating, "India's effort should be a voluntary one." Gandhi said that he was honored to find himself "one of the supporters of the resolution," adding, "I fully realize all that the resolution means and I tender my support to it with all my heart."[60]

Lieutenant Governor O'Dwyer returned from that meeting to the Punjab with the request that his province furnish two hundred thousand recruits. At a public meeting in Lahore in May, he won the unanimous approval of six hundred representatives of the province and of the Native States to meet the quota. The nationalist press offered one patriotic appeal after another. In Ferozepore *Punjabi Bhain* said in mid-May: "Indian women [should] help the Government in the defense of the country. They could urge their relations to go to the front and induce large numbers of men to come forward as recruits."[61] Mind you, none of the Indian troops raised in 1918 were bound for the Western Front—even though that was where Britain needed troops most. An April War Office directive to the commander-in-chief of the Indian Army stipulated, "Whatever units India can raise over and above her present establishment should be utilized in releasing British troops in minor theatres for service in France wherever this is possible."[62] Be that as it may, the biggest recruiting drive in the history of the British Raj to date was underway.

Propagandist of Empire

In the months that followed the Delhi war council, Mohandas Karamchand Gandhi emerged as one of the most forceful champions of the imperial war effort in India. In 1914 he helped raise a Field Ambulance Training Corps for Indian students residing in the United Kingdom. He wrote an editorial to the *Times*, calling readers' attention to the nearly 470 wounded Indian soldiers at Netley Hospital. "The need for Indian volunteer orderlies is greater than ever," he said. "In my humble opinion, it ought to be our proud privilege to nurse the Indian soldiers back to health."[63]

The War's Most Critical Phase

Gandhi returned to India at the start of 1915 and threw himself into national politics. He spoke out against the Press Act, indentured labor in South Africa, and racial discrimination in Canada. He led campaigns of satyagraha in Northern India. Let it not be said that he was at any point uncritical of the empire. But at the viceroy's war conference in Delhi in April 1918, he pledged that he would support the government's call for five hundred thousand fresh volunteers for the army.[64] Thereafter he set to work as an army mouthpiece, giving speeches, writing editorials, and distributing pamphlets. "I would like to do something which Lord Chelmsford [the new viceroy] would consider to be real war work," Gandhi wrote to J. L. Smaffey after the Delhi war conference. "I have an idea that, if I became your recruiting agent-in-chief, I might rain men on you. Pardon me for the impertinence."[65]

Gandhi hit the rails. "I am entering upon a big recruiting campaign," he wrote a beloved friend and comrade from the satyagraha struggle in South Africa. "My work has involved constant railway travelling."[66] By August he told a friend that he was "recruiting mad. I do nothing else, think of nothing else, talk of nothing else."[67] In a speech at Ras, Gandhi addressed his naysayers. "Some will ask, 'Why get killed in France?' But there is a meaning in being thus killed. When we send our dear ones to the battle-field, the courage and strength which they will acquire will transform all the villages."[68] Men and women in India died every year by the hundreds of disease such as cholera, forgotten by all but their relatives. "On the other hand, soldiers' death on the battle-field makes them immortal, if the scriptures are right, and becomes a source of joy and pride to those left behind." At a speech in Karamsad in mid-July, Gandhi said: "A seed must lose itself in earth in order that numerous seeds may spring up from it. Even so, from the ashes of the thousands dying for India, will spring up a living India."[69] Gandhi did not abandon his critical stance vis-à-vis the Empire. "I do feel that we shall truly serve the common cause if we help the Government with sepoys and yet give battle on their wrongdoings," he wrote in one letter.[70] Notwithstanding, Gandhi wanted to be the empire's champion in its hour of need.

How could a man who preached nonviolence reconcile that with his support for a war? He'd done so before, recall, in the South Africa War. Gandhi's friends asked him the same question. "I knew that my recruiting campaign was bound to pain friends for a variety of reasons," he wrote in July.[71] He was not unaware of the apparent contradiction and came to his own defense again and again. "There is no speech in which I have yet said, 'Let us go to kill the Germans.' My refrain is, 'Let us go and die for the sake of India and the Empire,'" he offered as one defense of his activities as a propagandist. "What do you say to my recruiting campaign?" he asked in a letter to H. S. L. Polak in August. "It is for me a religious activity undertaken for the sacred doctrine of ahimsa. I have made the discovery that India has lost the power to fight—not the inclination. She must regain the power and then if she will deliver to a groaning world the doctrine of ahimsa."[72] A leaflet Gandhi distributed in June 1918 offers as clear an articulation of his calculus as one might hope to find. For Gandhi, military service advanced what he saw as India's cause—swaraj—self-rule. It did this not just by endearing Indians to the British (he earnestly hoped it would). Military service would instill in Indians the virtues—courage, discipline, self-respect, manliness—prerequisite for an equal stake and equal say within the British Empire alongside the White Dominions. Gandhi's 1918 appeals for recruits were as much rooted in a rebuttal of the empire's gross racial hierarchies and political injustices as they were in shrewd political calculus and, at times, a frightening echo of martial race doctrine.

"Today we are a subject people," Gandhi began. "We do not enjoy all the rights of Englishmen." Where a white Australian, Canadian, or South African could rightly claim equal partnership in the empire, Indians could not. Equality necessitated "the ability to defend ourselves, that is, the ability to bear arms and to use them. As long as we have to look to Englishmen for our defense, as long as we are not free from the fear of the military, so long we cannot be regarded as equal partners with Englishmen." A man who did not know how to bear arms was unmanly, Gandhi asserted. And an unmanly man had no reason to expect equality from the British. "There can be no friendship between the brave and the effeminate. We are regarded as a cowardly people. If we want to become free from that reproach, we should learn the use of arms." Gandhi viewed military service as the shortest possible route to that end—winning the respect of white Britons. After all, he said, the respect of white Britons was the prerequisite for Indian self-government. "*Hence the easiest and the straightest way to win Swaraj is to participate in the defense of the Empire*," he argued. The sepoys were fighting on behalf of the empire, Gandhi said, "but they cannot be regarded as lovers of Swaraj, their goal is not Swaraj." Sepoys fought for prizes and honors and pay. "The help they render is not out of love for the country." Now, Gandhi reminded his readers, the Government of India had asked for five hundred thousand recruits. "They will certainly succeed in raising this number somehow," he said. "If we supply this number, the credit will be ours ... by enlisting in the army we help the Empire, we qualify ourselves for Swaraj, we learn to defend India and to a certain extent regain our lost manhood."[73]

"Conscription Would Have Been Infinitely Better"

Recruiting efforts in India in the latter part of 1918 surpassed all previous records. About half of the combatants raised in India joined the ranks of the Indian Army in the last year of the war.[74] "Up to the end the Punjab displayed the same grim resolution in meeting its obligations," O'Dwyer remembered. "In each of the months, August and September, 1918, over twenty-one thousand recruits were raised, surpassing all previous records."[75] Indeed, across all of India, nearly as many men joined the army in three months—between June and August 1918—as had joined the army in the war's opening two years. Was this the product of Gandhi's propaganda campaign?

Gandhi didn't think so. In the Kheda district in June 1918, Gandhi said that he expected "not 500 or 700 recruits but thousands."[76] Early returns in Gujarat proved frustrating. "No tangible result can yet be reported," he confessed. "Anyway no stone will be left unturned by me to obtain recruits in their thousands."[77] In the

Table 9. Total recruits obtained throughout India, January–August 1918

January	46,963
February	42,863
March	42,547
April	39,094
May	37,469
June	51,212
July	64,965
August	80,752

Source: Western and General Report No. 91, TNA CAB 24/152/16.

end Gandhi admitted that he had not persuaded even one man to enlist. "So far I have not a single recruit to my credit apart," he wrote in July 1918. "The task is most difficult. It is the toughest job I have yet handled in my life."[78] Things had not gotten any easier by the end of the month. "I find great difficulties in recruiting but do you know that not one man has yet objected because he would not kill. They object because they fear to die."[79] Before the close of the summer recruiting season, Gandhi collapsed from exhaustion. He remained in his sickbed through the end of the war and the start of the New Year.

But if this was not the product of Gandhi's efforts, what then best accounts for the Indian Army's windfall? Did these numbers reflect—as some had predicted at the war conference they might—a desire on the part of Indians to defend hearth and home? Patriotic feeling may explain in part what we see in table 9, but I would caution against granting it too much significance in the final analysis. India had a Central Recruiting Board in place in 1918 to better coordinate recruiting efforts across the provinces and spur on those with no real prior military experience. No such institution existed in the war's opening years. Recruiting efforts, which had been localized for most of the war, really were countrywide in 1918, so we should not be surprised that more men joined the army that year. It is also notable that at the height of the 1918 German offensive—late March, April, and May—recruiting efforts in India yielded their lowest returns. Army enlistments only really surged after the German advance had been checked. Recruiting efforts yielded their greatest returns in August 1918, when more than eighty thousand men joined the Indian Army. By that time the crisis had passed, and newspapers in India were reporting that an Allied victory was very nearly assured. "There is not a shadow of doubt that the ultimate victory is not with the Germans, but with the Allies and [the] Allies alone," reported the *Panjabee* on August 4.[80] The *Paisa Akhbar* told its Lahore readers that same day: "The end of the war is now in sight. It is true that Germany's back has not been broken yet, still her complete humiliation is to be the end."[81] What we may be seeing, therefore, is not a rush to defend hearth and home, but a last-ditch scramble to secure some of the war's economic windfall; to dip one's bucket in the well before the well dried up for good.

Ample evidence also reveals that what we are looking at in the recruiting numbers is the fruit of state-sponsored coercion. The Indian nationalist press began reporting as much in early 1918. That May a Lahore newspaper reported, "While the speeches of Mr. Tilak, Mrs. Annie Besant, Pandit Malaviya and Mahatma Gandhi, who are said to be very influential leaders, have failed to bring in recruits, not a few people in the Punjab are, without the aid of eloquent speeches, supplying large numbers of recruits by making use of personal and local influence."[82] After the war Gandhi investigated 1917–18 recruiting practices in the Punjab as part of a larger investigation ordered by the Indian National Congress to uncover the causes of the widespread civil unrest India experienced in 1919. In the course of that investigation, Gandhi found, "The evidence that we have collected and the judicial records that we have read conclusively prove that the methods adopted for securing recruits ... travelled far beyond the line of moral or social pressure; nor were these methods unknown to Sir Michael O'Dwyer." The "so-called volunteerism" that happened in 1918 "was in effect worse than conscription, because the voluntarism pressed only the weakest and permitted the strong to go scot-free."[83] At a meeting on May 4, 1918, just after the war conference at Delhi, Michael O'Dwyer relayed that the government looked to Punjab to recruit "200,000 men for the regular army, voluntarism if possible, conscription if necessary." His subordinate, Colonel Popham Young, outlined at that same meeting the method by which recruits could be found. "We shall fix quotas for each district, tehsil or village with reference to the material which is available, and shall in the great majority of cases obtain the number of men we require without resort to compulsion." But then Colonel Young continued, "When there has been a failure on the part of the people to choose their champions for the areas, Government will step in and make the choice for them."[84]

Starting in 1917, O'Dwyer applied the screws to any and every would-be holdout, all with the end goal of mustering money and manpower for the army. Judges showed leniency to defendants who had done their bit; they threw the book at those who had not. A magistrate at Cahkwal acquitted an accused criminal when he and his brother agreed to subscribe to a war bond. Another magistrate refused to hear one man's application for remission of income tax because that man apparently had not contributed to any war fund and because he had a son "whom he would not enlist."[85] O'Dwyer assigned to each district within the Punjab an enlistment quota. The entire civil administration went to work finding recruits. Recruiting returns in the Multan district at the end of 1917 stood at 759, or 1 man for every 586 in the district. By the end of November 1918, the number had risen to 4,636, or 1 man for every 93 in the district. Between April and October 1918 Punjab raised 77,728 recruits. Gandhi wrote in his report, "Instead of enlisting members of their own families, [the leading men in the district] tried to buy or coerce men of lower stratum."[86] In another region enlistees were promised "large sums" if they joined the colors, "500 or 1,000 rupees being the price of a recruit."[87] Gujranwala supplied the army 4,000 recruits between the start of the war and late 1917. Between just four months—December 1917 and March 1918—recruiters netted 5,000 new soldiers in Gujranwala. In those four months the price to "purchase" a recruit went up from 800 rupees to 1,000 rupees.[88] Villagers who resisted recruiting efforts were prosecuted under the Defense of India Act. Bureaucrats who did not meet their quotas were sacked. Other men were subjected to public beatings and humiliations. One man on a business trip to Hafizabad with his cousin witnessed a recruiting officer, his foot pressing down on the back of a man who was lying flat on the ground. The recruiter beat the young man on the side of the ribs with a shoe until the young man, crying out in pain, consented to joining the army. This sort of thing happened "practically every day," the witness reported.[89]

Tax collectors could be especially effective in securing manpower for the army. One man by the name of Muhammad Khan described in testimony he gave for the prosecution at a murder trial of a local *tahsildar* (tax collector) in the Shahpur district the methods by which the deceased had obtained army recruits. "The Tahsildar's method was to have a list of all men in a village prepared by the *Patwari* [government employee who keeps land revenue records]. When he had got the list, it was the Tahsildar's practice to go into the village and hear if any objections were taken to the selection of the recruits. It was his practice to ask a family of 3 or 4 brothers to provide one or two recruits for the army."[90] Another man from the Gujranwala district witnessed similar practices in his village. First the tahsildar would arrive and "by beat of drum" order that the men of the village were to present themselves the next morning at the village *diara* (public square). As it was harvest time "and also as the people were afraid of being forcibly taken as recruits," only a small group assembled. "The Tahsildar therefore fined some 60 or 70 persons. The total amount of fine was Rs. 1,600." Having made his point, the tahsildar now ordered all of the men of the village to assemble at Gujranwala, some eighteen miles away. Our witness testified, "When the people went there on the fixed date, they were made to stand in a row and 7 young men were picked out. This was done by Fateh Khan, Tahsildar. The other people were abused and beaten and told to bring more recruits."[91]

Some people went to great lengths in 1917 and 1918 to avoid serving in the Indian Army. Not all tahsildars could throw their weight around. Some were murdered. New recruits deserted from their recruiting centers—not exactly the behavior we might expect from willing volunteers. Almost twenty-seven thousand ran away in 1917; more than seventeen thousand were arrested.[92] An investigation conducted by the Indian National Congress found that fully half of the recruits raised in the Gujranwala District in 1917 and 1918 deserted. Young men in frontier districts crossed the border into independent Afghanistan, beyond the reach of the Government of India.[93] It remains quite difficult to know for certain what a peasant might have been thinking when he joined the army in late 1918. As O'Dwyer pointed out in his memoirs, "About half of the seven hundred thousand combatants raised in India came forward in the last year of the War, and as six to nine months' preliminary training were necessary to fit men for active service, few of these later recruits ever went to the front."[94] Their letters home, in other words, do not exist in any central file; they never passed through the hands of the censor in Boulogne. We can be sure of this, however. India's was not an all-volunteer army in 1918. It was the product of state-sponsored, Gandhi- and INC-endorsed coercion.[95]

8

Into the Face of Bayonets

> It is derogatory to national dignity to think of permanence of [the] British connection at any cost.... If the British connection is for the advancement of India we do not want to destroy it. But if it is inconsistent with our national self-respect, then it is our bounden duty to destroy it.
>
> —Gandhi, speech at Nagpur, December 28, 1920

Between 1914 and 1918 Indian soldiers deployed to every theater to which British imperial troops deployed. Indian sepoys and sowars held the lines in France and Belgium early in the war when the British Army was desperate for manpower. In the Persian Gulf Indian troops secured vital oil installations. They stormed beaches in East Africa. In 1915 Indians defended the Suez Canal and fought alongside Australians at Gallipoli. In Mesopotamia IEFD's operations unraveled and ended in defeat during the winter of 1915–16. But one year later Indian forces punched through Turkish fortifications and captured Baghdad. In 1918 Indian Army soldiers seized Palestine and knocked Turkey out of the war. During World War I, therefore, the Indian Army saved the British Expeditionary Force from annihilation, safeguarded British imperial installations, and expanded Britain's imperial holdings. Their soldiers having done these things between 1914 and 1918, what did Indians hope for when the war ended at long last? What political concessions were the British ready to grant? And why was Gandhi, who had actively supported the empire during the war as one of its propagandists, ready to say in 1920 that it was "derogatory to national dignity to think of permanence of [the] British connection at any cost"? Here, in this final chapter, I examine the expectations and disappointments brought on in the immediate postwar months. I reveal the actions taken by Indian troops in March and April 1919, when they were decisive in suppressing civil unrest in towns and cities across India. This was the moment Gandhi made his break from the empire, and the Indian National Congress at last shed its prewar moderate stance. Having successfully fought the king-emperor's battles abroad during World War I, Indian soldiers turned their rifles on Indian civilians in the war's aftermath. For India, the end of the war did not herald the start of peace. As one Indian Army general said at the time, "the battlefield of France or Amritsar is the same."

Home Rule

On November 11, 1918, Britain's war against Germany concluded with an armistice along the length of the Western Front. In East Africa Indian sepoys would continue to chase German and African soldiers under the command of Paul von Lettow-Vorbeck through the bush for a few more weeks. In northern Iraq sepoys were just ramping up counterinsurgency operations against the Kurds. But for many people following the war's events on British imperial home fronts that spanned the globe, the November 11 armistice on the Western Front meant the war was indeed over. Crowds thronged Trafalgar Square in London. In Manchester, England, munitions workers took to the streets in joyous celebration. "This is the great day—the great day of peace, hoped for, longed for, at times appearing remote, almost unattainable, yet never despaired of, resolutely pursued, at last conquered," ran an editorial in the *Manchester Guardian*. The peace was not just Britain's, readers were told: "it is the world's."[1]

The mood of India's nationalist press was no less jubilant or celebratory at the conclusion of hostilities. "India's rejoicings on the present occasion will . . . be no less than those of England or France or America," one newspaper proclaimed.[2] "The sanguinary universal war which owed its origin to Germany's greed for world-wide dominion and which was a conflict between humanity and barbarism, between civilization and cruelty, and between right and usurpation, has at last ended in the victory of the British

Government and its Allies," offered another Lahore newspaper. The victory of the Allies, the paper proclaimed, was a "triumph of truth over falsehood as to be without a parallel in the history of the world."[3] The end of the slaughter on the battlefield was certainly sufficient reason to rejoice. But members of India's nationalist press also looked forward to receiving at last the reward they believed India so richly deserved. "India has . . . proved her loyalty and devotion to the cause of the Empire by the most exacting test that could be laid down," wrote S. Aiyangar of the Lahore *Tribune*. "She has, therefore, by her deeds and sacrifices made good her claim to an equality within the Empire."[4]

When the Indian nationalist press talked about "equality within the Empire" at the end of World War I, it was articulating the aspiration Indian nationalists had voiced since the very start of the war four years earlier—namely, self-government in the form of parliamentary representation and Indian control of the executive authority of the state, all within the fabric of the British Empire. "There can be no denying the fact that India can make satisfactory progress only if she is granted self-government, that is, self-government under British rule," offered one Punjabi newspaper in 1915. "Without it the position of India in the world can never be raised."[5] Severing India's connection with Britain was not the goal. The goal was to elevate India's status and Indians' stature within the British Empire. "Mr. Gokhale said—and he knew his people well—he said that you are compelled to live in an atmosphere of inferiority that made the tallest of you bow your heads," Annie Besant said in her address before the Indian National Congress at Bombay in 1915. "These men who are here," Besant elaborated, "representatives of India from every part of the land, these men are not the children of savages emerging from barbarism, needing to be trained in the elements of Self-Government by a western nation." To rousing applause Besant said Indians "are children of heroes, the children of warriors, worthy to govern their own land-save for one reason: and that is that the very noblest amongst you seems to think himself inferior to the Englishmen around you."[6]

As the war progressed, nationalists healed old wounds. Bal Gangadhar Tilak and the "extremists," ousted by the moderates a decade earlier, were readmitted to the INC. In early 1916 Besant and Tilak founded the Home Rule League. Its object was to increase the pressure on the INC and on the British to grant self-government. As membership in the Home Rule League climbed to sixty thousand by 1917–18, Tilak claimed that if there were an end to racial discrimination, if Indians received swaraj, or Home Rule, the resultant pride Indians felt would bring thousands of new recruits forward.[7] The year 1916 also brought the INC and the All-India Muslim League together under the Lucknow Pact. Still the hope was for self-government within the British Empire, "that in the reconstruction of the Empire after the War India shall be lifted from the position of a dependency to that of an equal partner in the Empire with the Self-Governing Dominions," Besant articulated in her speech before the INC in December.[8]

In 1917 the war did as much as anything else to heighten the growing expectation among Indian politicians that their petitions would at long last receive a favorable hearing by British statesmen at the war's successful conclusion. As Indian troops consolidated their gains in the Middle East, the *Kisan* assured its readership in Lahore, "the services of Indians in the war have extorted the love and sympathy of British statesmen and even members of Parliament have been interested in the subject of Indian self-government. The question of Home Rule, which we are anxious to obtain but which we never expected to obtain for an indefinite period, has entered within the range of practical politics."[9] The end of tsarist rule in Russia in March 1917 heralded the beginning of "a new chapter" in history, reported the *Desh*. "That sacred day is approaching when all the men in the world will enjoy equal rights and will consider each other as brothers."[10] In April 1917 the United States entered the war. Speaking before a joint session of the U.S. Congress, President Woodrow Wilson declared that the Americans would wage war on Germany in order to make "the world safe for democracy." Indian nationalists and Home Rulers quickly saw that Wilsonian rhetoric would be useful for their struggle against

British autocracy.[11] Annie Besant printed and circulated copies of Woodrow Wilson's April 2 war message. When British authorities had her arrested under the Defense of India Act and charged her with "sedition," some of her supporters appealed directly to the U.S. president to intervene on her behalf. Wilson never did, but Home Rulers remained nonetheless hopeful that he would be a friend to their cause when hostilities ended. Then in August 1917 Edwin Montagu, the new secretary of state for India, articulated that "Responsible Government" was the goal for British India. Montagu had a profound distaste for the traditional Raj. He also had a wary eye on political developments underway in India. He and the new prime minister, David Lloyd George, therefore believed that India would do more for the imperial war effort "if her warm heart is touched." The Montagu Declaration was great news to Indian nationalists. "The news of Mr. Montagu's visit to India has given great pleasure to Indians and filled their minds with hope," one Amritsar newspaper put forth upon the arrival of the new secretary of state for India in South Asia.[12]

But where four years of war had certainly galvanized Indian national politics and aspirations, it had not fundamentally altered the INC's stand vis-à-vis the empire. Annie Besant's confinement in 1917 was short-lived. Upon her release she was elected president of the Congress. Besant spoke before its assembled members in Calcutta in December 1917. With the war entering its fourth year, Besant remained avowedly pro-war. When the war began, she said, India "saw in Great Britain the champion of Freedom, in Germany the champion of despotism. And [India] saw rightly." The Allied cause was just, she maintained. "For the true object of this war is to prove the evil of, and to destroy, autocracy and the enslavement of one Nation by another, and to place on sure foundations the God-given Right to Self-Rule and Self-Development of every Nation." To this end, Indian soldiers had made one decisive contribution after another on the battlefield. Besant reminded her audience that when the British Expeditionary Force deployed to France in 1914, for example, it was grossly outnumbered and outmatched by the German Army. It looked like the war might quickly be lost. But then the Indian Corps arrived. "India's sons," standing firmly on the soil of France, "were flung to the front, rushed past the exhausted regiments who cheered them with failing breath, charged the advancing hosts, stopped the retreat, and joined the British army in forming that unbreakable line which wrestled to the death through two fearful winters—often, these soldiers of the tropics, waist-deep in freezing mud—and knew no surrender."[13]

Besant was not a bullhorn for colonial rule, of course. If anything, the war years had stoked her fury and contempt for the Raj—for Britain's wanton plundering of India's treasure and natural resources; for the ineptitude with which the British prosecuted the war; for the Indian Army's wartime recruitment doctrine, one that by excluding Bengalis and Madrasis belonging to the middle classes in favor of Punjabi peasants had, she said, "emasculated the Nation." Besant saw through some of the hollow gestures the Indian Army liked to herald as far-reaching reforms. "The throwing open of Kings Commissions to qualified Indians should not be represented by a meagre nine," she said. "If English lads of 19 and 20 are worthy of King's Commissions—as the long roll of slain Second Lieutenants prove it—then certainly Indian lads, since Indians have fought as bravely as Englishmen, should find the door thrown open to them equally widely in their own country." So long as racism governed British policy, Annie Besant pledged that she would remain a formidable opponent of British policymakers. And yet even the fiery Annie Besant was not ready to make her break from the empire. If anything, she said, it was absolutely necessary for the future security of the empire that Indians be granted Home Rule. "I once said in England: 'The condition of India's loyalty is India's freedom.' I may now add: 'The condition of India's usefulness to the Empire is India's freedom.'"[14] England and India needed each other still, she said, "for prosperity in Peace as well as for safety in War. Mr. Montagu has wisely said that 'for equipment in War a Nation needs freedom in Peace.' Therefore I say that for both countries alike, the lesson of the War is Home Rule for India."[15]

Annie Besant's rhetoric might have been less conciliatory than that of some of her predecessors at the head of the INC, but she remained like them pro-empire. Thus when the war against Germany ended in November 1918, and the warring powers prepared for the postwar peace conferences at Paris, the scheme of the nationalists remained self-government within the empire, by means of persuasion and petition. "The question now is to what extent is India going to benefit by the principles for which she gave her lives and treasure, namely, the principles of justice and liberty, of the right of every nation to live an unmolested life of freedom and to grow," posited the new president of the INC, Madan Mohan Malaviya, in his December 1918 address. "The principles for which Great Britain and the Allies fought have now been embodied in the Peace Proposals of President Wilson." Self-government for India would, he said, "produce deep contentment and gratitude among the people of India and strengthen their attachment to the British Empire." But the INC would not have a voice at Paris. To be sure, the Government of India sent a delegation that could participate in deliberations where Indian interests were directly at stake. Secretary of State Montagu headed the government's delegation, accompanied by Sir S. P. Sinha and the Maharaja of Bikanir, Ganga Singh. Secretary Montagu estimated that the mere presence of separate Indian representation at Paris would appease the nationalists. India's status had "soared far more rapidly than could have been accomplished by any of our reforms," he said. This delegation, handpicked by the British, did not appease the nationalists, however. Ganga Singh had spent the war years in London speaking out against Indian self-government. The delegation of which he was a part was in Paris to represent the Government of India, not the Indian National Congress. Sinha and the maharaja were never going to press the powers in Paris for Indian Home Rule. In December 1918, therefore, the INC named its own delegates to Paris—Tilak and Gandhi. Tilak was already in London, where he was working to win sympathy from the Home Government for the Indian struggle. Gandhi was still recovering from his own pro-war propaganda campaign that previous summer. Neither made it to Paris for the opening of the peace conference in January 1919. British authorities denied Tilak's application for a passport to travel to Paris. Confined to his sickbed, Gandhi was barely in any condition to walk around his house. Tilak, for his part, did not give up hope. He sent petition after petition to the British delegation at Paris. The British delegation filed each away in a drawer, never to be seen again. By April Tilak was at a loss, if not entirely without hope. "Even a suggestion from the Conference—a hint—would be of great value and I have not yet grown hopeless about it," he wrote. Although the peace conference agreed that India would be a member of the newly created League of Nations, its delegates never took up the topic of Indian self-government and Home Rule in any formal fashion.

Rowlatt

With Indian aspirations coming to nothing in Paris, attention turned to India itself, where the viceroy's Legislative Council took up legislation in February 1919 enabling the Government of India to extend its wartime emergency powers into peacetime. Two proposed bills—the "Rowlatt Bills," as they were called—effectively suspended habeas corpus for any person charged with sedition. These laws reflected the Government of India's desire to govern through coercion in peacetime as it had during the war.[16] Among other things, the Rowlatt Bills stipulated that any person found in possession of a "seditious document"—defined as a document containing any writing or sign inciting violence against the Crown or its government, or inciting anyone to rebellion against the Crown or government—would be subject to prosecution and, if convicted by a panel of judges, subject to two years in prison, a fine, or both unless that person could prove that the document in question was in his possession "for lawful purposes." The language of the bills turned the whole system of justice on its head. From his sickbed Gandhi wrote, "This new offense alters one of the fundamental principles of British justice inasmuch as, instead of the prosecution having to prove the guilt of the accused, it is the latter who will have to establish his innocence. If I am charged with anything, how can I prove that I am not guilty? This can only mean that I shall be in jail."[17]

Where the gathering peace conference in Paris and the campaign for Indian self-determination had been the most prominent topics in the headlines of the Indian nationalist press in December and January, newspapers now shifted their focus to these impending laws.[18] The press was unsparing in its criticism of the Rowlatt Bills. One newspaper said, "It is monstrous... that legislation of that type should be introduced in India where British statesmen are so profuse in their talk of liberty and self-determination." Another newspaper described the Rowlatt Bills as "a bare-faced attempt on the part of a bureaucracy which has been demoralized by the exercise of unrestrained power to interfere with liberty." One Calcutta newspaper, *Amrita Bazar Patrika*, proclaimed on February 14, "the only parallel (to the Rowlatt Bills) ... furnished by history is that of a Nadir Shah on the pretext of some of his soldiers being killed in a bazaar affray, making over the city of Delhi to the rapine, lust and blood-thirstiness of his brutal soldiery." The *Bombay Chronicle* offered one article in which it said, "The Bills are dangerous to public safety, subversive of the rights of citizenship, improper for the subdual of revolution and a badge of crime and helotry on the people. India cannot and will not accept the mark of Cain on the forehead and be shamed among the nations of the earth." In Amritsar the *Waqt* published a cartoon showing "the Secretary of State in the act of handing the order of liberty to India, when a black cobra, released from a basket by Mr. Rowlatt, bites her."[19]

More than anything else, Rowlatt was Gandhi's moment of transformation. Still recovering from the debilitating exhaustion that had knocked him out of his recruitment campaign in 1918 and that had kept him in bed for months, Gandhi turned his attention to the proposed Rowlatt Bills. In a letter to Madan Mohan Malaviya, president of the INC, he wrote: "Unless we do something really big they [the Government] will not feel any respect for us. And we cannot hope to get anything from people who do not respect us."[20] The pending bills, he wrote V. S. Srinivasa Sastri in February 1919, "have stirred me to the very depths; and though I have not left my bed still, I feel I can no longer watch the progress of the Bills lying in the bed. To me, the Bills are the aggravated symptoms of the deep-seated disease. They are a striking demonstration of the determination of the Civil Service to retain its grip of our necks."[21] Aware of evidence of the Government of India's "determined policy of repression," Gandhi wrote that "civil disobedience seems to be a duty imposed upon every lover of personal and public liberty." To another friend Gandhi wrote, "The Rowlatt Bills have agitated me very much. It seems I shall have to fight the greatest battle of my life."[22]

Now Gandhi thrust himself into the center of Indian national politics. From his home in Ahmedabad, he began organizing a campaign of nonviolent civil disobedience, or *satyagraha*, in defiance of British law, and a nationwide *hartal*, or general strike. On February 24 he drafted "The Satyagraha Pledge." The Rowlatt Bills, he declared, "are unjust, subversive of the principles of liberty and justice, and destructive of the elementary rights of individuals on which the safety of the community as a whole and the state itself is based." Gandhi and those who took the vow of satyagraha pledged that in the event of the bills becoming law, "we shall refuse civilly to obey these laws and such other laws as a committee to be hereafter appointed may think fit, and we further affirm that in this struggle we will faithfully follow truth and refrain from violence to life, person or property."[23] He went public with his intentions that very same day, writing the viceroy, Lord Chelmsford, that the proposed laws rendered the proposed Montagu reforms "valueless."[24] In early March Gandhi embarked on a speaking tour, one that lasted the remainder of the month and took him from Bombay to Madras, from Tanjore to Nagapatam. He denounced the proposed Rowlatt Bills and explained to his audiences what he meant by satyagraha and what he believed the campaign would achieve. In a letter to the press widely reprinted, Gandhi explained, "Satyagraha ... is a process of purification and penance. It seeks to secure reforms or redress of grievances by self-suffering."[25] Gandhi called for a national day of fast and prayer on Sunday, April 6. "All work, except such as may be necessary in the public interest, should be suspended for the day," he instructed.

Hartal

On March 21, 1919, the Imperial Legislative Council in Delhi approved the Rowlatt Bills, extending the Defense of India Act into peacetime. Over the next several weeks, a wave of demonstrations, strikes, and civil unrest rocked Indian cities and towns. Protestors took to the streets in Delhi, Amritsar, Bombay, Lahore, and Ahmedabad. Gandhi was the figurehead to whom many demonstrators looked for inspiration and marching orders, but every demonstration took on its own life in response to local conditions and the available local leadership. Things kicked off on March 30. In Delhi tonga drivers disgorged their passengers. Demonstrators seized the central train station and pulled passengers off train cars. They choked the streets and the bazaars and shut down all economic activity as shopkeepers in the city's Muslim and Hindu neighborhoods shuttered their stores. In Gandhi's hometown of Ahmedabad, a city of four hundred thousand, demonstrators burned government buildings and chanted anticolonial slogans. "The British *Raj* is gone!" some shouted. "The King of England is defeated! *Swaraj* is established!" cried others. The demonstrations sent the civil and military authorities in India into a panic.[26] The Punjab government reported that a state of open rebellion existed in the Lahore and Amritsar districts. On April 10, Hindus and Muslims took to the streets of Amritsar in a show of solidarity, chanting "*Mahatma Gandhi ki jai!* [long live!]" and "*Hindu-Mussalman ki jai!*" They seized the railway station and post offices and cut telegraph wires. In Kasur, a town of some twenty-five thousand people outside Lahore, demonstrators marched carrying black flags representing the death of liberty and set fire to government installations. On April 14, in Gujranwala, a town of thirty thousand outside Lahore, people blocked trains from leaving the station, set fire to railway bridges, and burned the post office and district court. Government of India officials believed these "disturbances"—as they came to be called—represented the greatest threat to British rule in India since the 1857 Rebellion.[27] In mid-April the Punjab lieutenant governor, Michael O'Dwyer, declared martial law, effectively suspending habeas corpus in the province. This order lasted through June.

At the height of what the Government of India then believed to be a rebellion, protesters overwhelmed local authorities and civil police forces. Soldiers would therefore play a critical role in helping the government reestablish control. In Punjab this fact worried O'Dwyer considerably. "In the first place," he wrote, "we had very few troops in the Punjab. Those we had were about to be demobilized." Most of the troops available had been mustered in the last year of the war. They were only half-trained and lacked combat experience. Seasoned troops were on hand, but they were few and far between.[28] Regardless, the government had to make a way out of no way. Some former soldiers participated in the antigovernment demonstrations. Punjab housed anywhere from 100,000 to 150,000 demobilized men from the army at the time of the "disturbances." The Lyallpur district notably housed a fair number of military pensioners. Some of these ex-soldiers cut telegraph lines, rode the rails into Amritsar to participate in demonstrations, and distributed anti-British broadsides. O'Dwyer worried about these men. "With the high-spirited and adventurous Sikhs the interval between thought and action is short," he wrote, revealing that the war had done nothing to dissuade him of prewar racist stereotypes. "If captured by inflammatory appeals they are prone to act with all possible celerity and in a fashion dangerous to the whole fabric of order and constitutional rule."[29] In Lahore in early April an ex-sepoy spoke before a cheering crowd of twenty-five thousand Hindus and Muslims, telling them falsely that Indian regiments had mutinied and were marching on the city, that the soldiers had already killed some two hundred English soldiers, and that he himself had murdered six British troopers. In Amritsar a Sikh veteran spoke before a crowd on April 10, announcing the mutiny of Indian troops.

In most cases where government authorities deployed active-duty soldiers to suppress demonstrators, the troops obeyed their officers' commands. Soldiers arrived in Delhi on March 30, charged with containing the crowds then in control of the train station and spilling out onto the adjacent Queen's Road and the Queen's Garden (now Azad Park). Thirty sepoys, each armed with a rifle and twenty rounds of ammunition, set to work corralling the demonstrators, clearing them from the train station at bayonet point. Some demonstrators in the gardens collected stones and bricks to use as missiles. As these began to rain down on the Indian soldiers, officers issued the order to fire. A crack of gunfire sent demonstrators running for their lives through the park in the direction of the bazaar, Chandni Chowk, leaving behind the bodies of the dead and wounded. Indian soldiers pursued the crowd into the bazaar. There followed another crack of gunfire, followed by the screams of terrified civilians. Five more people were dead. The day's wounded numbered in the dozens. One soldier stationed in Delhi that day was Subedar Major Hamid Khan of the 55th Coke's Rifles—Mir Dast's old regiment. A Pathan resident of Hoti Mardan in Peshawar, Hamid Khan described the crowds he encountered as "threatening" and "bent on creating a disturbance." The sepoys of the 55th Rifles had their orders not to fire on demonstrators for any reason, "otherwise, perhaps some greater trouble might have occurred." And yet many of the sepoys in his regiment looked forward to a chance to clash with demonstrators. "The men of the regiment were very keen to go to the bazaar to put the bazaaris in their place," he recalled, "and whenever volunteers were called for twice the number fell in." Hamid Khan would have liked it had the government deployed troops sooner. "If the troops had been called out on the first sign of trouble, there would have been no *hartal*: it was only the seeming weakness of the Government that gave the mob courage."[30] One of Hamid Khan's Jamadar's, Ghulam Nabi, was of the same opinion. He described the demonstrators as "very aggravating" to the soldiers. "To my mind the crowd acted very foolishly during the *hartal*. We were quite prepared to deal with any active trouble, and the people would have derived no benefit from an attack on us."[31] Jamadar Jan Muhammad of the 69th Punjabis was also stationed in Delhi. "If Gandhi had been arrested at once," he said, "I think it all would have been nipped in the bud." Jan Muhammad applauded the army's use of lethal force on March 30. "Government action when it did come was decisive, and I think a great deal of further trouble was prevented by the action which was taken in firing on the crowd." He was not alone in thinking this. "This seems to be the opinion of the majority of the people I have spoken to on the subject and certainly of Indian officers and sepoys."[32]

Soldiers and civilians also clashed in Ahmedabad. One Indian soldier deployed to the city on April 10 recalled, "[Demonstrators] told me that we [the sepoys] were not Kshatriyas and to lay down our arms and join them." Pelted by stones, he fired into the crowd. On April 12 the sepoys received orders to fire on any gathering of over 10 individuals and to shoot at anyone out on the streets after dark. Troops shoot demonstrators throughout the day and into the next. In total, soldiers fired 609 rounds. They killed 28 demonstrators and wounded 123 others. A commission later appointed by the Government of India to investigate the causes of the uprisings concluded that "the use of military force [in Ahmedabad] was unavoidable, and the rioters alone were responsible for the casualties which ensured." As for the troops, they "behaved with praiseworthy restraint in most trying circumstances." A similar scene was then unfolding in Bombay where on April 12 Subedar-Major Kanhayalal Bahadur of the 97th Infantry, who had recently returned to India from overseas deployment, ordered the sepoys under his command to shoot at demonstrators. "The attitude of [the] crowds was extremely hostile and large numbers of the men were carrying sticks and stones," he said. The subedar-major ordered the crowd to disperse. "They gave no attention to this and shouted '*Gandhi Mahatma Li jai*' and one [man] and his party shouted out they wanted white men's flesh, and stones were thrown hitting many sepoys." Kanhayalal Bahadur gave his men the order to fire. Three demonstrators were wounded. This drove the crowd back. Kanhayalal Bahadur was satisfied that he and the men under his command had performed their duty.[33]

Troops deployed to Lahore on April 10. Gandhi had been arrested the previous day trying to travel to Delhi against government orders, and military and civil authorities expected the worst. Students assembled and marched on the government telegraph office. Soldiers guarding the office fixed bayonets and advanced into the crowd. Meanwhile at the Lohari Gate some fifteen thousand to twenty thousand demonstrators gathered. Government officials conceded that they had lost the city to demonstrators for the time being. On April 12 some eight hundred more troops entered the city. The government did not regain control of the situation until April 18. Authorities also temporarily lost control in Kasur, a town of twenty-five thousand in the Lahore district. Demonstrators shut down the town and government administration from April 11 through April 13 until troops regained the streets. In the town of Viramgam, outside Ahmedabad, demonstrators stormed the police station and the train station. They ripped up rails and burned passenger cars. Troops arrived on the evening of April 12 and cleared the streets. On April 14, when Lieutenant Governor O'Dwyer discovered that no troops were available to deploy to Gujranwala, he sent airplanes instead. Pilots bombed and strafed demonstrators, killing eleven and wounding twenty-seven.

In Amritsar Indian soldiers and their commanders set up conditions for what can only be described as a massacre. Gandhi's March 30 and April 6 general strikes went off without any confrontation between authorities and demonstrators in the city. Shops closed, protestors took to the streets, and the economic life of a city of 150,000 came to complete standstill without incident. But on April 9, Lieutenant Governor O'Dwyer ordered the deportation of two prominent nationalists under the Defense of India Act. In response, Hindus and Muslims took to the streets. They attempted to seize post offices and the railway station. On April 10, angry but unarmed demonstrators marched again. Parties of British troops and Indian sowars opened fire on the crowds, killing at least ten people. Risaldar-Major Fazal Dad Khan was in Amritsar that day. In the early afternoon of April 10, Fazal Dad Khan and the sowars under his command heard that crowds had murdered Europeans with clubs. Periodic gunfire—its source unknown—rattled the men. They were out of harm's way, ordered to secure the city's horse market. But at 2 p.m. they watched a detachment of British soldiers hurry past on its way to the telegraph office. "Thereafter, the sound of a volley fire was heard." At sundown, accompanied by two other cavalry soldiers, Fazal Dad Khan went in search "of some civil or military British officer," with every intention of telling him "that in the horse-market there were a number of Indian officers and sowars of various cavalry regiments, and that if we were given horses and arms, we should do patrol and picket work wherever necessary, or we should be given guns and cartridges to enable us to work as foot soldiers." The risaldar-major and nineteen other sowars were given rifles and fifty cartridges apiece and posted along the ramparts of Gobindgarh Fort in the city center.[34]

That night Lieutenant Governor O'Dwyer spoke to representatives of the martial races of the Punjab, and he did not hesitate, in Gandhi's words, "to incite them against the people." In this frightening excerpt from that speech, O'Dwyer effectively gave soldiers any and all permission they might require to gun down crowds of demonstrators.

> You have seen within the last few weeks how a law passed to safeguard the lives and property against . . . outbursts of anarchy and revolution—a law that is only to be brought into operation if, unfortunately, those conditions should arise—has by the persistent falsehood and misrepresentation of a small but noisy class been made to appear as a deadly weapon aimed at the people, whom it is intended to protect in situations of great emergency. . . . You can gather something of the motives of those behind that agitation from what took place a few days ago at Multan, when the Rowlatt Bill agitation was made a pretext for offering an insult to gallant Punjabi Mohammedans, Sikhs and Gurkhas, that had returned from the front after fighting the battles of India, and these insulters had, as we know, no martial spirit themselves and no appreciation for the valor and loyalty of those who had been safeguarding their hearths and homes. Their object is to attack Government and insult those who are true to their salt. Loyal men must and will oppose their evil designs. . . . Your cooperation with Government in this and similar matters will be as valued and as much appreciated as your memorable war services. . . .

Into the Face of Bayonets

The situation is for the moment critical, and prompt action on your part and that of Government is required. Government will do its duty without hesitation, and will support you in doing yours. Government will enforce the law, and if that leads to bloodshed, the responsibility is with those who make others break the laws.[35]

Hundreds of soldiers deployed to Amritsar overnight. Brigadier General Reginald Dyer arrived on April 11 and took charge. General Dyer was a man steeped in the tradition of colonial warfare, learned in previous campaigns in Burma, Persia, and Baluchistan. He believed that spectacles of brute force were needed in situations like the one to which he deployed in Amritsar in order to overawe and terrify the enemy into submission.[36] In O'Dwyer he had a ready co-disciple. The mood was tense on April 11, but both sides kept their distance out of respect for the funeral procession for those killed by soldiers on April 10. Troops patrolled the streets on April 12. The city's inhabitants seethed. Some spat on the ground as soldiers passed. A crowd formed at the Sultanwind Gate. There were shouts of "Hindu-Mussalman *ki jai!*" as troops set to work dispersing demonstrators at bayonet point. On the morning of April 13 General Dyer issued a proclamation that any gatherings of four or more people "would be looked upon and treated as an unlawful assembly and dispersed by force of arms if necessary." At the same time, demonstrators issued their own counter-proclamation, calling people to a meeting that afternoon at the Jallianwala Bagh, an enclosed public square. When General Dyer learned late that afternoon about the meeting, he assembled a force of fifty sepoys armed with rifles and hurried to the square. There he met a crowd of twenty thousand, peaceably assembled, unarmed, listening to a speech. Dyer deployed his men, and without giving the crowd any warning to disperse, he ordered his men to fire.

The square erupted into pandemonium. People panicked and fled for the exits. But the square was choked with people, and the exits became bottlenecks. Seeing this, General Dyer directed his men to fire "where the crowd was thickest." According to the general's own testimony, he ordered his men to do this, "not because [people in the crowd] were not going fast [enough]," but because he had "made up his mind to punish them for having assembled."[37] Dyer was intent on producing a massacre. One witness recalled the horrible scene that unfolded. "I saw hundreds of persons killed on the spot. The worst part of the whole thing was that firing was directed towards the gates through which the people were running out." People fought and clawed to get through the crowd, desperate to stay alive. "Many got trampled under the feet of the rushing crowds and thus lost their lives. Blood was pouring in profusion. Even those who lay on the ground were shot."

The troops fired without interruption for ten minutes. "I fired and continued to fire until the crowd dispersed, and I consider this is the least amount of firing which would produce the necessary moral and widespread effect it was my duty to produce if I was to justify my action," Dyer explained later. "If more troops had been at hand the casualties would have been greater in proportion. *It was no longer a question of merely dispersing the crowd*, but one of producing a sufficient moral effect from a military point of view not only on those who were present, but more especially throughout the Punjab. There could be no question of undue severity." In total, the Indian soldiers under Dyer's command fired 1,650 rounds. They killed 379 people, of whom 87 were villagers who had come into Amritsar from neighboring districts and could not possibly have heard the general's morning's proclamation. More than 1,000 people littered the ground wounded. When Dyer at last gave the order to cease fire, he withdrew, leaving those he had shot to fend for themselves. "The hospitals were open and the medical officers were there," he said later. "The wounded only had to apply for help. But they did not do this because they themselves would be in custody for being in the assembly."[38]

Lala Girdhari Lal, who witnessed the massacre, rushed to the square, when at last the troops withdrew, to see what he might do to help. "There were heaps [of bodies] at different places," he remembered. "The dead bodies of grown-up people and young boys also." People had had their heads shot off. Others lay on the ground, their arms or legs shattered. Some of the wounded scrambled to their feet and fled the square, only to collapse dead in the streets.[39] One could be forgiven for comparing the wreckage of the square to that of a battlefield. Indeed, the very next day General Dyer spoke before an assembly of Amritsar residents, municipal commissioners, magistrates, and merchants. "You people know well that I am a sepoy and soldier," he said. "Do you want war or peace? If you wish for war the Government is prepared for it," he threatened. "If you want peace, then obey my orders and open all your shops; else, I will shoot. For me the battlefield of France or Amritsar is the same."[40] It is possible that some of the Indian soldiers deployed to such cities as Delhi, Ahmedabad, and Amritsar in March and April 1919 felt similarly. For professional soldiers like Jan Muhammad, for example, shooting at demonstrators was what came with the job. "Their faith is pinned to the British government, which had provided an outlet for profitable employment," commented one British civil servant, referring to the Hindu Dogras of Punjab's eastern Kangra Hill District. "To put the matter on the lowest plane, a class in which practically every homestead had some connection with the military and government service . . . is fully aware of which side their bread is buttered."[41] Santanu Das writes, "We cannot forget the painful fact that the soldiers who obeyed the orders of General Dyer and gunned down the unarmed mob in Jallianwala Bagh on [April 13, 1919] were not British officers but Gurkha, Sikh and Pathan brothers-in-arms of our First World War soldiers."[42]

Gandhi, for his part, suspended the civil disobedience campaign on April 18. Some of his own supporters, alarmed at the violence experienced since the campaign began, urged that he call a temporary halt to the campaign. In the months that followed the disturbances, military and government authorities working in tandem carried out a ruthless crackdown on dissent. Newspapers were subjected to the strictest censorship. The *Partap*, which had been especially critical of the government in early April, was ordered to submit all of its articles to the government censors before going to press. It and a number of other Lahore newspapers ordered to submit the whole of their material to censorship suspended publication. The editors of the *Tribune* and *Partap* were tried before a Martial Law Commission; the former was sentenced to two years and the latter to a year and a half of imprisonment.[43] A number of newspapers printed outside the Punjab were banned from circulation in the province. Soldiers patrolled the streets in cities and towns across the Punjab. Military tribunals tried 2,537 people for actions connected to the disturbances, of whom 1,804 received convictions resulting in prison sentences. Many cases resulted in whippings.[44] Military authorities flogged Indians for seemingly minor infractions, such as breaking curfew.

There was a vicious racial animus at work in all of this. The Indian Army deployed to Indian cities to reimpose white supremacy. Military authorities ordered Indians to be tied to posts and whipped for, among other things, failure to salaam a British officer, for disrespecting a white man or white woman, for refusing to sell milk to a white man. In Gujranwala military authorities issued the salaaming order in late April. All Indian inhabitants of the district were required to salute or "salaam" any white man they passed on the street. In Amritsar General Dyer imposed a humiliating and cruel "crawling order." Policy stipulated than any Indian who wished to travel along a 150-yard stretch of road—past the site where a white woman had been attacked during the Amritsar uprising—could only do so under sepoy escort, while crawling, in Gandhi's words, "exactly like reptiles." Any attempt to lift the knees or belly off the road brought swift retribution—a crack from a rifle butt on the back or on the ribs. Cloth merchant Lala Megha Mal recalled how Indian sepoys ordered him to crawl the length of the street one evening as he attempted to return home from work. Rather than submit, the man turned and ran, sneaking home later under the cover of darkness. Another merchant, Jain Sabha Mandir, was not so lucky. He was made to crawl, and soldiers kicked him sharply with their boots and beat his arms and torso with the butt end of their rifles. Anyone who had to travel this road had no choice but to submit to this kind of abuse, the able-bodied as well as the sick, the elderly, and the blind. Why did General Dyer inflict such wanton violence upon Indian bodies? "I felt women have been beaten," he said. "We look upon women as sacred." So claimed the man whose soldiers gunned down Indian women at Jallianwala Bagh. Women were not sacred to General Dyer. White supremacy was sacred to General Dyer. As in 1915, when a racial panic led to the removal of white nurses from the Indian hospitals in Brighton, England, so too did General Dyer act to reimpose white supremacy in Amritsar. For eight days his "crawling order" was in effect; sepoy boots and rifles were the cudgel of racism.[45]

Parting Ways

In the wake of the events of March and April 1919, the Government of India appointed a committee to investigate the "disorders" and uncover what happened. Assembled in Delhi in late October 1919, the Hunter Commission began taking testimony from witnesses of the events in Delhi, Bombay, and the Punjab. The Indian National Congress cross-examined witnesses and called witnesses of their own, but they protested that the Government of India was unwilling to collect testimony from those imprisoned during the disturbances. In 1920 the Hunter Commission published its findings. In addition to outlining the numerous causes of the widespread unrest, the commission considered whether the army was justified in opening fire on demonstrators. Troops in Delhi opened fire on demonstrators on March 30 and again on April 17. The Hunter Commission ruled that the army's decision to fire on what it considered "mobs" was justified. "On all the occasions to which we have referred recourse was only had to firing after the patience of those entrusted with the duty of maintaining public peace and order had been sorely tried and all reasonable efforts had been made to induce the crowd to disperse peacefully," the commission report concluded. "In no case was firing continued longer than was necessary to achieve the legitimate object of restoring order and preventing a disastrous outbreak of violence."[46] Troops opened fire on demonstrators in Ahmedabad on April 11. "We are of the opinion that the measures taken by the authorities to deal with the disturbances were appropriate," the commissioners wrote in their report. "The use of military force was unavoidable, and the rioters alone were responsible for the casualties which ensued."[47] The troops, the commission found, "behaved with praiseworthy restraint in most trying circumstances." Soldiers opened fire in Amritsar in a few instances on April 10. Of one incident, the commission concluded, "In our opinion this resort to firing was completely justified as absolutely necessary in the circumstances and in no way exceeding the occasion."[48] Of another, it said, "We think that the order to fire was rightly given."[49] Even the decision to use airplanes to drop bombs on demonstrators in Gujranwala was ruled justified and reasonable.

Every decision to gun down demonstrators was deemed justified except that of General Dyer at the Jallianwala Bagh on April 13. His actions, the commissioned ruled, were "open to criticism in two respects. (First) that he started firing without giving the people who had assembled a chance to disperse, and (second) that he continued firing for a substantial period of time after the crowd had commenced to disperse." Note the careful wording. Firing into a crowd was not itself a problem. Indeed, the commission stipulated, had Dyer first issued a command to the crowd to disperse, and the crowd then disregarded his directive, then he would "have been justified in firing on the crowd, to compel it to disperse." As to the general's decision to fire for as long as he did, the commission ruled only that he had "committed a grave error" in judgment. "If necessary a crowd that has assembled contrary to a proclamation issued to prevent or terminate disorder may have to be fired upon; but continued firing upon that crowd cannot be justified because of the effect such firing may have upon people in other places," the commissioners ruled. "The employment of excessive measures is as likely as not to produce the opposite result to that desired." And finally, to the matter of Dyer's decision to make no provision for the wounded his actions had produced, the commission deflected criticism. "It has to be remembered . . . that [Dyer] was acting with a very small force." It never entered the general's head, moreover, that the hospitals were woefully unequipped to deal with such an emergency. The commission found, "It has not been proved to us that any wounded people were in fact exposed to unnecessary suffering from want of medical treatment."[50]

Condemnation of the Hunter Commission's findings by the Indian National Congress was swift and unequivocal. The INC rejected the Hunter Commission's report as "perverse and tainted with racial bias." Its members wanted General Dyer and Lieutenant Governor O'Dwyer brought up on charges and tried. Gandhi wrote up his own findings on the Punjab disturbances. In 1920 the INC adopted his conclusions. When crowds turned violent, Gandhi said, it was because their members had been killed and wounded by Indian troops. "The sight of the wounded persons and dead bodies inflamed the citizens who saw them," he wrote of things in Amritsar on April 10.[51] "Our study of the evidence ... led before Lord Hunter's Committee and the evidence collected by us, leads to the conclusion that there was no warrant for the firing. The authorities omitted all the intermediate stages that are usually resorted to in all civilized countries. There was no parleying, no humoring, and no use of milder force. Immediately the crowd became insistent, the order to fire was given." Gandhi wrote, "In this country, it has become too much the custom with the executive and the military never to run any risk, or, to put it in another way, to count Indian life very cheap."[52] Gandhi lay blame at the feet of Lieutenant Governor Michael O'Dwyer. "No other Head of Government in India laughed at the people on the 7th of April," Gandhi wrote. It was O'Dwyer's desire to provide "a day of reckoning." He created the conditions for a massacre, Gandhi said, by inciting the "martial races of the Punjab ... against the people." O'Dwyer "distorted facts, as for instance regarding the conduct of the people of Multan against the soldiers. We have investigated the incident and we have found that no insult was offered to the soldiers who passed through Multan."[53]

Delhi, Amritsar, and the tumultuous postwar years marked a decisive turning point in India's nationalist movement. Before the war the INC never openly challenged the legitimacy of the British Empire or its rule over India. Nationalists such as Gokhale wanted to moderate the terms of British rule, to be sure. They wanted self-government along the lines of that enjoyed by settlers in the White Dominions. They wanted racial equality for Indians. But the moderates and the INC never openly advocated independence. The events of March and April 1919 cemented a new direction for Gandhi and for the INC. During the war Gandhi extolled Indians to do what they could for the war effort. He gave speeches in India encouraging recruitment. After the events of the immediate postwar years, he wrote in *Young India* that it was "the duty of every Indian soldier . . . to sever his connection with the Government." The government was responsible for India's "economic, moral and political degradation." It had used its Indian soldiers to repress "national aspirations."[54] He preached civil disobedience, whatever the cost. "We must speak the Truth under a shower of bullets," he wrote in 1922. "We must band together in the face of bayonets."[55] By that time his readers had gained by way of painful experience the truth—those men firing the bullets, those men wielding the bayonets—those men were fellow Indians. In 1920 the INC changed its posture. That year the INC adopted Gandhi's policy of noncooperation, setting out to undermine British rule through campaigns of resistance.[56] In 1929 the INC pledged that it sought to eliminate British rule. The immediate postwar months in India marked the beginning of the end of the British Raj.

Conclusion

> Whence came [the Indian soldiers'] spirit of endurance and high endeavor? It came from the twin sources of an inborn and simple loyalty, of an instructed and very perfect discipline. Like the Roman legionary, they were faithful unto death. They had accepted a duty. They discharged it. More cannot be said: more need not be said.
>
> —Lord Birkenhead, secretary of state for India, speech delivered at the unveiling of the Indian Memorial at Neuve Chapelle, 1927

Among the warring powers in 1914–18, none drew more extensively on overseas colonial resources than Great Britain, and no overseas possession contributed more to Britain's imperial war effort than India. Indians provided money, materiel, and manpower. Some £100 million flowed directly from Indian coffers to the war in 1914. India spent another £20 to £30 million every year thereafter. Indian factories manufactured bullets, shells, saddles, and tents. Indian solders ate food produced in and exported from India, such as rice, dhal, and ghee. India exported to England wheat, rice, tea, leather, hides, oil seeds, raw jute, saltpeter, manganese, ore, and wolfram. Indian jute manufactured into sandbags in Dundee, Scotland, stopped bullets in Belgium and France. In terms of manpower, the Indian Army numbered some 160,000 Indian soldiers when the war began. By the close of 1919, the Indian Army recruited another 877,068 combatants and 563,369 noncombatants—the single greatest contribution made by any of Britain's colonies and dominions. More than one million Indian soldiers deployed overseas, to fronts in France and Belgium, to Egypt and East Africa, to Egypt, Palestine, and Mesopotamia. More than 89,000 Indians fought in France. Another 34,000 fought in

Conclusion

East Africa; 320,000 fought in Mesopotamia; more than 110,000 in Egypt and Palestine. This contribution in manpower spurred British wartime imperial ambitions in the Middle East all while providing the wartime British press ample fodder to feed the imperial imagination of Home audiences. But headlines that obscured the empire's longstanding commitment to racial inequality and exclusion did not lessen the commitment of British policymakers or battlefield commanders to defending white supremacy. And British racism cost thousands of Indian soldiers their lives during World War I, even as those men fought successfully on behalf of the British Empire. That many Indian soldiers remained nonetheless willing to inflict racist violence against Indian civilians in the war's immediate aftermath placed Indian national aspirations at loggerheads with British colonial rule. World War I was therefore a turning point in the history of British colonial rule in India, one in which the very racism upon which colonial rule was predicated would ultimately facilitate its undoing.

The Long Road Home

There were some soldiers—few in number, to be sure—who had flirted with switching their allegiance from the Indian Army to its king's enemies. These men were already the topic of discussion at the highest level before the close of the first year of the war when the Home Government began drafting plans for the eventual repatriation of Indian prisoners of war at the war's end. Vague reports reached the Home Government and Government of India that Indian soldiers held at Zossen had received "special treatment" at German hands. A May 7, 1915, telegram from the Government of India to the Foreign Office read that a German newspaper had "invited some Indians in Europe to go to Germany where they will be well paid for talking to captured Indian soldiers." Those soldiers deemed "most amenable to the talk" would be the first exchanged, "if and when exchange of prisoners with England begins." The Germans hoped these men would then "do their best to persuade other soldiers to revolt against the British." The Government of India warned the Foreign Office, "In the event of

Conclusion

exchange becoming [a] practical question or of Indian prisoners being permitted to escape, mental attitude of such Indians will require consideration."[1]

British concern for the stability of India—and for the "mental attitude" of Indian prisoners of war—intensified as the war dragged on. In mid-1915 a German expedition led by Lieutenant Oskar Ritter von Niedermayer reached Kabul, Afghanistan, where it tried to convince the emir to abandon neutrality and invade northwest India.[2] A handful of Indian sepoys—soldiers belonging to the 58th Rifles who deserted from their posts on the Western Front in March of that year—accompanied the team. The British, alerted to the expedition and its intentions, bought the emir's continued neutrality by increasing his annual stipend by £25,000. In mid-1917 the British intercepted another party made up of Germans, Austrians, Turks, and eleven Afghan sepoys (soldiers from the 58th Rifles and 20th Pathans) in a surprise raid in Shiraz, Persia.[3] Secretary of State for India Austen Chamberlain estimated there were still some seven hundred Indian soldiers interned in German prison camps. These men, he worried, had been exposed to "strongly hostile influences" and might contribute to growing unrest in India after the war. "There would seem to be a risk that some of these men when they return to their homes may become the willing tools of extremist and anarchist factions in India," he wrote.[4]

Intelligence smuggled out of the prisoner-of-war camps to British authorities corroborated the secretary's concerns. Subedar-Major Mala Khan spent most of the war in captivity after his capture on the Western Front in late 1914. During his time as an internee at Zossen in 1916, he compiled a list of thirty-five Indian sepoys from the 129th Baluchis, the 127th Baluchis, and the 58th Rifles who had "gone over to the enemy." He also created a list of Indian soldiers who were actively collaborating with the Germans in the camps, trying to spread sedition within the Indian ranks. He smuggled his lists out of the camp to the British, hiding them in the clothes of a sick Indian the German authorities had agreed to repatriate to England.[5] Other sepoys, sick from an outbreak of tuberculosis and repatriated to England prior to the end of the war, divulged

Conclusion

additional names from the comfort of their hospital beds. Cross-referencing these testimonies with the lists provided by Mala Khan, by October 1918 the British finalized a master list of ninety-two Indian prisoners of war who they believed had deserted to the enemy or given information or assistance to the enemy after their capture in France.[6] The India Office took this information and formulated an elaborate plan for handling the repatriation of Indian prisoners of war at the end of hostilities. Soldiers released on the Western Front would congregate at Marseilles. Those released by way of ports on the North Sea through neutral Holland passed first through London before rejoining their compatriots in southern France. At both sites the British separated the soldiers into four categories, based on the information they had gleaned earlier: (a) genuine prisoners of war; (b) declared deserters to the enemy; (c) those among (a) who were known to have taken up arms against the British or to have accepted service with the enemy; and (d) those among (a) who were believed to have been armed and equipped by propaganda and required watching in India. Protocol stipulated for (a) and (d), repatriation to India, where on arrival special arrangements would be made for (d); for (b), returned to unit for trial or to India in custody to await trial on return of unit from overseas or to be dispatched to a unit overseas if more convenient and evidence unobtainable in India; and (c) returned to India in custody pending collection of evidence against them.[7]

Prior to the November 1918 armistice, the Indian Soldiers' Fund worked to ensure the regular shipment of care parcels to former Indian prisoners of war as they slowly trickled across Western Europe to hospitals in London. "It is a matter of real importance that Indian prisoners of war should not return to their own country with any ground for regarding themselves as neglected by this Department."[8] In October 1918, forty-five Indian prisoners of war arrived in England, all of them sick with tuberculosis. "These men have been in captivity for several years, and from a political point of view it seems to us that proper arrangements should be made to meet them and look after them when they come to England," the Indian Soldiers' Fund urged the India Office. "It may make a

Conclusion

very bad impression in India when these men get back if they do not carry away with them a good impression of the way in which they have been treated in England, and we are sure that the India Office would not wish this."[9]

But failure on the part of the British to implement efficiently their own repatriation policy did leave some soldiers with lingering feelings that they had been mistreated by their imperial hosts after the war. Havildar Abdul Aziz Khan, an Afghan from Peshawar, enlisted in the Indian Army at the outbreak of the war, serving on the Western Front with the 9th Hodson's Horse. Captured by the Germans sometime in 1914 or early 1915, he spent the remainder of the war interned in Germany. At the end of the conflict he was repatriated to London, where he lived in a YMCA with a number of former Indian prisoners of war until 1919, when he finally received his ticket home to India. As far as the soldier was concerned, the war was over for him. But upon arriving in Bombay, Khan was arrested by the local authorities, suspected of having fed information to the Germans during the war. Khan wrote to a friend in England, "On 3rd May I landed in Bombay. Immediately I and another man, who also has come with me from England and is my countryman were put under arrest. I tried to know the reason of the sudden calamity and failed. Even till today nothing can I know but what I have gathered is that the government suspect me, why and how rests with the government."[10] Decisions concerning the repatriation of Indian prisoners of war were made on the spot. In the case of Havildar Khan, paranoia and circumstances on the ground in postwar India shaped policy more than any concrete evidence of Khan's wartime activities. A confidential memo from the Government of India to the India Office suggests that the British bungled the implementation of their own recommendations. It read: "The Government of India had been warned in regard to the possibility that the Germans had taken steps to tutor Indian prisoners of war for propaganda purposes" and that "they could not afford to run the risk of setting suspects at liberty, particularly at a time of internal disturbance and with trouble on the frontier of India." The chief commissioner and

Conclusion

agent to the governor general of the North-West Province, within whose jurisdiction Abdul Aziz Khan's home was situated, "was unwilling to allow men suspected of contamination to return to the North-West Frontier Province at [this] juncture."[11]

Khan's frustrations with the authorities in India appear warranted. His letter to an English friend prompted this letter, addressed by Mary Cruikshank to the War Office in August 1919:

> I beg to invite your attention to the enclosed true copy of a letter just received by a friend of mine from an Indian non-commissioned officer of the 9th Hodson's Horse. This man, Abdul Aziz Khan, who is of good family (his brother being Khan of Zaida near Peshawar) is an Afghan. He enlisted in the Indian Army for the war, & was for some time a prisoner of war in Germany. He was released & came to England in December or January of the last winter, & remained in London staying at a Y.M.C.A. hostel with other released Indian soldiers until April 1st when he left England with two other Indian soldiers & proceeded overland to Taranto, whence he sailed for India. During his stay in England, he was not, to my knowledge, under any suspicion, he appeared free to go anywhere he wished in London. He also paid a short visit to my friend in Leicestershire. Some weeks ago I saw a letter from him dated about June 25th in which he said he had been arrested on arrival at Bombay: the officer who arrested him refused to give any reason.[12]

Not long after Mrs. Cruikshank wrote to the War Office, Indian authorities released the havildar. "It has now been decided that it would not be in the interests of the service to retain Dafadar Abdul Aziz Khan and he has accordingly been discharged," noted a secret memo from the Government of India.[13]

Some of those Indian soldiers who collaborated with the Germans freely remained in Germany after the war. Sepoy Guli Jan deserted to the German trenches in March 1915 and served with Oppenheim's Indian Battalion in Constantinople before returning to Zossen toward the end of the war. In December 1918 he and nine other Indian prisoners of war secured funding from German agents formerly employed by Oppenheim's Intelligence Office and

Conclusion

secured housing and work in Berlin.¹⁴ In June 1920 two of his comrades, Mir Baz Khan and Mir Zamir, walked into the offices of the British Passport Control Officer in Berlin, requesting a written pardon from the British government and permission to return home to South Asia. Identifying themselves as Afghan Afridis of Khyber, they explained that they had deployed to the Western Front in 1914 as part of the Indian Corps. "We were engaged for about 2 years in the West Front," they said, and "fought faithfully for our King Emperor against the enemy." Redeployed to the Middle East in 1916, the men deserted to the Turkish lines. "It was impossible according to our religion to fight against our religion. Our religion forbids us to fight against a Muslim," they claimed, stipulating that at no point had they taken up arms against the British. "We have done nothing against our Government," they said. Presumably the Turks handed the men off to the Germans who brought the sepoys to Zossen. The sepoys pleaded their case, "During this long time we remained neutral and did not serve the British enemy." Now they were homeless, jobless, and hungry. "We hope you would be kindly enough to send for our Amnesty and feed us till we leave for our country. For this act of kindness we should pray for your long life and prosperity."¹⁵ The passport officer recommended that authorities grant the soldiers' request. "It is thought that under proper treatment they might be of use to Indian Intelligence, but in the hands of unscrupulous people in Berlin they might become a possible danger to the Empire."¹⁶ But the India Office did not agree. An internal memo noted, "The suggestion that the men who deserted to the enemy in the war should be pardoned, because of 'the possible danger to the Empire' involved in their stay in Germany, seems thoroughly unsound from the point of view of the effect produced on the men who did not desert."¹⁷

For all we know, Mir Baz Khan and Mir Zamir remained in Berlin. Other sepoys took matters into their own hands. Navigating the politically volatile Eurasian landscape, a few managed to return home again. Guli Jan returned to Afghanistan safely in 1921 by way of civil war–torn Russia and central Asia. That he did so with a German wife and their infant in tow makes his story all the more

Conclusion

exceptional. The Indian soldier vanishes almost entirely from the British archives after March 1915 when he deserted to the German trenches. In October 1923 his wife walked into the British Legation in Kabul and asked for permission to travel through India on her way to Europe by ship. (The Government of India refused her request.) She and Guli Jan met shortly after the war and lived together in Danzig until November 1920. They made their way to Afghanistan by way of Riga, Moscow, Tashkent, Kushk, Herat, and Kandahar. They reached Kabul on foot in March 1921.[18]

Remembering the Fallen

Thousands of the Indian soldiers deployed overseas during World War I never returned home. Official figures for the Indian Army count 53,486 dead and 64,350 wounded. More than 7,500 Indian soldiers died during their deployment in France. More than 16,000 were wounded. Slightly less than 3,000 soldiers died in East Africa, where another 2,000 were wounded. In Mesopotamia, more than 29,000 Indian soldiers died in the performance of their duty, and more than 32,000 were wounded. More than 4,000 soldiers died in Egypt and Palestine. Operations there claimed another 6,400 wounded. The remains of Indian soldiers who fought in World War I are therefore scattered across swaths of the earth's land surfaces in Europe, Asia, and Africa. Men died fighting for control of villages and towns up and down the Western Front. They died fighting just outside Ctesiphon in Iraq. The burial places of 3,293 Indian soldiers killed in France and Belgium are marked by headstones in 141 cemeteries. Walter Lawrence collaborated with a local maulvi in England during the war and arranged for Muslim burial near a mosque in Woking. In France the remains of sepoys who died of their wounds at the Jesuit College in Boulognue were interred at an Indian cemetery. "Cremation is most thorough," Lawrence observed in his final report to Kitchener in 1916, "and His Highness, the Raja of Ratlam, expressed his warmest thanks for the way in which the Hindus were cremated."[19] At the Zelobes Indian Cemetery at Lacouture, there are 108 graves of soldiers who fell between 1914 and 1915. La Chapellette Indian

Table 10. Total combatant Indians killed and wounded during the war

Theater	Dead from all causes		Wounded	
	Officers	Other ranks	Officers	Other ranks
France	176	5,316	404	15,893
East Africa	67	2,405	59	1,927
Mesopotamia	364	17,567	828	31,330
Egypt	74	3,713	135	6,286
Gallipoli	33	1,591	72	3,578
Aden	7	500	16	548

Source: Statistics of the Military Effort of the British Empire, 778.

Table 11. Summary of all Indian casualties

Died from all causes	53,486
Wounded	64,350
Missing	2,937

Note: The casualties include those deployed to war operations in France, East Africa, Mesopotamia, Egypt, Gallipoli, and Aden, as well as those deployed to Dunsterforce, Persia, Maskat, and the Indian frontier.

Source: Statistics of the Military Effort of the British Empire, 778.

Cemetery in Peronne contains the graves of 309 Indian cavalrymen and laborers who fell in 1917 and 1918. The names of 421 fallen Indian soldiers appear on the Menin Gate Memorial to the Missing at Ypres, to recall the appearance of the Lahore Division in Belgium in October 1914. The names of 4,842 Indian soldiers can be found on the Indian Memorial at Neuve Chapelle.[20] At a quiet little military cemetery in Zehrensdorf, thirty miles south of Berlin, lie the remains of 206 Indians who died while interned at the nearby Crescent Moon Camp.[21] These headstones and memorials in England, France, and Germany are reminders of the globality of World War I, that the conflict was a war of empire, one in which many thousands of imperial subjects paid the ultimate price.

Conclusion

After more than four years of slaughter, many people wondered how the world might possibly remember the rolls of dead, a fact not lost on scholars of World War I.[22] In March 1916 Walter Lawrence wrote to Lord Kitchener, "On historical, as well as on political grounds, it seems most desirable to erect worthy memorials to the Indians who fell so far from their homes."[23] When the Imperial War Graves Commission received its Royal Charter on May 21, 1917, it's vice-chairman, Fabian Ware, set to work preserving the graves of the dead not only for bereaved friends and relatives, but "to keep alive the ideals for . . . which they have laid down their lives . . . and to promote a feeling of common citizenship and of loyalty and devotion to Us [the monarch] and to the Empire of which they are subjects."[24] But the War Graves Commission never upheld its own stated principles. In East Africa the commission conserved the graves of white soldiers. Graves containing the remains of black Africans and Indians were permitted to deteriorate. The Indian memorial at Neuve Chapelle contains the names of close to five thousand Indian soldiers. In Basra, where the deaths of IEFD's soldiers are commemorated on the Memorial to the Missing of the Mesopotamia Expeditionary Force, unveiled in 1929, only the names of British and Indian officers appear. The Indian sepoys remain unnamed. The War Graves Commission did not anticipate Indian visitors in Mesopotamia. They did anticipate Indians and their families making the pilgrimage to France. So the Indian lives lost in France mattered; the Indian lives lost in the Middle East mattered less. But the lives of white British officers—be those the lives of men killed in France or the Middle East—those lives mattered.[25] So in this way monuments to the fallen were places where audiences could see and experience the ideologies and priorities of the British Empire. That this was the purpose for which the Indian memorial at Neuve Chapelle was built was evident at its unveiling ceremony in October 1927, when Indian soldiers returned to the Western Front.

Designed by Herbert Baker, the massive Indian Memorial at Neuve Chapelle was built as a sanctuary. Two carved tigers stand watch on either side of a magnificent pillar over a temple of the

Conclusion

dead, inscribed with texts in English, Urdu, Hindi, and Gurmukhi. A circular wall carved with Indian symbols encloses the space. "It was at Neuve Chapelle that [India's] troops made their first appearance in action on the Western Front in the third month of the war, when they distinguished themselves by taking the village, and a few months later, on March 10, 1915, when the position was again captured," the *Times* reminded its readers on the morning of the ceremony.

> In this engagement, the three days' battle of Neuve Chapelle, they fought with the greatest gallantry, and their losses, particularly in the successful assault on the Bois de Biez, were exceptionally heavy. Throughout the campaigns on this front the Indian troops were always heavily handicapped for a great part of the year in comparison with the rest of the King's Forces. Not only were the fighting conditions entirely different from the style of warfare to which they were accustomed, but for the majority of them the constant exposure to the rains and mud and bitter cold of the winter months in Western Europe was necessarily a far more trying experience than for their follow soldiers of British blood.[26]

The Earl of Birkenhead, secretary of state for India, orchestrated the unveiling and dedication ceremony. The day's events opened with a formal procession. The small contingent of Indian soldiers—about fifty, audiences read, "representing the various units engaged," Sikhs, Dogras, Garhwalis—stood at attention around the circular wall's inner periphery, surrounding the small crowd and platform from which each speaker took his turn. The Indian soldiers were there as window dressing. Smartly dressed and there for all to admire, for the cameras to capture, the men remained silent while others spoke to the assembled crowd on their behalf. No one thought to record the thoughts or opinions of the empire's soldiers on this occasion, one ostensibly dedicated to the memory of their fallen comrades. The presence of Indian soldiers was itself a reminder to British audiences that the empire owed "a great debt ... to our Eastern Colony." The *Evening Telegraph* reported, "No sooner was news of the outbreak of hostil-

Conclusion

ities flashed to India than detachments of stately Sikhs and of agile Gurkhas rallied to the Standard and pulled more than their weight in France."[27]

Lieutenant-General Sir Charles Anderson of the Indian Army offered the day's first remarks, followed by the Maharaja of Kapurthala, and then Marshal Foch, who, upon addressing the crowd, turned to the Indian soldiers and told them (in French) that here, at Neuve Chapelle in 1915, their Indian comrades "showed us the way, they made the first steps towards the final victory." M. Leon Perrier, French minister of colonies took the stand next, followed at last by Lord Birkenhead, who, in grandiloquent fashion, with all the self-serving rhetoric one should expect, rehashed and reemphasized for the small but nonetheless distinguished audience assembled a version of events British audiences had been telling themselves since sepoys first set foot on the shores of Europe in 1914. "In three respects," he stated, "while all who fought suffered greatly and wrought nobly, the endurance of the Indians was specially to be remarked." First, he said, the Indian soldiers fought thousands of miles from their homes, "in strange and unfamiliar surroundings." Second, sepoys and sowars "fought in a climate to which their bodies were not [acclimated]." Birkenhead said that he could still see the soldiers in his mind's eye, "shivering in those early and primitive trenches." Third, he offered, "these men who have died fought in a quarrel of which their understanding was less perfect than was that of those by whose side they contended." To what was owed the Indian soldiers' "spirit of endurance and of high endeavor?" Birkenhead asked. He answered, "It came from the twin sources of an inborn and simple loyalty; of an instructed and very perfect discipline. Like the Roman legionary, they were faithful unto death. They had accepted a duty. They discharged it. More cannot be said: more need not be said."[28] Buglers sounded the "Last Post" followed by a one minute of silence. Birkenhead placed wreathes at the foot of the pillar. After the ceremony the Indian soldiers traveled to England, where they were received by King George at Buckingham Palace. In November they left Europe, just as they had twelve years earlier.

Conclusion

Much more recently, British prime minister David Cameron reflected at length on the efforts his government was then undertaking to commemorate the war, in a speech delivered at the Imperial War Museum in London on the eve of the World War I centennial. "Why should we make such a priority of commemorations when money is tight and there is no one left from the generation that fought in the Great War?" he asked. For the prime minister, "the sheer scale of the sacrifice" of the 1914 generation was but one reason why he wanted "to make sure we really do this properly as a country." When the soldiers set out in 1914, they had no idea what awaited them on the battlefield. "For many, going off to war was a rite of passage." Many were excited, even, and confident that "they would eat better than they had when they were down the mines or in the textile mills." The horrors people encountered soon enough dashed all that. "Four months later, one million had died in the heavy artillery battles that actually came before the digging of the trenches," the prime minister said. Four years later, the death toll exceeded 16 million, nearly 1 million of them Britons. "To us, today, it seems so inexplicable that countries which had many things binding them together could indulge in such a never-ending slaughter, but they did," Cameron reflected. The war also claimed 70,000 Indians, Cameron said, alongside 60,000 Canadians, 60,000 Australians, 18,000 New Zealanders, and 27,000 Irish. "This was the extraordinary sacrifice of a generation," he posited, adding, "It was a sacrifice they made for us, and it is right that we should remember them."[29]

Though it is right that we should remember the past, let us strive to remember it for its complexity and its less-than-savory details.[30] Britain's was an imperial war effort, as the prime minister correctly reminds us. But Cameron's assertion that seventy thousand Indians died somehow for the sake of those standing in the prime minister's 2012 London audience is of course absurd. The prime minister's comment also represents a frightening echo of the kind of propaganda one might have read over and over again in wartime British newspapers. When in our effort to remember the past we begin regurgitating its propaganda, we are no longer commemorat-

Conclusion

ing history. Rather, we are propagating myth. And in this instance the prime minister's comment comes very close to propagating nostalgia for a particular vision of Britain's lost empire—not the empire as it was, one in which racism and white supremacy ran roughshod over black and brown bodies; but the empire as some of its self-satisfied cheerleaders and self-serving acolytes liked to imagine it, an empire whose colonial subjects were "determined to help win their Emperor's battles or die," as the *Times* gushed on October 2, 1914. And if indeed the prime minister offered British audiences anything in the way of that brand of empire nostalgia, we find ourselves too in a moment of empire amnesia, as Brexiters peddle in gross racial stereotypes and xenophobia, seeking among other things to write the colonial presence out of British history in favor of chest-thumping and jingoism. Although none of the Indian veterans of World War I remain alive today a century later, we need not let those peddling alternatively in nostalgia or amnesia have the last word. The historical record abounds with the voices of those who made the war. Those voices cry out to us, sometimes from unexpected places. They have lessons to teach. It is on us to listen.

NOTES

Introduction

1. Scott, *Weapons of the Weak*, xv.
2. "The Rally of the Empire," *Times*, September 10, 1914.
3. Schauwecker, *Aufbruch der Nation*, 371.
4. Jackson, *British Empire*.
5. Another twenty thousand people served in the Imperial Service Corps. See *Statistics of the Military Effort*, 777.
6. Morton-Jack, *Indian Army*, 152.
7. Neiberg, *Fighting the Great War*, 141.
8. Morton-Jack, *Indian Army*, 168–70.
9. Townshend, *Desert Hell*, 259.
10. Showalter, "Indianization," 145.
11. Jarboe, *War News in India*, 173.
12. *Statistics of the Military Effort*, 777.
13. *Statistics of the Military Effort*, 777. There is some discrepancy within the book. See also 756.
14. Kant, *India and the First World War*, 234–35.
15. Ramnath, *Haj to Utopia*; Streets-Salter, *World War One*.
16. Kolsky, *Colonial Justice in British India*.
17. Hughes, "German Mission to Afghanistan," 447–76.
18. Wagner, *Amritsar 1919*, chap. 12.
19. "A United Empire," *Times*, August 17, 1914.
20. *Young India*, October 6, 1921.
21. Manela, *Wilsonian Moment*, 175.
22. Das, "Sepoys, Sahibs, and Babus," 73.
23. See, for example, Government of India, *India's Contributions*; Moberley, *Campaign in Mesopotamia*.
24. See Alexander, *On Two Fronts*; Merewether and Smith, *Indian Corps in France*; Willcocks, *With the Indians in France*; Drake-Brockman, *With the Royal Garhwal Rifles*; Townshend, *My Campaign in Mesopotamia*; Gilbert, *Romance of the Last Crusade*.
25. Willcocks, *With the Indians in France*, xviii.
26. Chhina, qtd. in Jeffreys, foreword to *Indian Army*, xi.
27. See Das et al., "Global Perspectives on World War I."
28. Ellinwood and Pradhan, *India and World War I*.
29. Greenhut, "Imperial Reserve," 54–73; Greenhut, "Race, Sex, and War," 71–74; Greenhut, "Sahib and Sepoy," 71–74.
30. Farwell, *Gurkhas*; Farwell, *Armies of the Raj*.

Notes to Pages 12–31

31. Corrigan, *Sepoys in the Trenches*; McLain, "Indian Corps"; Morton-Jack, "Indian Army."
32. Omissi, *Sepoy and the Raj*; Omissi, *Indian Voices*.
33. Das, *Race, Empire*, 4.
34. Howe, *Race, War and Nationalism*; Smith, *Jamaican Volunteers*; Singh, *Testimonies of Indian Soldiers*.
35. See Jarboe and Fogarty, *Empires in World War I*; Gerwarth and Manela, *Empires at War*.
36. See Fogarty, *Race and War in France*; Visram, *Asians in Britain*; and Liebau et al., *World in World Wars*.
37. See Streets-Salter, *World War One*; Fawaz, *Land of Aching Hearts*; Gardner, *Siege of Kut-al-Amara*; Townshend, *Desert Hell*. See also Strachan, *First World War*; Strachan, *To Arms*; Strachan, *First World War in Africa*; Morrow, *Great War*; Neiberg, *Fighting the Great War*; Storey, *First World War*; Sondhaus, *World War One*.
38. See Kant, *India and the First World War*; S. Basu, *For King and Another Country*; K. Roy, *Indian Army and the First World War*; Morton-Jack, *Indian Army*; and Morton-Jack, *Army of Empire*.
39. Das, *India, Empire*; Imy, *Faithful Fighters*.
40. Singh, *Testimonies of Indian Soldiers*.
41. Jeffreys, *Indian Army*.
42. Omissi, *Indian Voices*, 4–8.
43. Singh, *Testimonies of Indian Soldiers*, 6.
44. Audoin-Rouzeau, *Men at War*.
45. Das, *India, Empire*, 13.
46. Singh, *Testimonies of Indian Soldiers*, 185.
47. See Stoler, *Carnal Knowledge and Imperial Power*; Ballantyne and Burton, *Bodies in Contact*.
48. Singh, *Testimonies of Indian Soldiers*, 81.
49. Note by the censor, March 20, 1915, India Office Record, British Library, London (IOR) L/MIL/17347.
50. Jarboe, *War News in India*, 10.
51. B. Anderson, *Imagined Communities*, 36.
52. "British at Neuve Chapelle," *Daily Record and Mail*, March 12, 1915.
53. Sinha, *Colonial Masculinity*, 6.
54. *Khalsa Sowar*, September 14, 1914, IOR L/R/5/195.
55. Jarboe, *War News in India*, 48.
56. Jarboe, *War News in India*, 36.
57. Das, *India, Empire*, 56.

1. Peasants into Sepoys

1. Omissi, *Sepoy and the Raj*, 4; Mazumder, *Indian Army*, 7.
2. Yong, "Sepoys and the Colonial State," 13–16; Omissi, *Sepoy and the Raj*, 5.
3. "The Mutiny at Allahabad," *Sheffield Daily Telegraph*, August 10, 1857.
4. "The Revolt at Benares," *Sheffield Daily Telegraph*, August 10, 1857.
5. "The Causes of the Mutiny in Bengal," *Times*, August 28, 1857.
6. Chowdhury, "Shocked by War," 21.
7. Chowdhury, "Shocked by War," 26.
8. Barkawi and Stanski, introduction to *Orientalism and War*, 3.
9. "The Mutiny at Allahabad," *Sheffield Daily Telegraph*, August 10, 1857.

10. Barkawi and Stanski, introduction to *Orientalism and War*, 26.
11. "The Sepoy Mutiny," *Brighton Gazette*, July 23, 1857.
12. MacMunn, *Armies of India*, 2.
13. MacMunn, *Armies of India*, 212.
14. Mazumder, *Indian Army*, 11.
15. Omissi, *Sepoy and the Raj*, 8.
16. Omissi, *Sepoy and the Raj*, 12.
17. Caplan, "Martial Gurkhas," 228.
18. "How the Punjab Was Saved," *Times*, January 12, 1858.
19. Streets-Salter, *Martial Races*, 8.
20. Omissi, *Sepoy and the Raj*, 19.
21. MacMunn, *Armies of India*, 2.
22. MacMunn, *Armies of India*, 129–30.
23. Yong, *Garrison State*, 70–71.
24. Constable, "Dalit Martial Race," 439.
25. Bourne, *Recruiting Handbook*, 40.
26. MacMunn, *Armies of India*, 142.
27. Yong, *Garrison State*, 75.
28. Yong, *Garrison State*, 74.
29. Bourne, *Recruiting Handbook*, 28.
30. Yong, *Garrison State*, 76.
31. MacMunn, "Romance of the Martial Races," 173.
32. Streets-Salter, *Martial Races*, chap. 4.
33. Frederick Roberts, foreword to MacMunn, *Armies of India*, xi.
34. Singh, *Testimonies of Indian Soldiers*, 13.
35. MacMunn, *Armies of India*, 132.
36. MacMunn, *Armies of India*, 151.
37. MacMunn, *Armies of India*, 138.
38. MacMunn, *Armies of India*, 139.
39. MacMunn, *Armies of India*, 139–40.
40. MacMunn, *Armies of India*, 143–44.
41. MacMunn, *Armies of India*, 148.
42. MacMunn, *Armies of India*, 151.
43. MacMunn, *Armies of India*, 165.
44. MacMunn, *Armies of India*, 136.
45. MacMunn, *Armies of India*, 148.
46. MacMunn, *Armies of India*, 213.
47. Wikeley, *Punjabi Musalmans*, 46.
48. MacMunn, *Armies of India*, 150–51.
49. MacMunn, *Armies of India*, 153.
50. Bourne, *Recruiting Handbook*, 48.
51. MacMunn, *Armies of India*, 211.
52. Anand, *Across the Black Waters*, 168.
53. Streets-Salter, *Martial Races*, 195.
54. Nandy, *Intimate Enemy*, 1–2.
55. Imy, "Fascist Yogis," 325.
56. Imy, "Fascist Yogis," 325.

57. Ellinwood, "Two Masculine Worlds Compared," 246–71.
58. IOR L/MIL/5/825/1.
59. IOR L/MIL/17347.
60. IOR L/MIL/17347.
61. IOR L/MIL/5/826/4.
62. Omissi, *Indian Voices*, 12.
63. IOR L/MIL/5/827/4.
64. Supplementary letters, January 10, 1917, The National Archives, Kew, UK (TNA) FO 383/288.
65. Singh, *Testimonies of Indian Soldiers*, 40.
66. Singh, *Testimonies of Indian Soldiers*, 42.
67. Morton-Jack, *Army of Empire*, 75.
68. Gandhi, *Collected Works of Mahatma Gandhi* (CWMG), 2:2.
69. Gokhale, *Speeches of Group Krishna Gokhale*, 707.
70. Searle, "'National Efficiency,'" 194.
71. Omissi, "India," 215–16.
72. Lake, *Drawing the Global Color Line*, 119.
73. *CWMG*, 1:362.
74. *CWMG*, 1:201.
75. Atkinson, "White Australia Policy," 12.
76. *Sydney Morning Herald*, qtd. in Atkinson, "White Australia Policy," 1.
77. Lake, *Global Color Line*, 315.
78. Ramnath, *Haj to Utopia*, 47.
79. *Hindu*, August 13, 1914, IOR L/R/5/195.
80. *Panjabee*, September 12, 1914, IOR L/R/5/195.
81. *Panjabee*, September 12, 1914.
82. *CWMG*, 1:186–204.
83. Desai and Vahed, *South African Gandhi*, 44.
84. Desai and Vahed, *South African Gandhi*, 91.
85. *CWMG*, 2:334.
86. *CWMG*, 2:421.
87. *CWMG*, 3:429.
88. *CWMG*, 4:193.
89. *CWMG*, 5:258.
90. Gokhale, *Speeches of Group Krishna Gokhale*, 707.
91. Lucas, *The Empire at War*, 158.
92. Tilak, *Bal Gangadhar Tilak*, 55–56.
93. Tilak, *Bal Gangadhar Tilak*, 58.
94. Tilak, *Bal Gangadhar Tilak*, 65.
95. *CWMG*, 2:334.
96. Sinha, *Colonial Masculinity*, 80.
97. Sinha, *Colonial Masculinity*, 94.
98. Sinha, *Colonial Masculinity*, 94.
99. Sinha, *Colonial Masculinity*, 69.
100. *CWMG*, 2:2.
101. *CWMG*, 2:210.
102. *CWMG*, 3:169–70.

103. *CWMG*, 3:469.
104. Jarboe, *War News in India*, 26.
105. Jarboe, *War News in India*, 23.
106. Jarboe, *War News in India*, 21.
107. Imy, *Faithful Fighters*, 229.

2. India's Splendid Rally

1. Brittain, *Testament of Youth*, 95.
2. Brittain, *Testament of Youth*, 96.
3. Brittain, *Testament of Youth*, 96–97.
4. Kant, *India and the First World War*, 15.
5. *Dipak*, September 22, 1914, IOR L/R/5/195.
6. *Dipak*, November 12, 1914, IOR L/R/5/195.
7. *Jhang Sial*, October 9, 1914, IOR L/R/5/195.
8. Holland, "British Empire," 114.
9. Hermann, *Arming of Europe*, 221.
10. Morton-Jack, "Indian Army," 337–38.
11. Hardinge, *My Indian Years*, 99.
12. Army Order of August 7, 1914, IOR L/MIL/7/17243. By the end of the war, the viceroy had "no figures to show how many deserters then took advantage of the King's pardon."
13. Farwell, *Gurkhas*, 86–87.
14. War Diary of the 58th Rifles, TNA WO 95/3948.
15. "Parliament and the War," *Times*, August 29, 1914.
16. *Observer*, August 8, 1914, IOR L/R/5/195.
17. Merewether and Smith, *Indian Corps in France*, 4–6; see also Das, "Ardour and Anxiety."
18. Lucas, *Empire at War*, 163.
19. *CWMG*, 14:284.
20. "A United Empire," *Times*, August 17, 1914.
21. Natesan, *All about the War*, 116.
22. MacMunn, *India and the War*, 55–62.
23. MacMunn, *India and the War*, 55–62.
24. Das, "Sepoys, Sahibs, and Babus," 73.
25. *Khalsa Sowar*, September 14, 1914, IOR L/R/5/195.
26. *Zamindar*, October 16, 1914, IOR L/R/5/195.
27. Natesan, *All about the War*, 114.
28. *Tribune* (Lahore), August 12, 1914, IOR L/R/5/195.
29. *Panjabee*, September 5, 1914, IOR L/R/5/195.
30. *Jhang Sial*, September 1, 1914, IOR L/R/5/195.
31. Ginsburg, *War Speeches*, 19–27.
32. Ramnath, *Haj to Utopia*, 48–49.
33. *Azadi*, September 11, 1914, IOR L/R/5/195.
34. *Panth Sewak*, September 18, 1914, IOR L/R/5/195.
35. Hardinge, *Speeches of His Excellency*, 293–313.
36. Hardinge, *Speeches of His Excellency*, 320.
37. Anand, *Across the Black Waters*, 12.
38. Anand, *Across the Black Waters*, 14.

Notes to Pages 67–76

39. Merewether and Smith, *Indian Corps in France*, 16.
40. "Indian Troops at Marseilles," *Birmingham Mail*, October 3, 1914.
41. *Birmingham Daily Mail*, October 3, 1914.
42. "With the Indian Force," *Daily Mirror*, October 7, 1914.
43. "Indians in Camp," *Times*, October 28, 1914.
44. Bibikoff, *Our Indians at Marseilles*, 85.
45. "India and Her Army," *Times*, August 31, 1914.
46. "Indian Troops in France," *Times*, October 2, 1914.
47. "Lord Roberts," *Manchester Guardian*, November 19, 1914.
48. Trevelyan, *India and the War*, 6.
49. B. Basu, *Why India Is Heart and Soul*, 8.
50. B. Basu, *Why India Is Heart and Soul*, 8.
51. "King's Message to Indian Troops," *Aberdeen Journal*, October 2, 1914.
52. Hodder, *Famous Fights*, ix.
53. Fischer, *Germany's Aims*, 121.
54. Geiss, *July 1914*, document 179.
55. Craig, *Germany*, 342.
56. Fischer, *Germany's Aims*, 120.
57. Lüdke, *Jihad Made in Germany*, 32.
58. Lüdke, *Jihad Made in Germany*, 63.
59. Strachan, *To Arms*, 696.
60. McMeekin, *Berlin-Baghdad Express*, 12.
61. McMeekin, *Berlin-Baghdad Express*, 13.
62. McMeekin, *Berlin-Baghdad Express*, 14.
63. Lüdke, *Jihad Made in Germany*, 116.
64. Lüdke, *Jihad Made in Germany*, 117.
65. McKale, *War by Revolution*, 50–52.
66. McMeekin, *Berlin-Baghdad Express*, 91.
67. McMeekin, *Berlin-Baghdad Express*, 91.
68. Baron Max von Oppenheim to Hans Freiherr von Wangenheim, September 16, 1914, Political Archives of the Foreign Office, Berlin (PAAA) R21071.
69. Ramnath, *Haj to Utopia*, 73.
70. Lüdke, *Jihad Made in Germany*, 119–20.
71. Ramnath, *Haj to Utopia*, 3.
72. Ramnath, *Haj to Utopia*, 8.
73. Ramnath, *Haj to Utopia*, 73–74.
74. Letter from Har Dayal, September 1914, PAAA R21074.
75. Paul Walter to the Foreign Office, August 7, 1914, PAAA R21070.
76. Walter, "Indien und der Weltkrieg," PAAA R21070.
77. Walter, "Indien und der Weltkrieg."
78. Telegram from Undersecretary Zimmermann to Wangenheim, August 28, 1914, PAAA R21070.
79. Wangenheim to Zimmermann, August 31, 1914, PAAA R21070.
80. Oppenheim to Wangenheim, September 24, 1914, PAAA R21072.
81. Oppenheim to Wangenheim, September 15, 1914, PAAA R21071.
82. Statement presented through the Indian Committee, Berlin, February 16, 1915, PAAA R21078.

83. *Observer*, November 4, 1914, IOR L/R/5/195.
84. *Prabhat*, October 24, 1914, IOR L/R/5/195.
85. "War with Turkey, Moslem Attitudes in India," TNA CO 323/638.
86. "War with Turkey."
87. "War with Turkey."
88. Telegram from the viceroy, January 29, 1915, IOR L/MIL/7/18846.
89. Telegram from the viceroy, January 29, 1915.
90. Telegram from the viceroy, January 29, 1915.
91. Secretary of State of India to the viceroy, February 1, 1915, IOR L/MIL/7/18846.
92. IOR L/MIL/17347.
93. IOR L/MIL/17347.
94. IOR L/MIL/17347.
95. Ramnath, *Haj to Utopia*, 50.
96. Ramnath, *Haj to Utopia*, 55-56.
97. Ramnath, *Haj to Utopia*, 59-60.
98. Ramnath, *Haj to Utopia*, 191.
99. Ramnath, *Haj to Utopia*, 193.
100. Governor to the Secretary of State for the Colonies, February 20, 1915, TNA ADM 1/8419/112. See also Streets-Salter, "Local Was Global," 539-76; and Singh, *Testimonies of Indian Soldiers*, chap. 5.
101. IOR L/MIL/17347.
102. IOR L/MIL/5/825/1.
103. Streets-Salter, *World War One*, 17-18.

3. In Flanders Fields

1. McCulloch, "Empire and Violence," 221.
2. Ellis, *History of the Machine Gun*, 92-93.
3. Kramer, *Dynamic of Destruction*, 79.
4. Kramer, *Dynamic of Destruction*, 38.
5. IOR L/MIL/5/825/3.
6. Wounded Sikh to a friend in India, January 20, 1915, IOR L/MIL/17347.
7. Wounded Sikh to a friend, February 3, 1915, IOR L/MIL/17347.
8. Jarboe and Fogarty, introduction to *Empires in World War I*, 5; Ferguson, *Pity of War*, 291.
9. Actually, about half of the soldiers deployed to Gallipoli wound up as casualties. As the overall number of soldiers deployed to Gallipoli was quite small—about three thousand—I'm treating that figure as something of an outlier.
10. *Statistics of the Military Effort*, 778.
11. Keegan, *First World War*, 129.
12. IOR L/MIL/5/825/1.
13. Merewether and Smith, *Indian Corps in France*, 30.
14. S. Basu, *For King and Another Country*, 62.
15. Willcocks, *With the Indians in France*, 83.
16. Keegan, *First World War*, 132.
17. S. Basu, *For King and Another Country*, 56.
18. Gardner, *Trial by Fire*, 191.
19. Merewether and Smith, *Indian Corps in France*, xviii.
20. Willcocks, *With the Indians in France*, 61.

Notes to Pages 87–93

21. K. Roy, *Indian Army and the First World War*, 81.
22. Willcocks to Fitzgerald, November 10, 1914, TNA PRO 30/57/52.
23. IOR L/MIL/5/825/1.
24. Report on the examination of Vice-Feldwebel Braun, November 23, 1914, TNA WO 157/597.
25. Report on the examination of 97 prisoners of war, November 25, 1914, TNA WO 157/597.
26. IOR L/MIL/17347.
27. Lewis to his mother, December 19, 1914, Imperial War Museum, London (IWM).
28. Lewis to his mother, December 19, 1914.
29. Neiberg, *Fighting the Great War*, 34–35.
30. Morton-Jack, *Indian Army*, 152.
31. Greenhut, "Imperial Reserve," 56.
32. Merewether and Smith, *Indian Corps in France*, 174.
33. S. Basu, *For King and Another Country*, 78.
34. Morton-Jack, *Indian Army*, 159.
35. Merewether and Smith, *Indian Corps in France*, 199.
36. Kant, *India and the First World War*, 117.
37. The First World War Diary of Brigadier P. Mortimer, January 13, 1915, IWM P253.
38. IOR L/MIL/5/825/1.
39. Censor's Report, January 23, 1915, IOR L/MIL/5/825/1.
40. S. Basu, *For King and Another Country*, 58.
41. Ali, *Our Heroes*, 34.
42. Ali, *Our Heroes*, 26.
43. "The Indian Soldiers in France," *Newcastle Daily Journal*, October 21, 1914.
44. "Indian Troops," *Observer*, October 31, 1914.
45. "Valour of the Indian Troops," *Times*, November 5, 1914.
46. "Magnificent Indians," *Aberdeen Evening Express*, November 10, 1914.
47. "The Indian Troops," *Western Daily Press*, November 10, 1914.
48. "Indians' Troops Charge," *Daily Mirror*, October 27, 1914.
49. "The Indian Charge," *Daily Mirror*, October 28, 1914.
50. "Indian Corps Captures German Guns," *Daily Mirror*, November 26, 1914.
51. "Les Indiens et les Ecossais," *Le Siecle*, November 14, 1914.
52. "Dash of the Indian Troops," *Times*, November 10, 1914.
53. Hodder, *Famous Fights*, xi–xvii.
54. "Indian Troops in Action," *Times*, November 21, 1914.
55. W. Anderson, *Cultivation of Whiteness*.
56. "The Indian Troops," *Liverpool Daily Post and Mercury*, October 3, 1914.
57. Willcocks, *With the Indians in France*, 194.
58. Doyle, *British Campaign in France*, 329–30.
59. Taylor, *Illustrated History*, 35.
60. Keegan, *First World War*, 130, 182.
61. Kant, *India and the First World War*, 42.
62. Merewether and Smith, *Indian Corps in France*, 500–504; Morton-Jack, *Indian Army*, 154–55.
63. Morton-Jack, *Indian Army*, 155.

Notes to Pages 94-102

64. Willcocks, *With the Indians in France*, 98-99.
65. Merewether and Smith, *Indian Corps in France*, 503.
66. Morton-Jack, *Indian Army*, 156.
67. "Indian Troops in Grand Health," *Evening Dispatch*, March 6, 1915.
68. Willcocks, *With the Indians in France*, 194.
69. IOR L/MIL/5/825/1.
70. Farwell, *Armies of the Raj*, 251; Morton-Jack, *Indian Army*, 171-75.
71. Willcocks to Fitzgerald, November 10, 1914, TNA PRO 30/57/52.
72. IOR L/MIL/5/825/1.
73. Morton-Jack, "Indian Army," 340-41.
74. Morton-Jack, *Indian Army*, 175.
75. Morton-Jack, *Indian Army*, 175.
76. Putkowski and Sykes, *Shot at Dawn*.
77. Ferguson, *Pity of War*, 346.
78. Censor's Report, May 1, 1915, IOR L/MIL/5/825/3.
79. Letter from Lieutenant Schniewind, January 13, 1915, PAAA R21077.
80. List A, Nominal Roll of Indian Prisoners of War, suspected of having deserted to the enemy or of having given information to or otherwise assisted the enemy after capture, October 24, 1918, IOR L/MIL/17/5/2403.
81. K. Roy, *Indian Army and the First World War*, 89.
82. S. Basu, *For King and Another Country*, 118.
83. Merewether and Smith, *Indian Corps in France*, 75-76.
84. Merewether and Smith, *Indian Corps in France*, 119.
85. Merewether and Smith, *Indian Corps in France*, 124.
86. Merewether and Smith, *Indian Corps in France*, 192.
87. IOR L/MIL/17347.
88. Note by the censor, February 3, 1915, IOR L/MIL/17347.
89. IOR L/MIL/17347.
90. War Diary of the 58th Rifles, TNA WO 95/3948.
91. War Diary of the 58th Rifles.
92. War Diary, I.E.F. "A," March 26, 1915, IOR L/MIL/1715/3093.
93. *Times*, November 26, 1914.
94. Extracts of leaflets for Indian troops, January 11, 1915, PAAA R21077.
95. Indian Corps Intelligence Summaries, February 1915, TNA WO 157/599.
96. IOR L/MIL/17347.
97. IOR L/MIL/17347.
98. IOR L/MIL/17347.
99. Interview by Paul Walter with deserters of the 58th Rifles, March 6, 1915, PAAA R21245.
100. Interview by Walter with deserters, March 6, 1915.
101. IOR L/MIL/5/825/4.
102. Morton-Jack, *Indian Army*, 187-219.
103. Keegan, *First World War*, 190.
104. IOR L/MIL/5/825/6.
105. Lloyd George, *War Memoirs*, 418.
106. Keegan, *First World War*, 192-93; Neiberg, *Fighting the Great War*, 74-77.

Notes to Pages 102–110

107. *Action Taken by the Indian Corps*, 3.
108. IOR L/MIL/5/825/2.
109. Keegan, *First World War*, 193.
110. *Action Taken by the Indian Corps*, 3.
111. Keegan, *First World War*, 194–95.
112. *Action Taken by the Indian Corps*, 4.
113. IOR L/MIL/5/825/2.
114. IOR L/MIL/5/825/2.
115. Keegan, *First World War*, 195.
116. *Action Taken by the Indian Corps*, 29.
117. IOR L/MIL/5/825/2.
118. IOR L/MIL/5/825/2.
119. IOR L/MIL/5/825/2.
120. IOR L/MIL/5/826/3.
121. IOR L/MIL/5/825/1.
122. IOR L/MIL/5/825/6.
123. Audoin-Rouzeau, *Men at War*.
124. IOR L/MIL/5/825/1.
125. IOR L/MIL/5/825/6.
126. IOR L/MIL/5/825/6.
127. IOR L/MIL/5/825/6.
128. IOR L/MIL/5/825/1.
129. IOR L/MIL/5/825/3.
130. IOR L/MIL/5/825/1.
131. Morton-Jack, *Indian Army*, 245.
132. Censor's Report, October 11, 1915, IOR L/MIL/5/825/6.
133. Ellinwood, *Between Two Worlds*, 375, 378, 389.
134. Ellinwood, *Between Two Worlds*, 389.
135. Ellinwood, *Between Two Worlds*, 381.
136. Ellinwood, *Between Two Worlds*, 390.
137. Ellinwood, *Between Two Worlds*, 389.
138. IOR L/MIL/5/825/6.
139. IOR L/MIL/5/825/6.
140. IOR L/MIL/5/825/6.
141. IOR L/MIL/5/825/6.
142. IOR L/MIL/5/825/6.
143. "After Neuve Chapelle," *Western Daily Press*, March 25, 1915.
144. *Western Daily Press*, March 22, 1915.
145. "Thrilling Deeds by Indian Warriors," *Daily Mirror*, August 16, 1915.
146. Alexander, *On Two Fronts*, 108.
147. Koller, "Representing Otherness," 135; Markovits, "Indian Soldiers' Experiences in France," 43–44.
148. Markovits, "Indian Soldiers' Experiences in France," 47.
149. IOR L/MIL/5/826/3.
150. Morton-Jack, *Army of Empire*, 260, 408.
151. Levine, "Battle Colors," 106.
152. Bush, "Gender and Empire," 90.

153. Stoler, "Matters of Intimacy," 893–97.
154. Markovits, "Indian Soldiers' Experiences in France," 29–54; Omissi, "Europe through Indian Eyes," 371–96.
155. IOR L/MIL/5/825/4.
156. IOR L/MIL/17347.
157. IOR L/MIL/5/825/4.
158. Morton-Jack, *Army of Empire*, 411.
159. Vice-consul at Boulogne to consulate at Lille, October 19, 1923, IOR L/PJ/6/1864, File 5661.
160. Censor's Report, April 24, 1915, IOR L/MIL/17347.
161. Censor's Report, June 26, 1915, IOR L/MIL/5/825/4.
162. Gardner, *Trial by Fire*, 176.
163. Gardner, *Trial by Fire*, 176.
164. Gardner, *Trial by Fire*, 177.
165. Havildar to sepoy in Malakand, May 31, 1915, IOR L/MIL/5/825/4.
166. Gardner, *Trial by Fire*, 177.
167. Gardner, *Trial by Fire*, 177.
168. Censor's Report, July 31, 1915, IOR L/MIL/5/825/4.
169. Censor's Report, August 21, 1915, IOR L/MIL/5/825/4.
170. Willcocks, *With the Indians in France*, 23.
171. Morton-Jack, *Army of Empire*, 519–23.
172. Millar, *Death of an Army*, 11.
173. Morton-Jack, *Indian Army*, 169.
174. Morton-Jack, *Indian Army*, 170; Millar, *Death of an Army*, 12.
175. IOR L/MIL/5/825/6.
176. IOR L/MIL/5/825/4.
177. Merewether and Smith, *Indian Corps in France*, 462.

4. Healing the Empire

1. Imperial War Conference memorandum, March 11, 1917, TNA CAB 24/7/5.
2. Mesopotamia Commission, *Report of the Commission*, 113.
3. Stevenson, *Cataclysm*, 168.
4. Future Operations in East Africa, TNA CAB 24/1/43.
5. Sehrawat, *Colonial Medical Care*, 192–93.
6. These perks included more efficient hospital administration, improved and cleaner surgical and recovery facilities, improved comfort, and quality nursing.
7. Sehrawat, *Colonial Medical Care*, 192–93.
8. Mesopotamia Commission, *Report of the Commission*, 105.
9. Mesopotamia Commission, *Report of the Commission*, 105.
10. Mesopotamia Commission, *Report of the Commission*, 95.
11. Mesopotamia Commission, *Report of the Commission*, 95.
12. Mesopotamia Commission, *Report of the Commission*, 95.
13. Reznick, *Healing the Nation*.
14. Arrangements made for Indian sick and wounded in England and France, March 8, 1916, TNA WO 32/5110.
15. Walter Lawrence to Lord Kitchener, December 31, 1914, TNA WO 159/17.
16. Visram, *Asians in Britain*, 180–92.

Notes to Pages 123–132

17. Merewether and Smith, *Indian Corps in France*, 49.
18. Merewether and Smith, *Indian Corps in France*, 199.
19. *Action Taken by the Indian Corps*, 28.
20. Morton-Jack, "Indian Army," 329.
21. Farwell, *Armies of the Raj*, 253.
22. IOR L/MIL/5/825/1.
23. Report by Lawrence, March 8, 1916, TNA WO 32/5110.
24. Lawrence to Kitchener, March 22, 1915, TNA WO 32/5110.
25. Visram, *Asians in Britain*, 171–72, 181.
26. *Times*, November 5, 1915.
27. Lawrence to Kitchener, March 22, 1915.
28. Commandant Kitchener Hospital to India Office, June 24, 1915, TNA WO 95/5110.
29. Report by Lawrence, March 8, 1916.
30. Lawrence to Kitchener, December 15, 1914, TNA WO 32/5110.
31. IOR L/MIL/5/825/1.
32. IOR L/MIL/17347.
33. Lawrence to Kitchener, April 30, 1915, TNA WO 95/5110.
34. War Diary of Kitchener Indian Hospital, TNA WO 95/5465.
35. Report by Lawrence, March 8, 1916.
36. Report by Lawrence, March 8, 1916.
37. Lawrence to Kitchener, December 15, 1914.
38. Report by Lawrence, March 8, 1916.
39. Lawrence to Kitchener, March 10, 1915, TNA WO 32/5110.
40. Lawrence to Sir Neville, March 3, 1915, TNA WO 32/5110.
41. Lawrence to Kitchener, March 22, 1915.
42. Brighton Corporation, "Hospital for Indian Soldiers," 13.
43. Lawrence to Kitchener, December 15, 1914, TNA WO 32/5110.
44. Lawrence to Kitchener, April 30, 1915, TNA WO 32/5110.
45. Letter from Alfred Keogh, n.d., TNA WO 32/5110.
46. Imy, *Faithful Fighters*, chap. 3.
47. IOR L/MIL/5/827/2.
48. Metcalf, *Aftermath of Revolt*, 47, 89, 107–8.
49. Lawrence to Kitchener, March 10, 1915.
50. Lawrence to Kitchener, February 15, 1915, TNA WO 32/5110.
51. *Times*, October 20, 1914.
52. "Wounded Indians at Brighton," *Times*, May 28, 1915.
53. Brighton Corporation, "Hospital for Indian Soldiers," 7.
54. Imy, *Faithful Fighters*, chap. 3.
55. Brighton Corporation, "Hospital for Indian Soldiers," 18.
56. S. Basu, *For King and Another Country*, 149–51.
57. Fell and Hallett, *First World War Nursing*, 11.
58. IOR L/MIL/7/17316.
59. IOR L/MIL/17/5/2016.
60. IOR L/MIL/17/5/2016.
61. Fell, "Nursing the Other," 170.
62. Fell, "Nursing the Other," 166.
63. Fell, "Nursing the Other," 166.

64. Baldwin, *Canteening Overseas*, 36–37.
65. IOR L/R/5/196.
66. Lawrence to Kitchener, August 5, 1915, TNA WO 32/5110.
67. Censor's Report, January 23, 1915, IOR L/MIL/5/825/1.
68. Lerner, "Psychiatry and Casualties," 18.
69. Mosse, "Shell-Shock," 101–8.
70. Winter, "Hospitals," 356.
71. IOR L/MIL/5/825/1.
72. Buxton, "Imperial Amnesia," 230.
73. Lawrence to Kitchener, December 15, 1914.
74. Buxton, "Imperial Amnesia," 234–35.
75. Lawrence to Kitchener, May 27, 1915, TNA WO 32/5110.
76. Lawrence to Kitchener, June 15, 1915, TNA WO 32/5110.
77. Singh, *Testimonies of Indian Soldiers*, 49.
78. Singh, *Testimonies of Indian Soldiers*, 53.
79. IOR L/MIL/5/825/1.
80. Scott, *Weapons of the Weak*.
81. IOR L/MIL/5/825/1.
82. Lawrence to Kitchener, February 15, 1915, TNA WO 32/5110.
83. Sikh to his father, March 17, 1915, IOR L/MIL/17347.
84. Lawrence to Kitchener, March 10, 1915, TNA WO 32/5110.
85. Lawrence to Kitchener, February 15, 1915, TNA WO 32/5110.
86. Lawrence to Kitchener, February 15, 1915.
87. IOR L/MIL/5/825/3.
88. Lawrence to Kitchener, June 15, 1915, TNA WO 32/5110.
89. IOR L/MIL/5/825/2.
90. IOR L/MIL/5/825/2.
91. Lawrence to Kitchener, June 15, 1915.
92. S. Basu, *For King and Another Country*, 122–26.
93. IOR L/MIL/5/825/4.
94. Morton-Jack, *Army of Empire*, 252–55.
95. IOR L/MIL/5/825/5.
96. IOR L/MIL/5/825/5.
97. IOR L/MIL/5/825/5.
98. Censor's Report, July 31, 1915, IOR L/MIL/5/825/4.
99. Lawrence to Kitchener, June 15, 1915.
100. Lawrence to Kitchener, June 15, 1915.
101. R. Anderson, "Logistics," 105.
102. K. Roy, *Indian Army and the First World War*, 257.
103. Mesopotamia Commission, *Report of the Commission*, 142.
104. R. Anderson, "Logistics," 111–14.
105. R. Anderson, "Logistics," 96.
106. R. Anderson, "Logistics," 139.
107. Gardner, *Siege of Kut-al-Amara*, 26.
108. Mesopotamia Commission, *Report of the Commission*, 20.
109. K. Roy, *Indian Army and the First World War*, 259.
110. The Strategical Situation in Mesopotamia, October 16, 1915, TNA CAB 24/1/33.

Notes to Pages 144–156

111. The Strategical Situation in Mesopotamia, October 16, 1915.

112. K. Roy, *Indian Army and the First World War*, 263.

113. Sarbadhikari, *On to Baghdad*. Extracts translated by Amitav Ghosh and available on his website, http://amitavghosh.com/blog/?cat=12.

114. Amitav Ghosh, "Shared Sorrows: Indians and Armenians in the Prison Camps of Ras al-'Ain, 1916–18" (blog), http://amitavghosh.com/blog/?cat=12.

115. Gardner, *Siege of Kut-al-Amara*, 31.

116. Sarbadhikari, *On to Baghdad*, qtd. by Ghosh.

117. Gardner, *Siege of Kut-al-Amara*, 38.

118. Sarbadhikari, *On to Baghdad*, qtd. by Ghosh.

119. Sarbadhikari, *On to Baghdad*, qtd. by Ghosh.

120. K. Roy, *Indian Army and the First World War*, 265.

121. Gardner, *Siege of Kut-al-Amara*, 43.

122. Gardner, *Siege of Kut-al-Amara*, 39.

123. Sarbadhikari, *On to Baghdad*, qtd. by Ghosh.

124. Sarbadhikari, *On to Baghdad*, qtd. by Ghosh.

125. Sarbadhikari, *On to Baghdad*, qtd. by Ghosh.

126. Mesopotamia Commission, *Report of the Commission*, 67; "Vincent-Bingley" Report, 155–56.

127. Callahan and Marston, "Neglected Soldiers," 26.

128. "Vincent-Bingley" Report, 157.

129. Mesopotamia Commission, *Report of the Commission*, 111.

130. Mesopotamia Commission, *Report of the Commission*, 111–14.

131. Mesopotamia Commission, *Report of the Commission*, 115.

132. Mesopotamia Commission, *Report of the Commission*, 115.

133. Final report by Walter Lawrence, March 8, 1916, TNA WO 32/5110.

134. Sehrawat, *Colonial Medical Care*, 234.

5. In the Hands of the Enemy

1. Letter from Major General C. Melliss, 1918, IOR L/MIL/7/18454.

2. Ferguson, *Pity of War*, 369.

3. Beveridge, "Report," TNA FO 383/39. Beveridge later republished the report in a book, *What Is Back of the War* (1916).

4. Audoin-Rouzeau and Becker, *14–18*, 71.

5. Speed, *Prisoners, Diplomats*, 10.

6. Jones, *Violence against Prisoners of War*.

7. Chickering, *Imperial Germany*, 184.

8. Ferguson, *Pity of War*, 371.

9. Doegen made no distinction between British and Indian soldiers in his tables showing the total number of prisoners captured by the Germans, lumping both together under the category "Engländer." See Doegen, *Kriegsgefangene Völker*.

10. Report on Zossen, August 16, 1915, PAAA R19354.

11. Report on Zossen, August 16, 1915.

12. Statement of Subadar Major Sher Singh Rana, 1st/4th Gurkha Rifles, TNA FO 383/390.

13. John French to the War Office, August 31, 1915, IOR L/MIL/7/13561.

14. Indian prisoners of war, December 15, 1915, IOR L/MIL/7/13561.

15. Merewether and Smith, *Indian Corps in France*, 503.

16. Merewether and Smith, *Indian Corps in France*, 459. A century has elapsed, and the frustrations of the war's contemporaries have not been settled. Historian Gerhard Höpp counted anywhere between five hundred and six hundred Indian prisoners of war in Germany. The estimates of other historians are higher, in the range of one thousand.
17. *Akhbar-I'-Am*, February 26, 1915, IOR L/R/5/196.
18. Godfrey to Bosanquet, December 3, 1914, TNA FO 383/39.
19. Höpp, *Muslime in der Mark*, 44–45.
20. Rudolf Nadolny to Foreign Office, March 27, 1915, PAAA R21245.
21. Ramadan at the Halbmondlager, July 25, 1915, PAAA R21250.
22. Undated, untitled document, PAAA R21246.
23. Indian Independence Committee Report, January 4, 1915, PAAA R21244.
24. Baron Max von Oppenheim to Foreign Office, February 4, 1915, PAAA R21244.
25. Report by J. B. Jackson, TNA PRO 383/65.
26. Plan for Muslim and Indian prisoners, February 27, 1915, PAAA R21245.
27. Höpp, *Muslime in der Mark*, 55.
28. Report on contents of *Hindustan*, n.d., PAAA R21256.
29. "Never forget about your oppression by the English," n.d., PAAA R21245.
30. Paul Walter to Oppenheim, December 12, 1914, PAAA R21244.
31. Memo by Oppenheim, October 1914, PAAA R21244.
32. Communication from E. B. Howell, October 21, 1915, IOR L/MIL/17347.
33. Report on Bairam Feast, October 25, 1915, PAAA R21252.
34. Ramsay to Lossow, November 9, 1915, PAAA R21252.
35. Foreign Office memo, January 20, 1916, PAAA R21253.
36. Indians sent to Turkey, March 3, 1916, PAAA R21254.
37. Report on the Halbmondlager, December 25, 1915, PAAA R21253.
38. Statement of Sher Singh Rana, TNA FO 383/390.
39. Indian Committee to Foreign Office, June 21, 1916, PAAA R21258.
40. To the Foreign Office, November 18, 1915, PAAA R21252.
41. Memo, May 27, 1915, PAAA R21246.
42. Report, January 25, 1916, PAAA R21253.
43. Statement of Sher Singh Rana, TNA FO 383/390.
44. Indian Committee to Foreign Office, January 14, 1916, PAAA R21253.
45. Fogarty, "Out of North Africa," 150.
46. Proctor, *Racial Hygiene*, 16–18.
47. "Die Moschee im Gefangenenlager," *Berliner Tageblatt*, July 9, 1915.
48. Stiehl, *Unsere Feinde*, 5.
49. Report on Prisoners' Camp in Germany, February 1915, TNA FO 383/39.
50. Report on Prisoners' Camp in Germany, February 1915.
51. Report from Zossen, March 14, 1916, PAAA R21255.
52. Report, January 25, 1916, PAAA R21253.
53. Indian Committee to Foreign Office, January 9, 1915, PAAA R21253.
54. Indian Committee to Foreign Office, January 9, 1915.
55. Indian Committee to Foreign Office, January 14, 1916, PAAA R21253.
56. Report, January 4, 1915, PAAA R21244.
57. Ferdinand Graetsch to Foreign Office, August 9, 1915, PAAA R21250.
58. Indian Committee to Foreign Office, May 29, 1915, PAAA R21246.
59. Report, January 14, 1916, PAAA R21253.

Notes to Pages 165–177

60. Report, January 4, 1915, PAAA R21244.
61. Indian Committee to Foreign Office, January 9, 1915, PAAA R21253.
62. Interrogation of Mohamed Arifan, January 20, 1915, PAAA R21245.
63. Interrogation of Mohamed Arifan, January 20, 1915.
64. Treatment of Indian Prisoners at Zossen, March 6, 1918, TNA FO 383/390.
65. Treatment of Indian Prisoners at Zossen, March 6, 1918.
66. Report, November 24, 1915, PAAA R21252.
67. Indian Committee to Foreign Office, December 23, 1915, PAAA R21252.
68. Indian Committee to Foreign Office, April 23, 1916, PAAA R21255.
69. Treatment of Indian Prisoners at Zossen, March 6, 1918.
70. Indian Committee to Foreign Office, December 23, 1915 PAAA R21252.
71. Indian Committee to Foreign Office, March 5, 1916, PAAA R21254.
72. Indian Committee to Foreign Office, April 28, 1916, PAAA R21256.
73. Treatment of British Prisoners of War in Turkey, IOR L/MIL/7/18737.
74. Townshend, *My Campaign in Mesopotamia*, 3.
75. Townshend, *My Campaign in Mesopotamia*, 4.
76. Townshend, *My Campaign in Mesopotamia*, 6–7.
77. Gardner, *Siege of Kut-al-Amara*, 62.
78. Townshend, *My Campaign in Mesopotamia*, 8.
79. Sarbadhikari, *On to Baghdad*, n.p.
80. Nikolas Gardner argues that Townshend did not understand Indian troops.
81. Townshend, *My Campaign in Mesopotamia*, 26.
82. Townshend, *My Campaign in Mesopotamia*, 26.
83. Townshend, *My Campaign in Mesopotamia*, 207.
84. Das, *India, Empire*, 262.
85. Townshend, *My Campaign in Mesopotamia*, 207.
86. Townshend, *My Campaign in Mesopotamia*, 27.
87. Sarbadhikari, *On to Baghdad*, 65–66.
88. Townshend, *My Campaign in Mesopotamia*, 43.
89. Sarbadhikari, *On to Baghdad*, qtd. by Ghosh.
90. Townshend, *My Campaign in Mesopotamia*, 49.
91. K. Roy, *Indian Army and the First World War*, 275.
92. Sarbadhikari, *On to Baghdad*, 75, qtd. by Ghosh.
93. Gardner, *Siege of Kut-al-Amara*, 139; Callahan and Marston, "Neglected Soldiers," 28.
94. Sarbadhikari, *On to Baghdad*, qtd. by Ghosh.
95. K. Roy, *Indian Army and the First World War*, 285.
96. Townshend, *My Campaign in Mesopotamia*, 168–69.
97. Sarbadhikari, *On to Baghdad*, qtd. by Ghosh.
98. Townshend, *Desert Hell*, 259.
99. Sarbadhikari, *On to Baghdad*, 92, qtd. by Ghosh.
100. Townshend, *My Campaign in Mesopotamia*, 237.
101. Sarbadhikari, *On to Baghdad*, qtd. by Ghosh.
102. Fawaz, *Land of Aching Hearts*, 182.
103. Fawaz, *Land of Aching Hearts*, 170.
104. Fawaz, *Land of Aching Hearts*, 202.
105. Townshend, *Desert Hell*, 307.
106. *Treatment of British Prisoners of War*, IOR L/MIL/5/775.

107. Information obtained from sick and wounded, September 1916, IOR L/MIL/5/775.
108. Sarbadhikari, *On to Baghdad*, qtd. by Ghosh.
109. *Treatment of British Prisoners of War*.
110. Townshend, *Desert Hell*, 318.
111. Memorandum, T. D. Cree, IOR L/MIL/7/18454.
112. Balakian, *Armenian Golgotha*, 294-98.
113. *Treatment of British Prisoners of War*.
114. *Treatment of British Prisoners of War*.
115. Sarbadhikari, *On to Baghdad*, 126, qtd. by Ghosh.
116. Sarbadhikari, *On to Baghdad*, 158, qtd. by Ghosh.
117. Information obtained from sick and wounded, September 1916, IOR L/MIL/5/775.
118. Civil Intelligence Officer, Karachi, July 23, 1917, IOR L/PS/11/129, 4700.

6. The Empire's Fighters

1. IOR L/MIL/5/825/6.
2. Ali, *Our Heroes*, 28-30.
3. Ali, *Our Heroes*, 35.
4. Additional Military Assistance from India, February 1917, TNA CAB 24/6/22.
5. Smith, "Loss and Longing," 250.
6. Morrow, *Great War*, 312.
7. Military Co-operation of Japan in the War, October 3, 1917, TNA CAB 24/28/6.
8. IOR L/MIL/5/827/2.
9. IOR L/MIL/5/827/2.
10. IOR L/MIL/5/826/3.
11. IOR L/MIL/5/827/2.
12. IOR L/MIL/5/826/2.
13. IOR L/MIL/5/826/4.
14. IOR L/MIL/5/827/2.
15. IOR L/MIL/5/827/2.
16. IOR L/MIL/5/827/2.
17. IOR L/MIL/5/825/2.
18. IOR L/MIL/5/827/3.
19. IOR L/MIL/5/827/2.
20. IOR L/MIL/17347.
21. Censor's Report, May 8, 1915, IOR L/MIL/5/825/3.
22. Censor's Report, November 13, 1915, IOR L/MIL/5/825/7.
23. IOR L/MIL/5/825/7.
24. IOR L/MIL/5/826/3.
25. *Prabhat*, April 3, 1915, IOR L/R/5/196.
26. IOR L/MIL/5/827/2.
27. IOR L/MIL/5/827/2.
28. IOR L/MIL/5/827/2.
29. IOR L/MIL/5/825/1.
30. IOR L/MIL/5/827/2.
31. IOR L/MIL/5/825/1.
32. IOR L/MIL/5/827/2.
33. IOR L/MIL/5/827/2.

Notes to Pages 194–206

34. IOR L/MIL/5/825/2.
35. IOR L/MIL/5/825/2
36. IOR L/MIL/5/827/2.
37. R. Anderson, "Logistics," 123.
38. Townshend, *Desert Hell*, 289.
39. Townshend, *Desert Hell*, 297.
40. Townshend, *Desert Hell*, 340.
41. K. Roy, *Indian Army and the First World War*, 309.
42. Barker, *First Iraq War*, 279–80.
43. K. Roy, *Indian Army and the First World War*, 310.
44. K. Roy, *Indian Army and the First World War*, 314.
45. IOR L/MIL/5/827/2.
46. Townshend, *Desert Hell*, 346.
47. Maude, *Operations*, IOR L/MIL/7/17407.
48. Maude, *Operations*.
49. K. Roy, *Indian Army and the First World War*, 314.
50. IOR L/MIL/5/827/2.
51. Barker, *First Iraq War*, 300.
52. Barker, *First Iraq War*, 311–12.
53. Lloyd George, *Memoirs*, 79.
54. Jarboe, *War News in India*, 154.
55. Jarboe, *War News in India*, 154.
56. Jarboe, *War News in India*, 155.
57. IOR L/MIL/5/827/3.
58. IOR L/MIL/5/827/2.
59. K. Roy, *Indian Army and the First World War*, 318.
60. Barker, *First Iraq War*, 337.
61. Maude, *Operations*.
62. K. Roy, *Indian Army and the First World War*, 337.
63. IOR L/MIL/5/827/3.
64. *Tribune* (Lahore), April 29, 1915, IOR L/R/5/196.
65. *Tribune* (Lahore), July 25, 1915, IOR L/R/5/196.
66. K. Roy, *Indian Army and the First World War*, 21.
67. Additional Military Assistance from India, February 1917, TNA CAB 24/6/22.
68. Memorandum, August 2, 1917, TNA PRO CAB 23/3/51.
69. Memorandum, August 2, 1917.
70. Jarboe, *War News in India*, 170.
71. *With a Highland Regiment*, n.p.
72. Morton-Jack, *Army of Empire*, 224.
73. "Australians and Indians," *Daily Graphic*, August 9, 1915.
74. CWMG, 15:89–90.
75. "War Pictures at the Hippodrome," *Rochdale Observer*, August 8, 1917.
76. "Photographs under Fire," *Reading Mercury*, April 6, 1918.
77. *Daily Mail*, June 27, 1917.
78. "Photographs under Fire."
79. *Liverpool Courier*, November 23, 1917.
80. "The Gurkhas at the Front," *Nottingham Evening Post*, March 9, 1917.

81. "War Pictures at the Cosy," *Derby Daily Telegraph*, January 30, 1917.
82. "A Film of Indian Warriors," *Times*, September 12, 1916.
83. "War Pictures at the Cosy."
84. "War Pictures at the Hippodrome."
85. IOR L/PJ/6/1454, File 3569.
86. IOR L/PJ/6/1454, File 3569.
87. IOR L/PJ/6/1454, File 3569.
88. K. Roy, *Indian Army and the First World War*, 103.
89. IOR L/MIL/5/827/6.
90. IOR L/MIL/5/827/6.
91. IOR L/MIL/7/18463.
92. India Office memo, December 24, 1917, IOR L/MIL/7/18463.
93. India Office letter, December 28, 1917, IOR L/MIL/7/18463.
94. Callahan and Marston, "Neglected Soldiers," 33.
95. Western General Report No. 91, TNA CAB 24/152/16.
96. Neiberg, *Fighting the Great War*, 141.
97. Neiberg, *Fighting the Great War*, 146–47.
98. Neiberg, *Fighting the Great War*, 147.
99. K. Roy, *Indian Army and the First World War*, 221.
100. K. Roy, *Indian Army and the First World War*, 223.
101. Showalter, "Indianization," 145.
102. K. Roy, *Indian Army and the First World War*, 224.
103. Creese, "Indian Cavalry in Palestine," 240.
104. IOR L/MIL/7/18463.
105. Minute of suggested reply, IOR L/MIL/7/18463.
106. Jarboe and Fogarty, *Empires in World War I*, 60.
107. IOR L/R/5/196.
108. IOR L/R/5/196.
109. IOR L/R/5/196.
110. Jarboe and Fogarty, *Empires in World War I*, 63.
111. Cabinet Memorandum on the Future Settlement of Eastern Turkey in Asia and Arabia, March 14, 1915, TNA PRO CAB 24/1/16.
112. Reynolds, *Long Shadow*, 96.

7. The War's Most Critical Phase

1. Ferguson, *Pity of War*, 198.
2. Neiberg, *Fighting the Great War*, 73.
3. Ferguson, *Pity of War*, 199.
4. Strachan, *First World War*, 121.
5. *Statistics of the Military Effort*, 374.
6. Mazumder, *Indian Army*, 465.
7. O'Dwyer, *India as I Knew It*, 219.
8. Yong, "Imperial Home-Front," 379.
9. O'Dwyer, *India as I Knew It*, 216.
10. Merewether and Smith, *Indian Corps in France*, 458.
11. IOR L/MIL/17347.
12. Merewether and Smith, *Indian Corps in France*, 455.

Notes to Pages 221–233

13. Lawrence to Kitchener, March 3, 1915, TNA WO32/5110.
14. Lawrence to Kitchener, June 15, 1915, TNA WO 32/5110.
15. *Siraj-ul-Akhbar*, March 15, 1915, IOR L/R/5/196.
16. Copy of a telegram from the viceroy to the India Office, June 5, 1915, IOR L/MIL/17347.
17. Censor's Report, April 24, 1915, IOR L/MIL/17347.
18. IOR L/MIL/5/825/1.
19. IOR L/MIL/17347.
20. IOR L/MIL/5/825/8.
21. IOR L/MIL/5/825/1.
22. IOR L/MIL/5/825/3.
23. IOR L/MIL/5/825/3.
24. O'Dwyer, *India as I Knew It*, 213.
25. Yong, "Imperial Home-Front," 374.
26. O'Dwyer, *India as I Knew It*, 219.
27. O'Dwyer, *India as I Knew It*, 221.
28. O'Dwyer, *India as I Knew It*, 223.
29. O'Dwyer, *India as I Knew It*, 223.
30. IOR L/MIL/17/5/2383; Government of India, *India's Contributions*, 237–43.
31. O'Dwyer, *India as I Knew It*, 198–99.
32. O'Dwyer, *India as I Knew It*, 216.
33. O'Dwyer, *India as I Knew It*, 226.
34. IOR L/MIL/5/825/1.
35. IOR L/MIL/5/826/4.
36. IOR L/MIL/5/826/4.
37. IOR L/MIL/5/826/4.
38. IOR L/MIL/5/826/4.
39. Streets-Salter, *Martial Races*, 223.
40. IOR L/MIL/5/826/4.
41. IOR L/MIL/5/826/4.
42. IOR L/MIL/5/826/2.
43. IOR L/MIL/5/826/4.
44. IOR L/MIL/5/825/1.
45. IOR L/MIL/5/825/1.
46. IOR L/MIL/5/825/1.
47. IOR L/MIL/5/827/4.
48. IOR L/MIL/5/827/4.
49. Das, *India, Empire*, 69.
50. Jarboe, *War News in India*, 146.
51. Jarboe, *War News in India*, 149.
52. Jarboe, *War News in India*, 148.
53. Jarboe, *War News in India*, 147.
54. See parliamentary speeches of David Lloyd George, https://api.parliament.uk/historic-hansard/people/mr-david-lloyd-george/1918.
55. Jarboe, *War News in India*, 188–89.
56. Jarboe, *War News in India*, 189.
57. Jarboe, *War News in India*, 192.
58. Jarboe, *War News in India*, 191.

59. *Proceedings of the War Conference*, 2–15.
60. *Proceedings of the War Conference*, 41.
61. Jarboe, *War News in India*, 198.
62. War Office to C-in-C, India, April 21, 1918, TNA CAB 24/50/1.
63. *CWMG*, 14:306.
64. *CWMG*, 17:5.
65. *CWMG*, 17:12.
66. *CWMG*, 17:91–92.
67. *CWMG*, 17:190.
68. *CWMG*, 17:100.
69. *CWMG*, 17:130.
70. *CWMG*, 17:90.
71. *CWMG*, 17:131.
72. *CWMG*, 17:174.
73. *CWMG*, 17:83–87.
74. O'Dwyer, *India as I Knew It*, 226.
75. O'Dwyer, *India as I Knew It*, 225–26.
76. *CWMG*, 17:86.
77. *CWMG*, 17:99.
78. *CWMG*, 17:119.
79. *CWMG*, 17:157.
80. Jarboe, *War News in India*, 204.
81. Jarboe, *War News in India*, 204.
82. Jarboe, *War News in India*, 199.
83. *CWMG*, 20:15.
84. *CWMG*, 20:16.
85. *CWMG*, 20:18.
86. *CWMG*, 20:22.
87. *CWMG*, 20:22.
88. Interview with Lieutenant-Colonel A. J. O'Brien, in Hunter, *Report of the Committee*, 5:24.
89. Written statement of R. C. Chopra, in Hunter, *Report of the Committee*, 5:130.
90. *CWMG*, 20:20.
91. *CWMG*, 20:23.
92. Das, *India, Empire*, 90.
93. Hunter, *Report of the Committee*, 3:90.
94. O'Dwyer, *India as I Knew It*, 226.
95. Showalter, "Indianization," 150.

8. Into the Face of Bayonets

1. "The Great Day," *Manchester Guardian*, November 12, 1918.
2. Jarboe, *War News in India*, 212.
3. Jarboe, *War News in India*, 212.
4. Jarboe, *War News in India*, 212–13.
5. *Desh*, December 10, 1915, IOR L/R/5/196.
6. Besant, *Congress Speeches*, 19.
7. Das, *India, Empire*, 58.

Notes to Pages 246-265

8. Besant, *Congress Speeches*, 21.
9. Jarboe, *War News in India*, 136.
10. Jarboe, *War News in India*, 157.
11. Manela, *Wilsonian Moment*, 78.
12. Jarboe, *War News in India*, 12.
13. Besant, *Speeches & Writings*, 292.
14. Besant, *Speeches & Writings*, 312.
15. Besant, *Speeches & Writings*, 312.
16. Wagner, *Amritsar 1919*, chap. 2.
17. CWMG, 17:313.
18. Manela, *Wilsonian Moment*, 168.
19. *Hunter Commission*, 59, IOR L/MIL/17/12/42.
20. CWMG, 17:279-80.
21. CWMG, 17:280.
22. CWMG, 17:281.
23. CWMG, 17:297.
24. CWMG, 17:298.
25. CWMG, 17:343.
26. Wagner, *Amritsar 1919*, chap. 4.
27. Wagner, *Amritsar 1919*, prologue.
28. *Hunter Commission*, 73.
29. *Hunter Commission*, 72.
30. Written statement of Hamid Khan, in *Disorders Inquiry Committee*, 1:186.
31. Written statement of Ghulam Nabi, in Hunter, *Report of the Committee*, 1:186.
32. Written statement of Jan Muhammad, in Hunter, *Report of the Committee*, 1:187.
33. Written statement of Kanhayalal Bahadur, in Hunter, *Report of the Committee*, 2:240.
34. Written statement of Fazal Dad Khan, in Hunter, *Report of the Committee*, 3:198-99.
35. CWMG, 20:7.
36. Wagner, *Amritsar 1919*.
37. CWMG, 20:61.
38. *Hunter Commission*, 31.
39. CWMG, 20:62.
40. CWMG, 20:65.
41. For an elegant summary of the experiences of Indian soldiers in the postwar years, see Morton-Jack, *Army of Empire*, 491-516.
42. Das, *India, Empire*, 408.
43. *Hunter Commission*, 86.
44. *Hunter Commission*, 81.
45. CWMG, 20:67-69.
46. *Hunter Commission*, 7.
47. *Hunter Commission*, 14.
48. *Hunter Commission*, 23.
49. *Hunter Commission*, 23.
50. *Hunter Commission*, 31.
51. CWMG, 20:52.
52. CWMG, 20:53.
53. CWMG, 20:8.

54. *Young India*, October 6, 1921.
55. *Young India*, January 5, 1922.
56. Manela, *Wilsonian Moment*, 175.

Conclusion

1. Telegram from the Government of India to the Foreign Office, May 7, 1915, TNA FO 383/62.
2. Niedermayer, *Im Weltkrieg vor Indiens Toren*.
3. Civil Intelligence Officer, Karachi, July 23, 1917, IOR L/PS/11/129, 4700.
4. Secret memo from Austen Chamberlain to the Governor General of India, August 11, 1916, IOR L/MIL/7/18501.
5. Statements of repatriated Indian Prisoners of War, December 16, 1918, IOR L/MIL/7/18501.
6. Statements of repatriated Indian Prisoners of War, December 16, 1918.
7. Paraphrase of a cipher telegram from War Section, A.H.Q., Simla, India, to the D.A.G., 3rd Echelon, G.H.Q., Indian Section, Rouen, France, November 15, 1918, IOR L/MIL/7/18501.
8. Letter from India Office to J. I. Macpherson, M.P., October 31, 1918, IOR L/MIL/7/18502.
9. Letter from the Indian Soldiers' Fund to the India Office, October 28, 1918, IOR L/MIL/7/18502
10. Letter from Havildar Khan to Ms. Fisher, IOR L/MIL/7/18501.
11. Confidential memo from the Government of India to the Secretary, Military Department, India Office, October 23, 1919, IOR L/MIL/7/18501.
12. Letter from Mrs. Mary Cruikshank to the War Office, August 10, 1919, IOR L/MIL/7/18501.
13. Confidential memo from the Government of India to the Secretary, Military Department, India Office, October 23, 1919, IOR L/MIL/7/18501.
14. Letter from Graetsch to the Foreign Office, December 11, 1918, PAAA R21262.
15. Letter from Passport Control Officer, Berlin, June 25, 1920, IOR L/MIL/7/18899.
16. Letter from Passport Control Officer, Berlin, June 25, 1920.
17. India Office, internal memo, 1920, IOR L/MIL/7/18899.
18. IOR L/PS/11/237, P4421/1923.
19. Report by Walter Lawrence to the Secretary of State for War, Lord Kitchener, March 8, 1916, TNA WO 32/5110.
20. Barrett, "Subalterns at War," 457.
21. Commonwealth War Graves Commission Records, Cemetery Report: Zehrensdorf Indian Cemetery, accessed July 27, 2012, http://www.cwgc.org/find-a-cemetery.aspx?cpage=1.
22. See Winter, *Sites of Memory*; and Mosse, *Fallen Soldiers*.
23. Report by Walter Lawrence to the Secretary of State for War, March 8, 1916, TNA WO 32/5110.
24. Lack and Ziino, "Requiem for Empire."
25. Barrett, "Subalterns at War," 457.
26. "India at Neuve Chapelle," *Times*, October 7, 1927.
27. "India's War Sacrifice in France—To-Morrow's Tribute," *Evening Telegraph*, October 6, 1927.
28. Rice, *Neuve Chapelle*, IOR V/27/281/33.

Notes to Page 279

29. David Cameron, "Speech at Imperial War Museum on First World War Centenary Plans," October 11, 2012, https://www.gov.uk/government/speeches/speech-at-imperial-war-museum-on-first-world-war-centenary-plans.

30. Hew Strachan, "First World War Anniversary: We Must Do More than Remember," *Daily Telegraph*, January 17, 2013, available at Legacies of War, University of Leeds, https://legaciesofwar.leeds.ac.uk/news/first-world-war-anniversary-we-must-do-more-than-remember-daily-telegraph-article-17th-january-2013-by-professor-hew-strachan/.

BIBLIOGRAPHY

Archives

British Newspaper Archive, housed at the British Library, London
Imperial War Museum, London (IWM)
India Office Record, British Library, London (IOR)
The National Archives, Kew, UK (TNA)
Political Archives of the Foreign Office, Berlin (PAAA)

Published Works

The Action Taken by the Indian Corps in the Battle of Neuve Chapelle March 10th to March 13th 1915. Simla: Government Central Press, 1915.
Alexander, H. M. *On Two Fronts: Being the Adventures of an Indian Mule Corps in France and Gallipoli.* New York: E. P. Dutton, 1917.
Ali, Sardar Asghar. *Our Heroes of the Great War.* Bombay: Times Press, 1922.
Anand, Mulk Raj. *Across the Black Waters.* Delhi: Orient Paperbacks, 2000.
Anderson, Benedict. *Imagined Communities: Reflections on the Origins and Spread of Nationalism.* London: Verso, 1983.
Anderson, Ross. "Logistics of the Indian Expeditionary Force D, 1914–18." In *The Indian Army in the Two World Wars*, edited by Kaushik Roy, 105–44. Leiden: Brill, 2012.
Anderson, Warwick. *The Cultivation of Whiteness: Science, Health and Racial Destiny in Australia.* New York: Basic Books, 2003.
Atkinson, David. "The White Australia Policy, the British Empire, and the World." *Britain and the World* 8, no. 2 (September 2015): 204–44.
Audoin-Rouzeau, Stéphane. *Men at War, 1914–1918: National Sentiment and Trench Journalism in France during the First World War.* Providence RI: Berg, 1992.
Audoin-Rouzeau, Stéphane, and Annette Becker. *14–18: Understanding the Great War.* New York: Hill and Wang, 2000.
Backhaus, Professor Dr. *Die Kriegsgefangenen in Deutschland.* Siegen, Leipzig, Berlin: Verlag Hermann Montanus, 1915.
Balakian, Grigoris. *Armenian Golgotha: A Memoir of the Armenian Genocide, 1915–1918.* New York: Vintage, 2009.
Baldwin, Marian. *Canteening Overseas, 1917–1919.* New York: Macmillan, 1920.
Ballantyne, Tony. *Orientalism and Race: Aryanism in the British Empire.* New York: Palgrave Macmillan, 2002.
Ballantyne, Tony, and Antionette Burton. *Bodies in Contact: Rethinking Colonial Encounters in World History.* Durham: Duke University Press, 2005.
Barkawi, Tarak, and Keith Stanski, eds. *Orientalism and War.* New York: Columbia University Press, 2013.

Bibliography

Barker, A. J. *The First Iraq War, 1914-1918: Britain's Mesopotamia Campaign*. New York: Enigma Books, 2009.
Barrett, Michèle. "Subalterns at War: First World War Colonial Forces and the Politics of the Imperial War Graves Commission." *Interventions* 9, no. 3 (2007).
Basu, Bhupendranath. *Why India Is Heart and Soul with Great Britain*. London: Macmillan, 1914.
Basu, Shrabani. *For King and Another Country: Indian Soldiers on the Western Front, 1914-18*. London: Bloomsbury, 2015.
Berghahn, V. R. *Germany and the Approach of War in 1914*. New York: St. Martin's Press, 1973.
Besant, Annie. *Congress Speeches of Annie Besant*. Madras: Commonweal Office, 1917.
———. *Speeches & Writings of Annie Besant*. Madras: G. A. Natesan, 1921.
Bhownaggree, M. M. *The Verdict of India*. London: Hodder & Stoughton, 1916.
Bibikoff, Massia. *Our Indians at Marseilles*. London: Smith, Elder, 1915.
Bourne, Walter FitzGerald. *Recruiting Handbook for the Indian Army*. Calcutta: Government of India, 1914.
Brittain, Vera. *Testament of Youth*. New York: Penguin, 2005.
Brown, Judith M., and Wm. Roger Louis. *The Oxford History of the British Empire*. Vol. 4, *The Twentieth Century*. Oxford: Oxford University Press, 2001.
Bush, Barbara. "Gender and Empire: The Twentieth Century." In *Gender and Empire*, edited by Philippa Levine. Oxford: Oxford University Press, 2007.
Buxton, Hilary. "Imperial Amnesia: Race, Trauma and Indian Troops in the First World War." *Past & Present* 241, no. 1 (November 2018): 221-58.
Callahan, Raymond, and Daniel Marston. "Neglected Soldiers." In Jeffreys, *Indian Army*, 17-39.
Caplan, Lionel. "Martial Gurkhas: The Persistence of a British Military Discourse on 'Race.'" In *The Concept of Race in South Asia*, edited by Peter Robb, 260-81. Oxford: Oxford University Press, 1998.
Chhina, Rana. *India and the First World War*. New Delhi: Centre for Armed Forces Historical Research, 2014.
Chickering, Roger. *Imperial Germany and the Great War, 1914-1918*. 2nd ed. Cambridge: Cambridge University Press, 2004.
Chowdhury, Arjun. "Shocked by War: The Non-Politics of Orientalism." In *Orientalism and War*, edited by Tarak Barkawi and Keith Stanski, 19-37. London: Hurst, 2012.
Conrad, Sebastian. *German Colonialism: A Short History*. Cambridge: Cambridge University Press, 2010.
———. *Globalisation and the Nation in Imperial Germany*. Cambridge: Cambridge University Press, 2010.
Constable, Philip. "The Marginalization of a Dalit Martial Race in Late Nineteenth- and Early Twentieth-Century Western India." *Journal of Asian Studies* 60, no. 2 (May 2001).
Cooper, Frederick, and Ann Laura Stoler. *Tensions of Empire: Colonial Cultures in a Bourgeois World*. Berkeley: University of California Press, 1997.
Corrigan, Gordon. *Sepoys in the Trenches: The Indian Corps on the Western Front, 1914-15*. Kent, UK: Spellmount, 1999.
Craig, Gordon A. *Germany, 1866-1945*. New York: Oxford University Press, 1978.
Creese, Michael. "The Indian Cavalry in Palestine, 1917-19." In Jeffreys, *Indian Army*, 231-48.
Crozier, Anna. *Practicing Colonial Medicine: The Colonial Medical Service in British East Africa*. London: I. B. Tauris, 2007.

Das, Santanu. "Ardour and Anxiety: Politics and Literature in the Indian Homefront." In *The World in World Wars*, edited by Heike Liebau et al., 341–67. Leiden: Brill, 2010.
———. *India, Empire, and First World War Culture: Writings, Images, and Songs*. Cambridge: Cambridge University Press, 2018.
———, ed. *Race, Empire and First World War Writing*. Cambridge: Cambridge University Press, 2011.
———. "Sepoys, Sahibs, and Babus: India, the Great War and Two Colonial Journals." In *Publishing in the First World War*, edited by M. Hammond et al., 61–77. London: Palgrave Macmillan, 2007.
Das, Santanu, Gerhard Hirschfeld, Heather Jones, Jennifer Keene, Boris Kolonitskii, and Jay Winter. "Global Perspectives on World War I: A Roundtable Discussion." *Zeithistorische Forschungen/Studies in Contemporary History*, no. 1 (2014), http://www.zeithistorische-forschungen.de/1-2014/id=5009.
Deacon, Harriet. "Racism and Medical Science in South Africa's Cape Colony in the Mid- to Late Nineteenth Century." *Osiris* 15, no. 1 (2000): 190–206.
Desai, Ashwin, and Goolam Vahed. *The South African Gandhi: Stretcher-Bearer of Empire*. Stanford: Stanford University Press, 2015.
Disorders Inquiry Committee, 1919–1920. 5 vols. Calcutta: Superintendent, Government Printing, 1920.
Doegen, Wilhelm. *Kriegsgefangene Völker*. Vol. 1. Berlin: D. Reimer, 1921.
Doyle, Arthur Conan. *The British Campaign in France and Flanders*. Vol. 1. London: Hodder & Stoughton, 1916.
Drake-Brockman, D. H. *With the Royal Garhwal Rifles in the Great War from August, 1914, to November, 1917*. London: Clarke, 1934.
Dudink, Stefan, Karen Hagemann, and John Tosh, eds. *Masculinities in Politics and War: Gendering Modern History*. Manchester: Manchester University Press, 2004.
Eksteins, Modris. *Rites of Spring: The Great War and the Birth of the Modern Age*. New York: Anchor Books, 1989.
Ellinwood, D. C., and S. D. Pradhan. *India and World War I*. New Delhi: South Asia Books, 1978.
Ellinwood, DeWitt C. *Between Two Worlds: A Rajput Officer in the Indian Army, 1905–21*. New York: Hamilton Books, 2005.
———. "Two Masculine Worlds Compared: The Army Cantonment and the Jaipur Rajput: Male Society in Late Colonial India." In *War and Society in Colonial India*, edited by Kaushik Roy, 246–74. New Delhi: Oxford University Press, 2006.
Ellis, John. *The Social History of the Machine Gun*. Baltimore: Johns Hopkins University Press, 1975.
Employment, Contrary to International Law, of Colored Troops upon the European Arena of War by England and France. Berlin: Foreign Office, 1915.
Farwell, Byron. *Armies of the Raj: From the Great Indian Mutiny to Independence, 1858–1947*. London: W. W. Norton, 1989.
———. *The Gurkhas*. New York: W. W. Norton, 1984.
Fawaz, Leila Tarazi. *A Land of Aching Hearts: The Middle East in the Great War*. Cambridge MA: Harvard University Press, 2014.
Fell, Alison S. "Nursing the Other: The Representation of Colonial Troops in French and British First World War Nursing Memoirs." In *Race, Empire, and First World War Writing*, edited by Santanu Das, 158–74. Cambridge: Cambridge University Press, 2011.

Bibliography

Fell, Alison S., and Christine E. Hallett, eds. *First World War Nursing: New Perspectives*. New York: Routledge, 2013.

Ferguson, Niall. *The Pity of War*. New York: Basic Books, 1999.

Fischer, Fritz. *Germany's Aims in the First World War*. New York: W. W. Norton, 1967.

Fogarty, Richard. "Out of North Africa: Contested Visions of French Muslim Soldiers during World War I." In Jarboe and Fogarty, *Empires in World War I*, 136–58.

———. *Race and War in France: Colonial Subjects in the French Army, 1914-1918*. Baltimore: Johns Hopkins University Press, 2008.

Friedrichsmeyer, Sara, Sara Lennox, and Susanne Zantop, eds. *The Imperialist Imagination: German Colonialism and Its Legacy*. Ann Arbor: University of Michigan Press, 1998.

Fromkin, David. *Europe's Last Summer: Who Started the Great War in 1914?* New York: Vintage Books, 2004.

Fussell, Paul. *The Great War and Modern Memory*. Oxford: Oxford University Press, 1975.

Gandhi, Mahatma. *Collected Works of Mahatma Gandhi*. 98 vols. New Delhi: Publications Division, Government of India, 1999. E-book.

Gardner, Nikolas. *The Siege of Kut-al-Amara: At War in Mesopotamia, 1915-1916*. Bloomington: Indiana University Press, 2014.

———. *Trial by Fire: Command and the British Expeditionary Force*. Westport CT: Praeger, 2003.

Geiss, Imanuel. *July 1914: The Outbreak of the First World War; Selected Documents*. New York: Scribner, 1968.

Gerwarth, Robert, and Erez Manela. *Empires at War, 1911-1923*. Oxford: Oxford University Press, 2014.

Gilbert, Vivian. *The Romance of the Last Crusade: With Allenby to Jerusalem*. New York: D. Appleton, 1928.

Ginsburg, Benedict W. *War Speeches, 1914-1917*. Oxford: Clarendon Press, 1917.

Gokhale, Gopal Krishna. *Speeches of Goap Krishna Gokhale*. Madras: G. A. Natesan, 1920.

Gooptu, Nandini. *The Politics of the Urban Poor in Early Twentieth-century India*. Cambridge: Cambridge University Press, 2001.

Government of India. *India's Contributions to the Great War*. Simla: Superintendent, Government Printing, 1923.

Greenhut, Jeffrey. "The Imperial Reserve: The Indian Corps on the Western Front, 1914-15." *Journal of Imperial and Commonwealth History* 12 (1983): 54–73.

———. "Race, Sex, and War: The Impact of Race and Sex on Morale and Health Services for the Indian Corps on the Western Front, 1914." *Military Affairs* 45, no. 2 (April 1981): 71–74.

———. "Sahib and Sepoy: An Inquiry into the Relationship between the British Officers and Native Soldiers of the British Indian Army." *Military Affairs* 48, no. 1 (January 1984): 15–18.

Gries, Rainer, and Wolfgang Schmale, eds. *Kultur der Propaganda: Ueberlegungen zu einer Propagandageschichte als Kulturgeschichte*. Bochum: Verlag Dr. Dieter Winkler, 2005.

Guha, Ranajit, and Gayatri Chakravorty Spivak, eds. *Selected Subaltern Studies*. New York: Oxford University Press, 1988.

Gullace, Nicoletta F. "White Feathers and Wounded Men: Female Patriotism and Memory of the Great War." *Journal of British Studies* 36, no. 2 (April 1997).

Gupta, Partha Sarathi, and Anirudh Deshpande, eds. *The British Raj and Its Indian Armed Forces, 1857-1939*. Oxford: Oxford University Press, 2002.

Hardinge, Charles. *My Indian Years, 1910-1916*. London: J. Murray, 1948.
———. *Speeches of His Excellency the Right Hon'able Baron Hardinge of Penshurst, Viceroy and Governor-General of India*. Madras: Thompson, at the Minerva Press, 1915.
Herrmann, David G. *The Arming of Europe and the Making of the First World War*. Princeton: Princeton University Press, 1996.
Hodder, Reginald. *Famous Fights of Indian Native Regiments*. London: Hodder and Stoughton, 1914.
Holland, Robert. "The British Empire and the Great War, 1914-1918." In *The Oxford History of the British Empire*. Vol. 4, *The Twentieth Century*, edited by Judith Brown and Wm. Roger Louis. Oxford: Oxford University Press, 1999.
Höpp, Gerhard. *Muslime in der Mark: Asl Kriegsgefangene und Internierte in Wünsdorf und Zossen, 1914-1924*. Berlin: Das Arabische Buch, 1997.
Horne, John, and Alan Kramer. *German Atrocities, 1914: A History of Denial*. New Haven: Yale University Press, 2001.
Howe, Glenford. *Race, War and Nationalism: A Social History of West Indians in the First World War*. Kingston, Jamaica: Ian Randle, 2002.
Hughes, Thomas L. "The German Mission to Afghanistan, 1915-1916." *German Studies Review* 25, no. 3 (October 2002): 447-76.
Hunter, William. *Report of the Committee Appointed in the Government of India to Investigate the Disturbances in the Punjab, etc.* 5 vols. London: H. M. Stationery Office, 1920.
Imy, Kate. *Faithful Fighters: Identity and Power in the British Indian Army*. Stanford: Stanford University Press, 2019. Kindle.
———. "Fascist Yogis: Martial Bodies and Imperial Impotence." *Journal of British Studies* 55 (April 2016): 320-43.
Jackson, Ashley, ed. *The British Empire and the First World War*. New York: Routledge, 2017.
Jarboe, Andrew Tait, ed. *War News in India: The Punjabi Press during World War I*. London: I. B. Tauris, 2016.
Jarboe, Andrew Tait, and Richard S. Fogarty, eds. *Empires in World War I: Shifting Frontiers and Imperial Dynamics in a Global Conflict*. London: I. B. Tauris, 2013.
Jeffreys, Alan, ed. *The Indian Army in the First World War: New Perspectives*. Solihill, UK: Helion, 2018.
Jensen, Geoffrey, and Andrew Wiest, eds. *War in the Age of Technology: Myriad Faces of Modern Armed Conflict*. New York: New York University Press, 2001.
Jones, Heather. *Violence against Prisoners of War in the First World War: Britain, France and Germany, 1914-1920*. Cambridge: Cambridge University Press, 2011.
Judd, Dennis. *The Lion and the Tiger: The Ride and Fall of the British Raj, 1600-1947*. Oxford: Oxford University Press, 2004.
Kant, Vedica. *India and the First World War: "If I Die Here Who Will Remember Me?"* New Delhi: Roli Books, 2015.
Keegan, John. *The Face of Battle*. New York: Penguin Books, 1976.
———. *The First World War*. New York: Vintage Books, 1998.
Killingray, David, and David Omissi, eds. *Guardians of Empire: The Armed Forces of the Colonial Powers, c. 1700-1964*. Manchester: Manchester University Press, 1999.
Koller, Christian. "The Recruitment of Colonial Troops in Africa and Asia and Their Deployment in Europe during the First World War." *Immigrants & Minorities* 26, no. 1-2 (March/July 2008): 111-33.

Bibliography

———. "Representing Otherness: African, Indian, and European Soldiers' Letters and Memoirs." In *Race, Empire and First World War Writing*, edited by Santanu Das, 127–42. Cambridge: Cambridge University Press, 2011.

———. *Von Wilden aller Rassen niedergemetzelt: Die Diskussion um die Verwendung von Kolonialtruppen in Europa zwischen Rassismus, Kolonial-und Militärpolitik, 1914-1930*. Stuttgart: Steiner, 2001.

Kolsky, Elizabeth. *Colonial Justice in British India: White Violence and the Rule of Law*. New York: Cambridge University Press, 2010.

Kramer, Alan. *Dynamic of Destruction: Culture and Mass Killing in the First World War*. Oxford: Oxford University Press, 2007.

Lack, John, and Bart Ziino, "Requiem for Empire: Fabian Ware & the Imperial War Graves Commission." In Jarboe and Fogarty, *Empires in World War I*, 351–75.

Lake, Marilyn. *Drawing the Global Color Line: White Men's Countries and the International Challenge of Racial Equality*. Cambridge: Cambridge University Press, 2008.

Lerner, Paul. "Psychiatry and Casualties of War in Germany, 1914–18." In "Shell-Shock," special issue, *Journal of Contemporary History* 35, no. 1 (January 2000): 13–28.

Levine, Philippa, ed. "Battle Colors: Race, Sex, and Colonial Soldiery in World War I." *Journal of Women's History* 9 (1998).

———, ed. *Gender and Empire*. Oxford: Oxford University Press, 2004.

Liebau, Heike, Katrin Bromber, Katharina Lange, Dyala Hamzah, and Ravi Ahuja, eds. *The World in World Wars: Experiences, Perceptions and Perspectives from Africa and Asia*. Leiden: Brill, 2010.

Lloyd George, David. *War Memoirs of David Lloyd George, 1914-1915*. Boston: Odhams Press, 1935.

Lucas, Charles Prestwood. *The Empire at War*. Vol. 5. Oxford: Oxford University Press, 1926.

Lüdke, Tilmann. *Jihad Made in Germany: Ottoman and German Propaganda and Intelligence Operations in the First World War*. Munich: Lit Verlag, 2001.

MacKenzie, John M. *Propaganda and Empire: The Manipulation of British Public Opinion, 1880-1960*. New York: St. Martin's Press, 1984.

MacMunn, George. *The Armies of India*. London: A & C Black, 1911; repr., Clifton, Bristol: Crecy Books, 1984.

———. *India and the War*. London: Hodder & Stoughton, 1915.

———. "The Romance of the Martial Races of India." *Journal of the Royal Society of Arts* 80, no. 4128 (January 1932).

Manela, Erez. *The Wilsonian Moment: Self-Determination and the International Origins of Anticolonial Nationalism*. Oxford: Oxford University Press, 2009.

Markovits, Claude. "Indian Soldiers' Experiences in France during World War I: Seeing Europe from the Rear of the Front." In *The World in World Wars: Experiences, Perceptions and Perspectives from Africa and Asia*, edited by Heike Liebau, Katrin Bromber, Katharina Lange, Dyala Hamzah, and Ravi Ahuja, 27–53. Leiden: Brill, 2010.

Marston, Daniel. *The Indian Army and the End of the Raj*. Cambridge: Cambridge University Press, 2014.

Mazumder, Rajit K. *The Indian Army and the Making of Punjab*. Delhi: Permanent Black, 2003.

McCulloch, Jock. "Empire and Violence, 1900–1939." In *Gender and Empire*, edited by Philippa Levine, 220–39. Oxford: Oxford University Press, 2007.

Bibliography

McKale, Donald M. *War by Revolution: Germany and Great Britain in the Middle East in the Era of World War I.* Kent OH: Kent State University Press, 1998.

McLain, Robert. "The Indian Corps on the Western Front: A Reconsideration." In *War in the Age of Technology: Myriad Faces of Modern Armed Conflict*, edited by Geoffrey Jensen and Andrew West, 167–93. New York: New York University Press, 2001.

McMeekin, Sean. *The Berlin-Beghdad Express: The Ottoman Empire and Germany's Bid for World Power, 1898-1918.* Cambridge MA: Harvard University Press, 2010.

Merewether, Lt-Colonel J. W. B., and Lt-Colonel Sir Frederick Smith. *The Indian Corps in France.* London: John Murray, 1918.

Mesopotamia Commission. *Report of the Commission Appointed by Act of Parliament to Enquire into the Operations of War in Mesopotamia, Together with a Separate Report by Commander J. Wedgwood.* London: H. M. Stationery Office, 1917.

Metcalf, Thomas. *The Aftermath of Revolt: India, 1857-1870.* Princeton: Princeton University Press, 1964.

———, ed. *Forging the Raj: Essays on British India in the Heyday of Empire.* Oxford: Oxford University Press, 2005.

———. *Ideologies of the Raj.* Cambridge: Cambridge University Press, 1994.

———. *Imperial Connections: India in the Indian Ocean Arena, 1860-1920.* Berkeley: University of California Press, 2007.

Millar, Ronald. *Kut: The Death of an Army.* London: Secker & Warburg, 1969.

Moberly, F. J. *The Campaign in Mesopotamia, 1914-1918.* London: HMSO, 1923.

Morrow, John H., Jr. *The Great War: An Imperial History.* New York: Routledge, 2004.

Morton-Jack, George. *Army of Empire: The Untold Story of the Indian Army in World War I.* New York: Basic Books, 2018.

———. *The Indian Army on the Western Front: India's Expeditionary Force to France and Belgium in the First World War.* Cambridge: Cambridge University Press, 2014.

———. "The Indian Army on the Western Front, 1914-1915: A Portrait of Collaboration." *War in History* 13, no. 3 (2006).

Mosier, John. *The Myth of the Great War.* New York: HarperCollins, 2001.

Mosse, George L. *Fallen Soldiers: Reshaping the Memory of the World Wars.* Oxford: Oxford University Press, 1990.

———. "Shell-Shock as a Social Disease." In "Shell-Shock," special issue, *Journal of Contemporary History* 35, no. 1 (January 2000).

Nandy, Ashis. *The Intimate Enemy: Loss and Recovery of Self under Colonialism.* New Delhi: Oxford University Press, 1983.

Natesan, G. A. *All about the War: The Indian Review War Book.* Madras: G. A. Natesan, 1915.

Neiberg, Michael S. *Fighting the Great War: A Global History.* Cambridge: Harvard University Press, 2006.

Nelson, Robert L. *German Soldier Newspapers of the First World War.* Cambridge: Cambridge University Press, 2011.

Nestel, Sheryl. "(Ad)ministering Angels: Colonial Nursing and the Extension of Empire in Africa." *Journal of Medical Humanities* 19, no. 4 (1998): 257–77.

Niedermayer, Oskar Ritter von. *Im Weltkrieg vor Indiens Toren: Dier Wüstenzug der deutschen Expedition nach Persien und Afganistan.* Hamburg: Hanseatische Verlagsanstalt, 1936.

O'Dwyer, Michael. *India as I Knew It, 1885-1925.* London: Constable, 1926.

Bibliography

Omissi, David. "Europe through Indian Eyes: Indian Soldiers Encounter England and France, 1914-1918." *English Historical Review* 122, no. 496 (2007): 371-96.

———. "India: Some Perceptions of Race and Empire." In *The Impact of the South African War*, edited by David Omissi and Andrew S. Thompson, 215-32. New York: Palgrave Macmillan, 2002.

———. *Indian Voices of the Great War: Soldiers' Letters, 1914-18*. New York: St. Martin's Press, 1999.

———. *The Sepoy and the Raj: The Indian Army, 1860-1940*. London: Macmillan, 1994.

Omissi, David, and Andrew S. Thompson, eds. *The Impact of the South African War*. New York: Palgrave Macmillan, 2002.

Pandey, Gyanendra. "The Long Life of Rumor." *Alternatives: Global, Local, Political* 27, no. 2 (2002): 165-91.

Proceedings of the War Conference Held at Delhi, 27th-29th April 1918. Delhi: Superintendent, Government Printing, 1918.

Proctor, Robert. *Racial Hygiene: Medicine under the Nazis*. Cambridge MA: Harvard University Press, 1988.

Putkowski, Julian, and Julian Sykes. *Shot at Dawn: Executions in World War One by Authority of the British Army Act*. Barnsley, UK: Leo Cooper, 1999.

Ramnath, Maia. *Haj to Utopia: How the Ghadar Movement Charted Global Radicalism and Attempted to Overthrow the British Empire*. Berkeley: University of California Press, 2011.

Report of the Committee Appointed in the Government of India to Investigate the Disturbances in the Punjab, etc. 5 vols. London: H. M. Stationery Office, 1920.

Reynolds, David. *The Long Shadow: The Great War and the Twentieth Century*. New York: W. W. Norton, 2013.

Reznick, Jeffrey. *Healing the Nation: Soldiers and the Culture of Caregiving in Britain during the Great War*. Manchester: Manchester University Press, 2004.

Rice, Stanley. *Neuve Chapelle: India's Memorial in France, 1914-1918*. London: Hodder & Stoughton, 1927.

Roy, Franziska, Heike Liebau, and Ravi Ahuja, eds. *When the War Began We Heard of Several Kings: South Asian Prisoners in World War I Germany*. New Delhi: Social Science Press, 2011.

Roy, Kaushik. *Indian Army and the First World War: 1914-18*. Oxford: Oxford University Press, 2018.

———. *The Indian Army in the Two World Wars*. Leiden: Brill, 2012.

———, ed. *War and Society in Colonial India*. Oxford: Oxford University Press, 2006.

Schauwecker, Franz. *Aufbruch der Nation*. Berlin: Frundsberg Verlag, 1929.

Scott, James C. *Weapons of the Weak: Everyday Forms of Peasant Resistance*. New Haven: Yale University Press, 1985.

Searle, Geoffrey. "'National Efficiency' and the 'Lessons' of the War." In *The Impact of the South African War*, edited by David Omissi and A. S. Thompson, 194-211. London: Palgrave Macmillan, 2002.

Sehrawat, Samiksha. *Colonial Medical Care in North India: Gender, State, and Society, c. 1840-1920*. Oxford: Oxford University Press, 2013.

A Short History in English, Gurmukhi and Urdu of the Royal Pavilion Brighton and a Description of It as a Hospital for Indian Soldiers. Brighton: King, Thorne and Stace, 1915.

Showalter, Dennis. "The Indianization of the Egyptian Expeditionary Force, 1917-18: An

Imperial Turning Point." In *The Indian Army in the Two World Wars*, edited by Kaushik Roy, 145–64. Leiden: Brill, 2012.
Singh, Gajendra. *The Testimonies of Indian Soldiers and the Two World Wars: Between Self and Sepoy*. London: Bloomsbury, 2014.
Sinha, Mrinalini. *Colonial Masculinity: The 'Manly Englishman' and the 'Effeminate Bengali' in the Late Nineteenth Century*. Manchester: Manchester University Press, 1995.
Smith, Richard. *Jamaican Volunteers in the First World War: Race, Masculinity and the Development of National Consciousness*. Manchester: Manchester University Press, 2004.
———. "Loss and Longing: Emotional Responses to West Indian Soldiers during the First World War." *Round Table: The Commonwealth Journal of International Affairs* 103, no. 2 (2014): 243–52.
Sondhaus, Lawrence. *World War One: The Global Revolution*. Cambridge: Cambridge University Press, 2011.
Speed, Richard B., III. *Prisoners, Diplomats, and the Great War: A Study in the Diplomacy of Captivity*. New York: Greenwood Press, 1990.
Statistics of the Military Effort of the British Empire during the Great War, 1914-1920. London: H. M. Stationery Office, 1920.
Stevenson, David. *Cataclysm: The First World War as Political Tragedy*. New York: Basic Books, 2004.
Stiehl, O. *Unsere Feinde: 96 Characterkoepfe aus deutschen Kriegsgefangenenlagern*. Stuttgart: Verlag Julius Hoffman, 1916.
Stoler, Ann Laura. *Carnal Knowledge and Imperial Power*. Berkeley: University of California Press, 2002.
———. "Matters of Intimacy as Matters of State: A Response." *Journal of American History* 88, no. 3 (December 2001): 893–97.
———. "Tense and Tender Ties: The Politics of Comparison in North American History and (Post) Colonial Studies." *Journal of American History* 88, no. 3 (2001): 829–65.
Storey, William Kelleher. *The First World War: A Concise Global History*. New York: Rowman & Littlefield, 2010.
Stovall, Tyler. "The Color Line behind the Lines: Racial Violence in France during the Great War." *American Historical Review* 103, no. 3 (June 1998): 737–69.
———. "National Identity and Shifting Imperial Frontiers: Whiteness and the Exclusion of Colonial Labor after World War I." *Representations* 84, no. 1 (November 2003): 52–72.
Strachan, Hew. *The First World War*. New York: Viking, 2003.
———. "The First World War as a Global War." *First World War Studies* 1, no. 1 (2010).
———. *The First World War in Africa*. Oxford: Oxford University Press, 2004.
———. *To Arms*. Vol. 1 of *The First World War*. Oxford: Oxford University Press, 2001.
Streets-Salter, Heather. "The Local Was Global: The Singapore Mutiny of 1915." *Journal of World History* 24, no. 3 (September 2013).
———. *Martial Races: The Military, Race and Masculinity in British Imperial Culture, 1857-1914*. New York: Manchester University Press, 2004.
———. *World War One in Southeast Asia: Colonialism and Anticolonialism in an Era of Global Conflict*. Cambridge: Cambridge University Press, 2017.
Taylor, A. J. P. *Illustrated History of the First World War*. New York: Penguin, 1964.
Tilak, Bal Gangadhar. *Bal Gangadhar Tilak: His Writings and Speeches*. Madras: Ganesh, 1919.
Townshend, Charles. *Desert Hell: The British Invasion of Mesopotamia*. Cambridge MA: Harvard University Press, 2011.

Bibliography

———. *My Campaign in Mesopotamia*. London: T. Butterworth, 1920.
Trench, Charles Chenevix. *The Indian Army and the King's Enemies, 1900–1947*. London: Thames and Hudson, 1988.
Trevelyan, Ernest J. *India and the War*. London: Oxford University Press, 1914.
Trumpener, Ulrich. *Germany and the Ottoman Empire, 1914–1918*. Princeton: Princeton University Press, 1968.
"Vincent-Bingley" Report. 1916. Appendix 1 in Mesopotamia Commission, *Report of the Commission Appointed by Act of Parliament to Enquire into the Operations of War in Mesopotamia, Together with a Separate Report by Commander J. Wedgwood*. London: H. M. Stationery Office, 1917.
Visram, Rozina. *Asians in Britain: 400 Years of History*. London: Pluto Press, 2002.
Wagner, Kim. *Amritsar 1919: An Empire of Fear & the Making of a Massacre*. New Haven: Yale University Press, 2019. Kindle.
Wikeley, James Masson. *Punjabi Musalmans*. Calcutta: Government of India, 1915.
Willcocks, James. *With the Indians in France*. London: Constable, 1920.
Winter, Jay. "Hospitals." In *Capital Cities at War: Paris, London, Berlin 1914–1919*, vol. 2, edited by Jay Winter and Jean-Louis Robert, chap. 10. Cambridge: Cambridge University Press, 2012.
———. *Sites of Memory, Sites of Mourning: The Great War in European Cultural History*. Cambridge: Cambridge University Press, 1995.
Winter, Jay, and Antoine Prost. *The Great War in History: Debates and Controversies, 1914 to the Present*. Cambridge: Cambridge University Press, 2005.
With a Highland Regiment in Mesopotamia, by One of Its Officers. Bombay: Times Press, 1918.
Yong, Tan Tai. *The Garrison State: The Military, Government and Society in Colonial Punjab, 1849–1947*. New Delhi: Sage, 2005.
———. "An Imperial Home-Front: Punjab and the First World War." *Journal of Military History* 64, no. 2 (April 2000): 371–410.
———. "Sepoys and the Colonial State: Punjab and the Military Base of the Indian Army 1849–1900." In *British Raj and Its Indian Armed Forces, 1857–1939*, edited by P. S. Gupta, 7–44. New Delhi: Oxford University Press, 2002.

INDEX

Aberdeen Evening Express, 90
Across the Black Waters (Anand), 37, 39, 66
Afghanistan, 9; deserters in, 242, 273; German expedition to, 269; and German propaganda, 72, 74, 232; Indian Army operations in, 27, 42
Afridis, 37, 78, 79; as deserters, 98-99, 101, 183, 273
Aga Khan, 76
Ahmedabad, 252, 253, 256
Akhbar-I'-Am (Jhelum), 156, 232
Aleppo, 169, 179, 182, 210, 211
Allenby, Edmund, 8, 210-12
Amritsar: crawling order in, 262; demonstrations in, 253, 254; massacre in, 10, 257-61; recruitment in, 220-21, 223
Arifan, Mahomed, 18-19, 157, 165-66
Armenian genocide, 179-80
armistice (November 11, 1918), 244
artillery, 57, 86, 97, 105
Asquith, Herbert Henry, 5, 62, 63
Australia, 43, 44-45, 65
Australians: casualties of, 279; at Gallipoli, 203; troops of, 202, 203, 217
Azadi (Lahore), 63

Baghdad, 6-7; capture of, 185, 195-96, 198-99; deserters in, 183; forced marches to, 177-78; hospitals in, 169, 178; 1915 offensive on, 115, 143, 144, 149; railway of, 181, 213
Bahadur, Kanhayalal, 256
Baluchis, 129th, 78, 88, 98, 124, 186
Baluchis, 130th, 77-78
Bareilly Brigade, 96
Basra, 7, 143; hospitals in, 141, 142, 148; memorial in, 276
Belgium, 88, 275
Bengal, 49
Bengal Army, 28, 32
Bengalee (Calcutta), 60
Bengali 49th Regiment, 230

Besant, Annie, 54, 245, 248; and Home Rule League, 22, 246; and Indian National Congress, 245, 247
Beveridge, Albert, 162-63
Bikaner, Maharajah of, 233
Birmingham Mail, 67
Boer War. *See* South African War
Bombay, 54, 77, 200, 226, 256
Bose, Bhupendranath, 69
Boxer Rebellion, 42, 51
Brighton, 123, 130, 137
Brighton Corporation, 129
Brighton Gazette, 31
Brighton Pavilion Hospital, 126, 128, 139
British Army, 43, 86, 95; and Army Act (1881), 41; and Battle of Amiens (1918), 155; recruitment for, 224
British Empire: and anticolonialism, 73, 161; and migration, 27; and racism, 50, 63; and recruitment, 216, 218; and reform, 48, 60, 236, 245; and "small wars," 42; soldiers of, 42, 56
British Expeditionary Force (BEF), 57, 86, 87
British India, 5, 28, 216
Brittain, Vera, 55

Calcutta, 29, 63
Canada, 45, 63, 218
censor of Indian mail, 13-14, 79, 81, 96, 97-98, 191, 223; and censorship, 15, 261-62; and communication with India Office, 134; and German propaganda, 158; and relations between Indians and French women, 111, 112, 113; and return of wounded soldiers to the front, 140
Chamberlain, Austen, 76, 78, 115, 149, 206, 269
Chandni Chowk, 255
Charles, Havelock, 121, 131
climate, 188; in France, 93, 107, 126, 278; and health care, 92, 122; in the Middle East, 142
Constantinople: Independence Committee activities in, 75; Indian soldiers in, 159, 163, 182; kaiser's visit to, 71

315

Index

convalescents, 123, 125, 126, 129
crawling order, 262–63
Crescent Moon Camp. *See* Zossen
Crewe, Lord, 58, 130
Ctesiphon, Battle of (1915), 145–46, 147, 172
Curzon, Lord, 43

Daily Graphic, 203
Daily Mail, 131
Damascus, 71
Dayal, Har, 73–74
Defense of India Act, 80, 241, 253
Dehra Dun Brigade, 103
Delhi, 29, 49, 253, 254–55, 263
Delhi War Conference, 233
desertions: in France, 96, 97–99; in Middle East, 174; pardon for, 58
disease, 118-19, 176
Dogras, 33, 36
dominions, 3; and immigration policy, 45, 65; and racism, 51, 204; soldiers from, 6, 217; and South African War, 43
Doyle, Arthur Conan, 93
Duff, Beauchamp, 143, 149, 185
Dyer, Reginald, 10, 259–61, 262–63, 264

East Africa, 119, 186, 188
East India Company, 29
Egypt, 71, 116, 209–10
Egyptian Expeditionary Force, 210

Festubert, Battle of (1914), 87, 97
France, 84–85, 101; arrival of Indian troops in, 66–67, 68; civilians of, 109–10, 111, 194; German offensives on (1918), 231–32; impressions of Indian soldiers in, 114, 186; Indian casualties in, 85, 88, 221, 274; presence of French colonial troops in, 58, 161; weather in, 15, 188; withdrawal of Indian Corps from, 108, 115–16
French, John, 87, 116, 156
frostbite, 105, 188

Gallipoli, 115, 203
Gandhi, Mohandas Karamchand: on Amritsar massacre, 258; on British Empire, 47–48; and civil disobedience, 252, 256, 261; and Delhi War Conference, 233, 234; and hartal, 253, 257; on Indian soldiers, 42, 49, 51; and nationalist movement, 204, 235, 249, 252, 265–66; recruiting campaign of, 234, 235–38; response of, to outbreak of war, 59, 125; response of, to Rowlatt Bills, 250, 251–53; in South Africa, 44, 46–48
Garhwalis, 36

Garhwal Rifles, 39th, 89, 186
George, David Lloyd, 5, 198, 210, 231–32
George V, King, 5, 58, 69, 127, 139, 247
German East Africa, 212
Germany: alliance of, with Turkey, 71–72, 76, 81, 159; army of, 52, 56, 57, 95, 155; artillery of, 86; casualties of, 104; colonies of, 212; Foreign Office of, 54, 72, 100; hospitals in, 135; Indian opinion on, 60, 77, 230, 233, 244, 247; offensives of (March 1918), 210, 231–32; prisoner-of-war camps of, 154, 155; propaganda of, 70, 72, 75, 99–100, 153, 156, 157–59, 166, 169, 268, 269, 271; racism in, 161; soldiers of, 86, 87, 90, 96, 190, 207; and support for Indian radicals, 72, 74, 167; use of poison gas by, 138; war aims of, 70–71, 72, 85
Ghadar Party, 73–74, 79–80
Girdwood, H. D., 204-7
Givenchy, Battle of (1914), 87
Gobindgarh Fort, 258
Gokhale, Gopal Krishna, 48, 49, 212
Gujranwala, 240, 241, 253, 257, 262
Gurkhas, 32, 91–92
Gurkhas, 1st/4th, 58, 88, 155
Gurkhas, 2nd/2nd, 155
Gurung, Suba Sing, 167

Haig, Douglas, 57, 104, 208
Hardinge, Charles, 64–65, 149, 185, 222, 226
hartal, 25, 252, 253–54
Home Rule, 246, 248
hospitals, 122, 124; in Aleppo, 182; in Baghdad, 178; in Basra, 141–42, 148, 176, 200; in England, 123, 125–26, 150–51; in France, 123; in India, 121–22; nurses at, 130–33; personnel of, 125; in the press, 128–29, 139; and propaganda, 122, 127, 128, 129–30; regimental, 120; soldiers' responses to, 137–38; station, 120; treating shell shock at, 133–34, 135
Howell, E. B., 13, 134
Hunter Commission, 263–65

immigration, 44–46, 65, 204
imperial brotherhood, 46, 47, 48
Imperial War Graves Commission, 276
indentured laborers, 43
India: and Central Recruiting Board, 238; and Defense of India Act, 80, 241, 247, 253; "disorders" in, 263; government of, 5, 6, 18, 120, 212, 250; and Home Rule League, 246; and *Komagata Maru*, 63–64; and Mesopotamia Commission, 142, 149; and Montagu reforms, 202, 247; and outbreak of war, 60–61; and

Index

Paris peace talks, 249; and press, 56, 261-62; and recruitment, 187, 219, 237, 240; and repatriation, 271; and Rowlatt Bills, 250; and rumors, 56, 222; and sedition, 79; and self-government, 22, 49, 54, 61, 245-46, 249; and tahsildars, 241; and volunteer battalion, 50

Indian Army, 5, 38, 41, 185, 200

Indian Corps, 12, 69, 83, 86, 88, 93, 102-4, 115, 123, 124, 141, 222

Indian Division, 3rd (Lahore Division), 58, 118, 148, 174, 198, 210

Indian Division, 6th, 7, 115, 118, 142, 144, 146, 147, 153

Indian Division, 7th (Meerut Division), 58, 118, 148, 174, 196, 210

Indian Independence Committee, 73-74, 158, 163, 167

Indian Medical Service, 94, 121, 144, 181

Indian memorials, 275

Indian National Congress, 48, 49, 54, 59, 239, 263, 265

Indian Opinion, 48, 51

Indian press, 19, 63, 198, 232

Indian princes, 5, 50, 59, 77, 233

Indian Rebellion (1857), 28-30, 31, 74

Indian soldiers: and artillery, 203; and British officers, 58, 86, 106, 146, 172, 201, 222, 262; care for, 94; casualties of, 8, 85, 88, 274; and cavalry, 6, 207-8; cemeteries for, 274; decorations of, 8; deployment of, to France, 61-62, 67, 85; deployment of, to Mesopotamia, 85, 115; desertion of, 96-100, 183; discipline of, 112; and French civilians, 109-11, 113; and health care, 119, 120-22, 141, 150-52; and Indianization, 209-10; and Indian officers, 41; and infantry, 6; and king's commissions, 200-203; letters of, 13-15, 188-95; loyalty of, 29, 37; and "martial races," 33; memorialization of, 276-79; mobilization of, 57-58; munity of, 78, 79-81; and Muslim troops, 76; and nationalist movement, 49-51; pay for, 38, 40, 137, 226-27; pensions of, 38, 160, 226; and postwar demonstrations, 254-58, 261; in the press, 3, 35, 89-93, 108, 232; prewar deployments of, 42; as prisoners of war, 155-56, 166, 169; and racism, 2, 106, 178; recruitment of, 32-33, 219-20, 221, 222, 224, 233, 239; as recruits, 38-39, 227-29; religion of, 81, 106, 164, 273; remittances for, 226; repatriation of, 270-74; as reservists, 28, 221; resistance of, 135-37; self-inflicted wounds of, 95; and South African War, 43; as

veterans, 79, 114; and viceroy's commissions, 200-203; and white troops, 203

Indian Soldiers' Fund, 93, 131, 156, 270

India Office, 107, 126, 128, 134, 208, 270

izzat, 40

Jacob's Horse, 36th, 190, 211

Jam-e-Jamshad (Bombay), 60

Jan, Guli, 272, 273

Japan, 42, 187-88

Jats, 33, 36, 220

Jerusalem, 71, 210

jihad: British responses to, 76; and German propaganda, 71, 99; response of Muslim troops to, 81, 165; sultan's call to, 9, 72

Jordan, 211

Jullundur Brigade, 10, 103, 123

Kabul, 74, 269, 274

Keogh, Alfred, 122, 128, 131

Khalsa Advocate (Amritsar), 230, 232

Khalsa Samachar (Amritsar), 230

Khalsa Sowar (Amritsar), 61

Khan, Fazal Dad, 257-58

Khan, Khudadad, 88-89, 131

Khan, Mala, 269-70

Kisan (Lahore), 22, 246

Kitchener, Horatio, 57, 115

Kitchener Indian Hospital, 123, 125, 126, 129, 134

Komagata Maru (ship), 63-64

Kut, Battle of (1915-16): and British capture, 143; and relief efforts, 149; and siege, 8, 148, 169-75; and surrender, 144; and treatment of prisoners, 24, 175-81

Lady Hardinge Hospital, 131

Lahore, 253, 254, 257

Lancers, 2nd, 208, 211

Lancers, 14th, 197

Lancers, 16th, 208

Lancers, 18th, 208, 211

Lawrence, Walter, 122, 123, 126, 134, 136, 221; and burial of soldiers, 274; letters of, to Horatio Kitchener, 124, 125, 150-51; and propaganda, 127, 138; and YMCA, 128

Light Infantry, 5th, 80-81

Loos, Battle of (1915), 101, 106, 107, 222

MacMunn, George, 33, 35-37, 195

Manchester Guardian, 67, 68, 244

Marseilles: Indian camp at, 68, 112; Indian Corps arrival at, 66-67; Indian hospital at, 123, 126, 127

martial races, 32, 35-36, 258

317

Index

masculinity, 39
Maude, Stanley, 185, 196–200
Meerut, 29
Megiddo, Battle of (1918), 8, 211
Mesopotamia: climate of, 178, 188–89; colonization of, 213; health care in, 118, 199; Indian Army operations in, 7, 18, 115, 141, 200; Indian casualties in, 85, 274; letters from, 189; memorials in, 276
Mesopotamia Commission, 120, 142, 148–50
Mir Dast, 138–40
Mir Mast, 96, 100
Monro, Charles, 185, 196
Montagu, Edwin, 202, 208–9, 212, 213, 247
Montagu Declaration, 247
Muhammad, Jan, 255–56
Muslims: and All-India Muslim League, 246; burial of, 274; and German propaganda, 9, 71, 158, 163; loyalty of, 77, 81; mutiny of, 80; objections of, to fighting fellow Muslims, 76, 78, 165, 174, 273; as prisoners of war, 156–57, 159, 273; as recruits, 220, 226
mutiny, 37, 41, 43, 78, 79, 80, 254

Natal, 44, 46
Natal Advertiser, 42, 51
Natesan, G. A., 11, 60
nationalism, 73, 164
Nepal, 32
Neuve Chapelle, Battle of (1915), 102–4, 108, 124, 126, 138
Newcastle Daily Journal, 89
New Zealand, 43, 45, 217
Nixon, John, 7, 115, 142–43, 144, 148, 149, 174, 195
North-West Frontier Province, 9, 33, 42, 79, 101, 220
nurses, 130–33

Observer (Lahore), 59, 76, 90
O'Dwyer, Michael, 19, 224–28, 234, 239, 240, 253, 257, 258–59
Oppenheim, Max von, 71, 72, 74, 157, 182
Ottoman Army, 71, 142, 146, 196–97
Ottoman Empire, 71, 212–13; alliance of, with Germany, 72, 100, 159; and Arab revolt, 214; infrastructure of, 175; and jihad, 72, 81; prisoner-of-war camps in, 181; and propaganda, 158, 163

Palestine, 8, 185, 209, 211
Panjabee (Lahore), 19–20, 46, 52, 61, 198, 232
Panth Sewak (Lahore), 63–64
Paris peace conference, 249

Pathans, 33, 36, 77–78
Peel Commission, 32
Persia, 163, 183, 189, 269
Persian Gulf, 42, 143
Prabhat, 52, 76, 192
Punjab: annexation of, 38; "disorders" in, 253, 254, 262; Ghadar activities in, 80; newspapers of, 21; recruitment in, 16, 29, 33, 38, 219, 220, 224, 226–27, 237, 240
Punjabis, 22nd, 17, 173
Punjabis, 66th, 145, 146, 173
Punjabis, 69th, 101, 173, 255

racism: British Empire and, 27, 42, 66, 110, 203, 248, 268; Gandhi and, 47; and health care, 133, 135; historiography of, 93; Indian Army and, 28, 43, 110, 146, 172; Indian nationalists and, 48; and postwar violence, 263, 268; and recruitment, 33; and representations of Indian soldiers, 36, 92, 254; and South African War, 43; white soldiers and, 106
Rajputs, 28, 34, 40
Ram, Ganga, 155
Rana, Sher Singh, 155, 160
Rawalpindi, 21, 220
recruiting handbooks, 34, 37
recruitment: in Britain, 217–18, 224; in India, 29, 31–32, 33, 222, 224, 226; nationalist response to, 232, 248, 251
regimental system, 120
religion, 106
Rifles, 55th, 100, 138, 140, 255
Rifles, 57th, 138
Rifles, 58th, 34, 58, 88, 96, 98, 99, 100, 164, 269
Rifles, 59th, 34, 107, 123, 155, 221
Roberts, Frederick, 33, 35
Rowlatt Bills, 250, 251–53
Royal Navy, 58
rumors, 29, 55, 56, 132
Russia, 32, 50, 246

Sannaiyat, Battle of (1917), 197–98
Sarbadhikari, Sisir, 55, 144–47, 171–72, 173, 174, 178, 181–82
satyagraha, 235, 252
sepoys. *See* Indian soldiers
Shanti (Rawalpindi), 232
Sheffield Daily Telegraph, 30
shell shock, 133–34, 135
sickness, 94, 142, 182
Sikhs, 32, 36, 63, 90, 219
Sikhs, 15th, 34, 88, 104, 123, 222
Sikhs, 47th, 88, 107, 123, 197, 221

318

Index

Sinai Peninsula, 7, 210
Singapore mutiny, 80–81
Singh, Amar, 106-7, 202
Singh, Darwan, 89
Singh, Ganga, 249
Singh, Suwai, 160
Siraj-ul-Akhbar (Jhelum), 222
Sirhind Brigade, 103
soldiers' letters, 13-14, 15-16, 19, 193, 223; describing France, 110-11; and desertion, 98; from hospitals, 130, 133, 135, 136; from India, 40, 126, 140, 190-91, 194-95, 229; from the Western Front, 81, 84, 88, 95, 100, 110, 114, 128, 191, 194; from Zossen, 156, 158-59
Somme, Battle of the (1916), 217
South Africa, 43-44, 45, 47, 236
South African War, 42, 43, 47, 49, 57, 154
sowars. *See* Indian soldiers
Suez Canal, 7, 71, 210
swaraj, 4, 49, 236, 237, 246
Sydney Morning Herald, 44
Sykes-Pikot Agreement, 214
Syria, 8, 179, 181, 210

Times (London), 3, 4, 20, 30; Gandhi's letter to the editor of, 125, 234; and Indian camps, 68; and Indian hospitals, 129; and Indian loyalty, 68, 206; and Indian soldiers, 90, 91; and martial races, 32; and Neuve Chapelle memorial, 277; and wounded Indians, 129
Tigris River, 7, 142, 171, 176, 196, 198
Tilak, Bal Gangadhar, 22, 49, 60, 246, 249-50
Townshend, Charles, 144, 146, 170-71, 172-74, 175
Treatment of British Prisoners of War, 176, 178-79
Tribune (Lahore), 21, 61, 201, 202, 245, 262
Turkey, Sultan of, 9, 71, 72, 100

United States, 42, 45, 246

venereal disease, 135
Viceroy's Commissioned Officers (VCOs), 200
Victoria Cross (VC), 83, 89, 139, 229
Vincent-Bingley Commission, 120, 121, 147

Walter, Paul, 73, 74, 158
Ware, Fabian, 276
War Office, 56, 130, 187, 202, 209, 217
Western Front, 61, 84-85, 94, 102, 119, 133, 155, 188, 207, 231, 244
white man's war, 43, 57
Wilhelm, Kaiser, 70, 71, 157
Willcocks, James, 69, 86, 87, 93, 95, 99, 112, 130
Wilson, Woodrow, 246
With the Empire's Fighters, 204-5

YMCA, 128, 272
Young India, 266
Ypres, Battle of (1914), 85, 86, 104, 155, 275

Zamindar (Lahore), 19, 21, 61
Zossen, 156-57; Afridi deserters in, 160; cemetery in, 275; deaths in, 168; health care in, 166; Indian Committee activities in, 158, 160, 161, 163, Indian prisoners in, 155-56, 157, 165-66; Indian volunteers in, 159, 163-64; jihad in, 158; mosque in, 157; and propaganda, 157-58, 159-61, 163; Ramadan in, 159; Sikh prisoners in, 165; visitors to, 157, 162

Studies in War, Society, and the Military

Military Migration and State Formation: The British Military Community in Seventeenth-Century Sweden
Mary Elizabeth Ailes

Managing Sex in the U.S. Military: Gender, Identity, and Behavior
Edited by Beth Bailey, Alesha E. Doan, Shannon Portillo, and Kara Dixon Vuic

The State at War in South Asia
Pradeep P. Barua

Marianne Is Watching: Intelligence, Counterintelligence, and the Origins of the French Surveillance State
Deborah Bauer

Death at the Edges of Empire: Fallen Soldiers, Cultural Memory, and the Making of an American Nation, 1863-1921
Shannon Bontrager

An American Soldier in World War I
George Browne
Edited by David L. Snead

Beneficial Bombing: The Progressive Foundations of American Air Power, 1917-1945
Mark Clodfelter

Fu-go: The Curious History of Japan's Balloon Bomb Attack on America
Ross Coen

Imagining the Unimaginable: World War, Modern Art, and the Politics of Public Culture in Russia, 1914-1917
Aaron J. Cohen

The Rise of the National Guard: The Evolution of the American Militia, 1865-1920
Jerry Cooper

The Thirty Years' War and German Memory in the Nineteenth Century
Kevin Cramer

Political Indoctrination in the U.S. Army from World War II to the Vietnam War
Christopher S. DeRosa

The Korean War Remembered: Contested Memories of an Unended Conflict
Michael J. Devine

In the Service of the Emperor: Essays on the Imperial Japanese Army
Edward J. Drea

American Journalists in the Great War: Rewriting the Rules of Reporting
Chris Dubbs

America's U-Boats: Terror Trophies of World War I
Chris Dubbs

The Age of the Ship of the Line: The British and French Navies, 1650–1815
Jonathan R. Dull

American Naval History, 1607–1865: Overcoming the Colonial Legacy
Jonathan R. Dull

Soldiers of the Nation: Military Service and Modern Puerto Rico, 1868–1952
Harry Franqui-Rivera

You Can't Fight Tanks with Bayonets: Psychological Warfare against the Japanese Army in the Southwest Pacific
Allison B. Gilmore

A Strange and Formidable Weapon: British Responses to World War I Poison Gas
Marion Girard

Civilians in the Path of War
Edited by Mark Grimsley and Clifford J. Rogers

A Scientific Way of War: Antebellum Military Science, West Point, and the Origins of American Military Thought
Ian C. Hope

Picture This: World War I Posters and Visual Culture
Edited and with an introduction by Pearl James

Indian Soldiers in World War I: Race and Representation in an Imperial War
Andrew T. Jarboe

Death Zones and Darling Spies: Seven Years of Vietnam War Reporting
Beverly Deepe Keever

For Home and Country: World War I Propaganda on the Home Front
Celia Malone Kingsbury

I Die with My Country: Perspectives on the Paraguayan War, 1864–1870
Edited by Hendrik Kraay and Thomas L. Whigham

North American Indians in the Great War
Susan Applegate Krouse
Photographs and original documentation by Joseph K. Dixon

Remembering World War I in America
Kimberly J. Lamay Licursi

Citizens More than Soldiers: The Kentucky Militia and Society in the Early Republic
Harry S. Laver

*Soldiers as Citizens: Former Wehrmacht Officers in the
Federal Republic of Germany, 1945-1955*
Jay Lockenour

*Deterrence through Strength: British Naval Power and Foreign Policy
under Pax Britannica*
Rebecca Berens Matzke

Army and Empire: British Soldiers on the American Frontier, 1758-1775
Michael N. McConnell

Of Duty Well and Faithfully Done: A History of the Regular Army in the Civil War
Clayton R. Newell and Charles R. Shrader
With a foreword by Edward M. Coffman

*The Militarization of Culture in the Dominican Republic,
from the Captains General to General Trujillo*
Valentina Peguero

A Religious History of the American GI in World War II
G. Kurt Piehler

Arabs at War: Military Effectiveness, 1948-1991
Kenneth M. Pollack

*The Politics of Air Power: From Confrontation to Cooperation in
Army Aviation Civil-Military Relations*
Rondall R. Rice

Andean Tragedy: Fighting the War of the Pacific, 1879-1884
William F. Sater

The Grand Illusion: The Prussianization of the Chilean Army
William F. Sater and Holger H. Herwig

Sex Crimes under the Wehrmacht
David Raub Snyder

In the School of War
Roger J. Spiller
Foreword by John W. Shy

*Empire between the Lines: Imperial Culture in British and French Trench
Newspapers of the Great War*
Elizabeth Stice

*On the Trail of the Yellow Tiger: War, Trauma, and Social Dislocation in
Southwest China during the Ming-Qing Transition*
Kenneth M. Swope

Friendly Enemies: Soldier Fraternization throughout the American Civil War
Lauren K. Thompson

The Paraguayan War, Volume 1: Causes and Early Conduct
Thomas L. Whigham

Policing Sex and Marriage in the American Military: The Court-Martial and the Construction of Gender and Sexual Deviance, 1950-2000
Kellie Wilson-Buford

The Challenge of Change: Military Institutions and New Realities, 1918-1941
Edited by Harold R. Winton and David R. Mets

To order or obtain more information on these or other University of Nebraska Press titles, visit nebraskapress.unl.edu.

www.ingramcontent.com/pod-product-compliance
Lightning Source LLC
Chambersburg PA
CBHW030607230426
43661CB00053B/1872